Our First Visit in America

Our First Visit in America

Early Reports from the Colony of Georgia 1732-1740

INTRODUCTION BY
TREVOR R. REESE

The Beehive Press
SAVANNAH, GEORGIA, 1974

LIBRARY OF CONGRESS CATALOG CARD NUMBER 74-84332

Contents

Introduction

BY early 1734, only a year after the first party of pioneer settlers reached Savannah, the population of Georgia exceeded five hundred and the foundations of a new British colony in America had been laid. The picture that historians have drawn of its inhabitants and early development is based partly on the papers of the Trustees, a group of men living in England and bearing primary responsibility for the province's government, and partly on accounts by officials, other inhabitants and travellers who observed conditions in the settlement at first hand. The Trustees' records necessarily provide the formal framework, but for an intimate and, presumably, more authentic impression of what life was like in the colony historians must turn to the papers of those who visited it or resided in it.

Peter Gordon, whose journal covers the initial, formative months of the settlement, was among the first civil officers appointed by the Trustees in November, 1732. Allegedly an upholsterer by trade, Gordon became a Bailiff and Conservator of the Peace and was to prove an unhappy choice. He was about thirty-four and looking for employment when he and his wife were selected to sail with the first emigrants to Georgia. Two children died on the voyage, and Gordon was one of ten who became ill with what was graphically described as "the bloody flux."[1] He fell ill again during the first year and returned to England in November, 1733, for medical attention. The Trustees seized the opportunity afforded by his presence in London to question him about the colony's progress, and were gratified by his sanguine report. A plan that he drew of Savannah was dedicated to the Trustees, who paid him sixteen guineas and ordered it to be engraved.[2]

Gordon's attitude appears to have changed when he arrived back in Georgia at the end of 1734 with his wife and two servants, his expenses having been met by the Trustees. Almost as soon as he set foot on Georgia soil again he was expressing dissatisfaction and talking of returning to the mother country. James Oglethorpe, who was in charge of the colony, and Thomas Causton, the Storekeeper, suspected that much of the grumbling and unrest among the settlers at this time was attributable to Gordon who evidently decided to assume the role of agent for conveying complaints on a variety of matters to the Trustees. He left Georgia a second time after only a brief stay and presented to the Trustees a memorial and letters by various hands protesting about conditions and some of the activities of the civil officers in the colony, especially Causton, Thomas Christie, the Recorder, whom he accused of selling rum, and Noble Jones, who counted carpenter, surveyor and Constable among his successive employments. The Trustees were annoyed that Gordon should have left the colony again without permission and were not sympathetic towards the complaints and criticisms he laid before them.[3] He never returned to Georgia, so that his journal covers less than two years of the early history of the province. He had left before the Trustees decided to give a first payment to the civil appointees there, and it has been conjectured

1. *Manuscripts of the Earl of Egmont: Diary of the First Earl of Egmont Viscount Percival, 1730–1747*, ed. R. A. Roberts (3 vols., Historical Manuscripts Commission, London, 1920–3), I, 364.

2. "A View of Savanah [sic] as it stood the 29th of March, 1734. P. Gordon inv. P. Fourdrinier, sculp."

3. Sarah B. Gober Temple and K. Coleman, *Georgia Journeys* (Athens, Ga., 1961), pp. 69–71.

that the manuscript was intended by Gordon to support a request for financial recognition of his services.[4] Much of it, however, is a criticism of the policies being pursued by the Trustees and foreshadows the literature of malcontents in Georgia in the 1740s,[5] but it also contains useful and interesting narrative and commentary on the founding period of the new colony.

The journals of Baron Georg Philipp Friedrich von Reck and the Reverend Johann Martin Bolzius, who led a band of Protestant exiles from Salzburg to Georgia, are of value partly because they give an insight into the attitudes and feelings of immigrants who were not British.[6] They describe in lyrical terms their landing and reception at Savannah, where Oglethorpe and the original settlers had established themselves, and they rhapsodize over Savannah the town, over the woods, over the fresh grass on the banks of the river, and over the singing of the birds. The Salzburgers founded the town of Ebenezer a little way up the Savannah River and were well served for many years by von Reck and Bolzius, although Bolzius, who remained their pastor until his death in 1765, was said to have buried four of his five children in seven years when he attempted rice planting in unhealthy conditions.[7]

Among the most informative of contemporary descriptions of life in the province is that contained in *A Voyage to Georgia begun in the year 1735*. Its author, Francis Moore, had served in West Africa as a writer for the Royal African Company engaged in the

4. E. Merton Coulter, ed., *The Journal of Peter Gordon 1732–1735* (Wormsloe Foundation Publications No. 6, Athens, Ga., 1963), pp. 19–20.

5. See *The Clamorous Malcontents: Criticisms and Defenses of the Colony of Georgia, 1741–1743* (Beehive Press, Savannah, 1973).

6. For the background to the Georgia emigration see J. M. Hofer, "The Georgia Salzburgers," *Georgia Historical Quarterly*, 18 (June 1934); F. F. Strauss, "A Brief Survey of Protestantism in Archiepiscopal Salzburg and the Emigration of 1732," *ibid.*, 43 (March, 1959); J. K. Mayr, "Die Emigration der Salzburger Protestanten von 1731–1732," *Mitteilungen der Gesellschaft für Salzburger Landeskunde*, 69–71 (1929–31); P. A. Strobel, *The Salzburgers and their Descendants* (1855; ed. E. D. Wells, Athens, Ga., 1953).

7. H. McCall, *The History of Georgia, containing brief sketches of the most remarkable events up to the present day* (2 vols., Savannah, 1811–16), I, 251.

traffic of Negro slaves to the West Indies, and had journeyed up the Gambia river six hundred miles into the interior making careful observations and drawings that he later published.[8] He spent nearly five years in Africa before going to Georgia in 1735, when he stayed for nine months, and again in 1738, when he stayed until 1743.

Moore's first voyage to Georgia in October, 1735, was in the company of forty families—Scots, Germans and English—who had been selected for their trustworthiness, industry and general suitability to the existing conditions of the projected fortress town of Frederica on the southern frontier of Georgia whose original plan he describes vividly and exactly. Moore's association with these families and his admiration for them conditioned his assessment of the colonial population in general, and he concludes that the most successful settlers were the most frugal and the least ostentatious. He is very critical of those who took their provisions from the public store but idled their time away in drinking and became the core of the discontented.

Moore was Storekeeper and Recorder in Frederica, which by 1740 had a population of nearly a thousand, a large proportion of whom were soldiers.[9] He and his wife were assigned a lot in the northern of the two wards into which the town was organized, and they erected both a brick and a wooden house. Moore was energetic and imaginative, and for a time acted as Oglethorpe's secretary and kept the accounts when the general was away on military duties.[10] He worked hard in Georgia, but the Trustees in London came to regard him as vain and dangerous when he questioned as-

8. *Travels into the Inland Parts of Africa, containing a description of the several nations for the space of six hundred miles up the . . . Gambia* (London, 1738). "Reisen in die inländischen Theile von Africa," in Johann J. Schwabe, ed., *Allgemeine Historie der Reisen zu Wasser und Lander* (21 vols., Leipzig, 1747–74), III.

9. T. R. Reese, *Frederica: Colonial Fort and Town. Its Place in History* (Fort Frederica Association, 1969), pp. 22, 51.

10. Oglethorpe to Trustees, May 18, 1736, C.O. 5/687 (Colonial Office Series 5, Vol. 687; Public Record Office, London).

pects of their policy. His appointment as Recorder was eventually revoked, and in 1743 he returned to England to publish his travels, bringing to them the keen, perceptive mind and facile pen that had been evident earlier in his writings on Africa.

Benjamin Ingham, who kept a short journal of his voyage to Georgia in 1736, had been an active member of the Methodist group at Oxford led by John and Charles Wesley. He equivocated over a request by John Wesley to accompany him to Georgia, but finally accepted and sailed with him in October, 1735, at the age of twenty-three. Ingham's journal describes the crossing of the Atlantic and his activities on board ship, where he began his clerical and educational duties by teaching the children and giving English language instruction to some Moravians. He reached St. Simon's Island in February, 1736, and there participated with Oglethorpe and the Wesleys in the founding days of the fortified frontier town of Frederica. He appears to have possessed strict ideas about the observance of the Sabbath, and his authoritarian concept of his moral responsibilities in the town eventually caused resentment. The esteem in which the inhabitants held him at first, he admits, gave way to ill will when they discovered that he "watch'd narrowly over them and reprov'd them sharply for their faults." Finding himself in increasing trouble, Ingham hastened back to Savannah and in February, 1737, returned to England.

John Wesley stayed on in Georgia for what proved to be a lamentable period in his distinguished career. His journal is a massive source for historians of the eighteenth century, but that portion of it relating to Georgia needs to be read carefully against the background of his unfortunate experiences in the colony. The inhabitants suspected that he had been sent by the Trustees for a clandestine purpose, and they were quickly upset by his autocratic manner and the establishment in Savannah of what they criticized as a High Church service. He made several trips to Frederica in the south, but won little support there either, and one woman threatened to shoot him. He then completely undermined his position by falling in love with the niece of the Storekeeper, Thomas Causton, a passionate and hot-tempered man who was later dismissed by the Trustees on suspicion of abusing his position in the province. The girl married someone else, and Wesley, spurned and disappointed, gave expression to his injured feelings by refusing her the sacrament of communion. The husband of the offended girl brought a suit for damages against Wesley, who flouted a magistrate's order forbidding him to leave the colony and slipped away to South Carolina one evening in December, 1737, in the company of a Constable, a Tythingman and a barber, reputed to be three of the most objectionable persons in Savannah.[11] The journal kept by Thomas Causton, the Storekeeper, sheds a little additional light on John Wesley's love affair, but it is useful principally for its detailed account of administration in Savannah by a man who was at the center of affairs until 1739 and was sometimes in charge of the colony when Oglethorpe was absent.[12]

George Whitefield, whose evangelizing period in America was as much a success as Wesley's had been a failure, was like Wesley a prolific writer and between 1738 and 1741 he published in several parts journals of his voyages to Georgia and activities there. Whitefield was appointed to Frederica in December, 1737, but in fact spent most of his time in Savannah. He was interested in education and was instrumental in opening a school at Savannah for girls and another at the village of Highgate for teaching English to French children so that they could attend Anglican services. His most considerable achievement, however, was the planning and construction on a five-hundred acre tract near Savannah of an orphanage school which he called Bethesda, and, although his attempt later to acquire a charter for it as a college failed, the orphanage remained dear to his heart and was always an inspiration to him in his work.[13] Whitefield's zeal carried him beyond his nominal office as the Anglican incumbent in Frederica, so that he became more a minister at large. He was popular but shocked some of

11. *Colonial Records of the State of Georgia*, ed. A. D. Candler (26 vols., Atlanta, 1904–16), IV, 40–1; hereafter cited as *Col. Rec. Ga.*

12. *Col. Rec. Ga.*, I, 305.

13. L. Tyerman, *The Life of the Rev. George Whitefield* (2 vols., London, 1876–7), I, 136, 350. *Col. Rec. Ga.*, I, 333–4.

the more conservative inhabitants by occasional unorthodoxy. He pleaded for justification by faith alone and inveighed against modern clergy as "slothful shepherds, dumb dogs, etc. who led their people dreaming on in a carnal security to destruction."[14] In June, 1740, he was reprimanded by the Trustees for proposing to erect looms and teach the orphans at Bethesda to weave. It was widely held in Britain at this time that the function of colonies was to supply raw material for the manufactures of the mother country, not to compete with it by manufacturing for themselves, and consequently the Trustees forbade looms to be set up in any part of Georgia.[15] Within a month of the reprimand, Whitefield was dismissed by the Trustees from his post as minister.[16] Whitefield had wandered through the other colonies on a series of preaching tours and left his Georgia parishes neglected. His experiences in Georgia, therefore, were only one aspect of his career in America, but Georgia provided him with the base he needed for his wider concerns and activities that helped to begin the period of religious revival in America known as the Great Awakening.

All these journals are valuable sources for historians of early Georgia and, in conjunction with the Trustees' records and correspondence, the diary of their first President, the Earl of Egmont, and the journal of their Provincial Secretary, William Stephens, provide a comprehensive picture of the colony's first decade. They portray a colony with a number of small, but growing, towns, notably Savannah, Augusta, Frederica, Darien and Ebenezer.[17]

14. *Col. Rec. Ga.*, IV, 504–5.

15. Instructions to bailiffs, June 6, 1740, C.O. 5/670, p. 443. Trustees to Whitefield, June 11, 1740, C.O. 5/667, pp. 341–4.

16. *Col. Rec. Ga.*, I, 373.

17. The Trustees' records and correspondence are deposited in the Public Record Office, London, at C.O. 5/636 *et seq.* and published in *Col. Rec. Ga.*; Egmont's diary has been published in three volumes by the Historical Manuscripts Commission, London, in 1920–3 (*supra*, footnote 1) and in *Col. Rec. Ga.*, V; Stephens's journals for 1737–41 is in *Col. Rec. Ga.*, IV and Supplement, and that for 1741–5 has been published as Wormsloe Foundation Publications Nos. 2 and 3, edited by E. Merton Coulter (Athens, Ga., 1958–9). Reference might also be made to *A New Voyage to Georgia by a young gentleman, giving an ac-*

Peaceful relations had been established with most of the neighboring Indians and trade with them was expanding. South Carolina was benefiting from its improved security against attack by Indians or Spaniards, and land on its southern borders which had previously lain waste and desolate was now cultivated and its value multiplied fourfold.[18] The initial achievements in Georgia were not as great as had been hoped for originally, but they were considerable, as can be deduced from the writings of early visitors to the colony and active participants in the venture.[19] Unfortunately, the colonists were not allowed to devote themselves wholeheartedly to the improvement of their tiny settlements. Discontented elements in the population were becoming vociferous, and the Spaniards in Florida were turning their eyes towards the unwelcome newcomers on their northern border.

Editorial Note

All documents have been printed here with only the following specific alterations. In manuscript journals, contractions have been expanded, some punctuation marks have been added and "ye" printed as "the." In the journals which were published contemporaneously, obvious typographical errors have been corrected. In John Wesley's journal, the final pages, which do not relate to Georgia, have been deleted. In George Whitefield's journal, some routine entries from the ocean voyage to America, his travels outside of Georgia and daily religious quotations have been deleted.

---

count of his travels in South Carolina (London, 1737) and *A Description of Georgia by a gentleman who has resided there upwards of seven years and was one of the first settlers* (London, 1741).

18. *Political State of Great Britain*, 48 (Nov., 1734), 470. "An Impartial Enquiry into the State and Utility of the Province of Georgia, 1741," *The Clamorous Malcontents*, p. 148.

19. See *The Most Delightful Country of the Universe: Promotional Literature of the Colony of Georgia, 1717–1734* (Beehive Press, Savannah, 1972).

Journal of Peter Gordon

As the Setling of Colony's has in all ages been esteemed a Prudent, and Praise worthy, un= dertaking, So we find from many Instances in History, that they have Often been attended with the Success that Such Noble and Generous undertakings deserved. Nor is it at all to be wondered at, That the Roman Colony's Suc= ceeded So greatly as they did, When we con= =sider them, first, as a People unaquainted with the many Vices. Which are at this time, but too Fashionable and Generall; And almost Strangers To Luxury and profussion of Living. Besides the Romans, were a People little aquainted with Traffick, and as yet arts, and Sciences,

Journal of Peter Gordon

AS the setling of Colony's has in all ages been esteemed a prudent, and praise worthy undertaking, so we find from many instances in history that they have often been attended with the success that such noble and generous undertakings deserved. Nor is it at all to be wondered at, that the Roman Colony's succeeded so greatly as they did, when we consider them, first, as a people unaquainted with the many vices, which are at this time, but too fashionable and generall; and almost strangers to luxury and profussion of living. Besides the Romans were a people little aquainted with traffick, and as yet arts and sciences hade made but a small progress amongst them, so that their minds were wholly bent upon improveing and cultivating their lands, as the only means they hade for their subsistance, nor hade as yet their governours any self interested views of raising private fortunes, and by that means prostituting justice, and oppressing the people to accomplish their base and unworthy ends. But on the contrary, laboured in common with the meanest, for their daily subsistance, which glorious example could not faile to inspire the breast of ever'y Roman to labour, and that with the utmost chearfulness.

This was the state of the Colony's in those dayes, and to which was owing the great progress and figure they made in the world.

The case now is certainly very different, because the people generally used in setling our moderne Colony's are a people who have either by misfortunes, or ill conduct, been reduced from plenty to a state of indigency and want. Or they are the idle and abandoned part of mankind, who were ever strangers to labour and industry, and who are always ready to enter upon any undertaking where they can be supplyed with a year's provissions, their darling idleness indulg'd for some part of that time, and their minds puffed up with mighty hopes and expectations of success. But alass when they enter upon the scene of action and feel the many hardships and difficulty's, such undertakings must for ever be attended with, their industrious resolutions are intirely defeated, and they beginn to wish themselves in any other place and if that cannot be accomplish'd, they return like a dog to his vomite, to gratify those vicious habits of idleness and drinking, which brought them to that unhappy state before. Thus farr I thought necessary to say of Colony's in generall and shall now proceed to the particulars of Georgia.

His Majesty having by his Royall Charter granted that tract of land lying between the rivers, Savanah and Altamaha, and now distinguished by the name of Georgia; to be setled and erected into a Colony and for that purpose hade approved of Trustees for carrying the project into execution. Nothing could be more conducive to the sucess of the undertaking than the choise that was made of so many worthy patriots, men distinguished for their extensive charity and benevolences to mankind to conduct and cary on the work. And who as a proof of their being intirely disinterested in the undertaking, hade at their own requestes bound themselves and their successors by the said Charter from receiving any benefite, what-so-ever from the said Colony.

The trustees, for so we must now call them, in order to be enabled to cary on so great a work, found it necessary to prepare the minds of the people for their charitable contributions, by publishing some account of their designs, and sometime after, reasons for establishing said Colony. Wherein was represented the excelence of the climate, the fruitfulness of the land, and the great plenty of all good things with which the country abounded, and likewise the great advantage the nation in generall would reap from such a setlement which was capable by that amount of producing silk and wine in such quantities, that in a short time there was the greatest reason to believe, would be able to answear our consumption, and by that means save to the nation imence sums of mony that is yearly laid out in forreign countries, for those commodities. And that at so small an expence as twenty pounds, an unfortunate family might not only be transported thither, but also put in a condition of supporting afterwards, and making a provission for posterity. Some other accounts, particularly one by Colonel Pury was published about that time, wherein it was represented as the Land of Promise, overflowing with the abundance of all good things necessary and desirable for the comfortable support of life, and those to be obtained with half the labour, industry and application, that is required here for the lowest subsistance. Many were led into errors by this falacious account which has been found by experience to have very litle truth, for its foundation, seem'd to be calculated only to answear the Colonel's private views; however, those accounts excited the curiosity and desire of great numbers of unfortunate people, to apply to the Trustees, to be of the number of those who should be sent in the first imbarkation, yet not withstanding the beautifull prospect that things cary'd by the accounts that were published, and the necesitious circumstances of those that applyed to the Trustees to be sent over. There were some thinking men amongst the number, who were unwilling to engage in the affair, before they were informed of the tenure by which they were to hold their lands, and of severall other circumstances relating to the Governement Consititution of the intended Colony.

To the first of which they were told by the Trustees that no larger quantity thane fifty acres was to be given to any persone sent over and assisted with a years provissions at the publick expence. Nor any quantity exceeding five hundred acres to any persone that should goe at their own expence to setle there, and cary with them the number of servants to occupy the land as is requir'd by their grant. That their lands were lyable to severall forfeitures, and that in case of dying without male issue their lands were to revert to the

Trustees. This gave occassion, to one of the people, who hade engaged to goe over in the first imbarkation, to represent to the Trustees, that as he hade only one child and that a daughter he could by no means think of going upon those terms, alledging that his daughter being equally dear to him as a sone, he could never enjoy eny peace of mind, for the apprehension of dying there, and leaving his child, destitute and unprovided for, not having a right to inherite or posses any part of his reall estate, or the improvements that he hade made upon it either by industry or expending the litle substance he hade brought from England with him for that purpose.

The Trustees, in consequence of this objection were pleased to indulge the first imbarkation, with the priviledge of nominating their heirs, male or female, related, or otherwise. This condesention of the Trustees, removed many of the difficulties, that were started by the first imbarkation, with regard to themselves. Tho there still remain'd great uneasiness amongst them, with regard to their posterity. For tho the Trustees hade given them the priviledge of naming their successors; yet as that was to be no law, and regarded only the first setlers they consider'd that their posterity, would find themselves in a much worse situation, by their estates reverting to the Trustees, in failure of male issue with all the improvements made upon it till the time of such revertion. And that tho the Trustees hade likewise assured them that upon any persons dying without male issue, and the next of kinn applying to them the right of inheritance should be given to him, provided that; he would occupy the same himself. Or otherwise, that they would give to the next heir applying, a consideration equall to the value of the said lands and improvements. Tho these promises were made by the Trustees yet they were not suffitient to remove the apprehensions of the people. Because they looked upon them, as things of courtisie only. And not such as they hade a right to claime, by the laws, and Consititution of the Colony; besides they considered, that tho the present Trustees were gentlemen of unblemished honour, and unspotted characters, yet they were mortall and in case of death, might be succeeded, by others, who would act upon quite different principles, and who instead of doeing justice, and adhearing to the rules and designs of the worthy gentlemen they succeeded, might have nothing in view but the pursuite of their own interests, by disposing of the lands and improvements, of those who should happen to die, and who hade ventured their lives [and] litle fortunes in making of their setlements, amongst their own friends and relations.

Nor were they at any certainty upon what terms they were to hold their lands, at the expiration of twenty years, when the deed of Trust granted by the King to the Trustees, expired, which was likewise a very great uneasiness to them. Yet not withstanding they chearfully sign'd an instrument prepar'd by order of the Trustees for that purpose whereby they oblidg'd themselves not to quitt the Colony in less thane three years without leave first obtain'd of the Chief Person in Power. That their labour should be in common till they hade erected houses sufficient for the whole and rais'd some other publick buildings for the service of the Colony, after which they received orders to repair on board of shipp, who thane lay at Gravesend, by the 9th of November [1732]. At the same time the Reverend Mr. [Samuel] Smith, one of the Trustees, made an excelent exhortation to the people, recomending to them in the strongest and most moving terms, brotherly love, friendshipp and sobriety.

Friday November the 17th, about eight in the morning we sail'd from Gravesend, on board the shipp Ann, Captain Thomas, Comander, bound for South Carolina, having on board 41 men, 27 women, and 28 children. The same day about noon we came to anchor, at the Bay of the Nore, with the wind at North by West. The 18th we weighed anchor, about five in the morning, with a fine gale, and gott into the Downs about noon, where we lay by to take in fresh provissions for Mr. Oglethorps use, which came on board. About three in the afternoon we thene bore away. Wind at North. In the evening we gott a breast of the South Foreland, and stood down chanell all night; in the morning the 19th the wind coming short, we stood in to the Downs again where we came to anchor, about eleven oclock. And being Sunday hade Divine Service, and a sermon preached by the Reverend Doctor Herbert who went as a voluntier in the expedition. About three in the afternoon, the wind coming about fair, we weighed anchor again and stood down chanell. The 20th were a breast of Beachy Head, with the wind at North by East. The 21st in the morning were a breast of the Isle of White [Wight] with a topsail gale at North by West. In the afternoon Mr. Warrens sone was baptis'd by the name of Georgia Marino, and Mr. Oglethorp having appoynted two Constables viz. Mr. Parker and Mr. Fitzwalter, ordered them to stand godfathers to the child, and Mr. Hodges's daughter godmother, Reverend Doctor Herbert, making an exhortation suitable to the occassion. Afterwards Mr. Oglethorp ordered five gallons of brandy to be made into a flipp which being equally divided was three quarts to each mess which consisted of five people, and to each mess was allowed half a fowl, with bacon, and greens, which was a very agreeable refreshment, our people having never been used to salt provissions before. The evening was spent, with mirth, and order and success to the intended Collony, and the Trustees. Healths went round chearfully.

The same afternoon, about four oclock we took our departure from Beverly Point, bearing North. About five leagues distant, in the evening Mr. Huges was taken ill, with fitts. The 26th about six in the morning Mr. Canons child about eight months old was found dead in the bed, and the same day about five oclock the child was putt in a wooden box, and buried in the sea, Doctor Herbert performing the prayers proper for the occassion. The 28th Mr. Oglethorp sent for me to the cabins, and told me that for the better regulation of our people, he hade besides the two Constables, appoynted four Tything Men, and that the Trustees hade been pleas'd to name me for the first, and desired that I should chuse which family's I best approv'd of to be in my Tything, and under my care, which I accordingly did. Our principle bussiness on board was to see that in the serving out of the provissions and other refreshments, (which was done, every day), each family, or mess, hade justice done them, and likewise that they should come regularly, and in their turns, to be serv'd and take particular care that no cursing, swearing, or any other indeceny's should be comitted. And to prevent the danger of fire, by having candles between decks in the night, Mr. Kilbery was appoynted Corporall, and to see that all the candles between decks were putt out ever'y night at eight oclock. And in case that any of the passengers should be suddenly taken ill, a watch was appoynted, of our own young men, who took it in their turns ever'y night to attend in the steerage with a lanthorne and candles.

December the 9th Mr. Hughes hade the misfortune of breaking his great toe, by the overturning of a scrutore in the cabine which was emediately sett by Doctor Cox, our surgeon, who made a perfect cure of it in a short time. This evening I was taken ill, and continued so till the 21st, which was Mr. Oglethorps birth day, upon which occassion, a sheep and some other fresh provissions was dress'd for our people, and a quantity of liquor given to drink the health of the day. After dinner we were diverted with cudgell playing and riding of skimingtons on account of Mrs. Coles having beat her husband. At night I hade a returne of my distemper, which continued till we came upon the coast of America. During my illness I received the utmost civilities from Mr. Oglethorp, Doctor Herbert, Captain Scott, and Captain Thomas, who all of them visited me constantly, and supplyed me with ever'y thing that was in their power, or wines and other refreshments.

January the 13th [1733] about nine in the morning we see two sails of shipps, and soon after we made land and stood for it, which we discovered in a short time to be Charles Town. Mr Oglethorp sent for me, and desired to know if my cloaths were on board, and if I could conveniently come at them, for that he intended to send me ashore with his complements to the Governour, and to bring of [off] a pilote. But being advised to fire guns, which is the usuall signall for pilotes to come off, and that it would give us the greater dispatch, it was accordingly done, but no pilote coming, Mr. Oglethorp resolved to goe himself, and sett off emediately from the shipp in the pinnace with six rowers, Mr. Amatiss, Mr. Kilbery, and two servants—about six he arrived at Charlestown, and returned on board the next day at noon, and brought with him Mr. Midletone one of the pilots belonging to the men of warr, stationed at Carolina.

This day we catched plenty of dog fish, black fish, angell fish, and severall other sorts, suffitient for all the people for severall dayes which was a welcome refreshment, they having lived chiefly upon salt provissions the whole voyage. At night about eleven oclock, we weighed anchor for Port Royall, but the wind coming short, we turned to the windward all night; and in the morning being the 15th found we hade only gained four leagues. The 17th about two in the afternoon, we were alarmed by a sloop who as soon as he perceived us standing along shore, emediately changed his course and bore down upon us, which looking very suspitious made us conclude the he must either be a pirate or Spanish Guard de Costa and that his intention was to plunder us, upon which Mr. Oglethorp order'd all our men upon deck, and the small arms to be brought up, and all the women and children to keep below, and not appear upon deck. In the mean time, while we were drawing our men up, and getting our arms loaded, and ready for our defence, Captain Thomas who commanded the shipp order'd his great guns to be charged, and all things ready on his part, continuing still our course. And the sloop bearing still down upon us and who by this time hade gott so near us that we could perseive he hade Jack Ensigne and pennant flying, which appear'd to us to be Spanish Colours, but being by this time pretty well provided for him, the Captain ordered the course to be hauled up in order to waite for him. As soon as he came within gun shott of us, the Captain order'd a gun to be fired across his stem, and we could perceive the ball to fall about a hundred yards a head of him, but that not bringing him too, as we expected it would, he ordered another to be fired, still nearer to him, which fell within a very small distance of him, upon which and fearing the next shott would be aboard him he thought proper to lower his top sails, and upon viewing us and finding we were so well provided for him both sides of the shipp being compleatly lined with armed men, he thought proper to gett upon a wind, and stand away the same course he was in when we perceived him first. The pilote whome we hade on board said he hade some knowledge of him that he hade been a pirate, and that he certainly would have plundered us hade he not found we were too strong for him. I cannot here omitt taking notice of the bravery of some of our women who when we expected every moment to come to an ingagement beg'd they might be assisting in handing us up arms amunitions, and what ever should be wanted, and that if it would be permitted they would come upon deck and fight as long as they could stand, while some of our men who hade been noted the whole voyage for noisy bullying fellows, were not to be found upon this occassion but sculked either in the hold or between decks.

The 18th came to an anchor in Port Royall river. The same evening Mr. Kilbery was sent to an island in the mouth of the river to gett what canoes he could, and returned to the shipp in the evening with one canoe and two men. The next morning Mr. Oglethorp and Doctor Herbert went up the river in the pinace to Beauford Town to provide periagaes to be assisting to us in debarking, and Captain Scott went with a party of six armed men in the canoe which was brought on board the night before, to secure those periagaes for owr use in their returne home who hade been imployed in carrying the Swiss under the command of Colonel Pury to their new setlement of Purisbourgh up Savannah River; and likewise to gett hutts built for owr accomodation in owr passage to Georgia. The same day sent owr boat with the pilote to find owr anchor, which we were oblidged to leave on Port Royall Barr. The day before in the evening they returned, and brought the anchor with them, but the wind being contrary, we could not gett up the river that night.

Saturday morning the wind being fair, we weighed anchor, but it coming very hazy, were oblidged to come too again. Clearing up in the afternoon we weighed again, and came to our moorings about five in the afternoon, within three miles of Beauford Town. About eight in the evening a canoe was sent on board by Mr. Oglethorp to let the Captain know that he intended to come on board with the first of the tide of ebb. About eleven oclock at night he arrived, and brought with him a large periagoe, ordered severall more to attend us the next morning, when we begane early to pack up our goods, in order for a generall debarkation. About noon, we were all safely landed at the new fort where we found by Mr. Oglethorps direction the barracks belonging to Captain Massys [Philip Massey] Independant Company clean'd out on purposs for owr reception, fires lighted, and provissions provided for owr refreshment. During owr stay here which was ten dayes, we were constantly visited by the planters of the country and diverted ourselves with fishing and shooting. Here our Tythings begane to mount guard. On Sunday we hade an excellant sermone preach'd by the Reverend Mr. Jones, minister of Beauford, under a tent which wee erected for that purpose, and likewise another adjoyning to it for the intertaining of the strangers of the better sort. Tuesday the 30th of January we begane about four in the morning to pack up our goods and putt them on board petiagores in order to proceed for Georgia. About eight we were loaded and under saile, but the tide being farr spent, and it blowing very hard we were oblidged to bear a way for a creek near a place call'd the look out, where we anchor'd and lay all night. Wednesday morning, about five we weighed anchor again, with a fair wind, and arrived at Jones's Island about six in the evening where we found hutts provided for us by Captain Scotts party. The same day the Indian hunters brought us in thirteen quarters of venison which was divided amongst us and dress'd for supper.

Next morning being the first of February, we sailed from Jones's Island, with a fair wind and arrived the same day at Yamacra Bluff in Georgia, the place which Mr. Oglethorp hade pitched upon for our intended setlement. As soon as we came near the Bluff, we were saluted by Captain Scott and his party, with their small arms, which we returned. And as soon as we landed, we sett emediately about getting our tents fixed, and our goods brought ashore, and carryed up the Bluff, which is fourty foot perpendicular height above by water mark. This by reason of the loos sand, and great height, would have been extreamly troublesome hade not Captain Scott and his party built stairs for us before our arrivall, which we found of very great use to us in bringing up our goods.

About an hour after our landing, the Indians came with their King, Queen, and Mr. Musgrave, the Indian trader and interpreter, along with him to pay their complements to Mr. Oglethorp, and to welcome us to Yamacraw. The manner of their aproach was thus, at a litle distance they saluted us with a voly of their small arms, which was returned by our guard and thane [then] the King, Queen, and Chiefs and other Indians advanced and before them, walked one of their generalls, with his head adorned with white feathers, with ratles in his hands (something like our casternutts) to which he danced, observing just time, singing and throwing his body into a thousand different and antike postures. In this manner they advanced to pay their obedience to Mr. Oglethorp, who stood at a small distance from his tent, to receive them. And thane conducted them into his tent, seating Tomo Chachi upon his right hand [and] Mr. Musgrave, the interpreter, standing between them. They continued on conference about a quarter of an hour, and thane, returned to their town, which was about a quarter of a mile distant from the place where we pitched owr camp, in the same order as they came. Not being able to compleate the pitching of our tents this night, and I being but lately recover'd from my illness, went to ly at the Indian town, at Mr. Musgrove, the interpreters house, with Doctor Cox and his family and Lieutenant Farringtone belonging to Captain Massy's Company, who hade order'd a handsome supper to be provided for us at Mr. Musgraves house.

As soon as the Indians were informed that we were come to Musgroves house, they begane to entertaine us with dancing round a large fire which they made upon the ground, opposite to the Kings house. Their manner of dancing is in a circle, round the fire, following each other close, with many antick gestures, singing and beating time, with their feet and hands to admiration. One of the oldest of our people, Doctor Lyons, having slept away from our camp and gott a litle in drink, found his way up to the Indian town and joyned with the Indians in their dance indeavouring to mimick and ape them in their antick gestures, which I being informed of, sent for him, and desired that he would emediately repair home to our camp. Otherwise I assured him I would aquaint Mr. Oglethorp with his folly. He promised me that he would. But being so much in liquor he returned again to the Indians and danced with them as before, which being told to me I ordered severall white men who were there to carry him home by force, it being of a very bad concequence that the Indians should see any follies or indiscretions in owr old men, by which they judge that our young men must be still guilty of greater, for they measure mens understanding and judgement according to their years.

Friday the 2d we finished our tents, and gott some of our stores on shore. The 3d we gott the petiagores unloaded, and all the goods brought up to the Bluff. Sunday the fourth, we hade Divine Service performed in Mr. Oglethorps tent, by Reverend Doctor Herbert with thanksgiving for our safe arrivall. Mr. Musgrove, the Indian trader, and his wife were present, and Tomo Chachi, the Indian King, desired to be admitted, which Mr. Oglethorp readily consented to and he with his Queen were seated in the tent. During the time of Divine Service, severall of the Indian warriors and others sate at a small distance from the tent, upon trees, and behaved very decently.

Munday the 5th Colonel Bull, being a gentlemen of great experience in making of setlements, was appoynted by the Governour and Councill of Carolina to come to us to be assisting with his advise, arrived in his own periagore from Charles Town and brought severall letters for Mr. Oglethorp from the Governour and Councill.

Wednesday the 7th we begane to digg trenches for fixing palisadoes round the place of our intended setlement as a fence in case we should be attacked by the Indians, while others of us were imployed in clearing of the lines, and cutting trees to the proper lengths, which was the 14 foot for the palisadoes. About noon a fire broke out in the guard room, which instantly consumed the same, and burnt severall chests that were in it belonging to owr people and likewise a hutt adjoyning to it belonging to Mr. Warren, whose things were likewise burned. It was with much diffuculty we gott the powder out of Mr. Oglethorps tent, which stood almost joyning to the fire, and which we preserved by taking it emediately down. After we hade gott the fire pretty near extinguished, one of the large pine trees near 100 foot high took fire and to prevent further damage we were obliged to cutt it down, and in the fall it broke too barrells of beef and one barrell of strong bear [beer] in pieces and damaged the end of one of owr tents. The whole damage amounted to about twenty pounds sterling.

Thursday the 8th each family hade given out of the stores, an iron pott, frying pan, and three wooden bowls, a Bible, Common Prayer Book, and Whole Duty of Man. This day we were taken of [off] from the palisadoes and sett about sawing and splitting boards eight foot long in order to build clapp board houses, to gett us under better cover till our framed houses could be built. This evening Mr. St. Julien, Mr. Whitaker, Major Barnwell, and Mr. Woodward arrived from Charlestown.

Friday our arms were delivered to us from the store viz. a musket and bayonett, cartrige box and belt to each persone able to cary arms. Sunday we were drawn up under owr arms for the first time, being divided into four Tythings, each Tything consisting of ten men, of which I was appoynted to command the first; Mr. Causton, the second; Mr. Jones, the third; and Mr. Goddard the fourth. I mounted the first guard at eight oclock at night, received orders from Mr. Oglethorp to fix two Centinells at the extream parts of the town who were to be relieved ever'y two hours and thane returning to the guard house, which we hade built of clapp boards, upon the most convenient part of the Bluff, for commanding the river both wayes. The next night at eight oclock I was relieved by Mr. Causton, who march'd to the guard house with his Tything under arms where I received him with my Tything drawn up before the guard with their arms rested.

Not withstanding that our guard duty was ever'y fourth night, yet we went directly from the guard to work in the woods, after owr names were called over, which was done ever'y morning at six oclock before Mr. Oglethorps tent, and if any persone did not at that time answear to his name, except hindred by sickness, was cutt of [off] from his dayes allowance of a pint of Madeira wine, which was allowed to every working man. About this time we hade excessive hard rains and almost continued thunder and lightening to a most astonishing degree. The rains were so violent, and came with such force, that it beat through our tents to that degree that we have been wett to the skinn in them severall times in a day. And to prevent our bedding from being wett, hade no other methode but by covering them with plates, dishes, bowls, and what other conveniency we hade to catch the rain in, which has often been so heavy that severall gallons has been catched in those vessells upon one bed, in the space of an hour.

As the country all round us was a continued forrest, and nothing to be seen but wood and water, the rains were very frequent and very severe. But as our people who were daily imployed in cutting down trees, and clearing the place which was intended for the town, advanced in their work, and hade cleared a pretty large space of ground, wee could perceive the rains not to be so frequent, nor so violent. Munday Mr. Oglethorp being informed that two fellows who hade broke out of Charles Town jayle, were in our neighbourhood, and hade killed severall catle, at Musgrave, the Indian traders cow penn, ordered two men with a large swivell gunn to watch near the side of the river all night to stopp their canoe in case they should attempt to pass, and if apprehended each man was to have a reward of ten pound currency from Mr. Oglethorp. The same evening Mr. Oglethorp desired us to draw up a letter of thanks to Mr. Whitaker and the other gentlemen, who hade generously made us a present of 100 head of catle to be equally divided amongst us. We drew the letter up, and had it signed by severall of our people, and went in a body and delivered it to Mr. Whitaker and the other gentlemen.

Tuesday early in the morning wee were all ordered under arms to salute those gentlemen before they sett out for Charles Town, which we did as they were going in to their boats, with three generall discharges and three husass. The same morning we see at a distance up the river, something like a canoe, which we supposed to be the two fellows who hade made their escape from Charles Town. Upon which Mr. Oglethorp ordered me to take two men along with me, in a canoe, and goe in quest of them. I chose Mr. Cristie and Mr. Cameron to goe along with me, and when we came to the place where we expected to find the fellows, we found that what appeared to us in town like a boate was a large tree floating down the river. Upon which we returned.

The 18th a servant maid belonging to Mr. Hughes was ordered to be brought before Captain Scott, Conservator of the Peace, where she was accused of a loose disorderly behaviour, and endeavouring to seduce severall other young women in the Colony, upon which she was ordered to be whipt at the carts taile, and returned to England to her friends, and in the mean time she was given in charge to the Constable. The 19th Mr. Oglethorp went in the scoutt boat to the Island Tybe in the mouth of our river to pitch upon a proper place for a small setlement for some people from Carolina who desired to be admitted under his protection, and to serve as a look out for our setlement. About four in the afternoon Colonel Pury arrived at the Indian town in a canoe from Purrisbourgh. I was ordered to take four of my guard with their arms, and waite upon the Colonel with the complements of the gentlemen and to give him an invitation to our camp. The Colonel returned their complements with great civility and desired me to aquaint the gentlemen that he would waite upon them presently. We were thane ordered all under arms, and when the Colonel arrived we saluted him with a generall discharge of our small arms. About seven in the evening Mr. Oglethorp returned in the scoutt boat from Tybe. This day our new crane was putt up.

Tuesday the 20th a warrant from Captain Scott came directed to me to see the sentence executed on the servant maid who some dayes before, was ordered to whipt, upon which I ordered four of my guard under arms to bring her out, a negroe being appoynted to whipp her. As soon as she was brought to the cart severall of our people interceded with Mr. Oglethorp in her behalf, who remitted that part of her sentence and sent her the same day out of the Colony onboard a petiagore bound for Charles Town in the care of Mr. Osbourne, the patroon. The 21st about two in the morning Doctor Herbert sett out for Charles Town, in the scoutt boat, accompanied by Colonel Pury and some of his people. The same day Mr. Kilbery sett out with a small party and an Indian guide, to apprehend the fellows who were in the woods, and hade been discovered by the Indians. About eleven at night he returned with the prisoners, who were emediately examined before Mr. Oglethorp.

One of them was English and the other a French man. The Frenchman denied all he was charged with, of having broke out of Charlestown jayle, and having committed severall roberies, and killed severall catle, in our neighbourhood. The English man confess'd most of what he was charged with, alledging that what catle they killed was only for their own subsistance, they having been in a most miserable way destitute of any manner of food in the woods, and must have inevitably perished hade they not done it. The French man was ordered into custody of the guard belonging to Captain Massy's Independant Company, ten of whome with a serjeant, were ordered to be assisting to us in Georgia. The other was ordered into custody of our guard.

The 22d. Mr. Fitzwalter, one of our people, arrived with fifty head of catle and other stores from Carolina. This catle was part of the hundred, which Mr. Whitaker and his friends hade made a present of to us. The 23d. the bell was hung at the end of the crane. The 25th the two prisoners were putt on board Captain Andersons petiagore to be sent to Beauford, and there to be delivered to Captain Watts, who was the commanding officer, and to be by him forwarded to Charles Town. The same day Mr. Oglethorp, Colonel Bull, and Tomo Chachi went up the river in order to give the Indians possesion of the lands alloted for their setlement, lying between the creeks six miles above us. About seven in the evening they returned to the camp. March the 1st the first house in the square was framed, and raised, Mr. Oglethorp driving the first pinn. Before this we hade proceeded in a very unsetled manner, having been imployed in severall different things such as cutting down trees, and cross cutting them to proper lengths, for clapp boards. And afterwards splitting them into clapp boards, in order to build us clapp board houses, which was the first design, but that not answearing the expectation, we were now divided into different gangs, and each gang had their proper labour assign'd to them and to be under the direction of one persone of each gang so that we proceeded in owr labour, much more regular thane before, there being four setts of carpenters, who hade each of them a quarter of the first ward, alloted to them to build, a sett of shingle makers, with proper people to cross cutt and splitt, and a suffitient number of negroe sawyers, who were hired from Carolina to be assisting to us. The same night, one redman, an Irish man, was ordered into custody of the guard on suspition of his being a spy and intending to goe to St. Augustine, a Spanish setlement, to informe them of the situation of owr affairs. But after frequent examinations, and nothing appearing against him, he was discharged.

Sunday the fourth, after Divine Service, we were ordered under arms, and the Tythings marched regularly into the wood, a small distance from the town, where Mr. Oglethorp ordered a mark to be fixed up, at a hundred yards distance to be shott at by all the men, and who ever shott nearest the mark, to have a small prise of seven or eight shillings value. This custome which was intended to train the people up to firing, and to make them good marksmen, was generally observed, for many Sundays afterwards. That being the only day we could be possibly spared from labour, and with some success. Thursday the 7th the Indian King & Chiefs desired a talk with Mr. Oglethorp, which he readily granted, and received them at a house which was fitted up on purpose for that occassion. Mr. Oglethorp being seated at the door, on a bench covered with blew cloath with Captain Scott on his right hand and Mr. Jon. Brian on his left, the Indians advancing with Mr. Musgrove, their interpreter, before them. Most of them hade their heads adorned with white feathers, in token of peace, and friendshipp. Before the King and other Chiefs, marched two warriors carrying long white tubes, adorned with white feathers, in their left hands, and ratles in their right hands, which was cocoa nutt shells, with shott in them, with which they beat time to their singing as they marched along, but before they reached where Mr. Oglethorp was they made severall stopps, and at each stopp they begane a new song, in which they recounted all the warlike exploits of their forefathers, which is all the records they have, and the only methode of handing down to posterity the history of their great men. When they came near the place where Mr. Oglethorp was, the two warriors, who carried the feathers, and ratles in their hands, advanced before the King and and other Chiefs singing and playing with their ratles and putting themselves in many antike postures. Thane, they came up to Mr. Oglethorp and the other gentlemen and waved the white wings they carried in their hands, over their heads, at the same time singing and putting their bodys in antike postures. Afterwards they fixed a lighted pipe of tobaco to the tubes which they held in their hands, and presented it to Mr. Oglethorp, who having smoaked severall whiffs they thane presented it to the other gentlemen, who observed the same methode which Mr. Oglethorp hade done. Thane they afterwards presented the same pipe to their King and two of their Chiefs, the King and each of the Chiefs smoaking four whiffs, blowing the first whiff to the left, the next to the right, the third upwards, and the fourth downwards. After this ceremony was over, they walked in to the house, the King being seated opposite to Mr. Oglethorp and the Chiefs on his right hand, thane Mr. Oglethorp desired the interpreter to ask the King, whether they desired to speak first. The King said they did, and bid the interpreter should say to Mr. Oglethorp, that they were glade to see him, and his people, safely arrived in this country and bid us hearty welcome to Yamacraw. Thane he said that with regard to one of his people, that hade been killed by the Uchis (another neighbouring nation of Indians) he would not take revenge without Mr. Oglethorps concent and approbation, (taking revenge is a terme they use, when they intend to declare warr). He thane said that he was not a stranger to the English, for that his father and grand father had been very well known to them. He afterwards presented Mr. Oglethorp with some deer skins, which is the most valuable, and indeed the only thing of value they have. Mr. Oglethorp after having assured them of his friendshipp, and utmost assistance and protection, made them some presents with which they were very much pleased. They afterwards returned to their own town in the same manner as they came.

Wee hade hither too continued very healthy, and proceeded in the publick labour with as much success and dispatch as could possibly be expected. But the weather beginning to be extreamly hott, and owr people haveing as yet no other water to drink but that of the river, which at high water was brackish, we did not long enjoy that happiness, for soon afterwards we begane to be very sickly, and lost many of owr people who died very suddenly.

Aprile the 6th Doctor Cox died very much lamented, being a generall loss to the Collony. He was a very useful and well experienced gentlemen. As the first persone that died, and we being thane, under a sort of a military government Mr. Oglethorp ordered that he should be buried in a military manner. All owr Tythings were accordingly ordered to be under arms, and to march regularly to the grave, with the corps, and as soon as he was interr'd and the funerall service performed we gave three generall discharges of owr small arms and during the time that we marched with the corps, and while the funerall office was performing, minute guns were fired from the guard house and the bell constantly toling. This military manner of burying was afterwards observed not only to all owr men that died, but likewise to owr women, till the people begane to die so fast that the frequent firing of the canon, and owr small arms, struck such terrour, in owr sick people (who knowing the cause, concluded they should be the next) that we have hade three or four die in one day which being represented to Mr. Oglethorp he ordered that it should be discontinued.

The Reverend Mr. Quincy arrived from England, and succeeded the Reverend Doctor Herbert, who some time before was returned but died in his passage. We hade now found out a spring of water, about half a mile distant from the town, which was of great service to the people. Soon after we discovered severall more. But to prevent the trouble of going so farr to fetch it Mr. Oglethorp ordered a well to be sunk in the midle of the town, not expecting to find water in less thane 40 or 50 foot. However before they hade sunk 25 foot we found plenty of water, which still continues to supply the town.

Mr. Oglethorp sett out in the scout boat for Charles Town in South Carolina, in order to apply to the Governour and Assembly, for some assistance towards carrying on the Colony, which having succeeded in, returned to Savanah, and brought severall gentlemen along with him to visit owr new Collony. During his absence an unlucky accident hade like to have hapned. Captain Scott to whome the command of the place was left, the civill goverment not being yet settled, having ordered a servant belonging to one Gray to attend him and the rest of the gentlemen that came to visit the Colony, Gray refused to send him, alledging that it was a very great hardship to have his property taken from him, which he looked upon his servant to be, and having infused this notion amongst the common people with whome he conversed, had formed a larg faction, who all agreed not to part with the servant, but would rather lose their lives in protecting him. This being whispered about, Captain Scott sent to me at night, when I went to relieve the guard and desired that I should take a file of my guard, with their arms, and goe and demand the servant, and bring him away. I accordingly chose two of the people I could best trust so, and came to the house where the servant was, but could not gett admittance for some time. At length the door was opened, and I went in with my men and demanded the servant, which the master refused, and the women who were in the house declared that there were twenty arm'd men without, ready to defend him in case any attempt was made to take him away by force. I told them the necesity I was under of obeying command, without no good order could possibly subsist, that tho I was determined not to goe without the servant, yet I was very unwilling to carry things to extreamity, and assured them that there was no intention of taking the servant from them, only to be assisting for a few dayes till Mr. Oglethorps returne, when I told them they might depend upon having any grievance redress'd as soon as he arrived. And their conduct in submitting to command, very much approved of, still I could not prevaille, by all the fair means I could possibly use, [convince them] so I resolved to carry it a litle farther, and with some small litle opposition I gott upstairs where the servant was, and ordered him to come down emediately, which with some reluctance he obey'd. But still the difficulty was to gett him out of the house, for they begane to be very clamorous, and sounded still resolved not to part with him. And I on the other hand was determined not to goe without him. And once more begg'd they would consider the concequence of opposing authority, that it would be deem'd mutiny and that they certainly would be punished as such, and at the same time assured them that if they would let the servant goe peaceably, in obedience to command, I gave them my word he should be returned to them in an hours time, and likewise promised that he should not receive any punishment. This at last they agreed to, and according to my promise the servant was returned in an hours time. So we happily gott over this affair which might have been attended with very fatall concequences.

On the [hiatus] a messenger arrived with an account that the Chiefs of the Upper Creeks and Uchi nations were arrived at Captains Bluff in their way to Savanah, upon which a house was ordered to be fitted up to receive them in, and the next morning they arived in a petiagore, having travell'd five hundred miles thro the woods to enter in to a Treaty of Friendshipp with Mr. Oglethorp, and receive the presents usuall on those occassions. There was to conduct them two Indian traders and interpreters, whom Mr. Oglethorp had sent up to the nations on purpose to bring them down. As soon as they arrived Mr. Oglethorp ordered me to goe to the water side and receive them at their landing, which I did and conducted them to the house where Mr. Oglethorp was to receive them. And Mr. Oglethorp being willing to show them owr strength, the great guns were fired as soon as they landed, which they seem'd much surprised at, many of them having never heard a cannon before, and all owr people being under arms lined the way on each side they were to pass thro from the Bluff to the house where Mr. Oglethorp was.

The Kings or Chiefs were seated on each side of Mr. Oglethorpe and the interpreters stood before, and the other Indians about four score in number satt on the floor, smoaking tobaco, and Mr. [John] Colleton and Mr. St. Julien, two gentlemen who came to visite us from Carolina, filled wine and were assisting during the time of the talk, which being ended, and they having received their presents, they retired each nation to a different camp, a small distance from the town where they continued a week, and were supply'd during that time with provisions from the Trustees stores.

About this time Mr. Oglethorp haveing some thoughts of returning to England, as soon as he could possibly gett things a litle setled and being desirious before his departure, to see what success the new scheme of government would have, declared his intentions of constituting the court (which was to be a Court of Record) and qualifying those persones who were appoynted to the magistracy, by a speciall comission from the Trustees before we left England, with (as it was believed) a discretionary power to continue or discontinue them as he found they were deserving. Accordingly the day was appoynted which was the 7th of July [1733], when the people being assembled together Mr. Oglethorp opened the Trustees Commission for appoynting the magistrates, and called and qualified them according to their rank, which was as follows: Peter Gordon, first Bailiff; William Waterland, second; Thomas Causton, third; Thomas Christie, Recorder; and Joseph Hughes, Register. The government of owr new setlement being thus modell'd, wee were now to act in a sphere different from any thing wee hade ever appear'd in before, the nature of which wee were but too litle aquainted with; and I cannot help saying not suffitiently qualified for offices of so great power and trust, as the disposall of such a number of peoples libertyes and properties, and even their lives, in as full a sense as any judge in England as has been suffitiently evidenced by severall instances.

The other inferior officers, such as Constables and Tything men, were to be appoynted occasionally by the magistrates as they found it necessary. And now all matters both civill and criminall were to be determined before the Court, which as I observed before, consisted of the magistrates I have already mentioned, with a jury of twelve freholders, who were to be properly summoned for that duty by the Recorder or Town Clerk.

This forme of government seem'd to be agreable enough to the people, who were generally satisfied with the decissions of the Court, in the litle matters, either about property or otherwise, which hade as yet been brought before them, but when they considered them as a sett of men, in whose hands and power their lives and fortunes were intrusted and that tho they should be ever so much oppress'd or aggrieved, there was no redress to be expected but by an application to the Trustees in England, which by reason of the distance, was looked upon as a tedious and uncertain relief, besides the danger of having their complaints rejected, and the representations of the people in power (against whome their complaints might probably be justly grounded) receiv'd by the Trustees, which consequently could not faile to throw them under their displeasure and make them be looked upon as a turbulant and restless people, for in the setling of Colony I say when they came to view the magistrates therefor in this light they begane thane naturally to reflect upon the qualifications and characters of those people who were thuss intrusted with the government of the Colony; and finding that tho they were men of fair reputation, yet as they hade never made the law's of their country their study and were almost as litle aquainted with them as they were themselves (nay some pretended to a much superior knowledge of the laws thane any persone in the administration), they therefor by no means looked upon them as people of concequence enough or suffitiently qualified for so great a trust as was reposed in them.

This naturally produced a disregard both for them and their proceedings and tho they could only express their dislikes in privatt caballs, yet it was a very great check to their industry and proceedings in their labour with that chearfulness they otherwise would have done. And what greatly contributed to their discontent was that one of the principle magistrates [Causton] hade the intire disposall and direction of the publick stores. By which all centered in him as having it in his power to starve the people into a compliance with his will and keeping from them the provissions alloted for them, if they in the least seem'd to disaprove or grumble at any measures he was disposed to take, but as there will be occassion to mention this hereafter in the memorialls I delivered to the Trustees, I shall proceed to consider the probability of succeeding in this new Colony, under the present Constitution and forme of Government and offer such reasons as I humbly conceive will be an enternall barr to the undertaking as long as the law's and regulations of the Colony continue in the same shape they are in at present.

The success of all Colony's must depend upon the industry of its inhabitants, in cultivating and improveing the lands that are alloted to them, in order to produce (in the first place) provissions for their own subsistance, and in the next place some comodities for exportation to foreign markets, without which no Colony can long subsist, tho ever so powerfully supported. In order therefor to encourage the people to answear this great end, it is absolutely necessary not to cramp or oppress their minds with any harsh laws, and particularly not to clogg their right of inheritance to the fruits of their labour and industry, with harder terms and more forfeitures thane their fellow subjects in the neighbouring Colonys are lyable to. And above all the greatest care should be hade to setle such a forme of government as is agreable to them, and corresponding with the laws of the country they have been brought up in. And the executive part of this government should be putt in the hands of persons fitly qualifyed, and who are not only distinguished for their superior capacities, humanities, and courage, but they should likewise be such as are in good esteem amongst and agreable to the people. If suffitient care be taken in these points and upon which I may venture to say the whole success depends, there is not in the least doubt but things would succeed (tho slowly) not withstanding the many hardships and difficulties such undertakeings must unavoidably be attended with.

But if on the contrary they should fall short of any of those necesary incouragements and the people find that they are upon a worss footing thane in any of owr Colonys in America it intirely unbends their minds from pursueing the principle thing of clearing and setling their lands; and they become quite tired of their undertakeing and many except those who by their places and oppressing the people, have an opportunity of amassing wealth, are kept by mere force wanting nothing but an opportunity of leaving the Colony and setling in some of the neighbouring provinces, which I know to be the case of many of the better sort of people as well as of the others, and who are only prevented from doeing it, by haveing exhausted the subsistance they brought with them, and necesarly oblidged to contract debts, which they are not in a condition of paying, and which is always found to be a suffitient reason for detaining them in the Colony.

But to proceed to the reasons which I apprehend will be a barr to the success of it I shall give but three, tho there are severall others which may not be so proper to be given. The first is the tenure by which the lands are held. The second is the prohibiting of negroes. And the third is the placing the government in the hands of people who are so farr from being qualified or equall to so great a trust that they are looked upon with the greatest scorne and contempt by ever'y persone who has either seen or heard of their administration.

As to the tenure of the lands the uncommon number of forfeitures contained in the grants, makes it almost impossible for any persone living to comply with them. And tho I am perswaded that no advantage would be taken if half the terms of the grants were not complyed with, yet the mere apprehension of it makes such an impression on the minds of the people that they must live in continuall fear of forfeiting their lands, knowing it almost impossible for them to comply with the conditions upon which they hold them. But this tho very discouraging is not near so fatall in its concequences as the setling the inheritance upon the male issue only and in failure of that to revert to the Trust, and thereby deprive daughters, brothers, and all other relations from enjoying what has been ever looked upon as a naturall right. This law is of its self alone suffitient to destroy the undertaking. For can any one imagine that a man who is posses'd of any property and who has that naturall tenderness and affection for his family and relations, which is common to mankind, would at the hazard of his own and their lives attended with a great expence and constant fatigue goe to setle in a country where if he chances to die without leaving a sone behind him, must have his lands with all the improvements he has made upon them, probably at a very considerable expense, revert to the Trust, and thereby leave his family, who hade been fellow labourers with him and shared in all his hardshipps so many sacrifises and unprovided for. Can one imagine I say that any man in his sences would goe to setle in any country upon those terms. The principle reasone that has been given for this law, is that by the inheritance descending in the male line, a suffitient number of men will be alwayes in the Colony to defend it in case of any attack, and that if the females should inherite, such a time might happen, when the whole Colony would be in the possession of women, and concequently defenceless and exposed a prey to any power who would invade her.

This reason how ever plausible it may appear at first has certainly no foundation in it, as has been suffitiently proved by instances, and can only be the child of some noted refiner of schemes. For supposing a man to die without male issue the Colony receives no emediate addition of strength by this, for that land would, must, doubtless be occupied by some persons already in the Colony or ly wast and neglected till the Trustee thought proper to dispose of it otherwise. And if they should think fitt to send people over from England to occupy that land, I cannot see how the Colony would receive any addition of strength even by that, because the Trustees have land enough in the Colony to give, without giving of that. Whereas on the contrary if the next of male kind or nearest male relation were to inherite (within a limited time) it would soon be occupied by some near relation, who would probably bring with him an additionall strength to the Colony, both of substance and people, which the Colony could never have received without such an accident, and in the mean time the relations who were upon the spott would make all the improvements they possibly could. This surely would be more agreable to justice and tend more to the advantage of the Colony thane to have the inheritance intirely cutt of [off] and the estates revert to the Trust, except the mansion house and one half of the inclosed lands, which the widdow's, in case there be any are intituled to the possession of, during their lives. But still the daughters would be in the same unhappy circumstances and cutt off from any hopes of inheriting or being provided for, upon a distant and most improbable supposition that a time might happen when the Colony would be wholely in the hands of women, and concequently defenceless.

European, and particularly English and other Brittish women, if they are sober and of good behaviour, are generally in good esteem and very valuable all over owr setlements both in the West

Indies and in America, and it is seldome known that a woman of any merrite, lives long single in these countrys, but have the good fortune of being married, often to great advantage. Thane I think it will naturally follow that if the right of inheritance were in the daughters, in failure of male issue it would be a means rather of strengthning the Colony thane of weakning it, because the incouragement of having a setlement would certainly bring many young men not only from owr neighbour Colonys but like wise from other parts to marry those daughters and setle in the Colony, which would evidently prove to be a very great advantage to the Colony. And it would likewise be the means of increasing greatly the number of inhabitants and setlers and of making those who are already there more easy in their minds and more dilligent and industrious in their setlements. For I am perswaded that this law is one of the reasons why so small a progress has been yet made in the Colony, and has certainly prevented many people of substance from going to setle there.

The second reasone is the prohibiting of negroes. I think it has hitherto been a received maxim in all owr southerne setlements, not only in the West Indies, but also in Carolina, that negroes are much more profitable to the planter (as being naturalisled to the extreame heats) thane any European servants whatsoever. And indeed daily experience showes that it is morrally impossible to doe without them, for it is to their labour joyned to their industry and good management of those who have hade the direction of them that owr Sugar Islands have made the great figure they have done, and to their labour is likewise owing the prodigious quantities of rice, which is yearly made in and exported from Carolina.

The reasons are very obvious: the first, because the climate is more naturall and agreable to them, and concequently they are less lyable to the distempers peculiar to hott country's by being daily exposed to the inclemency of the seasons. This is a truth so generally known that there needs nothing to be said to inforce it. The next reason is because they are much cheaper and more to be depended upon. For example, you purchass a new negroe, id est, a negroe just come from Guinea, for 20 pound sterling, which I take to be the midle price, given between the two extreams. This negroe we may suppose in the generall runn of negroes to be of a sound constitution and uncorrupted morralls, for it is certain that they are unaquainted with the many vices that are but too common amongst owr white servants, and almost in a state of inocency when compared to them and as he becomes your sole property, you may train him up in what manner you think will best answear your purpose, either to the field or to the house (which would not answear any end with a white servant, because his time is so short) and your negroe servant with good usage you may reasonably expect he will turne out a trusty and faithfull servant as long as he lives. For when ever it happens otherwise, it is too often owing to the barbarous cruelty their masters and overseers exercise over them, and I believe it has been observed by many people, as well as my self, that in proportion to the number of negroes and white servants, all over the West Indies and even in South Carolina the white servants generally turne out the worst. Nor can it be reasonably expected to be otherwise, because the common run of white servants that transport themselves to owr Colony's abroad by the help of owr agents for that purpose are generally the very scumm and refuse of mankind, trained up in all sorts of vice, often loaded with bad distempers and who leave their native country upon no other motive but to avoid the worss fate of being hanged in it. What can posibly be expected from such servants but that they would corrupt those you have before if they are not already as bad as themselves, for I am perswaded that of all the miserable objects on earth there is non make a worss figure thane the generall run of white servants abroad, owing intirely to their drunkeness and other vitious habits they hade contracted at home. On the contrary the negroes no where make a better appearance nor in the generall, doe I believe enjoy better health in their native country thane they doe in owr setlements.

The generall price of a common white servant, such as has not been brought up to any particular trade, is ten or twelve pounds, for which sum you have him bound to you by indenture for the terme of four years, during which time you are to supply him with such cloathing as is suitable to the country and usually given in such cases, and he must also be supplyed with provissions which you must likewise doe to your negroe servants, but with this difference that your plantation negroes (who are the only negroes I would be understood to mean) as they are the most usefull negroes. For I look upon the great number of domestick negroes that are kept in the towns, generally for ostentation and grandeur (which is a custome but too prevailing all over owr setlements) to be both an impolitick and unprofitable one, but there is this difference between your white and negroe servants, that your negroes, having a small spott of land alloted to them, which is the common methode, doe by their industry and at their spare hours not only raise provissions suffitient for their own subsistance, but many of them raise poultry and other litle things, which by selling at market often enables them to buy great part of their own cloathing, so that the expence the master is at in supporting his negroes is but very small.

White servants must be treated in a quite different manner, for as they have from their infancy been accustomed to live in a different manner to what the negroes doe, so they must be fed and cloathed much better and concequently at a much greater expence; otherwise you cannot expect to receive any satisfaction or advantage from their servitude. So that I may venture to affirme that the difference of the expence in supporting a white and a negroe servant for the terme of four years (which is the time that white servants are generally bound for) will amount near if not fully to the difference of the prime cost of the negroe and the summ you pay for the white servant for four years. From which it appears even in this point that the negroe is so much cheaper to the planters thane the white servant, as the price the negroe will sell for at the end of four years, which at a moderate calculation may be reackoned at one third more thane the prime cost because negroes that have been trained up for that time either to plantation or any other bussiness, as they become more expert and better aquainted with the particular bussiness they are bred to, because concequently more valuable, and that advantage redounds solely to the propriator of the negroe.

And on the other hand, if a white servant should happen to proove well, the master can reap no further advantage from him, but during the time of his servitude. So that I think it is very apparant that negroes are not only much fitter thane white servants for hott climates, but they are likewise much cheaper and more beneficiall to the planter in ever'y respect. Nay it is morrally impossible that the people of Georgia can ever gett forward in their setlements or even be a degree above common slaves, without the help and assistance of negroes. Because the people of Carolina, who are remarkable for their industry and who inhabite a country equally as fine and productive as Georgia, will at all times, by the help of their negroes be able to undersell the people of Georgia in any commodities they can possibly raise, at any market in Europe. Which I think is suffitiently proved by the small progress, that is as yet made in Georgia. For it is plain to ever'y one who has been there that what is done has been done meerly by dint of money which would have been quite otherwise if the same number of negroes hade been imployed in that Colony as there has been of white people, they would have been able long before this time, not only to have subsisted themselves, but would likewise made a considerable figure in their exports, neither of which the people of Georgia are able to doe, nor can the wisest man living say when they will while the constitution of the Colony remains upon the same footing it does at present.

The third reasone is the placing the Gouvernment of the Colonie in the hands of people that are not in any degree qualifyed for so great a trust as I hade the honour my self of being appoynted and continued First Bailiff for above two years (and till I apply'd to the Honourable the Trustees to have another appoynted in my room). I shall rather chuse to give some account of the magistrates and their gouvernment. From a letter wrote by a very worthy gentleman and friend, who was thane in Georgia, to his corrospondant in London, having obtained his leave for that purpose, and according as this shall be reviewed [I] shall be able to publish some other curious letters concerning the affairs of that Colony wrote by the same ingenious and other worthy friends. But at present shall content my self with giving you his sentiments of the magistrates and gouvernment rather thane speake my own, which I hope will be suffitient to show the evill concequences that attend a weak and disregarded gouvernment in an infant Colony.

Writing to his friend about some affairs relating to the Colony, he sayes,

Here is the cause that will confound us, the Chief Magistrate [Causton] we have here at present, who before he was advanced to this post and was only keeper of the publick stores, under the eye of Mr. Oglethorp, behaved himself in a modest civill manner and was really very dilligent and usefull in his place, is now so elated and puff'd up, his head so full of the dignity of his place and the honour and obedience the people are to pay him that in order to inforce this he runs into the most arbitrary and unjust proceedings, and those who doe not follow in with his measures, he procecutes with the utmost malice. Believe me what I say is not out of any personall pique, for his carriage to me has been very civill, and it is with reluctance that I make any complaint of him. But as the manifest good of the Colony requires it, I think it my duty. Nor shall I aledge any thing against him, but what I shall make evidently appear. If this humour of his amounted to no more thane what may be called a foible, a love of grandeur and ostentation, it would be excuseable, and whilst I apprehended it no worss I always discountenanced any complaints against him and advised all my friends to show him as much respect as he required, and thought it a stifness worthy of blame in them who could not bring their minds to it. And I shall not now alter my conduct in this respect, but whilst he continues in his post endeavour to make the people easy with him, tho I can't excuse him, as I have done because I have been my self a witness, together with the whole Court of a most flagrant piece of injustice, which I shall relate to you at large. But first must observe what a hardshipp the Colony is under, and those in particular who most stand in need of litle assistance and really deserves them, and yet cannot out of a principle of honesty or honour come into his measures. These are sure to have his frowns whilst mean worthless fellows, who can fawn and flatter are his favourites.

With what justice may we expect such a one will discharge the litle trust repoze'd in him, of dealing out the provissions according to nesescity's and deserts of the people. This requires more discretion and impartiality thane he seems disposed to exercise. I call it trust repoze'd in him because the others who are joyned with him (excepting Mr. Gordon, who is now in England) viz. two more, as well in dispensing of justice as in the other affair. Yet he has so absolutely made himself master of them that they are to be considered no more thane cyphers. We live in hopes of having shortly one of the gentlemen of the Trust or some other gentleman of worth amongst us, to take the gouvernment of the place upon him. The presence of such a one would be of vast service to us; nay I could almost say is absolutely necesary for upholding the Colony. There is a generall discontent with the present management, and I cannot say but very justly, for instead of an upright and faithfull dispensing of justice, instead of the magistrates being a terrour to evill doers and a praise to them that doe well.

Things are carried by prejudice and passion, by mean artifice and selfish designs of aquiring absolute power. Trick and cuning are universaly and deservedly esteem'd odious and detestable things in lessor matters, and why should they not appear much more so to honest and well designing men in maters of greater concequence in affairs of gouvernment and administration of justice, where the bad effects of them are more generall and lasting. Surely a persone must be farr gone in Machivilian principles to think them very criminall in one case and yet allowable and laudable in the other. It is certain that they can only serve the vile purposes of enslaving and destroying men, and I am sure the power that aims at those unworthy ends is not the power that is ordained of God.

You see here the sentiments of a very ingenious and worthy gentleman, which will be a great help in forming a right judgement of the gouvernment of the Colony. I shall now proceed to finish the journall during my stay in the Colony, for having by the hardshipps we underwent and living in a manner quite different from what I hade ever been accustomed to, contracted an illness which afterwards appear'd to be a fistula in ano, and owr surgeon Mr. Cox being dead, and no persone in the Colony from whome I could expect any relief, was oblidged to goe to Carolina, in order to gett the assistance of a surgeon there, who belong'd to Captain Massys Independent Company, where I continued three months during which time I was cutt three times and underwent incredible torture. But being informed by my surgeon that he hade compleated a cure, I returned to Savanah again, where in less thane a week I found my self so farr from being cured that I hade a returne of my illness worss thane ever, and there being litle hopes of meeting with a cure in that country I applyed to Mr. Oglethorp for leave to returne to England, which he granted, and wrote a letter along with me to George Heathcote Esq., one of the worthy Trustees recomending me to him and informing him in what manner I hade behaved my self.

And at the same time he assured me that by the next ship he would likewise write to the Trustees in generall in my behalf, which he could not at that time possibly doe, being so much hurryed in the affairs of the Colony that he hade scarce a moments time to spare, for at this time the Trustees hade not for some months heard from Mr. Oglethorp, nor know in what manner he was proceeding, so that he could not possibly write to the Trustees on my account only, without giving them at the same time, an account of the situation of affairs in the Colony, which would have required more time thane he could possibly spare thene.

November the 4th [1733] Gouvernour Johnston, Captain Massy, and Major Barnwell arrived at Savanah, to visite Mr. Oglethorp and the Colony, and the next morning Mr. Oglethorp ordered that the Corporation should waite upon the Gouvernour and the other gentlemen to welcome them to Savanah and to returne thanks to his Excellency for the favours he hade done to owr infant Colony, which we did and was received in a most obllidging manner. The same day his Excellency accompanied with Mr. Oglethorp and the other gentlemen sett out to visite Purisbourg and returned to Savanah the next day in their way to Charles Town.

November the eighth I sett out from Savanah, on my returne to England, and arrived at Charles Town the 12th and as soon as his Excellency, Gouvernour Johnston, to whome I brought letters from Mr. Oglethorp, heard of my arrivall, he with Captain Anson, who commanded one of His Majestys ships on that station, did me both honour of a visite at my lodgings, where they stayed above an hour and his Excellency invited me to dine with him the next day, which I did and during my stay received many civilitys from his Excellency and the gentlemen of Charles Town.

The 25th I sailed for England and arrived in London the 6th of January [1734]. As soon as I arrived, tho I was reduced to the weakest condition imaginable by my illness, yet before I putt my self under Mr. Chrisledons care to be cutt for my fistula, I delivered all the letters and packets I was charg'd with and particularly that from Mr. Oglethorp to George Heathcote, Esq, who was extreamly glade to hear from Mr. Oglethorp and have an account of owr proceedings in the Colony. I hope this worthy gentleman will pardon me if now I cannot omitt mentioning with the utmost gratitude the severall very kind offers of assistance he was so good to make me in my ilness and [illegible] and severall marks of friendshipp I have since received from him and his family.

I also waited upon Mr. [James] Vernon, another of the worthy Trustees, who was also extreamly kind and very curious in inquiring into the state of the affairs of the Colony. As soon as I was in a condition of stirring abroad after Mr. Chrisledon hade cutt my fistula, I waited upon the Trustees at their office, and gave them the best account I was able, of the situation of affairs in the Colony, and at the same time presented to them a view of the new Town of Savanah, its situation, and manner it was laid out in, as likewise the forme and elevation of all the houses and other publick buildings that were compleated at the time I left it. The Trustees seem'd pleased with it, and order'd me to gett a compleat drawing made of it, which I presented to them as soon as it was finished, and for which they ordered me a small present.

As soon as Mr. Oglethorp arrived in England, he gave me an account of what additionall buildings hade been raised since my coming away, and desired that I would have it printed and dedicated to the Trustees, in which I was assisted by a subscription of many of the Honourable Trustees and other noblemen and ladies. The Indian Chiefs who came over with Mr. Oglethorp, being soon to be sent home Mr. Oglethorp was very desirous that I should returne with them. Continued and confirmed in my office of First Bailiff, and at the same time and upon many other occassions, promised me his utmost friendshipp and assistance, I accordingly agreed to returne with the Indians, and applyed to Mr. Oglethorp, the affairs of the Colony being more emediately under his direction, for his instructions, in what manner I was to behave my self, in the execution of my office, looking upon my self not suffitiently qualified for the discharging an office of so great power without the assistance and particular directions of those I thought much better qualified thane my self. However, tho I frequently applyed for them yet I could never obtain any other thane not to oppose Mr. Causton in any steps he thought proper to take. This tho it gave me the greatest uneasiness, yet did not hinder me from persuing my resolution of returning.

And accordingly I imbarked at Gravesend on [a blank for the date, which was October 31] with the Indian Chiefs and about 50 Saltsburgers and as many English passengers, and arrived at Savanah in Georgia [a blank here for the date, which was December 27, 1734] where to my very great surprise I found the affairs of the Colony in the utmost confusion and so generall a dislike to the administration amongst the people, that many of them hade actually entered into one design before my arrival, of sending Mr. Causton, the principle magistrate, and against whom their complaints were chiefly grounded, home to England in irons. This design as soon as they heard of my arrivall they intirely laid aside in expectation that I was provided with full powers of redressing all their grievances, which from the knowledge they hade of me they assured themselves I would readily doe.

But not having received any particular instructions with regards to the execution of my office, tho I hade often applyed for them nor any power of inspecting into the publick stores, and seeing that justice was done to the poor people in the dispencing of them, which was one [of] the principle grievances complained of, I found that my power was not extencive enough effectually to relieve or redress them, tho it may be here objected that I being that

[End]

An Extract of the Journals of Mr. Commissary *Von Reck* and the Reverend Mr. *Bolzius*

A N

EXTRACT

OF THE

JOURNALS

OF

Mr. Commiſſary *Von Reck*,

Who Conducted the Firſt Tranſport of SALTZBURGERS to *Georgia*:

AND OF THE

Reverend Mr. *Bolzius*,

One of their MINISTERS.

Giving an Account of their VOYAGE to, and happy SETTLEMENT in that PROVINCE.

Publiſhed by the Direction of
The SOCIETY *for Promoting* CHRISTIAN KNOWLEDGE.

LONDON:
Printed by M. DOWNING, in *Bartholomew-Cloſe*.
M.DCC.XXXIV.

Extracts of Mr. *Von Reck*'s Journal From Dover *to* Ebenezer.

January 8. O. S. 1733-4.

HAVING a favourable Wind, we left *Dover*, and again set Sail. An universal Joy appeared amongst the *Saltzburgers*, who praised GOD that he had heard their Prayers.

Jan. 9. WE discovered at Noon the Isle of *Wight*.

Jan. 10, 11. AT Eleven in the Morning, having happily passed through the Channel, we left the Land's End.

THUS GOD was pleased to rejoice us, and give us Hopes, that, through the Continuance of his Mercy, the rest of our Voyage would be no less prosperous. May the LORD be pleased always to assist us; we are in his Hands, and to him we entirely trust our Souls and Bodies. Towards Night, the Wind increased so much, that it broke the Stay which held the Main-top-Mast; and we had been exposed to great Danger, if Divine Providence had not averted it.

Jan. 24. THE Weather was fine and pleasant. According to our Reckoning, we passed the Latitude of the *Canary* Islands, and through the adorable Mercy of the Almighty approached the Trade-Winds, which are reckoned to blow all the Year from the Eastward.

Jan. 25. We sung *Te Deum*, and praised the Almighty with our Lips and Hearts.

Jan. 26. God was pleased to give us very fair Weather, with the Continuation of the Trade-Wind.

Jan. 28. An Alarm of Fire caused a great Consternation in the whole Ship, but no ill Accident ensued. For my part, I think that God designed by this Alarm, to call us to Repentance; and to put us in mind of the Uncertainty of this Life, and the Eternity of the next. In reality, almost all became serious; and if they were not thoroughly converted, yet they could not help thinking with terror, how miserable must have been their Condition, had they by so sudden an Accident, been brought before the Tribunal of an offended and just God. Being recovered from our Fright, we [*Saltzburgers*] joined in our Praises unto the Lord, singing Hymns and Psalms, promising before him, never to offend his holy Majesty by any known Sin whatsoever.

Jan. 30. This Day we felt a great deal of Heat; and, for Refreshment, washed between the Decks, where the People lay, with Vinegar.

Jan. 31. A great Shower of Rain fell, and the Wind changed to *West.* Thus God confounds the Opinions of Men, and convinces them, that He is Almighty and Master of the Winds; for the Sailors, who had persuaded us, that the Trade-Wind blew constantly from the same Quarter, found now the contrary.

February 6. At Night, a tempestuous Wind arose, but God in his Goodness, held his Almighty Hand over us, and was pleased the next Day to give us a good Wind, which advanced us five or six Miles an Hour.

Feb. 16. At Two in the Afternoon, the Wind turned contrary *N.* by *W.* but being very gentle, the Sea was calm all that Night. It is remarkable, that *hitherto*, the contrary Winds have always been very gentle, and immediately followed by a Calm, so that we never went back.

Feb. 17. We had this Evening at Prayers *Psal.* l. 14. *Offer unto* God *Thanksgiving, and pay thy Vows unto the most Highest*; Which we heartily did, for all his loving Mercies vouchsafed unto us: and at the same time, we vowed a Vow, as *Jacob* did in *Gen.* xxviii. and the 20th Verse.

Feb. 18. At Two in the Afternoon, the Wind was strong at *S.* and soon after, it proved contrary, and extremely violent. I was very much surprized to see the Sea rise so high; a Tempest darkned the Sky; the Waves swelled and foamed; and every thing threatned to overwhelm us in the Deep. All the Sails were furled; the Violence of the Wind was so great, that it tore the Main Sail in pieces. Besides which, the Mate cried out, that the Water rose fast in the Hold: but though he spoke Truth, the Ship received no Damage. We sighed, we cried unto God, and prayed him to help us. He heard, and comforted us by some Passages of the Holy Scripture, as *Isa.* li. 15. *Psal.* xxxix. 7, 8. *Joh.* chap. xiv. and xvii.

Feb. 20. We saw a *Scotch* Ship, bound for *Charles-town*, and soon lost Sight of her again.

Feb. 27. Last Night we had the Wind contrary *W.S.W.* but God granted us a sweet Repose, and renewed our Strength, the better to undergo a Tempest, which a Wind at *W.* by *S.* brought upon us by Break of Day. This Storm was more dreadful than the other. One sees always Death present in a Storm, and is more sensibly convinced of this Truth, that there may be but a moment between Life and Death. Wherefore those who are not throughly converted to God, and assured of the Happiness of the Life to come, are the most miserable at Sea: for if they chance to perish, they perish in their Sins. We made *the Holy Scriptures* our Refuge, some Passages whereof did mightily comfort us, as *Isa.* liv. 7, 8. and the following verses, *Luk.* xviii. 7, 8. *Heb.* v. 7. *Mic.* vii. 18. Divine Mercy preserved us through our Saviour, and at Night the Wind abated.

March 1. As *Samuel* erected a Pillar which he called *Ebenezer*; so did we also erect in our Hearts an eternal Memorial of the divine Favours. I speak it in Truth, that I look upon it as the greater Mercy to my poor Soul, that God has vouchsafed to send me with the two Reverend Ministers, and the *Saltzburgers.*

Mar. 3. We were comforted, and our Hopes were revived by *Psal.* lxv. lxii. 12. xci. 93. *Isa.* xli. 13, 14. xliii. 12. xxxi. 5. and *Psal.* lxi.

Mar. 4. We sounded this Morning at six, and drew up some

Sand and Soil of *Carolina*; neither did the Water appear so black as before, but look'd yellowish. The Captain lay by to make an Observation, and was hindred by the Cloudiness of the Weather: but a Snow, bound from *Carolina* to *Pensilvania*, passed by us, and gave us an Account how the Land lay. The Captain told me, we were ten Leagues distant from the Shore.

Mar. 5. A *S.S.W.* arose, which carried us, through the Mercy of *Jesus Christ*, within sight of *Carolina*. We sung *Te Deum*, and the 66th *Psalm*, which was the Psalm for the Day, and seemed adapted to our Condition and Circumstances: and we trust it will be a Psalm of Remembrance to us upon the Day, which is to be celebrated every Year, as a Thanksgiving unto the Lord, for all his Mercies vouchsafed unto us. At Eleven in the Forenoon, we discovered the Coast of *Carolina*, all covered over with large Pine Trees. The Wind being *N.W.* by *W.* contrary, we could not reach the Point of *Charles-town*, so that we were forced, as we had been in our Voyage from *Rotterdam* to *Dover*, to stand off and on several times, in order to get more Wind. God acts with us, as he did with the *Israelites*: *Joshua* was to circumcise all those who were willing to enter into *Canaan*: so God is willing to circumcise, amend, and convert our Hearts, before he let us disembark. Towards Evening, we met an *English* Ship, which came from *Charles-town* this Afternoon, and was bound for *London*. He told us the agreeable News of Mr. *Oglethorpe*'s being safely arrived the Night before at *Charles-town*, in his Way to *England*, which mightily rejoiced and comforted us.

Mar. 6. At six in the Morning, the Wind blowing hard at *West*, we lost Sight of Land; though at Noon, the Wind coming to the *South*, we saw Land again: but Night approaching, we lay off and on.

Mar. 7. At Nine, there came from *Charles-town*, a Pilot on Board our Ship, we immediately cast Anchor; and at Ten, the Captain, the Reverend Divines, and I went into the Pilot's Boat. At one in the Afternoon, we came to *Charles-town*, where I immediately waited on his Excellency *Robert Johnson* Esq; and Mr. *Oglethorpe*. They were glad to hear that the *Saltzburgers* were come within six Leagues, all safe and in good Health, without the Loss of any one Person. Mr. *Oglethorpe* shewed me a Plan of *Georgia*, and gave me the Liberty to choose a Settlement for the *Saltzburgers*, either near the Sea, or further in the Continent. I accordingly accepted his Favour, and chose a Place 21 Miles from the Town of *Savannah*, and 30 Miles from the Sea, where there are Rivers, little Hills, clear Brooks, cool Springs, a fertile Soil, and plenty of Grass.

Charles-town is a fine Town, and a Sea-Port, and enjoys an extensive Trade. It is built on a Flat, and has large Streets; the Houses good, mostly built of Wood, some of Brick. Wheat Bread is very dear here, there being no Wheat Flour but what Gentlemen raise upon their Plantations for their own Use, and that is very good; or what they receive from the Northern Colonies, or from *England*; Rice is here excellent and cheap. There are five Negroes to one White, and there are imported generally 3000 fresh Negroes every Year. There are computed to be 30,000 Negroes in this Province, all of them Slaves, and their Posterity for ever: They work six Days in the Week for their Masters without pay, and are allowed to work on *Sundays* for themselves. Baptism is rarely here administer'd to the Children of the Negroes, and Marriage is not in use amongst them; but they are suffer'd promiscuously to mix, as if they were a Part of the Brute Creation. Being thus used, lays amongst them a Foundation of Discontent; and they are generally thought to watch an Opportunity of revolting against their Masters, as they have lately done in the Island of St. *John* and of St. *Thomas*, belonging to the *Danes* and *Sweeds*; and it is the Apprehension of these and other Inconveniencies, that has induced the Honourable Trustees for *Georgia*, to prohibit the Importation and Use of Negroes within their Colony.

Mr. *Oglethorpe* sent on Board our Ship, by the Pilot's Sloop, a large Quantity of fresh Beef, two Butts of Wine, two Tunn of Spring Water, Cabbage, Turnips, Radishes, Fruit, *&c.* as a present from the Trustees, to refresh the *Saltzburgers* after their long Voyage; for which Kindness (under God) we cannot be sufficiently thankful to them.

Mar. 8. We thought this Morning to have gone with the Pilot's Long Boat, on Board our Ship the *Purrysburg*, for the Captain had taken here a Pilot, to bring us into the River *Savannah*. Mr. *Oglethorpe* had given us for our Guide Mr. *Dunbar*, who knows the Country very well, and was already settled in *Georgia*, near the Place appointed for us. We thought, I say, to have gone this Morning; but the Boat was too much loaded, and the Wind, which was *E.S.E.* though favourable for *Georgia*, was contrary for us to reach our Ship. We returned to the Town, and lay there.

Mar. 9. WE beg'd of God, that he would permit us to go to our *Georgia*. We went away this Morning at ten, and got on Board our Ship at two in the Afternoon.

Mar. 10. GOD blessed us this Day with the Sight of our Country, our wish'd-for *Georgia*, which we saw at ten in the Morning; and brought us unto the *Savannah* River, and caused us to remember the Vows we had made unto him, if He did through his infinite Goodness bring us hither. We were to day very much edified with the xxxiid Chapter of *Genesis*, and the xxvith of *Leviticus*. At Noon, we cast Anchor because of the Tide: at eight, during the Evening Prayers, we enter'd the River of *Savannah*; and were shelter'd by the Divine Goodness, from all Dangers and Inconveniencies of the Sea. This River is in some Places broader than the *Rhine*, and from 16 to 25 Foot deep; and abounds with Oysters, Sturgeon, and other Fish. Its Banks were cloathed with fresh Grass; and a little beyond were seen Woods, old as the Creation; resounding with the Musick of Birds, who sung the Praise of their Creator.

Mar. 12. THE Magistrates of the Town sent on Board our Ship an experienced Pilot; and we were carried up to the Town of *Savannah* by 11 in the Forenoon. They returned our salute of five Guns with three; and all the Magistrates, the Citizens, and the *Indians*, were come to the River side. The two Divines, Mr. *Dunbar*, some others, and my self, went ashore in a Boat. We were received with all possible Demonstrations of Joy, Friendship, and Civility. The *Indians* reach'd their Hands to me, as a Testimony of their Joy also for our Arrival. The *Saltzburgers* came on shore after us; and we immediately pitch'd a Tent for them, in the Square of the Town.

I WENT to view this rising Town, *Savannah*, seated upon the Banks of a River of the same Name. The Town is regularly laid out, divided into four Wards, in each of which is left a spacious Square, for holding of Markets, and other publick Uses. The Streets are straight, and the Houses are all of the same Model and Dimensions, and well contrived for Conveniency: For the Time it has been built, it is very populous, and its Inhabitants are all White People. And indeed, the Blessing of God seems to have gone along with this Undertaking; for here we see Industry honoured, and Justice strictly executed, and Luxury and Idleness banished from this happy Place, where Plenty and Brotherly Love seem to make their Abode, and where the good Order of a Nightly Watch, restrains the Disorderly, and makes the Inhabitants sleep secure in the midst of a Wilderness. There is laid out, near the Town, by Order of the Trustees, a Garden for making Experiments, for the Improving Botany and Agriculture; it contains 10 Acres, and lies upon the River; and it is cleared, and brought into such Order, that there is already, a fine Nursery of Oranges, Olives, white Mulberries, Figs, Peaches, and many curious Herbs: besides which, there is Cabbages, Peas, and other *European* Pulse and Plants, which all thrive. Within the Garden there is an artificial Hill, said by the Indians, to be raised over the Body of one of their ancient Emperors. I had like to have forgot one of the best Regulations, made by the Trustees, for the Government of the Town of *Savannah*, I mean, the utter Prohibition of the Use of Rum, that flattering but deceitful Liquor, which has been found equally pernicious to the Natives and new Comers, which seldom fails, by Sickness, or Death, to draw after it its own Punishment.

Mar. 13. I went to see the *Indians*, and their King *Tomo-chachi*: I caused some Raisins, of which they are very fond, to be distributed amongst them. It is worth taking Notice of, that as we were at Evening Prayers, after our Return from the *Indians*, who have their Huts at 100 Paces distance from the Town, one of the *Saltzburgers* should tell us, that he was edified to Day by this Passage of St. *John*, that *God loved all the World*.

Mar. 14. MR. *Oglethorpe* had given Orders for three Horses to be ready for my Service, to take a View of the Country, and to ride to the Place where the *Saltzburgers* were to settle. I went this Morning at nine of the Clock, with a Constable and a Guide; but after we had gone a Mile or two, we enter'd some thick Woods, divided by deep Brooks of Water; and though we could with great Difficulty pass over some, yet there were others we could not pass; wherefore we returned back to the Town.

Mar. 15. I received the List of the Provisions and Tools for the *Saltzburgers*.

Mr. *Oglethorpe*, and Mr. *Jenys*, Speaker of the Assembly of *Carolina*, arrived at *Savannah*, from *Charles-town*; the first having out of Love to our *Saltzburgers* put off his Journey to *England*, being resolved to see them settled before he went. Having informed him, that the Floods had made it impossible for me to pass the Woods by Land; he said he would go himself, to shew me the Country, and see what Place I would choose. The Speaker desired to accompany him, and I did my self the Honour to make one of the Company. He sent to the *Indian* King, to desire two *Indians* to hunt for him in the Journey; who not only granted them, but his chief War Captain, *Tuskeneoi*, out of Civility to Mr. *Oglethorpe*, came along with them to accompany us. We went on Board a ten-oar'd Boat, to the Place where a House was building by Mr. *Musgrove*, * six Miles up the *Savannah* River.

Mar. 16. Having slept well in a Tent which we pitched under the Shade of a Tree, by the River side last Night, I accompanied Mr. *Oglethorpe* on Horseback, and the Speaker and others went by Water.

If you ask, how a Country that is covered with Wood, and cut with Rivers and Morasses, is passable; I must acquaint you, that since the Colony was settled, the Ways were marked by Barking of the Trees, to shew where the Roads should go, and where the Rivers were passable. After passing through a Morass covered with Canes, we came to an unfordable River, through which the *Indians* swam our Horses, and we crossed over upon a great Tree, cut down for that Purpose: The Tree was cut down so as to lie across the River, and serve for a Bridge. And after riding some Leagues in the

* Who afterwards came to *England*, Interpreter to *Tomo-cha-chi*.

Woods, we passed another River. Night overtaking us, we were obliged to take up our Quarters upon a little Hill, round a Fire with the *Indians*, who brought us a wild Turkey for our Supper.

Mar. 17. We continued our Journey, and set out by Break of Day, and at nine arrived at the Place where the *Saltzburgers* were afterwards settled. I shall here give a short Description of it. The Lands are inclosed between two Rivers, which fall into the *Savannah*. The *Saltzburg* Town is to be built near the largest, which is called * *Ebenezer*, in Remembrance that God has brought us hither; and is navigable, being twelve Foot deep. A little Rivulet, whose Water is as clear as Crystal, glides by the Town; another runs through it, and both fall into the *Ebenezer*. The Woods here are not so thick as in other Places. The sweet Zephyrs preserve a delicious Coolness, notwithstanding the scorching Beams of the Sun. There are very fine Meadows, in which a great Quantity of Hay might be made with very little Pains: there are also Hillocks, very fit for Vines. The Cedar, Walnut, Pine, Cypress, and Oak, make the greatest Part of the Woods. There is found in them a great Quantity of Myrtle Trees, out of which they extract, by boiling the Berries, a green Wax, very proper to make Candles with. There is much Sassafras, and a great Quantity of those Herbs of which Indigo is made, and Abundance of *China* Roots. The Earth is so fertile, that it will bring forth any thing that can be sown or planted in it; whether Fruits, Herbs, or Trees. There are wild Vines, which run up to the Tops of the tallest Trees; and the Country is so good, that one may ride full gallop 20 or 30 Miles an end. As to Game, here are Eagles, Wild Turkies, Roe-Bucks, Wild Goats, Stags, Wild Cows, Horses, Hares, Partridges, and Buffaloes.

From hence I returned to the Town of *Savannah*, through *Abercorn*, a Village newly settled by Order of the Trustees, upon the *Savannah* River, near where the *Ebenezer* falls into it.

Mar. 22. Mr. *Oglethorpe*, after a great deal of Fatigue, returned this Morning to *Savannah*; every thing was immediately prepared for his Departure, and he really thought to have gone this After-

* The Stone of Help.

noon; but the Multiplicity of Affairs, the Complaints which were made before him, and several other Things which fell out together, kept him back till to-morrow.

Mar. 23. AND then He went away. All the People were so concerned at it, that they could not refrain their Tears, when they saw Him go, who was their Benefactor and their Father; who had carefully watched over them, as a good Shepherd does over his Flock, and who had had so tender a Care of them, both by Day and by Night; and they were the more afflicted, that the Fatigues and Difficulties of so long a Voyage, left them very small Hopes of seeing Him again.

Mar. 24. *Sunday.* WE were spiritually comforted by receiving the Holy Communion.

Mar. 27. MR. *Jones*, who is a Surveyor, and I, went away this Night in a small Boat, for *Abercorn*, in order to go from thence to seek and clear the River *Ebenezer*. It thunder'd and lighten'd; and the Wind being contrary and strong, we could go up no higher than *Musgrove*'s Land; where we lay under the Canopy of Heaven, upon the bare Ground, having made a good Fire to warm our benumbed Limbs; for tho' it be hot here in the Day-time, yet it is cold in the Night.

Mar. 28. AFTER Breakfast, we continued our Journey, and came at Noon to *Abercorn*. At five in the Afternoon, we entered into a small River, but at nine at Night, we perceived that it was lost among the Trees and Marshes. We entered the same Night into another River, more towards the *W.* very large, and having a good Stream, adorned with Woods on each side of it. At last, we reach'd a rising Ground, where we landed; we cut some Canes, made a Fire, lay round it, and God granted us a good Rest.

Mar. 29. WE went farther up the River, but not without great Difficulties.

Mar. 30. TOWARDS Night we came out of the River, which fell into the *Savannah*, 8 Miles above *Purrysburg*; so our Design was frustrated, by missing the River *Ebenezer*, and we returned the same Night to *Abercorn*, where we staid.

Mar. 31. WE arrived this Afternoon at *Savannah*.

April 1. We put on Board a Sloop, Provision for three Months, with necessary Tools, and the Baggage of the *Saltzburgers*.

Apr. 2. We all went on Board the little Sloop, but found it was too much loaden; wherefore I went with only a few of the Men, and was obliged to leave the rest in the Town.

Apr. 3. We came to the Village of *Abercorn*, at Four in the Afternoon: from hence, we were forced to carry our Provision and Baggage to *Ebenezer* by Land.

Apr. 4. I stay'd at *Ebenezer*, and could not but commend the Diligence and Industry of the nine *Saltzburgers*, who were come before, and whose Labour God had given a Blessing unto. They had erected two good Tents, made of the Barks of Trees, one of which was 40 Foot long; and had cut down abundance of Trees, in order to breathe a free Air: and besides all that, they were obliged in the greatest Heats, almost every Day, to walk to *Abercorn*, which is 12 Miles; and to carry their Utensils and daily Provision, upon their Backs. After this, God was pleased, to shew us a more convenient Road than the other, by which we avoided one of the greatest Brooks.

Apr. 5. I returned to wait the Arrival of the other *Saltzburgers*, who were to follow us immediately.

Apr. 7. The rest of the *Saltzburgers* arrived.

Apr. 8. Mr. *Bolzius* made ardent Prayers, that our Saviour would assist us in our Beginning, and bless our Labours with Success.

Apr. 9. We began to make a Bridge over a Brook, and finished it.

Apr. 10. In the Morning we went on cutting and cleansing.

Apr. 12. *Good Friday*. God was pleased to take to himself, the Soul of one of our People, called * *Lackner*. The Resignation and sweet Death of this Man, who expired the same Day that Jesus Christ did on the Cross, did not fail to touch every one, and raise in us a fervent Desire of enjoying soon the same Felicity, with our Saviour, in the Heavenly Jerusalem. We put up a Box, for the Relief of the Poor, and of the poor Children of the Indians; and as the first Foundation, we put in to it the Deceased's Money, which though but small, we pray God to increase.

* See a more full Account in Mr. *Bolzius*'s Journal.

Apr. 13. THE Reverend Mr. *Bolzius* made a Funeral Oration upon the Words of St. *Paul* in the xith Chap. to the *Hebrews*, ver. 8, 9, 10. which suited the Deceased in every respect. At the Place of Interment, he made a very moving Exhortation, from *Heb.* iv. ver. 9, 10, 11.

Apr. 14, and 15. *Easter.* GOD was pleased to awaken our Zeal for his Service, and to animate us to more ardent Endeavours to enter through the strait Gate into the Kingdom of Heaven, and to pass through this Vale of Miseries, Troubles, Sufferings, and Persecutions, to the eternal Felicity which is prepared for Those who shall remain faithful unto the End, and who shall fight and overcome.

Apr. 16. OUR *Saltzburgers* continued to work upon the Road.

Apr. 18. OUR People had made Sledges; I caused Horses to be put to them, and we brought Provisions to *Ebenezer.*

Apr. 19. THIS Day the *Saltzburgers* finished the Way for Carriages; which surprized the *English* mightily, to see they had compassed it in so short a Time; having built seven Bridges over several Rivers, besides cutting the Thickets and Trees that were in the Way; and this for the Length of 12 Miles, from *Abercorn* to *Ebenezer.*

WE found before my Tent a strong white Horse; and as we wanted Horses, and knew not from whence he came, nor to whom he belonged, we received him with Thankfulness to GOD.——I received Letters from Captain *Mackpherson*, that he would soon deliver us at *Ebenezer* the Oxen which Mr. *Oglethorpe* had bought of him on our Arrival, to supply the *Saltzburgers* with fresh Meat.

Apr. 22. WE found another Horse in the Woods to-day, which proved very fit for our Service. We found also very good Honey in a hollow Tree, which very much refreshed us. Parrots and Partridges make us here a very good Dish. The Earth is of several sorts, some sandy, some black, fat and heavy, and some of a claiey nature. The first is good for Potatoes and Pease; the second for all sorts of Corn; and the third for to make Bricks, Earthen Ware, *&c.* And the Meadows and Valleys are good for feeding Cattle, Rice, and *Indian* Corn: So that we might hope, with the Blessing of GOD, for plentiful Harvests every Year; if there were more People who would apply themselves to the Tilling of the Ground.

Apr. 24. THE Inhabitants of the Island of *Edistow*, having given 30 Cows for the Use of the Colony of *Georgia*, Mr. *Oglethorpe* order'd them to be sent up to the *Saltzburgers*.

Apr. 27. WE sent every Day loaded Sledges to *Ebenezer*.

Apr. 29. I WENT this Day from *Abercorn*, in order to take my Leave of *Ebenezer*, and begin to build a Chapel.

May 1. I HAD Lotts drawn for the Places for the Houses in the Town of *Ebenezer*; through which all the Commerce from *Savannah* by Land to *Carolina* must pass.

May 2. A SLOOP brought us ten Cows and Calves, from the Magistrates of *Savannah*, by Mr. *Oglethorpe*'s Order.

May 5. I RECEIVED by the * Post Letters from Mr. *Oglethorpe*, acquainting me, That we were to receive Twenty Cows and Calves, ten Sows, with Corn for to feed them, and some Fowls and Ducks.

May 9. A Sloop brought us ten† Casks full of all Sorts of Seeds; GOD be praised for it. We do not deserve, O LORD, all the loving Kindnesses thou hast done to thy Servants.

May 10. THE Indians brought us a Deer, which mightily refresh'd our *Saltzburgers*.

May 12. *Sunday*. WE prepared ourselves for the Celebration of a Thanksgiving, to morrow, to Almighty GOD, for his safely bringing us hither. The Chapel was quite finished, so that we could Worship our GOD in it.

May 13. MR. *Bolzius* made a Discourse upon these Words of *Jacob*; LORD, *I am not worthy of the least of all thy Mercies, and of the Truth which thou hast shewed to thy Servant*, Gen. xxxii. 10. The lx^th^ *Psalm*, ver. 9, 10. the lxvi^th^, and cvii^th^, were quoted, and expressed livelily our own Condition. I spake to the People in the Afternoon, and put them in mind of GOD's Kindnesses, by an Enumeration of them, according to my Observations. I read the 26th Chapter of *Leviticus*, and the 28th, 29th, of *Deuteronomy*. I applied them to the Congregation, and we made a strict Covenant with GOD, to serve Him for the future, with a more fervent Zeal, to give Him all that

* A Messenger goes by Land every 14 days, from *Charles-town* to *Savannah*, through *Ebenezer*.

† Which were sent from *Savannah*.

is his, to walk uprightly before his Face, to seek only the Kingdom of God, and its Righteousness, and we renewed the Vows we had made, when at Sea. Have Mercy on us, O our Saviour; Guide us by thy Holy Spirit, into the Paths of Truth; and grant unto us, the Grace to perform in Truth and Sincerity, all that we have promised and sworn unto Thee. After that, I took my Leave of them, and left them some Rules for their Direction, and was very much concerned, at my leaving such good Christians, and good Friends.

Extract of the Reverend Mr. *Bolzius*'s Journal, from Their Arrival in *Carolina*.

Thursday, *March* 7.

THOUGH the Wind is fair, the Ship will not go into *Charles-town* Harbour, but lie at Anchor, till we get a Pilot to carry us to *Georgia*.

WE have Liberty to go with our Captain in a Boat to *Charles-town*, where we intended to get our Habits made: But finding no Taylor here that understands it, we must endeavour to find one at another Place. *Charles-town* makes a fine Shew at a Distance in the Sea, and is very regularly built. What we observed here is as follows:

1. THAT every thing in this Place is very dear, except some sort of Victuals.

2. THAT they have here Money made of Paper, the Value of which is express'd upon it with Letters: and though you give the People Gold or Silver Coin, yet they give you the Change in Paper. This Money is current over all *Carolina*.

3. THAT notwithstanding almost every Thing is dear here, any Body that will work may get his Living.

4. THAT there are more Black than White People here; who all are kept to Work, but not to Christianity. Few are Baptized; the rest live like Brutes, in relation to the Seventh Commandment.

They are brought hither from *Africa*, by the whole Ship-loads, to be sold.

5. THAT the Weather is very hot here. In the Beginning of the Spring all Trees are in Blossom, and the Gardens full of Cabbage, Turneps, Radishes, Sallad, and other Fruits.

6. THAT we found here some *Germans*, who were very glad of our Arrival, and will come to us, in order to receive the Sacrament.

7. THAT three Weeks ago, a rich loaden Ship lying before this Town, was burnt to Ashes, by the Carelessness of a Boy.

8. THAT the Black Slaves are about 30,000 in *Carolina* only. A credible Man told us, that about two Months ago, in the two Islands of St. *Thomas* and St. *John*, belonging to the Swedes and *Danes*, the Black Slaves had killed all the White People; the former being more numerous than the latter.

9. THAT Mr. *Oglethorpe* received us with great Kindness, and went with us to the Governor, a very good Man, where we dined. Mr. *Oglethorpe* told us many good Things of the Heathens that were to be our Neighbours: That they were good and friendly to every Body; but if they were offended, they calmly demanded Satisfaction three several times; which if denied them, they used no more Words, but never forget the Offence, and will revenge themselves many Years after. If a Man behaved himself friendly to them, he could have of them what he pleased.

MR. *Oglethorpe* took Care likewise of the *Saltzburgers*, and sent on Board the Ship a whole Ox killed, Wine, fresh Water, and Garden Fruit. He also sent a Man to serve the People, and to bring us to *Georgia*, because he knew the Way.

Friday, *March* 8.

WE went off with the Sloop, in order to go to our Ship again, but the Wind being contrary, we were obliged to turn back.

Saturday, *March* 9.

THIS Day we came to our People again, which caused great Joy. We found them all in good Health, and they had edified each other by the Word of GOD; which gave us great Comfort, when they told us of it at the Evening Prayers.

Sunday, *March* 10.

BLESSED be the LORD, that he has brought us within the Bounds of *Georgia*, upon the Sunday *Reminiscere*; the Gospel of which Day tells us, "That our Blessed Saviour came to the Borders of the Heathen, after he had been persecuted in his own Country." He hath done great Things for us. He comforts our Bodies with wholesome Food. And lying, in fine and calm Weather, under the Shore of our beloved *Georgia*, where we heard the Birds sing melodiously, every Body in the Ship was joyful. Among others, we compared with this Gospel the xxxii[d] Chapter of *Genesis*, in which we find that the traveling *Jacob*, (1.) Remembers the many Blessings of GOD, and gives Him Thanks for them. (2.) That indeed he was afraid of his Brother: but at last, (3.) By Prayers and Tears, (collated with *Hos*. xii. 4.) was delivered from all Fear, and received the Blessings of *Christ*, (collated with *Ephes*. i.) The second Part especially was enlarged upon, because some were afraid of being invaded by the Enemies in their Country, as hath been told, (*vid. Gen*. xxxi. 24. collated with ver. 29.) Likewise, *When a Man's Ways please the* LORD, *he maketh even his Enemies to be at Peace with him*.

Monday, *March* 11.

THE Captain, to lighten the Ship, order'd that all Casks of fresh Water should be emptied, which we had now no more Occasion for. Before that time, the Captain was so sparing of the Water, that the People could not quench their Thirst; and now he is obliged to spill so many Casks full.

Savannah, Tuesday, *March* 12.

AT the Place of our Landing, almost all the Inhabitants of the Town of *Savannah* were gather'd together; they fired off some Cannons, and cried Huzzah! which was answer'd by our Sailors, and other *English* People in our Ship, in the same manner. Some of us were immediately fetch'd on Shore in a Boat, and carried about the City, into the Woods, and the new Garden belonging to the Trustees. In the mean time, a very good Dinner was prepared for us: And the *Saltzburgers*, who had yet fresh Meat in the Ship, when they came on shore, they got very good and wholesome *English* strong Beer. And besides the Inhabitants shewing them a great deal of Kindness, and the Country pleasing them, they were full of Joy, and praised God for it. We, the Commissary, and Mr. *Zwefler* the Physician, were lodged in the House of the Reverend Mr. *Quincy* *, the *English* Minister here.

Wednesday, *March* 13.

OUR *Saltzburgers* were lodged in a Tent, pitch'd on purpose for them, till Mr. *Oglethorpe*'s Arrival from *Charles-town*. A *Jew* invited our *Saltzburgers*, and treated them with a good Rice-Soop for Breakfast. And GOD hath also moved the Hearts of several others here, to be very good and hospitable to us. The Country, as the Inhabitants say, is very fruitful; and the Land chose by us, which is about 21 *English* Miles from hence, is still better. All that is sowed, grows in a short Time.

Thursday, *March* 14.

LAST Night we Prayed on shore for the first time, in the *English* Chapel, made of Boards, and used for divine Worship, till a Church can be built; the Use of which is allowed us, during our Stay here. The Inhabitants join with us, and shew much Devotion. The *Jews* likewise, of which there are 12 Families here, come to Church, and seem to be very devout: They understand the *German* Tongue. Though the Chapel is but of Boards, it is very convenient, and pleases the *Saltzburgers*.

THIS Afternoon, we were carried to a Camp, which some *Indian* Hunters had in this Neighbourhood, who were in such a Condition as made our Hearts bleed; for in the Absence of their Chiefs (who were gone to meet Mr. *Oglethorpe*) they had much disordered themselves with drinking of Rum, a Liquor very pernicious to them, and which has occasioned the Death of great † Numbers. They were painted with red, and made strange Postures. The most part of them are marked with blue Figures on their Necks, Faces, and

* The Missionary sent to *Savannah*, at the Expence of the Incorporated *Society for Propagating the Gospel in Foreign Parts*.

† This, among other Reasons, has given occasion to the Trustees, to prohibit the Use of *Rum* in the Province of *Georgia*.

Bodies. They have Beads about their Necks, and Rings, or coloured Feathers in their Ears. The *Saltzburgers* had been with them, who likewise were touched with this Spectacle. In this Affliction, we went to Prayer, and unexpectedly met with this Sentence; *For* GOD *so loved the World, that He gave his only begotten Son*, &c. which so greatly moved our Hearts, that we gave GOD thanks for his holy Gospel, especially because we had seen the *Indians* Misery for want of the Gospel. At the same Time we conceived great Hopes, that God will shew plainly that he hath loved and still loves the World. In which good Hopes we were strengthned by the lxxii[d] *Psalm*, which was read; and pray'd that GOD would have Mercy upon these poor Heathens, as he hath had upon others: we shall pray for them. By human Means it will not be easy to help these People, because it will be very difficult to learn their Language.

Friday, *March* 15.

THIS Day Mr. *Oglethorpe* arrived here, and received our *Saltzburgers* and us in a very friendly manner; and we dined with him. He will speedily give Orders that our People shall go to the Place intended for their Settlement. He being very sollicitous that these poor *Indians* should be brought to the Knowledge of GOD, has desired us to learn their Language; and we, with the Blessing of GOD, will joyfully undertake the Task. The *Indian* Language, from the best Information we can get, containeth not above One Thousand primitive Words; and can best be written with *Greek* Letters, because of the long and short Vowels; and some of their Sounds, cannot be expressed by any other Alphabet but the *Greek*. They say, that all Nations descend from two Brothers: that one of them, the Ancestor of the *Indians*, was red; and the other, the Ancestor of the *Europeans*, was white. 'Tis probable, these their Thoughts are grounded upon the History of *Esau* and *Jacob*. They had known nothing of Drunkenness, if they had not learn'd it of the Christians. They give each other several Names of Honour, according to the Time and Circumstances, as a Title or Reward; whereby they encourage young People to Valour, Industry and Fidelity.

THEY have some Religion, believing a Supreme Being, which

they call *Sotolycatè*, * who is in all Places; though they would not teach us the Word, by which they express the Name of GOD in their Language. They believe that from this Supreme Being comes every Thing, especially Wisdom. They use no Ceremonies, nor outward religious Exercises, except at a solemn Festival held once a Year. They worship no Idols; however they sing some Songs about the ancient Heroes. They are unwilling to talk to profane People about Religion. They are very ambitious: for which Reason they make War, but not to gain Land. They love to be praised; though they seem to turn it off, and transfer it to others. They shew great Respect to old People, to whom one must speak first, before one can speak to the young People. If any one dishonours them, they are not to be reconciled. They account themselves to be rude and ignorant, but are desirous to be better instructed. Of *Indians* they have several Nations, the best among which are the *Creeks*, who talk one Language. One of the other Nations, who are called *Uchees*, are much inclined to Robbing and Stealing; but these *Creeks* are Honest, Serviceable, and Disinterested. He that does a Kindness to them, they will remember for ever. And they likewise are willing to give what one desires of them, though they should want it themselves. If Mr. *Oglethorpe* was to desire one of them to go with him to *England*, or any other Place, he would be willing; unless he had an old Father, who was helpless, and wanted his Assistance. They love one another, so that they venture their Lives for one another. They abhor Adultery: They provide for the Poor, the Widows, and Orphans. In their Language are no Words which denote obscene Things, or Oaths; unless they learn them from the *Europeans*. Their Kings do not reign with absolute Power, but give Counsel. The King proposes to the Old Men, and the Old to the Young Men; after which it is put in Execution. They do not contradict one another with vehemence, but endeavour to agree; and if that cannot be, the Superiors are not angry. The King's Office is, to divide the Time; to tell the Season when to go a Hunting, when to Planting, and when to Harvest. Likewise He is to attend the Sick, give them Physick, provide for Widows: and these are called,

* Literally translated, *He who sitteth Above.*

KINGS OF PEACE. When a King is not fit for his Office, they choose another. The Wisest is their King; who doth not distinguish himself from others by Clothes. Besides These, they have War Captains. They give the King the Tenth of all they have. If a Present is made to the King, he doth not keep it, but distributes it among all, and keeps nothing for himself; and afterwards they give him back the Tenth Part, or pretty near it. The Widows do not cut their Hair, nor tie it up, but let it hang loose. Every Nation hath a peculiar way of cutting their Hair, whereby they are distinguished. They honour Mr. *Oglethorpe* as their Father, and ask his Advice in all their Circumstances: He understands somewhat of their Language.

OUR *Saltzburgers* have often been admonished very earnestly to abstain from drinking a certain intoxicating Liquor like Brandy, called *Rum*; which is made of Molosses, in the Islands of the *West-Indies*, &c. because this Liquor hath occasion'd the Death of many People. Some good Persons, who lately visited our *Saltzburgers*, are much pleased with their Devotion, and with the whole of their Behaviour; and on that Account, prophesy much Good to the Country.

Saturday, *March* 16.

IN the Forenoon, an *English* Minister, belonging to the Garrison of *Port Royal*, was at our Church; and after Service, went with us to our Lodgings. He was glad to see us, and our *Saltzburgers*, and assured us of his constant Friendship and Assistance; and he will take Care to get our Habits made, and buy what is wanting in *Charles-town*. We intend to receive the Sacrament in *Savannah*, for which we prepare our selves, and our Congregation.

BY Mr. *Oglethorpe*'s Fatherly Care, our *Saltzburgers* have got their Provision for a Fortnight before-hand, as Bread, Rice, Flower, Meat, Pease, and Sugar: Afterwards, they are to have it for 3 Months, so that they can divide and use it as they please, every one according to their Family. Besides this, Mr. *Oglethorpe* hath given every one six Pound of Bread, as a Present, and assured them of his further Affection and Care. Which Goodness makes the People rejoice, and bless GOD. Mrs. *Rothe*, who hath been some

Days sick, and is near her Time, hath all that she asks for, out of the Storehouse. Orders were likewise given for our Maintenance; but we told them, we had received our Salary; and therefore we desired nothing, but that this Benefaction might be bestowed upon others.

Sunday, *March* 17.

THOUGH it is but yet the Beginning of the Spring here, it hath for some Days past been hot, which makes the Nights, Mornings, and Evenings more pleasant. To every House is allotted a good Spot of Ground, of which the People make Gardens, where they may have all sorts of Fruit and Herbs. But at present there is very little Greens in them, because they have but lately been made. All Houses and Gardens are laid out in a Mathematical Equality; which will make a fine Shew, when they come to Perfection. The People have Horses, Cows, Fowls, *&c.* in plenty; yet Milk, Eggs, and other Victuals, (except Pork) is much dearer here than in *Germany*; because, They do not care to kill the Cattle, rob the Calves of the Milk, nor take the Eggs, for fear of lessening the Breed. For as the Settlement is but new, they are eagerly desirous of increasing their Stock; and the Cows go Day and Night in the Woods, with Bells on their Necks; The greatest Labour, is the cutting down and clearing away of the Trees, for the Country is all covered with Woods.

Monday, *March* 18.

ONE of us dined this Day with an *English* Merchant, where the *English* Minister was present; and in their Discourse they talk'd of the *Saltzburgers*, whom they commended very much, as being laborious and religious, whereby they gave a good Example to the Inhabitants here. They came twice a Day from their Tent to our Chapel, where we preach the Word of GOD to them, and pray with them an Hour: And several *English* People being also present, we have perceived that they admire them, because they answer our Questions so readily, and use the Bible, old and young. We wish that every one of our Congregation had a Bible, * then GOD would give more Blessing to our Devotion.

* *N. B.* Bibles have been sent.

Tuesday, *March* 19.

MR. *Oglethorpe* went last *Friday* with the Commissary, Mr. *Zwefler*, Mr. *Gronau*, and a *Saltzburger*, to the Place where we are to live with our *Saltzburgers*, in order to shew them the Ground where they are to build their Houses. This Day the Commissary and Mr. *Zwefler* return'd back, and inform'd us much of the Goodness and Fertility of the Ground, as also of the Goodness of the *Indians*. When they promise a Thing, they keep their Word, and would rather die than go from it. If they find one in a Lye, they account him unworthy to look upon, or shake Hands with. An Old Man, one of the Wisest among them, believed, and told them, That the Supreme Being would soon send them some Person that would shew them the right Way to Wisdom, (by which they mean Religion) though He might not live to see it. They seldom ask for any Thing of any Body; but if one offers them any Thing, they do not refuse it. They love Equality; and will be pleased with our *Saltzburgers*, who both eat and labour in common. They very much observe Peoples Behaviour: They hate self-interested People. They reckon themselves all Gentlemen, and will do nothing but what they think to be generous: They account labouring and working for Hire to be a Slavery: therefore they will not work for Gain. They reckon it a Shame to wear Breeches. When they go a Hunting, they wear Boots of woollen Cloth. Some of them are willing to send their Children to our School: Of these Children we shall by degrees learn some Words. Mrs. *Musgrove*, * who lives here, and is Daughter of an *English* Man by an *Indian* Woman, and speaks the *Creek* Language, is a very good Christian, and gave the *Indians* some Notions of the Holy Scriptures.

WE have learn'd some Words of their Language; for instance, *τὺτκα*, Fire; *αββε*, the Sun; *ζυκκω*, House; *σιλλιπαικα*, the Heel; *αφατικα*, Stockings; *ιφουα*, a Dog.

WE designed to celebrate the Memory of our Arrival here, and to receive the Sacrament all together; but we hear, that to-morrow Morning eight young Men of our *Saltzburgers* are to go to our Set-

* She is Wife to Mr. *Musgrove*, the Interpreter before mentioned.

tlement, in order to build some Houses against the Arrival of the Women, Children, and the rest of the *Saltzburgers*; therefore these few are to receive the Sacrament to-morrow Morning early. We prepared them this Day, according to the Form used in the *German* Chapel in St. *James*'s in *London*. Three *Indians* were present, who behaved with great Decency and Reverence. Mr. *Oglethorpe* going to *Purrisburg*, took with him one of us, *viz*. Mr. *Gronau*, and recommended to him to preach to the *Germans* there, which he accordingly did. There are three Families of our *Lutheran* Confession. And Mr. *Gronau* having preached before them out of *Gal*. ii. 20. they were very glad, and resolved to come constantly to our Settlement, which is but a * few Miles from *Purrisburg*, to hear the Word of GOD, and to receive the Sacrament. They reckon the *Saltzburgers* very happy, in having their own Ministers, for at *Purrisburg* they are now without a Minister.

Wednesday, *March* 20.

THIS Morning early, Mr. *Zwefler* and eight *Saltzburgers*, who were to go today to build the Houses, received the Sacrament, in presence of some others of our People. After a Psalm was sung, and Prayers said, a Sermon was preached before them out of *Matt*. xxii. 1. (1.) Of the great Mercy of GOD towards Men: (2.) Of the Way how to become meet for his Mercy. After this, the Communion was perform'd. The *English* Minister was present at the Communion; and yesterday likewise, when Mr. *Rothe*'s Child was Baptized, who was born here since our Arrival: He was very much pleased with our Communicants, and the whole Order of our Divine Service; and afterwards, at the House of one of the Magistrates, who had invited him and one of us to Breakfast, he spoke in a very Christian manner of our Communion. The rest of the *Saltzburgers* are to receive the Sacrament next *Sunday*.

MR. *Oglethorpe* hath desired that one of us should go with the eight *Saltzburgers* to our Settlement, in order to preach the Word of GOD to them, before they go to work, and after. And because I am much taken up with writing Letters, and am to administer the

* Three *German* Miles.

Sacrament to the *Saltzburgers* who remain here, Mr. *Gronau* hath taken this Journey upon him.

THE *Saltzburgers* have (as the other Settlers in *Georgia*) received a Gift from the Trustees, of Arms, Household Goods, and working Tools, *viz.* Kettles, Pots, Dishes, Saws, Axes, Shovels, &*c.*

Thursday, *March* 21.

THE *Jew* and his Wife, who were before mention'd, are so very willing to serve us and the *Saltzburgers*, that it surprises us; and are so honest and faithful, that the like is hardly to be found, as appears by the following Example. The *Jew*'s Wife had by Mistake, and in the dark, taken of a *Saltzburger*'s Wife a Crown piece for a Half-Crown piece, because the *Saltzburger*'s Wife had given her it for no more: when the next Day the *Jew* saw the Money, and his Wife told him she had taken it for half the Value, he went to the *Saltzburger*'s Tent, and asked for the Woman, and paid her the other Half-Crown with these Words; "GOD forbid I should have any Goods in my House that are not my own, for it will have no Blessing." This made a great Impression on the *Saltzburgers*.

BECAUSE these *Jews* shew a great Love for us, and have promised to see us at our Settlement, we hope we shall preach the Gospel of *Jesus Christ* to them with good Success. They were both born in *Germany*, and talk good *German*. They have taken very well what we hitherto have spoke to them.

Friday, *March* 22.

THIS Day Mr. *Oglethorpe* arrived here again, to the great Satisfaction of all the Inhabitants. He is to go to-morrow Night from hence to *Charles-town*, and from thence to embark directly for *London*.

Saturday, *March* 23.

MR. *Oglethorpe* did intend to depart from hence yesterday in the Evening, but many Complaints, and other Business of Importance happening, his Departure was deferr'd till this Morning. From what Knowledge we have of Him, we conclude, that He hath a great Esteem for GOD's holy Word and Sacraments, and a great

Love for GOD's Servants and Children, and wishes to see the Name of CHRIST glorified every where. GOD hath also blessed his Presence and Undertakings in these Countries. And the People being well perswaded of his Fatherly Mind, and indefatigable Labour for their Welfare, his Departure was very sorrowful to them. GOD bless Him, and bring Him well home, and hear all our Prayers for Him. He hath taken all possible Care of us.

THIS Afternoon, we held a Preparation with the rest of the *Saltzburgers* for the Holy Sacrament, preaching to them upon the Words of *Joel*, ii. 32.

Sunday, *March* 24.

THIS Day, at receiving the Holy Sacrament, Almighty GOD was pleased in an extraordinary manner to comfort the Hearts of the Auditors, *viz.* the Commissary Mr. *Von Reck*, and the rest of the *Saltzburgers*.

Tuesday, *March* 26.

IT is a great Pleasure to us, that Mr. *Oglethorpe* approved of our calling the River, and the Place where our Houses are to be built, *Ebenezer*; 1 Sam. vii. 12. *Then Samuel took a Stone, and set it between Mizpeh and Shen, and called the Name of it Ebenezer; saying, Hither-to hath the* LORD *helped us.* Which Denomination is already known among the People that live hereabout. This Word hath at our Arrival here, and when we were yet on board the Ship, made us joyful to the Praise of GOD, and will do it for the future as often as we name the Name of our Town or River, or hear it named.

THIS Afternoon, an *Indian* Man, that is married, * cut both Ears and Hair off from an *Indian* Woman, his Wife, for being too familiar with a white Man. Mr. *Oglethorpe* hath left Orders behind him, to send our *Saltzburgers* to *Ebenezer* as soon as possible. The Commissary went this Morning with some Men to the River of the same Name, in order to take out the Trees that lie in it, and hinder Boats from going up, that our Baggage may be carried thither by Water.

* This is the usual Punishment for Adultery amongst the *Indians*. The White Man was tried by a Jury at *Savannah*, found guilty, and punished severely: With which piece of Justice, the *Indians* were greatly satisfied.

Friday, *March* 29.

YESTERDAY and to-day we had cold Weather, which is very surprizing to us, because the Weather hath for some time been rather too hot: This cold Weather is a Blessing of GOD; since the Vermin and little Flies, which incommoded us much, have been destroyed thereby.

Saturday, *March* 30.

As, by the Help of GOD, we are now at more Ease, and in better Order, we can take more Care of the Education of the Children; who come daily several times to our Room, where they are taught proper Texts out of the Holy Scripture, and are Catechized. At Prayers, all is repeated in the Presence of the grown People, whereby they are edified; as well as by the Catechism, and Texts of the Holy Scripture, that are explained unto them. As soon as we come to our *Ebenezer*, we shall also begin to teach them Reading and Writing.

Sunday, *March* 31.

TO-DAY the Commissary and labouring People returned from the River *Ebenezer*, where he had found so much Difficulty, that nothing was done; and we are to make a Way by Land, which seems to be an Impossibility. GOD, who hath hitherto help'd us to overcome all Difficulties, help us in this Case.

Monday, *April* 1.

OUR *Saltzburgers* have had given to them, from the Publick Magazine, by Order of the Honourable Trustees, Provision again for three Months; and of every thing so plentifully, that we cannot enough praise GOD for it. Besides the Provision, they have had an Addition of Houshold Goods, and Tools, for Building Houses, Tilling the Ground, and Arms and Ammunition, for Defence. And though We two gave Mr. *Oglethorpe* to understand, that we did not desire any Victuals, but would be contented with our Salary, and leave that Benefaction for our *Saltzburgers*, yet the same Provision hath been given to us as to the *Saltzburgers*. This Benefaction came in good time; because the most Part of our Salary was spent in Necessaries, as Clothes, Houshold Goods, &*c*.

Tuesday, *April* 2.

A HOUSE being built at our *Ebenezer* for the *Saltzburg* Women and Children, all our Baggage was to-day put on Board a Shallop; which was so filled therewith, that there was no room for the People. Therefore I, (*Bolzius*) the Physician, and the *Saltzburgers*, must stay here some Days longer. Several of the *Saltzburgers* were displeased that they could not go with their Goods; however, they were soon appeased. Mr. *Causton*, one of the Magistrates, who hath the Inspection of the Store-house here, hath given unto the *Saltzburgers* Provision for fourteen Days more, because the former is sent on Board the Shallop; prais'd be GOD for this new Benefaction.

Wednesday, *April* 3.

THE *Jew*, of whom mention hath been made above, hath shewn us and the *Saltzburgers* so much Goodness, that we could desire no more; and though we offered him a Sum of Money for his Labour and Pains, yet he refused to accept of it: Wherefore the *Saltzburgers*, that are still here, resolve to Till his Ground, and to clear it of Trees, and so make good again what he hath neglected for their Sake. We have had several Discourses with him concerning Judaism, and given him some Passages out of the Holy Scripture to consider on, which seemed to make a strong Impression on him. He and his Wife are pleased with the *Saltzburgers* Brotherly Conversation, and Christian Behaviour; and he talking of it to us; we told him, that thereby he might learn, that the Christian Doctrine is a holy Doctrine, and that those *Jews* who Blaspheme, did commit great Sin, which he should take Care not to do; but pray to GOD incessantly, to shew him the Way to Salvation: then he would soon attain to the Knowledge of Truth. They both fear GOD, and desire to come to Salvation; and we hope to GOD, that he will also bring these People to the Knowledge of his Son. He was pleased, especially, when we told him, that hitherto we had shewn our People out of *David*'s Psalms, that tho' the *Jews* were now afflicted for their Sins; yet it was to be hoped, that soon the Time will come, in which GOD would raise this his People out of the Dust, Contempt and Sorrow, and make them happy again for *Messiah*'s Sake, both which he assented to; and when we asked him out of *Hos.* iii. 5. Who is King *David*? He answered, The LORD *Messiah*, whom they would call upon in the latter Days.

Thursday, *April* 4.

THE Indians come often to see us; they tell us many Indian Words; shewing us the Things we want to know in their Language. It hath happened very well for our *Saltzburgers*, that they were obliged to stay here some Days longer, for they have got by it a good deal of Linen Cloth, Shoes, and other Things.

Friday, *April* 5.

LAST Night, the Vessel which carried our Things to *Ebenezer*, came back; so that we, and the rest of our Baggage, can also go thither. GOD be praised for all the Good we have received in this Place.

Saturday, *April* 6.

ONE of our Congregation, namely *Lackner*, is grown dangerously Sick, so that according to all Appearances, he hardly will recover; he is troubled with the Diarrhœa, and Shortness of Breath, and very weak; Mr. *Zwefler* the Doctor, assists him as much as possible; we and the *Saltzburgers* would be very sorry if he should die, for he is a godly Man, and a Man of very good Sense, useful in every thing; GOD do with him as he pleases.

Abercorn, Sunday, *April* 7.

TO-DAY we arrived at a Village, called *Abercorn*, upon the River *Savannah*, where we must stay till a Road is made by Land to our *Ebenezer*; because at present, the Trees hinder the Passage thither by Water. Certain wicked People having maliciously spoken false Things of our Place of Settlement, not only that it was impossible to make a Way thither, but also that the Ground was Barren Sand, and exposed to the Invasion of the Enemies. We shewed in the Afternoon Sermon, out of the Gospel upon this Day, *Palm-Sunday*, *Mat.* xxi. the Nature of CHRIST's true Disciples, *viz.* to go whither the LORD sends them, notwithstanding, it seemed difficult and contrary to Reason. That it is GOD's way, to lead his Children through crooked and strange Paths, and then to bring them to a happy End. In the Application, almost the whole 26th Chapter of *Leviticus* was read to them, and it was shewn to them how we must do, if we will have a fruitful Country, Security against Enemies, *&c. viz.* we must live constantly in the Fear of GOD; on the contrary, that the Reason of Dearths, Barrenness of Soil, and Invasion of Enemies, was Ungodliness, *&c.* And since GOD has sent us in the Beginning of this *Passion-Week*, so near our temporal Country, we told them, that GOD who does all Things at his Time, and for our Good; thereby doubtless intended, *First*, That CHRIST and his Sufferings should be before their Eyes, and in their Hearts, throughout the whole Course of their Lives; and through them they should seek Wisdom and Righteousness, Sanctification and Redemption. *Secondly*, That they as Christians, should continually crucify their Flesh, with the Affections and Lusts; and that the World must be crucified unto them, and they unto the World. *Thirdly*, That they also should prepare themselves for a *Passion-Week*, in time, because GOD's Children must have Trouble and Affliction in this World, inward and outward, whereby they become like their Redeemer, which is the highest Honour, *Apoc.* vii. 14. To this plain Discourse, GOD gave his Blessing, and the People resolved to go farther, in the Name of GOD, whither He would send them; for they trusted in Him, that He would remove all Difficulties and Sorrow.

Monday, *April* 8.

NOTWITHSTANDING it rained this whole Day, by Intervals, very hard, the *Saltzburgers* have made a pretty good Beginning, in making the Way; after having at the Place of their first Work, implored GOD for his Blessing and Assistance. This Work being for the Publick Good, and for the Benefit of all *Carolina* and *Georgia*, the Commissary is resolved to desire the Honourable Trustees, that a second Year's Provision might be given to the People, because they must at present work as it were for the Publick, and cannot begin to Till their Ground so soon. All who are able, now work with pleasure.

Tuesday, *April* 9.

THE Wind being to-day Northerly, cooled the Air; which is strange to us, because we expected continual hot Weather in this Country. We all make shift, by Day and Night, as well as we can: The *Saltzburgers* have pitched two Tents; and we, the Ministers, live with two *English* Families, in a Hut in which we cannot sit dry when it rains, besides other Inconveniencies; it being low, and the Doors on both sides continually open, yet Providence preserves our Health. The chief Labour in *Georgia* is, that they must cut down the Woods, of which the whole Country is full, before they can Till the Ground. Here most of the Trees are Oak, but in other Places there are more Fir-trees, Walnut-trees, *&c.* likewise Frankincense, Vines, Sassafras, aromatick Herbs, *&c.*

Wednesday, *April* 10.

THE *Saltzburgers* take great Pains, and the Commissary labours hard in making the Way to *Ebenezer*. GOD reward his Christian Love.

Thursday, *April* 11.

MR. *Gronau* came from *Ebenezer* to us, and returned; because those *Saltzburgers* who are already there, must have the Word preached unto them.

Friday, *April* 12.

THIS Day we kept holy for the Honour of our Redeemer.

Saturday, *April* 13.

Lackner having been long sick, died last Night of a Phisick and a wasting Fever: He died in the Lord, whom he loved with his whole Heart, in Health and in Sickness. His Departure from this World was so quiet and still, that those who sat up with him in the Tent, did not perceive it. For a great while he longed for this Rest, and departing this Life; for which purpose he received the holy Sacrament with very great Desire and Devotion, not long ago in *Savannah*. He was a Man of good Sense, which he also employed to what was good: He was continually reading the holy Scriptures; prayed without ceasing, and by his peaceable and Christian Behaviour, he gave a good Example to others; his Example having been edifying to all the *Saltzburgers*, (for which Reason he was heartily beloved by them) we thought proper to make mention of his Christian Life, and happy Departure out of this World, at Prayers in the Morning; and to employ it to a general Edification. For this Purpose we chose *Heb.* xi. 8. He was to have had a Coffin made for him: but the *Saltzburgers* thought it unnecessary, being accustomed to bury no Body in a Coffin, but Women that die in Child-bed: So they dressed the Corps, after it was washed, in his own Cloaths, laid him upon a Board, and after he was brought to his Grave, in an orderly Procession, they wrap'd him up in a Cloth, and let him down into the Ground. Before he was carried out, the Hymn was sung, *Since nothing is more common than to die*, &c. and Prayers said this *Saturday*, remember'd us of GOD's Rest after finishing the Creation, and of our Saviour's Rest after his Sufferings: and gave us occasion to think on the Rest which all GOD's Children are to expect, according to the Words, *Heb.* iv. 9, 11. And before we left the Grave, we gave the People some short Precepts, Comfort and Admonition, to which GOD was pleased to vouchsafe his Blessing.

Sunday, *April* 14.

THE Death of *Lackner*, and the Preaching of the Word of GOD on that occasion, prepared our Congregation for the present *Easter* Holy-days; so that the first Day thereof was spent in great Devotion, though we are yet in an unsettled State; we wish that all Ministers of the Gospel were blessed with such a Flock; They pray for us, that GOD will give us Grace and Wisdom to preach the Gospel in its purity. During the Sermon, they are as attentive, as if they would devour every Word we spoke. After Sermon, we observe with pleasure, that they retire separately to pray to GOD, to convert the Word they have heard, to their Soul's Spiritual Nourishment: and by their Behaviour, we find that they are not only Hearers, but Doers of the Word. And they look upon it as a great Mercy, that the Word of GOD is preached pure to them; so they would (as they say) reckon it a great Punishment, if it should be taken from them, or one of us his unworthy Servants should die.

Tuesday, *April* 16.

THE deceased *Lackner* hath left a little Money, with which we have made a Beginning of a Box for the Poor, with the *Saltzburgers* Consent: GOD be pleased to accept this small Beginning, and increase it with his Blessing.

THE Commissary is gone to *Savannah*. Our *Saltzburg* Men are gone to *Ebenezer*, having taken some Kitchen Furniture with them; and will, with the Blessing of GOD, continue to work in making the Way with all Diligence.

Wednesday, *April* 17.

MR. *Gronau* came to-day back again here to *Abercorn*. The Men sent up from *Carolina* by the Trustees Order, to saw Boards for the Building six Houses for us in *Ebenezer*, have made a good Beginning.

Thursday, *April* 18.

WE intended this Afternoon to see the *Saltzburgers* at work; but finding they were advanced far, made us afraid we should not come to *Abercorn* again, and we turned back. One must take care not to go into the Woods without a Guide. The whole Country is covered with Wood; and if one loses sight of the Trees that are marked, whereby the Way is known, one is in danger of being lost; as hath happened to two *Germans*, belonging to *Purrisburg*.

Friday, *April* 19.

THIS Day hath been very remarkable and comfortable; GOD hath not only edified Old and Young, by the hearing of his Word, but also shewn us plain Proofs of his Fatherly Care; *First*, Our *Saltzburgers* have brought the Road to Perfection, which some thought impossible; and are gone to *Ebenezer*, to give GOD Thanks for his Mercies, and to begin to Work there. *Secondly*, A * certain Captain (left by Mr. *Oglethorpe*, with his Troops, to have an Eye upon the Behaviour of the *Spanish Indians*) sent a Letter to the Commissary, desiring that a Pasture Ground might be inclosed for some Oxen, which he would send soon for the *Saltzburgers*. *Thirdly*,

* Oxen sent up by Captain *Mackpherson*, pursuant to the Trustees Order, for supplying the *Saltzburgers* with fresh Provision.

When the Way was made, we wanted Horses to bring our Baggage and Victuals to *Ebenezer*; but God, who knew our Want, ordered it so, that * four Horses were sent us from *Pallachoccolas*†; and a young strong Horse, that had no Master, coming to *Ebenezer*, was brought to us. *Fourthly*, A ‡ certain Man, who lives amongst the *Indians*, not far from *Ebenezer*, sent us some Seeds, though he does not know us.

Saturday, *April* 20.

BECAUSE there is not yet any Malt made here, the *Saltzburgers* have learnt of the *English* People, to Brew a sort of Beer of Molosses, with Sassafras, and the Tops of Firr-Tree, instead of Hops, which they boil in a Kettle with Water; some add Indian Corn: The Inhabitants here reckon this Liquor to be wholesome, and the drinking of Water unwholesome; but we prefer the Water to this Mixture, and find our selves well after it; sometimes we mix it with a little Wine. Yesterday in the Evening, we had much Thunder, with hard Rains, for an Hour; during that time, we sung some Hymns, and edified our selves out of the 29th *Psalm*, and 1 *Sam.* xii. out of which, we considered the great Glory and Mercy of GOD.

Sunday, *April* 21.

TOWARDS the Evening, it Thunder'd, with hard Rain, which about ten o'Clock grew very vehement, and continued a long time. We and the *Saltzburgers* were very much incommoded by the Rain, that pierced thro' the Hut; however it did none of us any Harm.

Monday, *April* 22.

THE Weather clearing up, the People began to pack up their Baggage, to carry it to *Ebenezer*. We all are glad, that GOD at last will help us out of our present inconvenient Circumstances at *Aber-*

* Horses sent by Mr. *Oglethorpe*, over Land, from *Charles-town* to *Georgia*, being the Gift of his Excellency Governour *Johnson* to the Trustees.

† *Pallachoccolas* is the Name of a Fort, built upon the *Savannah* River, about 20 Miles above *Ebenezer*.

‡ Mr. *Augustine*, a *Welch* Gentleman, who since Mr. *Oglethorpe*'s Arrival, is settled at *Westbrook*, and built a House there, being 8 Miles from *Ebenezer*.

corn, into our Solitude, where we can serve him, and do our Business without hindrance. The Name of our Temporal Country, puts us in Mind of GOD's Blessings, and incites us to praise Him as often as we hear it named. We find in the Woods Spinage, Onions, Hyssop, and other useful Herbs, of which we do not know the Names, but are very good for the Pot, or Sallad. At leisure time, we shall apply our selves, together with our Physician Mr. *Zwefler*, who is a good Botanist, to examine the Herbs, and communicate the Knowledge of them to others.

THE Commissary being desirous to forward the Spiritual as well as the Temporal Welfare of the People, and being better qualified to instruct the * *French*, because he understands their Language, made this Afternoon, a Trial of his Talents, in a most pathetick Exhortation to a Christian Behaviour; which he performed to Admiration.

Tuesday, *April* 23.

HERE are Bees, and great Quantities of Honey, in the Woods, which has as agreeable a Taste as that made in *Germany*; and the *Saltzburgers* will make Hives, and gather the Bees. Here is also abundance of Fish, Fowl, and Venison.

Wednesday, *April* 24.

GOD hath moved the Hearts of our Benefactors, who have made a Present to our *Saltzburgers* of 30 Cows, and will send them free hither; 12 of them arrived here last Night; GOD be praised for this Benefaction. The Way to *Ebenezer* is grown deep, by the hard Rain; which makes it troublesome for the poor People, to carry their Baggage and Provision thither. Having as yet no Waggons, our People make use of a Sledge, till a Waggon is made; but it will cut very deep in the Ground, and be tiresome, especially, because the Horses that are sent us, are lean, and not used to draw. A *Saltzburger*, named *Mittensteiner*, who rode into the Woods, is not yet come back; he being simple, we fear he is lost; several Men, who know the Woods, are sent to find him; A Cannon hath likewise been discharged four times for his Direction, but he hath not been

* There are some *French* Families settled at *Abercorn*.

seen again yet. GOD seek this lost Sheep, and hear our Prayers for him: He is a good Christian, and a good Workman.

Thursday, *April* 25.

WE edified our selves out of *Exodus* 19th, and 20th, and the 18th *Psalm*.

Friday, *April* 26.

THE Horse which *Mittensteiner* rode into the Wood, came back this Afternoon, without his Rider; the Horse would have brought him back, if he had given him the Bridle. GOD have Mercy upon him, and grant that this Example may make others more circumspect. The Horse coming back without his Bridle, and the Man being not used to ride, and very simple, makes us fear he is killed with a Fall from the Horse.

Sunday, *April* 28.

PART of the *Saltzburgers* being in *Ebenezer*, and part of them in *Abercorn*; one of us performs the Service in *Ebenezer*, the other in *Abercorn*, GOD hath not yet heard our Prayers, which we have made in Publick and Private, for the lost *Mittensteiner*, we having had no News of him yet. The LORD's Will be done.

Tuesday, *April* 30.

ALL this Afternoon, we have had a warm and fruitful Rain.

Wednesday, *May* 1.

THE Carriage of our Baggage and Provision goes on very slow, and troublesome, because of the Rain, and deep Road.

Thursday, *May* 2.

SOME Days ago, an *Indian* Man, with his Wife and Children, arrived here in a little Boat, not far from *Abercorn*; and because we had shewed him some Kindness, he brought us this Morning a Deer, part of which we gave to our *Saltzburgers* that are here, and other People; and he came again towards Evening, and brought us half another Deer.

Friday, *May* 3.

TO-DAY arrived a Sloop from *Savannah*, which brought us ten great Casks of all sorts of Seeds, for our *Saltzburgers* to sow their Fields and Gardens with. God be praised for this Blessing.

Saturday, *May* 4.

To-day arrived the Cows and young Calves lately promised to our *Saltzburgers*. The Cattle are very wild; so that it is troublesome to bring them to *Ebenezer*, because they are used to run about Night and Day in the Woods.

Ebenezer, Tuesday, *May* 7.

Mr. *Oglethorpe*, who on account of some Business of Importance was not gone from *Charles-town*, sent a Letter to the Commissary, assuring him of all Care and Affection towards the *Saltzburgers*; and that besides the Cattle they had received already, He had ordered Hogs, Turkies, Geese, Ducks and Fowl, to be delivered to the *Saltzburgers*, as a Gift from the Trustees, and that the Magistrates of *Savannah* would send us, whatever We, the Ministers and the Commissary, should think needful for the *Saltzburgers*. To-day I had the Happiness of seeing *Ebenezer*; having been detained, on account of three sick People, in *Abercorn*, Mr. *Gronau* being in *Ebenezer*. The good People are already much advanced in Tilling the Ground; and to the End that they may advance better, two and two work together, to assist one another. The Place they have chosen to build on, is very pleasant and fruitful. They had liberty to choose a Place where they pleased.

Wednesday, *May* 8.

The People in *Abercorn*, as well as in *Ebenezer*, are troubled with Loosnesses. It is thought, that drinking too much in hot Weather, is the Reason of it. They are too bashful to tell it in the Beginning, when the Evil might be prevented. Some have had great Benefit by our Physick. We assist them in their Sickness: we wish we were able to serve them more. The River-Water will not agree with us nor the *Saltzburgers*; it being full of Trees and Leaves: wherefore we intended to dig a Well; but Providence ordered it so, that we found a Brook, which rises out of a little Hill, and hath good and wholesome Water, and saves us that trouble. This put us in mind of the Words, *Before they call, I will answer*.

Thursday, *May* 9.

A Tabernakle is to be made of Boards, till a Church can be built.

Friday, *May* 10.

THE many Benefactions Spiritual and Temporal, which we have received, and daily do receive from our kind and charitable Benefactors, oblige us to give GOD Thanks on a particular Day; for which purpose we have chosen next *Monday*.

Saturday, *May* 11.

GOD sent us this Day a very fruitful Rain for the Benefit of the Fields of the *Saltzburgers*, who work diligently. They are strengthned in their Belief, seeing they have not been mistaken in their Hopes; that they should not want for Rain: tho' some People would prophesy the rainy Time was already past, and the *Saltzburgers* had done ill in sowing their Seed in a sandy Ground.

Monday, *May* 13.

THIS Day was by the Consent of the Congregation, appointed for a Holy-day of Thanksgiving; on which our People met twice in remembrance of GOD's Blessings, and praised him for them in publick. In the Forenoon's Sermon, were explained the Words of the travelling *Jacob*, which during our Voyage, and here in *Ebenezer*, have been very comfortable to us, out of *Gen*. xxxii. 10. and thereby shewn, (1.) The Blessings GOD hitherto had shewn us; (2.) Our Duty, according to the Example of *Jacob*. Instead of an Introduction, we used the 107th Psalm, out of which we shewed our former Circumstances, and present Duty, which GOD also hath blessed. In the afternoon, we intended to explain the words 2 *Cor*. v. 9, 10. but it could not be done, because the Commissary, who was to go away next day, would take his leave of the *Saltzburgers*, and give them some good advice before his departure; which was very moving on both sides, and caused many tears. GOD bless the good man, and send him the Fruits of our earnest Prayers, and of all His Labour of Love and Faithfulness to us.

FINIS

A Voyage to *Georgia*.

A

VOYAGE

TO

GEORGIA.

Begun in the Year 1735.

CONTAINING,

An Account of the Settling the Town of FREDERICA, in the Southern Part of the Province; and a Defcription of the SOIL, AIR, BIRDS, BEASTS, TREES, RIVERS, ISLANDS, *&c.*

WITH

The RULES and ORDERS made by the Honourable the TRUSTEES for that SETTLEMENT; including the Allowances of Provifions, Cloathing, and other Neceffaries to the Families and Servants which went thither.

ALSO

A Defcription of the Town and County of *Savannah*, in the Northern Part of the Province; the Manner of dividing and granting the Lands, and the Improvements there: With an Account of the AIR, SOIL, RIVERS, and ISLANDS in that Part.

By FRANCIS MOORE, *Author of* Travels into the Inland Parts of *Africa*.

LONDON:

Printed for JACOB ROBINSON in *Ludgate-Street*, 1744.

A Voyage to *Georgia*; begun the 15th of *October*, 1735.

HE Trustees for establishing the Colony of *GEORGIA* in *America*, ordered a new Town to be built in that Colony, and an Embarkation to be made for that Purpose. They were pleased to appoint me to be Keeper of the Stores.

The following Rules were given for the Embarkation, *viz.*

RULES *for the Year* 1735.

The Trustees intend this Year to lay out a County, and build a new Town in *Georgia*.

They will give to such Persons as they send upon the Charity,

To every Man, A Watch-Coat,
A Musket and Bayonet,
An Hatchet,
An Hammer,
An Hand-saw,
A shod Shovel or Spade,
A broad Hoe,
A narrow Hoe,
A Gimlet,
A drawing Knife,
An Iron Pot, and a pair of Pot-hooks,
A Frying-pan,
And a publick Grindstone to each Ward or Village.

Each working Man will have for his Maintenance in the Colony for one Year,

312 *lib.* of Beef or Pork, 104 *lib.* of Rice, 104 *lib.* of *Indian* Corn, or Pease, 104 *lib.* of Flower, 1 Pint of Strong-beer a Day to a Man when he works, and not otherwise, 52 Quarts of Molasses for brewing Beer, 16 *lib.* of Cheese, 12 *lib.* of Butter, 8 *oz.* of Spice, 12 *lib.* of Sugar, 4 Gallons of Vinegar, 24 *lib.* of Salt, 12 Quarts of Lamp-Oil, and 1 *lib.* of Spun-Cotton, 12 *lib.* of Soap.	To be delivered in such Proportions, and at such Times, as the Trust shall think proper.

To the Mothers, Wives, Sisters, or Children of such Men, for one Year, that is to say, to every Person of the Age of 12 Years, and upwards, the following Allowance:

260 *lib.* of Beef or Pork, 104 *lib.* of Rice, 104 *lib.* of *Indian* Corn, or Pease, 104 *lib.* of Flower, 52 Quarts of Molasses, for brewing Beer, 16 *lib.* of Cheese, 12 *lib.* of Butter, 8 *oz.* of Spice, 12 *lib.* of Sugar, 4 Gallons of Vinegar, 24 *lib.* of Salt, 6 Quarts of Lamp-Oil, Half a Pound of Spun Cotton, and 12 *lib.* of Soap.	To be delivered as before.

For every Person above the Age of Seven, and under the Age of Twelve, half the said Allowance; being esteemed half an Head.

And for every Person above the Age of Two, and under the Age of Seven, one Third of the said Allowance; being esteemed one Third of an Head.

The Trustees pay their Passage from *England* to *Georgia*; and in the Voyage they will have in every Week four Beef Days, two Pork Days, and one Fish Day; and their Allowance served out daily as follows:

On the Four Beef Days.

Four Pounds of Beef for every Mess of 5 Heads,
And two Pounds and a half of Flower,
And half a Pound of Suet, or Plumbs.

On the Two Pork Days.

Five Pounds of Pork, and Two Pints and an half of Pease,	For every 5 Heads

And on the Fish Day.

Two Pounds and an half of Fish, and half a Pound of Butter,	For every 5 Heads. The whole at 16 *oz.* to the Pound.

And allow each Head seven Pounds of Bread, of fourteen Ounces to the Pound, by the Week. And three Pints of Beer, and two Quarts of Water (whereof one of the Quarts for drinking, and the other for Dressing the Ship-Provisions) each Head, by the Day for the Space of a Month; and a Gallon of Water (whereof two Quarts for drinking, and the other two for dressing the Ship-Provisions) each Head, by the Day after, during their Voyage.

The said Persons are to enter into the following Convenants before their Embarkation, *viz.*

That they will repair on Board such Ship as shall be provided for carrying them to the Province of *Georgia*; and during the Voyage will quietly, soberly and obediently demean themselves, and go to such Place in the said Province of *Georgia*, and there obey all such Orders as shall be given for the better settling, establishing, and governing the said Colony.

That for the first twelve Months from landing in the said Province of *Georgia*, they will work and labour in clearing their Lands, making Habitations and necessary Defences, and in all other Works for the common Good and publick Weal of the said Colony; at such Times, in such Manner, and according to such Plan and Directions as shall be given.

And that they, from and after the Expiration of the said last-mentioned twelve Months, will, during the two succeeding Years, abide, settle, and inhabit in the said Province of *Georgia*, and cultivate the Lands which shall be to them and their Heirs Male severally alotted and given, by all such Ways and Means, as according to their several Abilities and Skills they shall be best able and capable.

And such Persons are to be settled in the said Colony, either in new Towns, or new Villages.

Those in the Towns will have each of them a Lot 60 Feet in Front, and 90 Feet in Depth, whereon they are to build an House, and as much Land in the Country, as in the whole shall make up fifty Acres.

Those in the Villages will have each of them a Lot of 50 Acres, which is to lye all together, and they are to build their House upon it.

All Lots are granted in Tail Male, and descend to the Heirs Male of their Bodies for ever. And in case of Failure of Heirs Male, to revert to the Trust, to be granted again to such Persons, as the Common-Council of the Trustees shall think most for the Advantage of the Colony; and they will have a special Regard to the Daughters of Freeholders who have made Improvements on their Lots, not already provided for, by having married, or marrying Persons in Possessions, or entitled to Lands in the Province of *Georgia*, in Possession, or Remainder.

All Lots are to be preserved separate and undivided, and cannot be united, in order to keep up a Number of Men equal to the Number of Lots; for the better Defence and Support of the Colony.

No Person can lease out his House or Lot to another, without Licence for that Purpose; that the Colony may not be ruined by Absentees receiving, and spending their Rents elsewhere. Therefore each Man must cultivate the same by himself or Servants.

And no Person can alienate his Land, or any Part, or any Term, Estate, or Interest therein, to any other Person or Persons, without special Licence for that Purpose; to prevent the uniting or dividing the Lots.

If any of the Land so granted shall not be planted, cleared or fenced with a Worm-fence or Pails six Feet high, during the Space of ten Years from the Date of the Grant; then every Part thereof not planted, cleared, or fenced as aforesaid, shall belong to the Trust, and the Grant, as to such Parts, shall be void.

There is reserved for the Support of the Colony, a Rent-charge for ever of two Shillings *Sterling* Money for each fifty Acres; the Payment of which is not to commence until ten Years after the Grant.

The Wives of the Freeholders, in case they should survive their Husbands, are, during their Lives, entitled to the Mansion-house, and one half of the Lands improved by their Husbands; that is to say, inclosed with a Fence of six Feet high.

All Forfeitures for Non-residence, High-Treason, Felonies, *&c.* are to the Trustees for the Use and Benefit of the Colony.

Negroes and Rum are prohibited to be used in the said Colony; and Trade with the *Indians*, unless licens'd.

None are to have the Benefit of being sent upon the Charity in the manner above-mentioned; but,

1. Such as are in decayed Circumstances, and thereby disabled from following any Business in *England*; and who, if in Debt, must have Leave from their Creditors to go.

2. Such as have numerous Families of Children, if assisted by their respective Parishes, and recommended by the Minister, Church-wardens and Overseers thereof.

The Trustees do expect to have a good Character of the said Persons given; because no Drunkards, or other notoriously vicious Persons will be taken.

And for the better enabling the said Persons to build the new Town, and clear their Lands, the Trustees will give Leave to every Freeholder to take over with him one Male Servant, or Apprentice, of the Age of eighteen Years and upwards, to be bound for not less than four Years; and will by way of Loan to such Freeholder, advance the Charges of Passage for such Servant or Apprentice, and of furnishing him with the Cloathing and Provision hereafter mentioned; to be delivered in such Proportions, and at such Times as the Trust shall think proper; *viz.* with

A Pallias, and Bolster, and Blanket for Bedding.

A Frock and Trowzers of Linsey Woolsey, a Shirt and Frock, and Trowzers of Osnabrigs. } For Cloathing.

A Pair of Shoes from *England*, and two Pair of Country Shoes.

And 200 Pounds of Meat, and 342 Pounds of Rice, Pease, or *Indian* Corn for Food for a Year.

The Expence of which Passage, Cloathing, and Provision, is to be repaid the Trustees by the Master, within the third Year from their Embarkation from *England*.

And to each Man-servant, and the Heirs Male of his Body for ever, after the Expiration of his Service, upon a Certificate from his Master of his having served well, will be granted Twenty Acres of Land, under such Rents and Agreements as shall have been then last granted to any others Men-servants in like Circumstances.

PROVIDED, that in case any Person shall disobey such Orders as they shall receive, a Deduction shall be made of the Whole, or any Part of the above Provisions.

Signed by Order of the Common-Council of the Trustees for establishing the Colony of Georgia *in* America, *this Second Day of* July, 1735.

BENJ. MARTYN, *Secretary*.

THE Trustees examined at their Office such Persons as applied to them for the Benefit of the Charity, and out of them chose those who had the best Characters, and were the truest Objects of Compassion.

They acquainted those that they had chosen, that they must expect to go through great Hardships in the Beginning, and use great Industry and Labour in order to acquire afterwards a comfortable Subsistence for themselves and Families; that they gave them Lands, and a Year's Provisions, but that those Lands were uninhabited Woods; that they must lye without Cover till they could build Houses for themselves, live upon salt Meat, drink Water, work hard, keep Guard for Fear of Enemies, clear and plant Ground before they could reap any Harvest; that the Country was hot in *Summer*, and that there were Flies in Abundance, and that Thunder-storms were frequent in that Season; that Sicknesses were dangerous to those who drank distilled Liquors, and that

Temperance was not only necessary to preserve their Substance, but their Health also; that if they put their Trust in God, and were temperate and industrious, they might establish themselves and Families in a comfortable Way upon Lands of their own; but if they thought they should not be able to go through those Difficulties, they advised them by no means to undertake the Voyage.

Several were dishearten'd, which discover'd that they had pleaded Necessity without Reason, and that they were able to live in *England*. The Places of those who were deterr'd from going, were fill'd up with others; for there were a great many more petition'd to go than there was room for. Besides the *English*, there were a Number of persecuted *German* Protestants, under the Conduct of Mr. *Vonreck* and Capt. *Hermsdorf*. The whole Embarkation, *English* and Foreigners, together with the Missionaries to the *Indians*, amounted to 227 Heads, making 202 People upon the Trust's Account, besides Mr. *Oglethorpe*, the Gentlemen with him, and his Servants, whose Passages he himself paid.

There were two Ships freighted, the *Symond*, of 220 Ton, Capt. *Joseph Cornish*, and the *London Merchant*, about the same Burden, Capt. *John Thomas*. There was sufficient Quantity of Provisions for some Months put on board, likewise Arms, Cannon, Ammunition, and all kinds of Tools for Husbandry, and Necessaries for Families.

One of his Majesty's Sloops, under the Command of Capt. *James Gascoigne*, was ordered to assist the Colony, and to carry over Mr. *Oglethorpe*, who intended to inspect the Settlement; but he chose rather to go on board one of the Ships, tho' crowded with the Colony, that he might be able to take care of the People in their Passage.

On the 14th of *October* I set out from *Parliament-stairs*; about Four in the Afternoon I arriv'd at *Poorfleet*, where I dined, and staid during the Flood; after which I reach'd *Gravesend* about Midnight. There I lay, and the next Day went on board the *Symond*, Capt. *Joseph Cornish*, where the Passengers upon the Trust's Account had been for some Days. I immediately took an Account of the Stores.

On the 19th a Boy, as he was playing, fell overboard: A Man being near him, and seeing him fall, throw'd him a Rope, and he got in again. We waited for the coming down of the *London Merchant.*

On the 20th the *London Merchant,* Capt. *John Thomas,* with Part of the Colony on board, join'd us at *Gravesend.* I went and took an Account of her Cargo. The same Day Mr. *Oglethorpe,* with Mr. *Johnson,* Son to the late Governor of *South Carolina,* and several other Gentlemen, who intended to accompany him in the Voyage, came on board. In the Afternoon we weigh'd, and went down to the *Hope.*

On the 21st we sail'd from the *Hope,* and got within three Miles of the Buoy of the *Nore.*

On the 23d a thick Fog came upon us: We made shift to get to the Buoy of the *Nore,* and anchor'd on the *Kentish Flats,* being not able to proceed farther.

On the 25th it blew fresh against us, and we got but little forwards.

On the 26th, early in the Morning, we arrived at the *Horse-shoe Hole,* where we anchor'd for some time, and then setting sail we got to *Margate-Road.*

On the 27th we arrived at *Deal,* and were forced to come to an Anchor in the *Downs.* We set on shore a Servant belonging to one of the Colony, it being discover'd that he had the Itch.

On the 28th it blew hard against us. The same Day died a Child of eight Months old, being Daughter to one of the Colony. She was dangerously ill before she came on board.

On the 30th the Wind continued to blow hard; but Mr. *Oglethorpe* insisting with the Captains to sail, we ventur'd out, and found the Wind less, and more favourable at Sea.

On the 1st of *November* we put into *St. Helen*'s, in order to meet the Man of War, whom we expected to be ready. It being near Night the Ships came to Anchor, and a Gentleman was sent to *Spithead* to inquire after the Man of War: He return'd about Midnight with Advice, that she was in *Portsmouth* Harbour, and not yet ready.

On the 2d the Ships sail'd for *Cowes Road,* and Mr. *Oglethorpe* went to the Man of War Sloop. As the Ships pass'd by *Spithead* they saluted the Admiral's Ship, which she returned.

We were detain'd at *Cowes*, by contrary Winds, till the 10th of *December*; for though we twice broke ground, and once sail'd as far as *Yarmouth Road*, yet were we forced back again. This Delay was not only very tedious to the People, but very expensive to the Trust; since there were so many hundred Mouths eating, in Idleness, that which should have subsisted them till their Lands were cultivated; and that they were also losing the most useful Season for that Purpose.

In this time the Refreshments design'd for the Voyage were expended, and we were forced to lay in more at an excessive Price, by reason that the Squadron at *Spithead* had made every thing dear.

Mr. *Johnson*, Son to the late Governor of *South Carolina*, was taken ill here of a Fever, which prevented his going the Voyage. This was a great Disappointment; for if he had gone to *Carolina*, as intended, a Man of his Interest and good Sense being at *Charles-Town*, whilst Mr. *Oglethorpe* was at the Southward, might have prevented the Misunderstandings which afterwards happen'd.

On the 10th of *December*, the Wind at E. S. E. and a moderate Gale, we, in Company with the *Hawk*, the *London Merchant*, and about forty Sail more, who had been forced to stay by the long Continuance of contrary Winds, stood out for Sea.

When we had pass'd the *Needles* the Pilot left us. The *London Merchant* lay by a little for three of the Passengers, who happen'd to be gone to *Portsmouth* when the Wind came fair; but it was all to no Purpose, for they not coming up in time, were left behind.

On the 12th we parted with the *Hawk*, the Wind blowing very hard.

I believe a Journal of the Winds and Days of the Month will be but dry to the Reader, and that it may divert him more to hear which way our floating Colony were subsisted, and pass'd their time on board.

We had Prayers twice a Day. The Missionaries expounded the Scriptures, catechised the Children, and administer'd the Sacrament on *Sundays*; but Mr. *Oglethorpe* shew'd no Discountenance to any for being of different Persuasions in Religion. The Dissenters, of which there were many on board, particularly the *Germans*, sung Psalms and served God in their own way. Mr. *Oglethorpe* had laid in a large Quantity of live Stock, and other Refreshments, (though he himself seldom eat any but Ship's Provisions:) Not only the Gentlemen his Friends eat at his Table, but he invited, thro' the whole Passage, the Missionaries and the Captain of the Ship, who together made twelve in Number.

All those who came upon the Trust's Account were divided into Messes; and, besides the Ship's Provisions, the Trustees were so careful of the poor People's Health, that they put on board Turnips, Carrots, Potatoes, and Onions, which were given out with the salt Meat, and contributed greatly to prevent the Scurvy. The Ship was divided into Cabbins, with Gang-ways, which we call Streets, between them. The People were disposed into these by Families; the single Men were put by themselves. Each Cabbin had its Door and Partition. Whenever the Weather would permit, the Ship was clean'd between Decks, and wash'd with Vinegar, which kept the Place very sweet and healthy. There were Constables appointed to prevent any Disorders, and every thing was carried so easily, that during the whole Voyage there was no Occasion for punishing any one, excepting a Boy, who was whip'd for stealing of Turnips.

When the Weather permitted, the Men were exercised with small Arms. There were also Thread, Worsted, and Knitting-needles given to the Women, who employ'd their leisure time in making Stockings and Caps for their Family, or in mending their Cloaths and Linnen.

Mr. *Oglethorpe*, when Occasion offer'd, call'd together all those who were design'd to be Freeholders, recommended to them in what Manner to behave themselves, acquainted them of the Nature of the Country, and how to settle it advantagiously.

We went South as far as the 19th Degree of North Latitude, in order to fetch the Trade Winds, so that about *Christmas* it was as hot as in *June*. Our People grew sickly: Mr. *Oglethorpe* himself visited them constantly; and when it was proper he let them have

Fowls for Broth, and any Refreshments of his own. We had a very good Surgeon, and I observed that Carduus Vomits gave the Sick great Relief; If that did not do, Bleeding and some Powders which the Doctor gave, (which were chiefly either Compositions of Salt of Wormwood, or testaceous Powders) had such Effect, that, by the Blessing of God, not one Soul died from the time we left the *Downs* to our Arrival in *Georgia*. Instead of lessening our Number we increased, for on the Passage there were four Children born.

Whenever the Weather was calm enough to permit it, Mr. *Oglethorpe* went on board the *London Merchant*, to see that the like Care was taken of the People on board her, with whom we kept Company all the Way.

Having run before the Trade Wind till we had got Westing sufficient, and being as far South as 20 Degrees, we were obliged to stand Northwardly to fetch *Georgia*, which lies in the Latitude of 32; so that we had a second Winter, for we found the Weather cold as we came near the Coast of *Georgia*.

On the 26th of *January* it blew so hard, that we were obliged to lie-to under a reef'd Main-sail. We shipp'd several Seas, one of which fill'd the great Cabbin, though the dead Lights were up; and another splitted our Main-sail, which was quite new: We soon unbent it, and brought the Ship to under her Mizen.

On the 2d of *February*, at Noon, we saw three Sails standing E. N. E. We bore up to them, and soon after spoke with the *Pompey*, Capt. *Rowse*, bound for *London* from *Carolina*. He lay by, whilst Mr. *Oglethorpe* wrote Letters to *England*, which he sent by him.

On the 4th we found we had pass'd the Stream of the Gulph of *Florida*. We sounded, and found Ground with 50 Fathom of Line, being the Banks of *Georgia*, which shoal gradually to Shore, at that time about 30 Leagues distant. In the Evening we saw Land, which proved to be the Island of *Tybee*. We lay off and on all Night.

On the 5th we ran in, and made *Tybee* plain. Capt. *Dymond*, of the *Peter and James*, came out to us in his Boat, and brought a Pilot with him. He carried us over the Bar with the first of the Flood, finding 19 Foot Water in the shoalest Part. We came to an Anchor within *Tybee*.

Mr. *Oglethorpe* went ashore to see what Progress was made in the Light-house: He found the Foundation had been piled, but the Brick-work not rais'd. The Materials which he had left saw'd at *Savannah*, were brought down, but nothing set up. He had left one *Blythman*, a Carpenter, a very ingenious Workman, in charge to build it allowing him ten Men for his Assistance; and fearing that if he left any one to controul the Carpenter, (who naturally must understand less of it) it might have prevented the Work; therefore he left it in the Carpenter's Charge, at his Peril. Mr. *Oglethorpe* calling him to account for this scandalous Neglect, he had nothing to say in Excuse, but that he had used men in clearing away the Trees, that the Beacon might be the more conspicuous; that a great deal of time had been taken up in piling the Foundation, and in bringing down and landing the Timber; that he had made a great many more Braces than at first had been thought necessary; but that the chief Reason of his Delay arose from his Men's not working; that Rum was so cheap in *Carolina*, from whence they easily got it, that one Day's Pay would make them drunk for a Week, and then they neither minded him nor any thing else. I heard Mr. *Oglethorpe*, after he return'd to the Ship, say, that he was in doubt whether he should prosecute the Man, who is the only one here able to finish the Work, and thereby leave the Work undone, and lose the Materials, which were all ready; or else forgive what was past, and have the Beacon finish'd. He took the latter Counsel, and agreed with him for a Time certain, and a Price certain, appointing Mr. *Vanderplank* to see that the Work advanced according to the Agreement; and not to pay, but proportionably to what should be done. This Beacon is 25 Foot wide at Bottom, 90 Foot high, and 10 Foot wide at Top. It is of the best of Pine, strongly timber'd, raised upon Cedar Piles, and Brickwork round the Bottom. It will be, when raised, of great Service to all Shipping, not only to those bound to this Port, but also to *Carolina*; for the Land of all the Coast, for some hundred Miles, is so alike, being all low and woody, that a distinguishing Mark is of great Consequence.

There is an Island call'd *Peeper*, lying in the Mouth of the *Sa-*

vannah River, between which and *Tybee* there is a very good Harbour. In the Evening we came to Anchor there, where lay the following Ships: The *Prince of Wales*, Capt. *Dunbar*, the *Two Brothers*, Capt. *Thomson*, and the *Peter and James*, Capt. *Dymond*, who were all on the Trustees Account, with Stores and Men for the Southward Settlement, and obliged to stay on Demurrage, by reason of our being unluckily delay'd by contrary Winds at *Cowes*. Mr. *Oglethorpe* employ'd all Hands to discharge them, that he might stop the Expence of Demurrage as soon as possible. All the Ships saluted Mr. *Oglethorpe* with their Cannon on our coming to Anchor; after which he sent an Express to *Charles-Town*, and to Lieut. *Delegal*, (who commanded the King's Independent Company at *Port Royal*) for the Company to repair to *St. Simon*'s.

We learnt from Capt. *Dunbar*, who had brought over 170 *Highlanders*, that Capt. *Hugh Mackay* was set out for the *Alatamaha* River; he being gone first with Part of the Men, and having left the Families to follow after.

That there had been several Reports spread amongst the *Highlanders*, by the Suttlers who brought them Provisions, that the *Spaniards* and *Indians* would certainly destroy them; notwithstanding which they went up.

On the 6th, early, Mr. *Oglethorpe* set out for *Savannah*; but he first carried the People on shore upon *Peeper* Island, and shew'd them where to dig a Well, which they did, and found Plenty of fresh Water. He was received at *Savannah* by the Freeholders under Arms, and under the Salute of 21 Cannons, which we heard plainly, being about ten Miles distance.

After Mr. *Oglethorpe* was gone to Savannah, most of the Colony went ashore upon *Peeper Island*, where I found an Eagle's Nest on a Fir-tree; we cut it down, and found an Egg in it, in which was a young Eagle. In the Evening the People found another Spring, and also a Pond of fresh Water, which they used for washing their Linnen. A small Sloop passed by us for *Savannah*, bound thither with Provisions from *Carolina*.

On the 7th, all our Women went ashore on *Peeper Island* to wash their Linnen. A Boat came down from *Savannah* with some fresh

Beef, Pork, Venison and other Refreshments, sent by Mr. *Ogle-thorpe* for the People on board this Ship and the *London Merchant.* In the Evening we had a smart Shower of Rain, which wetted our good Women to the Skins before they could get aboard.

On the 8th, some Boats with Suttlers came on board with Provisions to sell to the Passengers. They privately brought some Rum; which being discover'd, the Officers who were left by Mr. *Oglethorpe* to keep Orders on board, during his Absence, order'd the same to be staved; which was accordingly complied with. The Boat returned which had been sent to *Port Royal*, with Answer, that the Refreshments which had been bespoke from *England*, for the Use of the Colony, were not ready. She immediately proceeded up to *Savannah*, having Packets of Letters for Mr. *Oglethorpe*, who in the Evening return'd from thence in a Scout-boat. This was a strong-built swift Boat, with three swivel Guns and ten Oars, kept for the visiting the River-Passages, and Islands, and for preventing the Incursions of Enemies, or Runaways, from whence it is call'd Scout-boat. The Crew is composed of Men bred in *America*, bold and hardy, who lie out in the Woods, and upon the Water Months together, without a House or Covering. Most of them are good Hunters or Fishers. By killing Deer and other Game they can subsist themselves, in case their Provisions should fail; but indeed, on these Sea-islands, no one can starve, since if, at the worst, a Man was lost, there are Oysters and Shell-fish enough to subsist him.

Mr. *Oglethorpe* brought with him fresh Meat, and other Refreshments in Plenty, which he distributed to the new Comers, consisting of fresh Beef, fresh Pork, Venison, wild Turkeys, soft Bread, (the Word soft is put to distinguish it from Biscuit, because at Sea they call Biscuit, Bread) Strong-beer, Small-beer, Turnips, and Garden-greens; and this in such Plenty, that there was enough for the whole Colony for some Days. This was doubly agreeable to the Colony, both because they found the Comfort of fresh Food after a long Voyage, and also that a Town begun within these three Years, by People in their own Circumstances, could produce such Plenty; from whence they hoped themselves should be in as good or better a Condition within that Time. The People were not a little surprised at the News, which came by the Boat, that Mr. *Vonreck* and the *Germans* did not go to the Southward with them. This is the more extraordinary, because Mr. *Vonreck* said, that he went up to *Ebenezer* to get some more Men from thence, who are acquainted with the Colony, to increase the Strength of the new Town. But this did not daunt our Inhabitants (that were to be) of *Frederica* (for so our Town was to be called) though to be sure, the losing half our Number was a great Lessening of our Strength. The Reason, we heard, he gave for the *Germans* going up to *Ebenezer* and not with us, was, that they might have the Benefit of the two Ministers, who were settled at *Ebenezer*, and that they might not divide the Congregation. Others of the *Germans* did not care to go to the Southward, because, they said, Fighting was against their Religion, and they apprehended Blows might happen there. But Captain *Hermsdorf* came to Mr. *Oglethorpe*, and desired that he might be put upon every Occasion of Service, if there was any, and that he would never forsake him, but serve with the *English* to the last. Mr. *Oglethorpe* told him, that the Stories of War were quite groundless; that there was as little Danger to the Southward, as to the Northward; that the *Indians* were at Friendship with us, and the *Spaniards* at Peace; and that as we would not molest them, it was not to be supposed that they would break the Peace, and attack us. Yet still, Caution was the Mother of Safety, and therefore it was fitting to keep the Men to Arms and Discipline; and for that Purpose he should be glad of his Assistance.

It was intended when we came from *London*, that these two Ship should have sailed into *Jekyl Sound*, and have landed the Colony, and all the Stores, at the Place where the Town was to be built; and for this Purpose, there had been an Agreement made to pay Demurrage for the Loss of Time there. The Captains did not care to venture down, and gave many Reasons. Capt. *Cornish* perceiving the great Damage that must arise to the Trust by their Ships not going down, proposed, that if Mr. *Oglethorpe* would send down Captain *Yokeley* with the *James*, to discover the Channel, they would go down, and in, he piloting of them. Captain *Thomas* agreed to the same Proposal, and Mr. *Oglethorpe* accordingly agreed with Captain *Yokeley*.

Mr. *Oglethorpe* seemed very uneasy at their not going to *Frederica* at once, but did not care to force them; the Words of the Agreement being not quite clear, and there was no sworn Pilot, who could take charge of the Ships in; for one *Miller*, the Pilot, who had surveyed that Entry, by Mr. *Oglethorpe*'s Order, was gone from *Savannah* before his Arrival; and *Kilbury*, another Pilot, who knew the same, was dead, and the Man of War was not yet arrived, whom we depended upon to have gone in first.

Mr. *Oglethorpe* spoke to the People to prevent their being terrified with false Reports. There seemed to be little need of it, for they were all zealous to settle a Town of their own, and trusting entirely to him, were not at all apprehensive of any Danger; but were fearful of staying and losing their Time at *Savannah*.

After three Hours stay, he set out for *Savannah* and took me along with him. About Midnight we arrived there, but being then High-water, and the *German* Ministers who were to go with him to *Ebenezer*, not caring to go by Night, he could not go forward as he intended, some of the Boatmen being ill, and the Freshes strong. He lay that Night at a House which he hires at *Savannah*; it is the same as the common Freeholders Houses are, a Frame of sawed Timber, 24 by 16 Foot, floored with rough Deals, the Sides with feather-edged Boards unplained, and the Roof shingled.

On the 9th, I heard that the *Saltzburghers* at *Ebenezer* were very discontented; that they demanded to leave their old Town, and to settle upon the Lands which the *Indians* had reserved for their own Use; and this was the Occasion of Mr. *Oglethorpe*'s going up in such haste at a Time when he could be ill spared from the Ships. He set out this Morning-Tide, with several Gentlemen, and the *Saltzburghers* Ministers, and went by Water to Sir *Francis Bathurst*'s, where part of Captain *Mackay*'s Troop of Horsemen, lately come out of the *Indian* Country, lay: There he took Horse for *Ebenezer*.

When he was gone, I took a View of the Town of *Savannah*; it is about a Mile and Quarter in Circumference; it stands upon the flat of a Hill, the Bank of the River (which they in barbarous *English* call a *Bluff*) is steep, and about 45 Foot perpendicular, so that all heavy Goods are brought up by a Crane, an Inconvenience designed to be remedied by a bridged Wharf, and an easy Ascent, which in laying out the Town, care was taken to allow room for, there being a very wide Strand between the first Row of Houses and the River. From this Strand there is a very pleasant Prospect; you see the River wash the Foot of the Hill, which is a hard, clear, sandy Beach, a Mile in Length; the Water is fresh, and the River 1000 Foot wide. Eastward you see the River increased by the Northern Branch, which runs round *Hutchinson's Island*, and the *Carolina* Shore beyond it, and the *Woody Islands* at the Sea, which close the Prospect at 10 or 12 Miles Distance. Over against it is *Hutchinson's Island*, great part of which is open Ground, where they mow Hay for the Trust's Horses and Cattle. The rest is Woods, in which there are many Bay-trees 80 Foot high. Westward you see the River winding between the Woods, with little Islands in it for many Miles, and *Toma Chi Chi*'s *Indian* Town standing upon the Southern Banks, between 3 and 4 Miles distance.

The Town of *Savannah* is built of Wood; all the Houses of the first 40 Freeholders are of the same Size with that Mr. *Oglethorpe* lives in, but there are great Numbers built since, I believe 100 or 150, many of these are much larger, some of 2 or 3 Stories high, the Boards plained and painted. The Houses stand on large Lotts, 60 Foot in Front by 90 Foot in Depth; each Lott has a fore and back Street to it; the Lotts are fenced in with split Pales; some few People have Pallisades of turned Wood before their Doors, but the Generality have been wise enough not to throw away their Money, which in this Country, laid out in Husbandry, is capable of great Improvements, though there are several People of good Substance in the Town, who came at their own Expence, and also, several of those who came over on the Charity, are in a very thriving way; but this is observed, that the most substantial People are the most frugal, and make the least Shew, and live at the least Expence. There are some also who have made but little or bad Use of the Benefits they received, idling away their Times, whilst they had their Provisions from the publick Store, or else working for Hire, earning from 2 Shillings, the Price of a Labourer, to 4 or 5 Shillings, the Price of a Carpenter, *per diem*, and spending that Money in Rum and good Living, thereby neglecting to improve their Lands, so that when their Time of receiving their Provisions from the Publick ceased, they were in no Forwardness to maintain themselves out of their own Lands. As they chose to be Hirelings when they might have improved for themselves, the Consequence of that Folly forces them now to work for their daily Bread. These are generally discontented with the Country; and if they have run themselves in Debt, their Creditors will not let them go away till they have paid. Considering the Number of People, there are but very few of these. The Industrious ones have throve beyond Expectation; most of them that have been there three Years, and many others, have Houses in the Town, which those that Let, have for the worst, 10 *l. per Annum*, and the best let for 30 *l.*

Those who have cleared their 5 Acre Lotts, have made a very great Profit out of them by Greens, Roots and Corn. Several have improv'd the Cattle they had at first, and have now 5 or 6 tame Cows; others, who to save the Trouble of Feeding them, let them go into the Woods, can rarely find them, and when they are brought up, one of them will not give half the Quantity of Milk, which another Cow fed near Home will give. Their Houses are built at a pretty large Distance from one another, for fear of Fire; the Streets are very wide, and there are great Squares left at proper Distances, for Markets and other Conveniences. Near the River-side is a Guard-house inclosed with Palisades a Foot thick, where there are 19 or 20 Cannons mounted, and a continual Guard kept by the Free-holders. This Town is governed by 3 Bailiffs, and has a Recorder, Register, and a Town Court, which is holden every six Weeks, where all Matters Civil and Criminal are decided by grand and petty Juries, as in *England*; but there are no Lawyers allowed to plead for Hire, nor no Attornies to take Money, but (as in old times in *England*) every Man pleads his own Cause. In case it should be an Orphan, or one that cannot speak for themselves, there are Persons of the best Substance in the Town, appointed by the Trustees to take care of the Orphans, and to defend the Helpless, and that without Fee or Reward, it being a Service that each that is capable must perform in his Turn. They have some Laws and Customs peculiar to *Georgia*; one is, that all Brandies and distilled Liquors are prohibited under severe Penalities; another is, that no Slavery is allowed, nor Negroes; a Third, that all Persons who go among the *Indians* must give Security for their good Behaviour; because the *Indians*, if any Injury is done to them, and they cannot kill the Man who does it, expect Satisfaction from the Government, which if not procured, they break out into War, by killing the first white Man they conveniently can. No Victualler or Alehouse-keeper can give any Credit, so consequently cannot recover any Debt. The Free-holds are all entailed, which has been very fortunate for the Place. If People could have sold, the greatest part, before they knew the Value of their Lotts, would have parted with them for a trifling Condition, and there were not wanting rich Men who employed Agents to Monopolize the whole Town: And if they had got Numbers of Lotts into their own Hands, the other Free-holders would have had no Benefit by letting their Houses, and hardly of Trade, since the Rich, by means of a large Captial, would underlet and undersell, and the Town must have been almost without Inhabitants, as *Port Royal* in *Carolina* is, by the best Lotts being got into a few Hands.

The mentioning the *Laws* and *Customs* leads me to take notice that *Georgia* is founded upon Maxims different from those on which other Colonies have been begun. The Intention of that Colony was an *Asylum* to receive the Distressed. This was the charitable Design, and the governmental Views besides that, was, with Numbers of free white People, well settled, to strengthen the southern Part of the *English* Settlements on the Continent of *America*, of which this is the Frontier. It is necessary therefore not to permit Slaves in such a Country, for Slaves starve the poor Labourer. For if the Gentleman can have his Work done by a Slave who is a Carpenter or Bricklayer, the Carpenter or Bricklayers of that Country must starve for want of Employment, and so of other Trades.

In order to maintain many People, it was proper that the Land should be divided into small Portions, and to prevent the uniting them by Marriage or Purchase. For every Time that two Lotts are united, the Town Loses a Family, and the Inconveniency of this shews itself at *Savannah*, notwithstanding the Care of the Trustees to prevent it. They suffered the Moiety of the Lotts to descend to the Widows during their Lives: Those who remarried to Men who had Lotts of their own, by uniting two Lotts made one be neglected; for the strength of Hands who could take care of one, was not sufficient to look to and improve two. These uncleared Lotts are a Nusance to their Neighbours. The Trees which grow upon them shade the Lotts, the Beasts take shelter in them, and for want of clearing the Brooks which pass thro' them, the Lands above are often prejudiced by Floods. To prevent all these Inconveniences, the first Regulation of the Trustees was a strict *Agrarian* Law, by which all the Lands near Towns should be divided, 50 Acres to each Freeholder. The Quantity of Land by Experience seems rather too much, since it is impossible that one poor Family can tend so much Land. If this Alottment is too much, how much more inconvenient would the uniting of two be? To prevent it, the Trustees grant the Lands in Tail Male, that on the expiring of a Male-Line they may regrant it to such Man, having no other Lott, as shall be married to the next Female Heir of the Deceased, as is of good Character. This manner of Dividing, prevents also the Sale of Lands, and the Rich thereby monopolizing the Country.

Each Freeholder had a Lott in Town 60 Foot by 90 Foot, besides which he has a Lott beyond the Common, of 5 Acres for a Garden. Every ten Houses make a Tything, and to every Tything there is a Mile Square, which is divided into 12 Lotts, besides Roads: Each Free-holder of the Tything has a Lott or Farm of 45 Acres there, and two Lotts are reserved by the Trustees in order to defray the Charge of the Publick. The Town is laid out for two hundred and forty Freeholds; the Quantity of Lands necessary for that Number is 24 Square Miles; every 40 Houses in Town make a Ward, to which 4 Square Miles in the Country belong; each Ward has a Constable, and under him 4 Tything Men. Where the Town-Lands end, the Villages begin; four Villages make a Ward without, which depends upon one of the Wards within the Town. The Use of this is, in case a War should happen, that the Villages without may have Places in the Town, to bring their Cattle and Families into for Refuge, and to that Purpose there is a Square left in every Ward, big enough for the Out-wards to encamp in. There is Ground also kept round about the Town ungranted, in order for the Fortifications, whenever Occasion shall require. Beyond the Villages, commence Lotts of 500 Acres; these are granted upon Terms of keeping 10 Servants, *&c.* Several Gentlemen who have settled on such Grants have succeeded very well, and have been of great Service to the Colony. Above the Town is a Parcel of Land called *Indian Lands*; these are those reserved by King *Toma Chi Chi* for his People. There is near the Town, to the East, a Garden belonging to the Trustees, consisting of 10 Acres; the Situation is delightful, one half of it is upon the Top of a Hill, the Foot of which the River *Savannah* washes, and from it you see the *Woody Islands* in the Sea. The Remainder of the Garden is the Side and some plain low Ground at the Foot of the Hill, where several fine Springs break out. In the Garden is variety of Soils; the Top is sandy and dry, the Sides of the Hill are Clay, and the Bottom is a black rich Garden-Mould well watered. On the North-part of the Garden is left standing a Grove of Part of the old Wood, as it was before the arrival of the Colony there. The Trees in the Grove are mostly Bay, Sassafras, Evergreen Oak, Pellitory, Hickary, *American* Ash, and the Laurel Tulip. This last is looked upon as one of the most beautiful Trees in the World; it grows straight-bodied to 40 or 50 Foot high; the Bark smooth and whitish, the Top spreads regular like an Orange-tree in *English* Gardens, only larger; the Leaf is like that of a common Laurel, but bigger, and the underside of a greenish Brown: It blooms about the Month of *June*; the Flowers are white, fragrant like the Orange, and perfume all the Air around it; the Flower is round, 8 or 10 Inches diameter, thick like the Orange-flower, and a little yellow near the Heart: As the Flowers drop, the Fruit, which is a Cone with red Berries, succeeds them. There are also some Bay-trees that have Flowers like the Laurel, only less.

The Garden is laid out with Cross-walks planted with Orange-trees, but the last Winter, a good deal of Snow having fallen, had killed those upon the Top of the Hill down to their Roots, but they being cut down sprouted again, as I saw when I returned to *Savannah*. In the Squares between the Walks, were vast Quantities of Mulberry-trees, this being a Nursery for all the Province, and every Planter that desires it, has young Trees given him *gratis* from this Nursery. These white Mulberry-trees were planted in order to raise Silk, for which Purpose several *Italians* were brought, at the Trustee's Expence, from *Piedmont* by Mr. *Amatis*; they have fed Worms, and wound Silk to as great Perfection as any that ever came out of *Italy*: But the *Italians* falling out, one of them stole away the Machines for winding, broke the Coppers, and spoiled all the Eggs, which he could not steal, and fled to *South-Carolina*. The others, who continued faithful, had saved but a few Eggs when Mr. *Oglethorpe* arrived, therefore he forbade any Silk should be wound, but that all the Worms should be suffered to eat through their Balls, in order to have more Eggs against next Year. The *Italian* Women are obliged to take *English* Girls Apprentices, whom they teach to wind and feed; and the Men have taught our *English* Gardeners to tend the Mulberry-trees, and our Joyners have learned how to make the Machines for winding. As the Mulberry-trees increase, there will be a great Quantity of Silk made here.

Besides the Mulberry-trees; there are in some of the Quarters in the coldest part of the Garden, all kinds of Fruit-trees usual in *England*, such as Apples, Pears, *&c*. In another Quarter are Olives, Figs, Vines, Pomegranates and such Fruits as are natural to the warmest Parts of *Europe*. At the bottom of the Hill, well sheltered from the North-wind, and in the warmest part of the Garden, there was a Collection of *West-India* Plants and Trees, some Coffee, some Cocoa-nuts, Cotton, Palma-christi, and several *West-Indian* physical Plants, some sent up by Mr. *Eveleigh* a publick-spirited Merchant at *Charles-Town*, and some by Dr. *Houstoun*, from the *Spanish West-Indies*, where he was sent at the Expence of a Collection raised by that curious Physician Sir *Hans Sloan*, for to collect and sent them to *Georgia*, where the Climate was capable of making a Garden which might contain all kinds of Plants; to which Design his Grace the Duke of *Richmond*, the Earl of *Derby*, the Lord *Peters*, and the Apothecary's Company contributed very generously; as did Sir *Hans* himself. The Quarrels amongst the *Italians* proved fatal to most of these Plants, and they were labouring to repair that Loss when I was there, Mr. *Miller* being employ'd in the room of Dr. *Houstoun*, who died in *Jamaica*. We heard he had wrote an Account of his having obtain'd the Plant from whence the true *Balsamum Capivi* is drawn; and that he was in hopes of getting that from whence the *Jesuits Bark* is taken, he designing for that Purpose to send to the *Spanish West Indies*.

There is a Plant of Bamboo Cane brought from the *East Indies*, and sent over by Mr. *Towers*, which thrives well. There was also some Tea-seeds, which came from the same Place; but the latter, though great Care was taken, did not grow.

Three Miles from *Savannah*, within Land, that is to say, to the South, are two pretty Villages, *Hampstead* and *Highgate*, where the Planters are very forward, having built neat Huts, and clear'd and planted a great deal of Land. Up the River also there are several other Villages, and two Towns, not much better than Villages, on the *Georgia* Side, and one call'd *Joseph's Town*, which some *Scotch* Gentlemen are building at their own Expence, and where they have already clear'd a great deal of Ground. Above that is *Ebenezer*, a Town of the *Saltzburghers*. On the *Carolina* Side is *Purysburgh*, chiefly inhabited by *Swiss*. There are also a Party of Rangers under the Command of Capt. *McPherson*, and another under the Command of Capt. *Æneas M'Intosh*; the one lying upon the *Savannah* River, the other upon the *Ogeechie*. These are Horsemen, and patrole the Woods to see that no Enemy *Indians*, nor other lawless Persons, shelter themselves there.

There were no publick Buildings in the Town, besides a Storehouse; for the Courts were held in a Hut 36 Foot long, and 12 Foot wide, made of split Boards, and erected on Mr. *Oglethorpe*'s first Arrival in the Colony. In this Hut also Divine Service was perform'd; but upon his Arrival this time, Mr. *Oglethorpe* order'd a House to be erected in the upper Square, which might serve for a Courthouse, and for Divine Service till a Church could be built, and a Work-house over-against it; for as yet there was no Prison here.

Two Ships lay close to the Town, the *James*, Capt. *Yokely*, in the

Trustees Service, waiting for our Arrival, (with Provisions) and another Ship from *Bristol*, Capt. *Dickens*, Commander, loaded with Passengers. The Water is not only deep, but thoroughly shelter'd from Hurricanes, and, being fresh, there are no Worms; an Advantage few Ports have in *America*.

On the 10th I went on board the *Two Brothers*, Capt. *Thomson*, and unloaded her, sending some Part of her Cargo up to *Savannah* Store, and the Remainder on board the *James*, Capt. *Yokely*, who, on the Unwillingness of the other Ships, as before mention'd, Mr. *Oglethorpe* engaged to go and try the Entrance of *Jekyll Sound*, his Ship being but about 100 Tons Burden.

On the 11th Mr. *Oglethorpe* return'd from *Ebenezer* to *Savannah*, where he found Capt. *Yokely*, not ready to sail. I heard that he had given Leave to the *Saltzburghers* to remove from *Old Ebenezer* to a Place call'd the *Red Bluff*, upon the River *Savannah*. Some People had infused such Notions into them, that they were obstinately resolv'd to quit *Old Ebenezer*, where they had very good Houses ready built, a pleasant Situation, a fine Range for Cattle, and a good deal of Ground clear'd. Mr. *Oglethorpe* in vain advised them against the Change, and told them, that Sickness would naturally follow the clearing a new Town; but they insisting, he granted their Request. Mr. *Oglethorpe*, in this Journey, pursuant to the Trustees Orders, and to save Expence, reduced Mr. *Patrick Mackay*'s Company that was come down from the *Indian* Nation. He call'd at *Purysburgh*, on his Return from *Ebenezer*.

On the 12th Mr. *Oglethorpe* went from *Savannah* down to the Ships at *Tybee*, having first raised 50 Rangers and 100 Workmen, and sent Capt. *M'Pherson* with a Parcel of his Rangers over Land, to support the *Highlanders* on the *Alatamaha* River. These *Highlanders*, under the Command of Capt. *Hugh Mackay*, were settled on the *Alatamaha* River, within one Mile and a half of where Fort *King George* formerly stood, and where his Majesty's Independent Company had been garrison'd for several Years. The Want of Supplies and Communication with *Carolina*, obliged them to abandon the Garrison and destroy the Fort: Therefore the first thing was to open a Communication by Land, that the like Distress might not again happen. Mr. *Oglethorpe* order'd Mr. *Walter Augustine* and Mr. *Tolme* to survey the Country from *Savannah* to the *Alatamaha*, to know where a Road might be most conveniently made; and appointed Mr. *Hugh Mackay*, junior, with ten Rangers to escort them, and two Pack-horsemen to carry Provisions for them. *Toma Chi Chi* also sent some *Indians* with them.

On the 14th *Toma Chi Chi*, *Scenauky* his Wife, *Tooanahowi* his Nephew, and several Attendants, came down to visit Mr. *Oglethorpe* on board the *Symond*, carrying with them Venison, Milk, Honey, and other *Indian* Refreshments.

Toma Chi Chi acquainted Mr. *Oglethorpe*, that he had sent up to the *Creek* Nation Notice of his Arrival by two chief Men, who had staid on purpose for some Months, they having so long expected him. That he had sent a Party of *Indians* to assist Capt. *Mackay* at the *Darien*: That the *Uchee Indians* complain'd that Cattle were pass'd over into their Country, contrary to the Capitulation; and that Planters had come and settled Negroes there.—Part of these Cattle belong'd to the *Saltzburghers*, who had pass'd over the *Ebenezer* River into the *Uchee* Lands; and the rest, as also the Negroes, belong'd to some of the Inhabitants of *South Carolina*. Upon this the following Orders were issued to Capt. *Æneas M'Intosh*, *viz.*

Tybee Road, 14*th Feb.* 1735-6.

Being inform'd by the *Indians*, that several Persons, contrary to the Treaties with them made, have carried over Cattle and Negroes, and have planted on the *Georgia* Side of the River: You are hereby authoriz'd and requir'd to give Notice to the same Persons to withdraw their Horses, Cattle, and Negroes out of *Georgia*; and if within three Days they do not withdraw their Negroes, you are to seize and bring the Negroes to the Town of *Savannah*, and deliver them to the Magistrates there; and Proceeding shall be had, if they leave their Cattle beyond the said Term.

(*Copy*) *James Oglethorpe.*

This Day Mr. *Oglethorpe* sent up the Act, intituled, *An Act for maintaining the Peace with the* Indians *in the Province of* Georgia, *prepared by the Hon. Trustees for establishing the Colony of* Georgia *in* America, *and approved by his most Excellent Majesty King* George *the Second in Council, on the 3d Day of* April, *in the Year of our Lord* 1735, *and in the* 8*th Year of his Majesty's Reign*, to *Savannah Town*, (alias *New Windsor*) and from thence to every Trader amongst the *Indians*, and Notice was given them to conform thereunto.

Scenauky presented the Missionaries two large Jars, one of Honey, and one of Milk, and invited them to come up to their new Town at *Yamacraw*, and teach the Children there; and told them, that the Honey and Milk was a Representation of their Inclinations. The same Evening, having done my Business on board Capt. *Thomson*, I went down to the Ships in the Scout-boat. About Midnight came to anchor at *Tybee* a Sloop from *New York*, call'd the *Midnight*, loaded with Provisions.

On the 15th, Capt. *Yokely* not being yet come down, Mr. *Oglethorpe* was much concern'd at the Delay, which was of great Damage to the poor People, who, by not being on their Lands, were losing the best Season both for building and improving (which is the Winter.) Besides, we were apprehensive that the *Spanish Indians* might undertake something against the *Highlanders*, if they were not strengthen'd; who also might be uneasy at finding themselves not supported; and that the *Spaniards* themselves might perhaps take Possession of the Mouths of the Harbours, and drive off and conquer the *English Indians*, who were then, and had long been in Possession of those Islands, and to whom they belong'd for several Ages. The Danger of Sickness, and Damage of Goods, besides the Expence and Hazard of sending the People in open Boats, was very great; and if no Vessel lay in the Entrance, if the *Spaniards* should come up with the smallest Ship, they might entrench themselves under the Shelter of the Ship's Cannon, in spite of all that the *English Indians* could do. Mr. *Oglethorpe* spoke to both the Captains to go and anchor at the Entrance of *Jekyll Sound*, and go in with Boats (which he would furnish, and go with himself) sound the Bar, and carry their Ships in. They remonstrated the Danger and Impossibility of Merchants Ships making Discoveries. At last this Expedient was thought of; to buy the Cargo of the *Midnight* Sloop, who arrived last Night, on Condition that she should go into *Jekyll Sound*, and deliver the Cargo at *Frederica* in the *Alatamaha*.

Capt. *Cornish* and Capt. *Thomas* consented to go on board the Sloop, and in her to try the Entrance, and promised then to come back and carry their Ships in, who, in the mean time, would lie in Safety in *Tybee* Harbour. Mr. *Oglethorpe* agreed for the Cargo; the Master of the Sloop, one *Barnes*, being a brisk Man, and very willing to undertake the Discovery of the Entrance, seeing it was for the publick Service. Mr. *Oglethorpe* order'd Mr. *Horton* and Mr. *Tanner*, with 30 of the single Men of the Colony, on board the Sloop, with Cannon, Arms, Ammunition, and Tools for entrenching, with whom Capt. *Cornish* and Capt. *Thomas* went down by Sea to meet him at *Frederica*; himself going down by the Channels within the Islands. Such Diligence was used, that the Sloop sail'd by Eight the next Morning. Mr. *Oglethorpe* order'd from *Savannah* the Workmen that he had engaged there; also more *Indians* from *Toma Chi Chi*; and those *Indians* who were already down, to rendezvous at certain Posts, where he might send for them as Occasion should require.

On the 16th in the Evening, Mr. *Oglethorpe* set out in the Scout-boat, through the inland Channels, to meet the Sloop at *Jekyll Sound*. He carried with him Capt. *Hermsdorf*, two of the Colony, and some *Indians*. Capt. *Dunbar* also accompanied him with his Boat. I was left with the Ships, having Charge of their Cargoes.

On the 17th, Capt. *Yokely* came down to *Tybee* from *Savannah*.

On the 18th, he began to take Beef and other Provisions out of Capt. *Dymond*, for *Frederica*; and before he had compleated his Cargo, the Wind came about, so that he could not get out.

Before Mr. *Oglethorpe* set out for the Southward, Lieutenant *Delegal*, who at that Time commanded his Majesty's independent Company at *Port Royal*, waited upon him, pursuant to his Letter, to acquaint him with the Circumstances of the Company, and what Provisions would be necessary for their Subsistence, and what Boats for their Embarkation, that Company being ordered to St. *Simons*.

A Gentleman with Letters to the Governor of *Augustine*, from the Person charged with the King of *Spain*'s Affairs at the Court of *England*, came over in the Ship *Symond*. Mr. *Oglethorpe*, before he went to *Alatamaha*, left orders with Major *Richard* of *Purysbourg* to conduct that Gentleman in a six-oar'd Boat, being the best then to be got, to *Augustine*; and also by the same Occasion sent a Letter to that Governor.

Mr. *Spangenberg* acquainted Mr. *Oglethorpe*, that several *Germans* with whom he had an Influence were gone to *Pensilvania* instead of *Georgia*, and that he would go thither and fetch them, to be an Increase of Strength to the Colony. Mr. *Oglethorpe* told him, that he would not inveigle any from another Colony; but if Mr. *Penn*, the Proprietor of that Province was desirous they should come away, he was willing to receive them; therefore he gave Letters for Mr. *Penn* to Mr. *Spangenberg*.

On the 19th, Major *Richard* set out for St. *Augustine*, with the Gentleman for that Place.

Whilst Mr. *Oglethorpe* was absent, the Colony that remained with us were employed, some in helping to build the Beacon at *Tybee*, and some in hunting and fishing; they all went daily on shore to *Peeper Island*, but none went up to *Savannah*, nor no Boats came to them without Licence, for fear some unwary People should be drawn to spend what little they had in buying Refreshments, and lest they should make themselves sick, by drinking Drams and eating Trash. They had plenty of fresh Provisions and good Beer provided for them, which made this Restraint not inconvenient. They washed their Linnen and drest their Meat on shore with Fires made of Cedar and Bay Trees, which to People new come from *England*, seemed an extraordinary Luxury. On the Shore were Oyster-Banks, dry at low-water, where they took as many as they pleased, the Oysters being very good.

I observed here a kind of long Moss I had never seen before; it grows in great Quantities upon the large Trees, and hangs down 3 or 4 Yards from the Boughs; it gives a noble, ancient and hoary Look to the Woods; it is of a whitish green Colour, but when dried, is black and like Horse-hair. This the *Indians* use for wadding their Guns, and making their Couches soft under the Skins of Beasts, which serve them for Beds. They use it also for Tinder, striking Fire by flashing the Pans of their Guns into a handful of it, and for all other Uses where old Linnen would be necessary.

On the 23d, Colonel *Bull*, one of his Majesty's Council in *Carolina*, arrived here in his own Perriagua, with Letters from the Lieutenant-Governor, Council and Assembly of that Province for Mr. *Oglethorpe*. I offered him the Ship's great Cabbin, and all Provisions and Necessaries, but he refused it, having himself a Cabbin fitted up with all Conveniences aboard his own Perriagua; howsoever he did us the Favour to dine on board.

Nothing remarkable happened on board till Mr. *Oglethorpe* returned from the Southward, which was on the 25th in the Evening. I had from one who went along with him, the following Account.

The Scout-boat went along through Channels, between the Islands and the Main; these Channels are in some Places above a Mile, and in others not above 200 Yards wide. In many Places, the Woods of Pines, Ever-green-Oaks, and Cedar-Trees grow close to the Water-side, which with the clear sea-green Colour and Stillness of the Channels, sheltered by the Woods, is very delightful to the Eye. In other Places, on the Banks, are wide Marshes, so hard that Cattle feed upon them, though at some of the very highest Spring-tides they are just covered with Water. We passed between the Island of *Wilmington* and the Main; upon the latter, we landed at one Mr. *Lacy*'s, where 5 Gentlemen of 500 Acre Lotts have built their Houses together, that they might be the more easily fortified, which they are with Palisades well flanked with several Pieces of Cannon. They with Masters and Servants make the Garrison, and in all Times of Apprehension do regular Duty; one of the Masters, with Proportion of Servants, mounting Guard each Night. They have cleared above 100 Acres of Land round the Fort. They have Milk, Cattle, Hogs, Garden-stuff, and Poultry in such Plenty, that they sent at different Times several Bushels of Eggs down to *Frederica*. This Fort commands the Water-passage between the Islands to *Savannah*. It stands high, the Banks of the River being about 18 Foot perpendicular from High-water Mark; the Bottom is a Clay mixed with Iron-stone, and is the only Place an Enemy can land at from the Southward. It is but 4 Miles from *Savannah* by Land, though 16 by Water; and the Ridge of Pine Groves reaching all the Way from the one to the other, it is passable for Horses and Carriages by going a little round about to follow the Course of the open Groves. Mr. *Lacy* has there set up Pot-ash-Works, and made some for Trial; but finding that he could make more Advantage of the same Labour by sawing

Timber for the Sugar-Islands, and splitting Staves for the *Madera*, he does not now go on with the Pot-ash, till he can have more Strength of Hands. Here we met a Boat from *Savannah* with Workmen for the Southward; they were most of them *Germans* and *Swiss*, raised at *Purysburg*; the Boat being full of Men and heavy loaded, we outwent her. From this Fort we saw the Island of *Skidoway*, being 4 Miles Distance down a wide Channel; we stopt at the northwardmost Point of that Island, where there is a Village, a Guard-house, and Battery of Cannon: The Free-holders of the Island perform Guard-duty at the Battery. The Land of this Island is very rich; the Inhabitants have cleared about 30 Acres, but propose doing much more this Year, since there will be Settlements to the Southward of them, for they have been much hindered by continual Alarms. This Island is about 12 Miles long, and 4 wide. Leaving *Skidoway* on the Left, and the Mouths of *Vernon* and *Ogeechee* Rivers on the Right, we passed forward, and still kept through Channels, as before, sometimes crossing wide Sounds (for so the Boatmen here call the Gulphs of the Sea which run into the Land, and the Entrances of the Rivers.) There are 3 or 4 Sounds to be passed, which in blowing Weather are dangerous to those open Boats. I believe, where we passed, St. *Catherine's* is above two Leagues wide. The Tides of Flood carried us up along-side the Islands, and the Tides of Ebb down to the Sea. Mr. *Oglethorpe* being in haste, the Men rowed Night and Day, and had no other Rest than what they got when a Snatch of Wind favoured us. They were all very willing, though we met with very boisterous Weather. The Master, Capt. *Ferguson* is perfectly acquainted with all the Water-passages, and in the darkest Night never missed the Way through the Woods and Marshes, though there are so many Channels as to make a perfect Labyrinth. The Men vied with each other, who should be forwardest to please Mr. *Oglethorpe*. Indeed, he lightened their Fatigue, by giving them Refreshments, which he rather spared from himself than let them want. The *Indians* seeing the Men hard laboured, desired to take the Oars, and rowed as well as any I ever saw, only differing from the others, by taking a short and long Stroke alternately, which they called the *Yamasee Stroke*. I found this was no new Thing to the *Indians*, they being accustomed to row their own Canoes, Boats made out of a single Tree hollowed, which they manage with great Dexterity.

When we came near the Mouths of the *Alatamaha*, we met a Boat with Mr. *Mackay* and Mr. *Cuthbert* (who is Lieutenant of the *Darien*) coming from the *Darien* to *Savannah*. They were very agreeably surprised to find Mr. *Oglethorpe* on board us. They returned to the *Darien*, taking Captain *Dunbar* with them, whilst we stood the shortest way to St. *Simons*. Mr. *Cuthbert* told us, that one of the Highlanders met with an Orange-tree full of Fruit on *Duboys Island*; he was charmed with the Colour, but could not get them by reason of the Height of the Tree, which was so full of Thorns, that there was no climbing it, so he cut it down and gathered some Dozens.

On the 18th in the Morning, we arrived at the Island of St. *Simons*. We were ordered to look to our Arms, new prime our Swivel-Guns, and make every thing ready for fear of Accidents: We also landed the *Indians*, who soon met a Party of their Friends, who informed them a Ship was come into St. *Simons*, but that they did not know what she was, nor would not speak to the People, having been ordered by their chief War Captain, in case they saw any Ship come in, not to shew themselves to them, but to watch the Men if they landed, and not to hurt them, but to send him notice. That they had sent to him, he being upon *Sapola Island*. We stood down one of the Branches of the *Alatamaha*, close under the Reeds, so as not to be seen till we fully discovered what they called a Ship, to be the *Midnight Sloop*. They were very joyful at our Arrival, and we also not a little pleased to hear that the Captains of our Ships said that they had found Water enough to bring in their Ships, excepting one Place. That there was 16 or 17 Fathom within the Harbour; that the Entrance was very easy, except one Place on the Barr, where they had found it shoaly by reason of a Spit of Sand, which they had not Opportunity in coming in to try round, but would go down in the Sloop, and the first calm Day did not doubt finding a good Channel round the Spit. Mr. *Horton*, Mr. *Tanner*, and the Men were all brisk, and in good Health. Mr. *Oglethorpe* immediately set all Hands to work, mark'd out a Booth to hold the Stores, digging the Ground three Foot deep, and throwing up the Earth on each Side by way of Bank, raised a Roof upon Crutches with Ridge-pole and Rafters, nailing small Poles across, and thatching the Whole with Palmetto-leaves. When the Sloop came first up, the Ground was cover'd with long Grass. Mr. *Tanner* fired it, and it destroy'd all Vermin, and made the Country round clear, so as not to be only pleasant to the Eye, but convenient for walking.

Mr. *Oglethorpe* afterwards laid out several Booths without digging under Ground, which were also covered with Palmetto Leaves, to lodge the Families of the Colony in when they should come up; each of these Booths were between thirty and forty Foot long, and upwards of twenty

Foot wide. Mr. *Oglethorpe* made a Present to Captain *Barnes* for having come in the first to this Port; and Captains *Thomas* and *Cornish* both said, they did not doubt but they should bring in their Ships.

We all made merry that Evening, having a plentiful Meal of Game brought in by the *Indians*.

On the 19th, in the Morning, Mr. *Oglethorpe* began to mark out a Fort with four Bastions, and taught the Men how to dig the Ditch, and raise and turf the Rampart. This Day and the following Day were spent in finishing the Houses, and tracing out the Fort. The Men not being yet very handy at it, we also in this Time unloaded the Sloop, and then she went down to discover the Channel.

On the 22d a Perriagua from *Savannah* arrived here with Workmen, and some Provisions and Cannon. These were *English*, who rowing hard, had passed the Boat with *Germans*, which did not come up whilst we were here.

We set out for *Darien*, 16 Miles from *Frederica*, up the Northern Branch of the *Alatamaha*, leaving Mr. *Hermsdorf* and the *Indians* here, and Mr. *Horton*'s Party, which was now augmented to 50 Men. Mr. *Tanner* went along with us. We arrived there in about 3 Hours. The *Highlanders* were all under Arms on the Sight of a Boat, and made a very manly Appearance with their Plads, broad Swords, Targets and Fire-arms. Captain *Hugh Mackay* commands there. He has mounted a Battery of four Pieces of Cannon, built a Guard-house, a Store-house, a Place for Divine Service, and several Huts for particular People. One of their Men dying, the whole People join'd, and built a Hut for the Widow. The *Highlanders* were not a little rejoiced to hear that a Town was going to be settled, and a Ship come up so near them; and also, that they had a Communication by Land to *Savannah*, Capt. *M'Pherson* having been here with a Party of Rangers from thence. Capt. *Mackay* invited Mr. *Oglethorpe* to lie in his Tent, where there was a Bed and Sheets (a Rarity as yet in this Part of the World.) He excused himself, chusing to lie at the Guard Fire, wrapt in his Plad, for he wore the *Highland* Habit. Capt. *Mackay* and the other Gentlemen did the same, tho' the Night was very cold.

The *Scotch* have met with a great deal of Game in the Woods, particularly wild Turkeys, of which they have kill'd many. There was a Party of *Toma Chi Chi*'s *Indians* there, who agreed mighty well with the *Highlanders*, and fetch'd them in Venison. They have a Minister, Mr. *M'Leod*, a very good Man, who is very careful of instructing the People in religious Matters, and will intermeddle with no other Affairs.

This Town stands upon a Hill on the Northern Branch of the River *Alatamaha*, on the main Continent of *America*. The Country behind it is high and healthy, and very fit for Cattle, tho' not so good for Corn. The Land near the River is fruitful, and a River falls into the *Alatamaha* about half a Mile above the Town, on both Sides of which is excellent good Land. The Timber upon the high Land, behind the Town, is some of the best in *Georgia*.

We left Mr. *Tanner* there, and then set out for the Ships, going down to *Duboys Island*, and from thence coming back the same way that we went. I take the whole Distance by the Channels, from *Tybee* to *Frederica*, to be about 130 Miles, tho' it is but 60 Miles South upon the Globe.

On the 25th Capt. *Yokely*, in the *James*, who had not sail'd all this while, seeing that Mr. *Oglethorpe* was come back, sail'd in the Night, without sending any Word, or waiting for farther Orders; so that we knew nothing of it till we saw him the next Morning, too far over the Bar to send any Message to him.

Col. *Bull* acquainted Mr. *Oglethorpe*, that, pursuant to his Desire from *England*, he had agreed for some hundreds of Cattle to be deliver'd on the *Savannah* River for the Trustees; and that the Price of Cattle was much risen since. Indeed, the Prices of Cattle and Provisions rose every Day after our Arrival, insomuch that Rice, which Mr. *Oglethorpe* had bought, when he came over with the first Colony, for 35 *s.* Currency *per* hundred, was now sold for 3 *l.* Currency in *Carolina*; and a Cow with its Calf, which then would have been sold for 10 *l.* Currency, fetch'd now from 15 *l.* to 20 *l.*—Col. *Bull* also acquainted him of his having bespoke Boards, Timbers, and Boats, according to the Orders of the Trustees; that Part of them was ready, and the rest would soon be so. This Timber was design'd for building Barracks; but for want of Boats to bring it down, the Year was far advanced before we could get it to *Frederica*.

On the 26th the Captains *Cornish* and *Thomas* return'd in their Yawl. Before they came on board the Ship, I saw Disappointment in their Countenances. They brought up a Draught of the Bar, and declared they had not time to discover it sufficiently to carry in their Ships; but that they had found Water enough for the *James*, and the

Peter and James, to go in. They farther told us, that there were great Fires on the Main over-against *Frederica*, which were supposed to be made by the *Spanish Indians*; which was only a groundless Apprehension, for these Fires were made by the *Creek English Indians*.

Mr. *Oglethorpe* finding it impossible to prevail with the Ships to go to *Jekyll Sound*, call'd the Freeholders together, acquainted them with the new Difficulties of 130 Miles Passage in open Boats, which might take up 14 Days, and could not be perform'd in less than six; that they must lie the Nights in Woods, with no other Shelter than what they could get up upon their Arrival, and be exposed to the cold frosty Nights, which were not then over, and perhaps hard Rains; that there might go by Sea, on board the *Peter and James*, as many as that Ship could contain; but that it would not hold near their Number: That (considering the Difficulties of the Southern Settlement, almost insuperable to Women and Children, of which they had great Numbers) if they were desirous thereof, he would permit them to settle at *Savannah*, and the neighbouring Lands.

He gave them time to consult their Wives and Families, and appointed them to meet him again in two Hours. When they return'd, they acquainted him, That as they came to make a Town and live together, they had all been resolved before they came from *England*, and in their Passage had confirm'd their Resolutions, and would not foraske one another; but desired Leave to go all together, and settle the Town of *Frederica*, as was first promised: That Brothers, Sons, and Servants were gone before them, and it would look very base, and be very inconvenient to forsake them, or send for them back: That they all desired to go through the inland Passage together, and were well contented to lie without Cover not only for six Days, but for a much longer time, since it was no more than what they expected before they left *England*.

The *Symond* and *London Merchant* not proceeding to the Southward, occasion'd a new Expence and Trouble; for besides the Demurrage during the Delay, whilst the Captains gave Hopes of going, these two large Ships were now to be unloaded into the *Peter and James*, which could not carry above 100 Tuns; therefore Sloops and other Vessels were to be freighted to carry the Remainder to *Savannah*, the only Place where there was Houseroom enough to keep the Goods dry, until they could be sent to the Southward as Occasion should serve.

We wanted a great many Periaguas for to carry the Families to the Southward through the Channels between the Islands. They daily arrived, some from *Savannah*, some from *Port Royal*, and some which return'd from having carried down the *Highlanders* to the *Darien*, and the Workmen to the Southward; so that we had soon enough, and by the First of *March* had put the Remainder of the Colony on board them.

These Periaguas are long flat-bottom'd Boats, carrying from 20 to 35 Tons. They have a kind of a Forecastle and a Cabbin; but the rest open, and no Deck. They have two Masts, which they can strike, and Sails like Schooners. They row generally with two Oars only; but upon this Occasion Mr. *Oglethorpe* order'd spare Oars for each Boat, by the Addition of which, and the Men of the Colony rowing, they perform'd their Voyage in five Days, which a single Periagua is often fourteen Days in doing. Mr. *Oglethorpe* accompanying them with the Scout-boat, taking the Hindermost in tow, and making them keep together; an Expedient for which was the putting all the strong Beer on board one Boat, which made the rest labour to keep up with that; for if they were not at the Rendezvous at Night, they lost their Beer.

On the 2d of *March* the Periaguas and Boats, making a little Fleet, with the Families on board, all sail'd with the Afternoon Flood, Mr. *Oglethorpe* in the Scout-boat accompanying them. I was left on board, in order to load the *Peter and James*, Capt. *Dymond*, with Things the most immediately necessary for *Frederica*, and to unload and discharge the *Symond* and *London Merchant.*

On the 3d I hired a Schooner belonging to Mr. *Foster*, one of the Freeholders of *Savannah*, to carry up Part of the Cargoes; and I set on shore at *Tybee* the Bricks, and such other Parts of the Cargoes as could not get Damage by Wet, to lie there till Occasion should offer to carry them down, and thereby saved the Charges of carrying them to *Savannah* and down again. I got the Ships Boats to help to unload, Craft being very scarce, by reason of so many Boats sent down to the Southward with the Colony.

On the 11th I discharged the Ships *Symond* and *London Merchant*, having this Day made an End of unloading them. The *Peter and James* being loaded, we now waited for a Wind to sail to *Frederica.*

On the 17th we set sail with the Morning Tide, in Company with the *Symond* and *London Merchant.* As soon as we were over the Bar we parted, they for *Charles Town*, and we for *Frederica.* In the Evening the Wind shifted, and we came to an Anchor, the Sea being very smooth, and but little Wind.

On the 18th the Wind came about, and we stood to the Southward two Days; at which time we stood in for the Land, and made a woody Island: The Land seem'd high about the Middle. We stood in within two Miles: It look'd pleasant, the Beach being white Sand, the Woods lofty, and the Land hilly. We daily saw several Smoaks and Fires all along the Shore, which were made by the friendly *Indians*, by Mr. *Oglethorpe*'s Order. At Noon we had an Observation, and found we were in 31 d. 20 m. being 20 Miles to the Southward of *Frederica*, for the Entrance of *Jekyl* Sound, is in 31 d. 0 m. We turned to the Northward, and on the 22d in the Evening, we made the opening between *Jekyl* Island and St. *Simons.* We came to an Anchor that Evening, and the next Morning being the 23d, we stood into the Opening, and found a good Channel between the Breakers all the way to *Jekyl* Sound, at the Entry of which, Captain *Yoakley*'s Boat came off to us. We ran directly up to *Frederica*, and anchored close to the Shore in 3 Fathom Water, where lay the *James* Captain *Yoakeley.*

I went on Shore, where I found Mr. *Oglethorpe* was gone to the *Spanish* Frontiers, and I was surprised to find that there was a Battery of Cannon mounted, which commanded the River, and the Fort almost built, the Ditches being dug round, though not to their Width, and the Rampart raised with green Sod. Within the Fort a very large and convenient Store-house, 60 Foot in Front, and to be 3 Stories high, was begun, with a Cellar of the same size underneath, and one Story already raised above Ground. The Town was building, the Streets were all laid out; the main Street, that went from the Front into the Country, was 25 Yards wide. Each Freeholder had 60 Foot in Front, by 90 Foot in Depth, upon the high Street, for their House and Garden; but those which fronted the River had but 30 Foot in Front, by 60 Foot in Depth. Each Family had a Bower of Palmetto Leaves, finished upon the back Street in their own Lands: The Side towards the front Street was set out for their Houses: These Palmetto Bowers were very convenient Shelters, being tight in the hardest Rains; they were about 20 Foot long, and 14 Foot wide, and in regular Rows, looked very pretty, the Palmetto Leaves lying smooth and handsome, and of a good Colour. The whole appeared something like a Camp; for the Bowers looked like Tents, only being larger and covered with Palmetto Leaves instead of Canvas. There were 3 large Tents, two belonging to Mr. *Oglethorpe*, and one to Mr. *Horton*, pitched upon the Parade near the River.

Mr. *Oglethorpe* had divided the Colony into Parties, one cut Forks, Poles, and Laths for building the Bowers, another set them up, a Third fetched Palmetto Leaves, a fourth thatched, and a Jew Workman, bred in the *Brazil*, and had come from *Savannah*, taught them to do this nimbly and in a neat manner. Mr. *Oglethorpe* had appointed some Men who knew the Country to instruct the Colony in Hoeing and Planting; and as soon as the Bowers were finished, a Party was set to that Work, and the rest were hired by him to work at the Fort, by reason that a great Part of the Workmen were not yet come up. It was so late in the Year, he hoped little from any Planting, therefore what he ordered to be done, was rather to teach the Colony against another Season, than from any Advantage likely to arise from it, and he employed the Men of the Colony to work at the Fort that they might get something to help to subsist themselves the next Year. There was Potatoes and *Indian* Corn in the Ground, and they were planting more; there was some Flax and Hempseed, which came to little, being too late set. And it is an Observation that all *Europe* Grains should be sowed rather before Winter, that they may shoot and cover the Ground;

for if they are sowed in Spring, the Weather coming hot upon them, the Blades shoot at once into Height, and not shading the Roots, the Heat of the Sun dries them up. But when the Winter has checked the Growth of the Blade, the Plant spreads, and covering the Ground thick, shades it from the parching Sun, and thereby keeps a Moisture underneath, which prevents the Roots from being dried up. There was Barley, Turnips, Lucern-Grass, Pumpkins, Water Melons, and several other Seeds sown or sowing daily; all was for the whole Colony, the Labour was in common, though they were assisted by several Workmen hired from *Savannah*. I was the more surprised to see a Team and six Horses ploughing, not having heard any thing of it before; but it was thus: Messieurs *Walter Augustine* and *Tolme*, escorted by Mr. *Hugh Mackay*, had pursuant to their Orders surveyed from *Savannah* to *Darien*, and had made a Plan of it, and Mr. *Hugh Mackay* had brought these Horses then with him, which were embarked in *Periaguas* from *Darien* to *Frederica*. They reported that the *Indians* had accompanied, assisted, and hunted for them in their Survey; and that they had met some Camps of friendly *Indians*, besides those which *Toma Chi Chi Mico* sent with them; that they had found the Country passable for Horses, but to keep the Horse-road they were obliged to go round about, and head several Vallies which were too rich and wet to be passable, therefore that Road was 90 Miles round; but that the Road might be carried so as to make it but 70; that there were two Rivers to be swam over, and some boggy places. The News they brought had been no small Joy to the People of *Frederica*, since they had a Communication from the *Darien* by Land, open to *Savannah*, and consequently to all the *English* Colonies of *North America*.

Frederica is situated in the Island of St. *Simons*, in the middle of an *Indian* Field, where our People found 30 or 40 Acres of Land cleared by them. The Ground is about 9 or 10 Foot above High-water Mark, and level for about a Mile into the Island; the Bank is steep to the River, which is here narrow, but deep, and makes an Elbow, so that the Fort commands two Reaches. The Woods on the other side this Branch of the *Alatamaha* are about three Miles

Distance. All that three Miles is a plain Marsh, which by small Banks might easily be made Meadow; when I was upon it, it was so hard that a Horse might gallop, but most part of it is flooded at very high Tides. The open Ground on which the Town stands, is bounded by a little Wood to the East, on the other Side of which is a large *Savannah* of above 200 Acres, where there is fine Food for Cattle. To the South, is a little Wood of red Bay-trees, live Oaks, and other useful Timber, which is reserved for the Publick Service. In the Fort also are some fine large Oaks preserved for Shade. To the North are Woods, where the People have leave to cut for Fire and Building, for all that Side is intended to be cleared: To the West is the River, and the Marshes beyond it, as I said before. The Soil is a rich Sand mix'd with Garden-mould, the Marshes are Clay. In all Places where they have tried, they find fresh Water within 9 Foot of the Surface. The Grass in the *Indian* old Field was good to cut into Turf, which was very useful in Sodding the Fort.

The Woods on the Island are chiefly Live-Oak, Water-Oak, Laurel, Bay, Cedar, Gum and Sassafras, and some Pines. There are also abundance of Vines grow wild in the Woods; one called the Fox-Grape, from a kind of Muscadine Taste, is as large and round as a Duke-Cherry, and fleshy like it, but the Stones are like the Grape. This kind of Grape does rarely grow in Clusters, but singly like Cherries. The other Grape is black in Clusters, small, thick skinned, big stoned, but pleasant enough: It seems to be the *Bourdeaux* Grape, wild and unimproved; they are ripe about *September*, but a Quantity sufficient to make a true Experiment of Wine (which can hardly be done under 60 Gallons) is hard to be got, because the Bears, Rackoons and Squirrels eat them before they are ripe, and as they run up very high Trees, it is difficult or almost impossible to get to the Tops of them where the best grow. These Grapes are common to the Woods in most parts of *America*. But there is on St. *Simons*, a wild Grape much nearer the *Europe* Vine, the Fruit being exactly the same as the common white Grape, though the Leaf is something different. The Birds and wild Animals like it so well, that they suffer it seldom to ripen. All the Vine

Kinds seem natural to the Country. The *China* Root produces a kind of Bind or Briar; and the Melon, Water-Melon, Cucumber, Kidney-Bean, Pompkin and Gourd, all thrive wonderfully.

The Island abounds with Deer and Rabits; there are no Buffaloes in it, though there are large Herds of them upon the Main. There are also a good many Rackoons, a Creature something like a Badger, but somewhat less, with a bushy Tail like a Squirrel, tabbied with Rings of brown and black. They are very destructive to the Poultry.

I heard that there were Wolves and Bears, but saw none. There are great Numbers of Squirrels of different Sizes, the little Kind the same as in *England*, a lesser than that, not much bigger than a Mouse, and a large grey Sort, very near as big as a Rabit, which those who are accustomed to the Country say, eats as well. There are wild Cats which they call Tigers; I saw one of them which the *Indians* killed, the Skin was brown, and all of one Colour, about the Size of a middling Spaniel, little Ears, great Whiskers, short Legs, and strong Claws.

Of the Wild-Fowl Kind, there are wild Turkeys, though but few of them upon the Island, but Plenty upon the Main. This Bird is larger than the tame Turkey, and the Cock is the beautifullest of the feathered Kind; his Head has the red and blue of the Turkey, only much more lively and beautiful, his Neck is like the Cock Pheasant's, his Feathers also are of the same Colour with those of that Bird, glittering in the Sun as if they were gilded; his Tail is as large, though it hath not so fine Eyes in it as the Peacock's hath. At first, before they were disturbed by our People, they would strut in the Woods as a Peacock does. I have heard some say, that upon weighing, they have found them to exceed 30 Pound; I never weighed any, but have had them very fat and large; they are delicious Meat, and are compared to a tame Turkey, as a Pheasant is to a Fowl. I saw no Partridges upon the Island, though they are plenty upon the Main. Turtle-Doves the Woods swarm with, which are excellent Food. There are also great Numbers of small Birds, of which a black Bird with a red Head, the red Bird, or *Virginia* Nightingale, the mocking Bird, which sings sweetly, and the

Rice-Bird, much resembling the *French Ortelan*, were the chief; the rest are too numerous to describe.

Of Water Fowl, in Winter there are great Abundance; besides the common *English* Wild Goose, Duck, Mallard and Teal, there is a kind of Wild Goose like the Brand Geese, and Ducks of many kinds, hardly known in *Europe*. There is a Hooping Crane, a Fowl with grey Feathers five or six Foot high, Numbers of the Heron Kind of different Species and Colours, some small ones of the most beautiful White, which are called Poor Jobs, from their being generally very lean. Of Birds of Prey, there are the Land and the Sea Eagle, with different Kinds of Hawks: There are also Numbers of Pelicans and Cormorants.

Of Reptiles, the Crocodile, which seems to be the chief, abounds in all the Rivers of *Georgia*; they call them Alligators. I have seen some of these I believe 12 Foot long. A Number of vulgar Errors are reported of them; one is, that their Scales are Musquet-proof; whereas I have frequently seen them killed with small Shot; nay, I have heard from people of good credit, that when they have found one at distance from the Water they have kill'd him with Sticks, not thinking him worth a Shot. And Mr. *Horton* more than once has struck one through with a Hanger. The Watermen often knock them on the head with their Oars as they sleep upon the Banks; for they are very sluggish and timorous, though they can make one or two Springs in the Water with Nimbleness enough, and snap with Strength whatever comes within their Jaws. They are terrible to look at, stretching open an horrible large Mouth, big enough to swallow a Man, with Rows of dreadful large sharp Teeth, and Feet like Dragons, armed with great Claws, and a long Tail, which they throw about with great Strength, and which seems their best Weapon, for their Claws are feebly set on, and the Stiffness of their Necks hinders them from turning nimbly to bite. When Mr. *Oglethorpe* was first at *Savannah*, to take off the Terror which the People had for the Crocodiles, having wounded and catch'd one about twelve Foot long, he had him brought up to the Town, and set the Boys to bait him with Sticks, the Creature gaping and blowing hard, but had no Heart to move, only turned about his Tail and snapt at the Sticks, till such time as the Children pelted and beat him to Death. At our first coming they would stare at the Boats and stand till they came up close to them, so that Mr. *Horton* killed 5 in one Day; but being frequently shot at they grew more shy. They destroy a great deal of Fish, and will seize a Hog or a Dog if they see them in the Water; but their general Way of preying is lying still, with their Mouths open and their Noses just above Water, and so they watch till the Stream brings down Prey to them: they swallow any thing that comes into their Mouths; and upon opening them Knots of light Wood have been found in their Guts. They rarely appear in Winter, being then in Holes. They lay Eggs, which are less than those of a Goose: They scrape together a Number of Leaves, and other Trash, of which Nature has taught them to chuse such as will foment and heat; of these they make a Dunghill, or Hot-Bed, in the midst of which they leave their Eggs, covering them over with a sufficient Thickness. The Heat of the Dunghill, help'd by the Warmth of the Climate, hatches them, and the young Crocodiles creep out like small Lizards.

Next to the Crocodile is the Rattle-Snake, a Creature really dangerous, tho' far from being terrible to look at. The Bite is generally thought mortal, and certainly is so, if Remedies are not in time applied. The *Indians* pretend to have perform'd wonderful Cures, and boast an infallible Secret, but it is generally believ'd that the hot Season of the Year, and the Rage of the Rattle-Snake increase the Force of the Poison, and that the Bite is more or less dangerous according to the Part; and those who are bit with the least dangerous Circumstances are cured by the outward Applications of the *Indians*. Mr. *Reeves*, who was Surgeon to the Independent Company at *Port Royal* has, by a regular Course of Medicine, cured most of those who were carried to him and bit by Rattle-Snakes. I can say less of this, because (thank God) there has not been one Person bit by a Rattle-Snake in the Colony of *Georgia*. I have seen several of these Snakes which were kill'd at *Frederica*, the largest above two Yards long, the Belly white, and the Back of a brown Colour; they seem to be of the Viper Kind, and are of a strong Smell, somewhat like Musk. The Rattles are Rings at the

End of their Tails of a horny Substance; these shaking together make a Noise, which with their strong musky Smell gives cautious People Notice where they are. They are not so nimble as some Snakes are, therefore do not remove out of the Way, which is generally the Occasion of Bites when they happen; for they naturally in their own Defence snap at what treads near them. To prevent this, those who walk the Woods much, wear what they call *Indian* Boots, which are made of coarse woollen Cloths, much too large for the Legs, tied upon their Thighs and hang loose to their Shoes.

Besides the Rattle-Snake, there are some others whose Bite is dangerous; there are also many others, as the Black, the Red, and the Chicken Snake, whose Bites are not venomous.

On the 24th, I resolved to keep the Cargoes on board, and landed nothing but as it was actually wanted. There was a Booth for a Storehouse on Shore, with a Cellar to it; but the Cargo of the *Midnight* Sloop had filled that. There were also some other Booths where the Colony lodged till they had made their own Bowers, but there being already a great many Goods and Provisions come up, there was not Room enough in all for them, and we were much distress'd for want of Room, many Things being damaged by not having Cover to put them under. I therefore thought it best to keep the Cargoes on board both Ships, and take Things out as we had Occasion.

On the 25th in the Evening Mr. *Oglethorpe* return'd from the *Spanish* Frontiers, and some Difficulties having arose about settling the Bounds of the Dominions belonging to the Crowns of *Great Britain* and *Spain*, to make the following Transactions intelligible it will be necessary to describe the Situation of the Province of *Georgia*, and also to give an Account of his Expedition to the Frontiers, from whence he now return'd.

The *Missisippi* River parts these Bounds, the Mouths and Heads of which are possess'd by the *French*, who have Garrisons and considerable Forces up that River as far as the *Chickesaws* Country. To the East of that River there are four great Nations of *Indians*:

1. The *Chocktaws*, some of which lie on the other Side the River,

and some on this. These Mr. *Oglethorpe* in his first Voyage to *Georgia* gain'd to admit of *English* Traders. They are about 5000 Warriors on the East Side of the River.

2. The *Cherickees*, a Nation who inhabit the Mountains upon the Southern Heads of the *Savannah* River, amounting to about 3000 Warriors.

3. The *Chechesaws*, who lie upon the *Missisippi* River, between the *Cherikees* and the *Chocktaws*, who have long been Subjects to the Crown of *England*, and who hinder the *French* Communication up that River with their Northern Colonies of *Canada*. And,

4. The *Creeks*, who are bounded by the *Chickesaws* and *Cherikees* upon the North, the *Chocktaws* upon the West, the *Florida-Indians* upon the South, and who to the Eastward reach as far as the Ocean. These are divided into several Towns and Nations, one of which is commanded by *Toma Chi Chi*, who was in *England*. To these belong'd all the Islands upon the Sea, and the Main-Land from the Mouth of the *Savannah* to the *Chocktaws* and the *Florida-Indians*. The *Creeks* did by Treaty grant the Lands which the *English* now possess in *Georgia* near *Savannah*, and for it receiv'd Presents. The Sovereignty was in the Crown of *Great Britain* ever since the Discovery of them by Sir *Walter Raleigh*. All *Carolina* bounded by the River *St. John*, was the *Carolina* granted to the Proprietors in the *English* Possession at the Treaty of 1670. They also conceded several Islands, reserving to themselves certain Portions of Land on the Main, as also the Islands of *St. Catharine*, *Sapola* and *Ossaba*. They granted those of *Tybee*, *Warsaw*, *Skidoway*, *Wilmington*, *St. Simons*, and all those to the Southward of it as far as *St. John*'s River to the Colony. The *Creek Indians* were Allies or rather Subjects to the Crown of *Great Britain*, and did, with the Assistance of the *English* in the Year 1703, beat the *Spaniards* as far as *St. Augustine*, and besieged that Place. But though the Siege was raised, the *Creek Indians* still kept Possession of all the Lands on the North of *St. John*'s River, but had made a Treaty with General *Nicholson* (who commanded by Commission from King *George* the First in those Countries) that no private *Englishman* should possess the Property of any Land to the South or West

of the River *Savannah*, without Leave first had from the *Indians*.

The first Thing Mr. *Oglethorpe* did in his first Voyage, was to obtain the Grant from the *Indians*; and upon a Meeting of all the Upper and Lower *Creeks*, upon *Toma Chi Chi*'s Return from *England*, they confirm'd the Grant of all the Islands (those reserved as above excepted) also of all the Lands upon the Continent as far as the Tide flowed, and two Hours Walk above it. In Pursuance of this Agreement *Toma Chi Chi* came down with a Party of *Indians* to shew Mr. *Oglethorpe* how far their Possessions reach'd. The Day he arrived he presented ten Bucks to the whole Colony, which were divided after the *Indian* Manner to all equal. Every Day more *Indians* came in from different Quarters, where they had been hunting: At last Mr. *Jonathan Brian* brought down a new Scout-Boat with ten Oars. Mr. *Oglethorpe* having heard no News of Major *Richard*, and the Boat sent to *Augustine*; and being inform'd by his *Indians*, that great Number of the *Florida Indians* were sent for up to their Town; and also having Advice from *Charles Town*, that they heard from *Augustine* that the *Spaniards* were preparing to dislodge us, he resolved to go down and see the Frontiers, and inquire what was become of his Boat and Men, and at the same time to restrain the *Indians* from hurting the *Spaniards*; who seemed very eager so to do, under the Pretence of hunting the Buffaloe. Knowing there was a Passage through which Boats might come round the Island, and perhaps might destroy the Colony in one Night, he made Captain *Yoakley* anchor below the Town, who was very alert and kept a good Look-out, and having some Cannon, and supported by a Battery from the Land, was above a Match for open Boats. He designed also to build a Fort upon the Boat Passage, but the *Indian* Company not being yet come, he had no Men to garrison it. The *Highlanders* very chearfully offer'd themselves for that Service. He order'd a large *Periagua* to bring them down from the *Darien*.

On the 18th of *April* he set out with the two Scout-Boats with *Toma Chi Chi Mico* and a Body of *Indians*, who tho' but few, being not forty, were all chosen Warriors and good Hunters. Mr. *Oglethorpe* did not care for having too many, lest their Strength should encourage them to Hostilities with the *Spaniards*, which it was his Business to avoid. Rowing across *Jekyl* Sound he went up another Branch of the *Alatamaha*, to see what Passages might lie that Way for Boats, and encamp'd in a Grove of Pine Trees upon the Main, where were many Trees fit for Masts to the largest Ships. They made up three Fires, one for the *Indians*, one for the Boat-Men, and one for the Gentlemen. Mr. *Oglethorpe* lay, as he usually does, in the Woods under a Tree, wrapt up in a Cloak, near a good Fire. Mr. *Horton*, Mr. *Tanner*, and the rest of the Gentlemen lay round the Fire in the same Manner.

The next Day soon after Day-Break they discover'd the *Periagua*, which made a fine Appearance, being full of Men: Captain *Hugh Mackay*, who commanded them, had been indefatigable in making this Dispatch; there was on board thirty *Highlanders* and ten other Men, a Party of the Independent Company, lately reduced, who had come over Land to *Darien* under the Command of Ensign *Hugh Mackay*, as before-mention'd: They had with them Tools for Entrenching, and Provisions. That Afternoon they saw an Island, which the *Indians* formerly call'd *Wissoo*, in *English*, *Sassafras*. This is over-against *Jekyl-Island* on the South; the North West End of it rises fifty Foot or upwards above the Water, like a Terras, a Mile in Length, cover'd with tall Pine Trees. The Western Extremity of this Hill commands the Passage for Boats from the Southward, as the Northern End of the Island does the Entry for Ships.—Here they met with some Bark-huts, which our friendly *Indians* some time since had built for their Lodging when they hunted there.—They saw a great many Deer and a wide *Savannah* lying at the Foot of the Hill, extending near two or three Miles: So that from the Western Point they could discover any Boat that came from the Southward for several Miles.

Mr. *Oglethorpe* upon the extream Western Point of the Hill, the Foot of which is wash'd on the one Side by the Bay and by the Channel that goes to the Southward on the other, mark'd out a Fort to be call'd *St. Andrew*'s, and gave Captain *Hugh Mackay* Orders to build it; leaving with him the *Periagua* and all that came in it, and also some *Indians* to hunt and shoot.

Mr. *Oglethorpe* proceeded on the next Morning with the two Scout-Boats, and *Toma Chi Chi* and his *Indians*; who new-named this Island *Cumberland*, in Memory of his Royal Highness the Duke, who had been very gracious to them, particularly to *Tooanahowi*, Nephew to *Toma Chi Chi*, to whom his Royal Highness had given a Gold Repeating-Watch, which *Toonanahowi* holding in his Hand, said, *The Duke gave us this*

Watch, that we might know how the Time went, and we will remember him at all Times, and therefore will give this Island this Name: Or Words to that Purpose. They encamp'd that Night on the South End of *Cumberland*, and the next Morning discover'd another Island beyond it, between which and the Main, they row'd thro' very narrow and shoaly Passes amongst the Marshes. To this Island Mr. *Oglethorpe* gave the Name of *Amelia*, it being a beautiful Island, and the Sea-shore cover'd with Myrtle, Peach-Trees, Orange-Trees, and Vines in the wild Woods. They row'd across a fresh-water River, a Branch of the *Alatamaha*, and that Night *Toma Chi Chi* chose to encamp upon a Ground where there were but a few straggling Pine-Trees, and the Land being clear for half a Mile round, and thick of Shrubs and Palmettoes: His Reason was, that if any *Florida-Indians* were out there, they would be discover'd, if they approached in the Night, by the Noise of the Palmetto Leaves; and (says he) *You being* Englishmen, *who are used to fight in open Ground, I chuse this as being most to your Advantage.*

Next Morning he conducted them through several Channels till they came to two Rocks cover'd with Cedar and Bay-Trees, and climbing to the Tops of those Rocks, he shew'd them a wide River, which was *St. John*'s, and a House or Hut on the other Side, saying, *That is the* Spanish *Guard. All on this Side that River we hunt: It is our Ground. On the other Side they hunt; but as they have lately hurt some of our People, we will now drive them away. We will stay behind these Rocks, where they cannot see us, till Night, and then we will fall upon them.*

Mr. *Oglethorpe*, with much Difficulty, prevail'd with the *Indians* not to attack the *Spaniards*; for some of them are related to those that had been kill'd the Winter before, by the Detachment from *Augustine*; and one of them, *Poyeechy* by Name, had then been wounded by the *Spaniards*. At last the *Indians* were prevail'd upon to return to the *Palmetto Ground*, where he promised to meet them. And not caring to trust them single, lest they should turn back and do Mischief to the *Spaniards*, he order'd Mr. *Horton*, with one of the ten-oar'd Scout-boats, to attend upon them; and with the other Boat he himself went into *St. John*'s River, intending to inquire of the *Spanish* Guards what was become of the Boat and Men he had sent to *Augustine*.

The Hut which they saw from the Rocks, was the upper *Spanish* Look-out; but seeing no People, they concluded it deserted; therefore stood down to the lower Look-out.

The Boatmen fancied they saw a Battery of Cannon; for there appear'd some black Things, which they thought look'd like Guns at a great Distance; but Mr. *Oglethorpe* desir'd to see them nearer.

As they stood in, they proved to be Cows lying down among the Sand-hills. There were no People at the Look-out, so they went down to the Sea, and rounding the Point *St. George*, passing between that and *Talbot Island*, came to the Rendezvous at the *Palmetto Ground*, where they met Mr. *Horton* in the Scout-boat, and some Boats of *Indians*; but *Toma Chi Chi*, with two Boats, was gone on.

About four Hours in the Night their Centry challeng'd a Boat; and *Umpeechy*, one of those who had been in *England*, answer'd, and at the same time leap'd on shore with four others, and ran up to the Fires where Mr. *Oglethorpe* then was.

They seem'd in such a Rage as is hardly to be describ'd:—Their Eyes glow'd, as it were, with Fire; some of them foam'd at the Mouth, and moved with such Bounds, that they seem'd rather possess'd.

Mr. *Oglethorpe* ask'd *Umpeechy* what the Matter was: He said, *Toma Chi Chi has seen Enemies, and has sent us to tell it, and to help you.* Being ask'd why the *Mico* did not come back himself; he said, *He is an old Warrior, and will not come away from his Enemies, who hunt upon our Lands, till he has seen them so near as to count them. He saw their Fire, and therefore sent to take care of you, who are his Friends. He will make a Warrior of* Tooanahowi; *and before Day-light will be reveng'd for his Men, whom they kill'd whilst he was gone to* England. *But we shall have no Honour, for we shall not be there.* The rest of the *Indians* seem'd to catch the raging Fits, at not being present. Mr. *Oglethorpe* ask'd if he thought they were many; he said, yes, he thought the Enemies were a great many, for they had a great Fire upon a high Ground, and the *Indians* never make large Fires, but when they are so strong as to despise all Resistance.

Mr. *Oglethorpe* immediately order'd all his People on board, and they row'd very briskly to where *Toma Chi Chi* was, being about four Miles distance.

They found him and his *Indians* with hardly any Fire, only a few Sparks behind a Bush, to prevent Discovery. They told him, they had been to see the Fire, and had discover'd seven or eight white Men; but the *Indians* they believed had camp'd farther in the Woods, for they had not seen them: But *Toma Chi Chi* was going out again to look for the *Indians*, whom, as soon as he discover'd, he intended to give the Signal to attack both Parties at once: One half of his Men creeping near, and taking each their Aim at those whom they saw most awake, and as soon as they had fir'd to run in with their Hatchets; and at the same time those who had not fir'd should run in with their loaded Arms, that, if they knew once where the *Indians* were, they could be sure of killing all the white Men; since, they being round the Fire, were easily seen, and the same Fire hinder'd them from seeing others.

Mr. *Oglethorpe* strove to dissuade them from that Attempt; but with great Difficulty could obtain of them to delay a little time, they thinking it argued Cowardice. At last they got up, and resolved to go in spite of all his Endeavours; on which he told them, *You certainly go to kill them in the Night, because you are afraid of seeing them by Day: Now I do not fear them. Stay till Day, and I will go with you, and see who they are.*

Toma Chi Chi sigh'd, and sat down, and said, *We don't fear them by Day; but if we don't kill them to-night, they'll kill you to-morrow.* So they staid.

By Day-break Mr. *Oglethorpe* and the *Mico* went down with their Men, and came up to the Fire, which they thought had been made by Enemies, which was less than a Mile from where the *Mico* had pass'd the Night. They saw a Boat there, with a white Flag flying, and the Men proved to be Major *Richard* return'd from *Augustine.*

The *Indians* then seem'd asham'd of their Rage, which inspir'd them to kill Men before they knew who they were.

The same Day they return'd towards *St. Andrew*'s, and not having Water enough, thro' the Narrows of *Amelia*, the Scout-boats were obliged to halt there; but the *Indians* advanced to the South End of *Cumberland*, where they hunted, and carried Venison to *St. Andrew*'s.

Mr. *Oglethorpe* arriving there, was surpriz'd to find the Fort in a Forwardness; the Ditch being dug, and the Parapet raised with Wood and Earth on the Land-side, and the small Wood was clear'd fifty Yards round the Fort. This seem'd to be the more extraordinary, because Mr. *Mackay* had no Engineer, nor any other Assistance in that Way, but the Directions left by Mr. *Oglethorpe*: Besides it was very difficult to raise Works here, the Ground being a loose Sand; therefore they used the same Method to support it as *Cæsar* mentions in the Wars of *Gaul*, laying Trees and Earth alternately, the Trees preventing the Sand from falling, and the Sand the Wood from Fire.—He return'd Thanks to the *Highlanders*, and offer'd to take any of them back; but they said, that whilst there was Danger they desired Leave to stay. But he order'd two along with him, they having Families at *Darien*, to whom he thought it would be agreeable for them to return. From thence he return'd to *Frederica* with the white Men, and the Scout-boats.

Next Day, being the 26th, the *Indians* arrived, and camp'd by themselves near the Town, and made a War-dance, to which Mr. *Oglethorpe* went, and all his People. They made a Ring, in the Middle of which four sat down, having little Drums made of Kettles, cover'd with Deer-skins, upon which they beat and sung: Round them the others danced, being naked to their Waists, and round their Middles many Trinkets tied with Skins, and some with the Tails of Beasts hanging down behind them. They painted their Faces and Bodies, and their Hair was stuck with Feathers: In one Hand they had a Rattle, in the other Hand the Feathers of an Eagle, made up like the Caduceus of *Mercury*: They shook these Wings and the Rattle, and danced round the Ring with high Bounds and antick Postures, looking much like the Figures of the Satyrs.

They shew'd great Activity, and kept just Time in their Motions; and at certain times answer'd, by way of Chorus, to those that sat in the Middle of the Ring. They stopt, and then stood out one of the chief Warriors, who sung what Wars he had been in, and describ'd (by Actions as well as by Words) which way he had vanquish'd the Enemies of his Country. When he had done, all the rest gave a Shout of Approbation, as knowing what he said to be true. The next Day Mr. *Oglethorpe* gave Presents to *Toma Chi Chi* and his *Indians*, and dismiss'd them with Thanks for their Fidelity to the King.

The 28th we received Advice, that Capt. *Gascoigne*, with the Man of War Sloop the *Hawk*, was got up to the Town of *Savannah*, she having suffer'd much in her Passage, being near lost by Stress of Weather. Capt. *Gascoigne* desiring a Pilot that knew *Frederica* Bar, there being none but Capt. *Dymond*, or Capt. *Yokely*, that could undertake it, Mr. *Oglethorpe* prevail'd with Capt. *Dymond* to leave his Ship and go to *Savannah*, to bring the *Hawk* into *Frederica*.

Major *Richard* gave an Account, that he was cast away before he could get to *Augustine*; that Part of their Baggage was lost, but the Boat and Men were saved; that having scrambled thro' the Breakers, and walk'd some Leagues through the Sands, they were met by Don *Pedro Lamberto*, a Captain of Horse, and by him conducted to the Governor, who received him with great Civility; and that the Reason of his long Stay was, to get the Boat repair'd. He brought Letters from Don *Francisco del Moral Sanchez*, Captain General of *Florida*, and Governor of *St. Augustine*, to Mr. *Oglethorpe*, who call'd together the Freeholders, and communicated to them the Contents of the Letters, to prevent the ill Impressions that idle Reports might occasion. There were first great Compliments, thanking him for the Letters he had received by Don *Carlos Dempsey* and Major *Richard*: Next complaining that the *Creek Indians* had fallen upon the *Spaniards*, and defeated some of them; that he daily expected farther Hostilities from them, and desired him to restrain them.

Major *Richard*, by Word of Mouth, told him, That the Governor expected an Answer back in three Weeks; that he had treated him with the greatest Civility, and desir'd him to bring it; and that the Governor had sent Advice to the *Havannah* of our Arrival.

By private Advices Mr. *Oglethorpe* was inform'd, that notwithstanding these Professions, the Governor of *Augustine* had sent to buy Arms at *Charles Town*, and was preparing to arm the *Florida Indians*, in order to join the *Yamasee Indians*, and to send them, together with a Detachment of the *Spanish* Garrison, to dislodge us; and that the complaining of Hostilities from the *Creeks* was only to give a Reason for such an Action, and lay upon us the Blame of having begun the War; that the Garrison of *Augustine* consisted of five Companies, sixty Men each, and forty Horse, and that the Inhabitants of the Place amounted to above two thousand Men, Women, and Children; and that they expected Troops would be sent from the *Havannah*, as soon as the Message would arrive; but that they thought they had enough already to dislodge us.

These private Advices Mr. *Oglethorpe* did not communicate to the People; but being doubtful of what the Event might be, in case he should be attacked before the Arrival of the Man of War, and the Independent Company, he concluded to arm a Periagua, that was a good Boat, to fit her out with Twenty Oars, and four Swivel-Guns, and to send her to the River *St. John's* with a Scout-Boat in Company, called the *Marine Boat*; and by patroling in that River to hinder the *Indians* from passing it, and thereby from giving pretence of Hostilities to the *Spaniards*; and such a Patrole was the only way to prevent the *Indians* falling upon the *Spaniards*, against whom they were very inveterate. He also designed that they should erect a Fort upon the Passages by the Island *St. George*, that the Periagua under the Shelter of those Guns might very easily hinder any Boats from coming through the Island-Passages, and send the Scout Boat to give the Alarm, which by signals of Smoak would reach *St. Andrews*, he ordering another Scout-Boat to cruise between *Amelia* and *Cumberland*.

The keeping the two Ships in the River, with the Assistance of the Land Batteries, would prevent any Ships from coming up from the Sea but under a great Disadvantage. He spoke to *Toma Chi Chi Mico*, who sent off Parties of the *Indians* into the Woods to strive to meet with the other Creek Hunters, and desire them not to hurt the *Spaniards*, till a Conference was held before Mr. *Oglethorpe*, who would see to get Justice done to them, but to keep in the Neighbourhood of *Frederica*, on the Main, to see that the *Spanish* Horse did not pass to *Darien*, and to be ready, in case they attacked us, to make a Body. *Toma Chi Chi* leaving most of his Men, returned to *Yamacraw* in all haste, in order to bring down more *Indians*. Men were chiefly wanted for this Disposition; but Mr. *Oglethorpe* made use of such Men as were hired for Workmen, and willing to serve on that Occasion.

The People went on with building the Storehouse but slowly, Hands being taken off for building the Fort, and it was farther delay'd for want of Boards and Stuff, those which were bought in *Carolina* not coming up. Mr. *Oglethorpe* had the Works round the Fort frased or palisaded with Cedar Posts, to prevent our Enemies turning up the green Sod. He also had Platforms of Two-Inch Planks laid for the Cannon upon the Bastions, and took in a Piece of Marsh Ground which lay below the Fort, with a Work called the Spur, the Cannon in which are upon a level with the Water's Edge, and make it impossible for any Boat or Ship to come up or down the River without being torn to Pieces.

He had a Well dug in the Fort, where we found tolerable good Water, and in Plenty. The People having no Bread, and Biscuit being dear and necessary for the Boats Service, there was an Oven built, and Mr. *Oglethorpe* bought off the Time of an indented Servant, who was a Baker, and he baked Bread for all the Colony, they giving him their Allowance of Flower, and he returning to them the same Weight in Bread, the Difference made by the Water and Salt being his Gain. Fresh Bread was a great Comfort to the People. The *Indians* also brought us in Plenty of Venison, which was divided as far as it would go, instead of Salt Provisions, to the Sick first, then to the Women and Children, and lastly, to the strong young Men. Whenever Venison failed, we killed Poultry, Hogs, or Sheep for the Sick.

Twenty-eighth of *March*, Mr. *Robert Ellis* arrived here in a Boat from *Savannah*. Mr. *Oglethorpe* received him with great Civility, upon Account of Mr. *Penn*, Proprietor of *Pensilvania*, who had sent to the poor People of the Town of *Savannah*, at the Beginning of that Settlement, one hundred Barrels of Flower, as a Present, which had been of very great Service and Relief to them. We bought of Mr. *Ellis* several Provisions which the Colony had occasion for.

The 30th, Mr. *Oglethorpe* agreed with Mr. *Jonathan Brian* to furnish him with eighteen Hands to assist him in cutting Roads through that Part of *Georgia*, which is from the River *Savannah* to the River *Ogeechee*, and for that Purpose, to begin, by making a Road passable from his own House in *Carolina* to the River *Savannah*, and thereby carry all Things along with him, that were necessary, for the Support of the Men. In the Evening Mr. *Bryan* and Mr. *Barnwell* set out for *Carolina*, of their own accords promising, that if we should be attacked, they would come down with a large Number of Volunteers from thence. We also received advice from *Savannah*, that the Chiefs of the *Cheehaws*, and another Town of the Creek *Indians*, were arrived there, and would come over to our Assistance in case any body disturbed us in our Settlements.

The 31st, Mr. *Horton*, who had 500 Acres of Land granted by the Trustees, went to take Possession of it, being on the other side the Branch of the *Alatamaha*, and about six Miles below the Town. Mr. *Oglethorpe* ordered one of the Scout-Boats to carry him: The

Captain was left ill ashore. He found the Land exceeding rich. The Scout-Boat having Orders to fire a Swivel-Gun by way of Signal, that we might know how the Lands bore from the Town, the young Fellow who fired the Gun, loading it again and again, fired it three times by way of Rejoicing, and at the third Fire the Gun being overloaded, burst, and the Splinters wounded him very dangerously in the Brain. Mr. *Horton* returned with the Boat and wounded Man directly, and notwithstanding the Surgeons took all possible care of him, he died the next Day, being the first Man that died at *Frederica*.

The 2d of *May*, Mr. *Horton* was sent down with a Scout-Boat to escort a Periagua loaded with Ammunition, Cannons, Boards for Platforms, and other Necessaries for St. *Andrews*, together with a Message to Ensign *Mackay*, to come up to consult upon the present Posture of Affairs, and to bring with him such of the Highlanders whose Interest in Planting required their Return to *Darien*; and during his Absence to leave Mr. *Cuthbert* to command at St. *Andrews*.

Boats daily arrived from *Savannah*, or *Port Royal*, with Fowls, Hogs, and other live Stock, for the Use of the Colony; and those from *Savannah* seldom came without some Volunteers to offer their Service to Mr. *Oglethorpe*, upon the present Apprehension. And all the Inhabitants of their Town, and this Province, show'd the greatest Readiness to do every thing necessary for the general Defence. And he was forced to send positive Orders to prevent those who had Plantations from coming down to the Southward, lest thereby they should lose their next Harvest; and both they and the People of *Port Royal* thought, it was better to dispute with the *Spaniards* here, than stay for the Event, being thoroughly satisfied that if the *Spaniards* dislodged this Settlement, they must of course be destroyed.

Mr. *Oglethorpe* received a Letter from *Augustine* by way of *Charles Town*, giving an Account that there had been an Alarm there, that they hourly expected Ships to their Assistance from the *Havannah*; that the General had beat to Arms, and the Trumpet sounded to Boot and Saddle; that all the Horse, and a Detachment of Foot, were marched out; and that the *Pohoia* King of the *Florida*'s was expected in a little more than a Month, with a great Number of *Indians*; that the *Spaniards* had not Arms for them, but that there were Proposals made by some Persons who were Runaways from *Carolina*, to buy at *Charles Town* Arms, Ammunition and Presents both for them and the Creek *Indians*, the *Spaniards* intending to gain the Upper Creeks from the *English* Interest. They had also sent to buy Provisions at *New York*, in order to have sufficient to maintain the Troops that they expected from the *Havannah*.

He received at the same time a Letter from *Don Carlos Dempsey*, by the Governor of *Augustine*'s Order, acquainting him that the *Indians* had fallen upon a Post of theirs, called *Picolata*, and killed some of their Men, and that he from thence seemed to conclude, that the *Indians* would not molest them unless they had some private Countenance.

Upon these Advices, to restrain the *Indians*, and prevent any Pretence of a Rupture upon their Account with the *Spaniards*, Mr. *Oglethorpe* hasten'd the sending out the Marine-Boats; and he also sent an Express to hasten the Independent Company from *Port Royal*, and the Man of War from *Savannah*.

On the 10th in the Evening Ensign *Delegal* arrived with a Detachment of 30 Men of the Independent Company under his Command, all active willing young Fellows; they had heard from *Charles Town* of the general Report of the *Spaniards* Intention to dislodge us; Mr. *Delegal* had made them row Night and Day, relieving their Oars with the Soldiers, in order to come up time enough for Service. Mr. *Oglethorpe* went immediately on Board them, and for fear of losing time, suffered none to land, but ordered Provisions and *English* strong Beer, to be carried on Board and distributed amongst the Soldiers. As also a Present of Wine to Ensign *Delegal*. They went forward with the same Tide of Ebb, and Mr. *Oglethorpe* went down with the Scout-Boat, and posted them upon the East Point of the Island, which projects into the Ocean, a pleasant and healthful Place, open to the Sea Breezes. There is a Beach of white Sand for four or five Miles long, so hard that Horse Races might be run upon it. It commands the Entry of *Jekyl* Sound, in such a manner that all Ships that come in at this North

Entry, must pass within shot of the Point, the Channel lying under it, by reason of a Shoal which runs off from *Jekyl* Island. Having pitched upon the Ground for a Fort, Mr. *Oglethorpe* ordered a Well to be dug, and found good Water; after which he returned to *Frederica.*

On the 13th in the Evening the *Marine* Boat and a *Periagua,* with Men and Provisions for three Months, together with Arms, Ammunition and Tools, sailed to the Southward. On board her was Major *Richard,* with Answers from Mr. *Oglethorpe* to the Captain General of *Florida's* Letters, acquainting him, that being greatly desirous to remove all occasions of Uneasiness, upon his Excellency's frequent Complaints of the Incursions of the *Indians* into the *Spanish* Dominions, Mr. *Oglethorpe* had sent down some armed Boats to patrole the Rivers which separate the King of *Great Britain's* Dominions from those of *Spain,* to hinder any lawless Persons from sheltring themselves in the *British* Dominions, and from thence molesting his Catholick Majesty's Subjects, and to restrain the *English Indians* from invading them. He returned him Thanks for his Civilities, and express'd his Inclination for maintaining a good Harmony between the Subjects of both Crowns; and that pursuant to his Excellency's Desire, he has sent back Major *Richard,* together with an *English* Gentleman, to wait upon his Excellency.

This Body of Men was commanded by Captain *Hermsdorf,* and under him by Mr. *Horton,* the latter of whom had Orders to go with Major *Richard* to *Augustine;* and Captain *Hermsdorf* had Orders, after having fortified the Parts which commanded the Pass by Water, to make the Boats patrole up the River *Saint John,* to prevent our friendly Indians from passing the Rivers, and advise all they met to return to Mr. *Oglethorpe* at *Frederica.*

The 16th we receiv'd Advice from Fort *Saint Andrews,* that they had seen some Ships out at Sea. This Day also return'd some Men whom Mr. *Oglethorpe* had sent to look out a Way by Land to the Sea-Point, which they had found, and brought Advice from Ensign *Delegal,* that he had already cast up a small Entrenchment, mounted some Cannon, and had seen some Ships lying off and on, and, as they thought, heard several Guns fire at Sea, but so very distant as not to be quite certain. We began to be apprehensive that the *Hawk* was intercepted, and the rather, because a Decked Boat, which had been set out a Month from *Charles Town* for this place, was not yet arrived; and this was increas'd by an account from a Sloop, which came from the Northward, that she had seen a large Ship out at Sea that seemed to make towards her, but she standing in for shoal Water heard no more of her.

Upon this all hands were set to work upon the Fortifications, Mr. *Oglethorpe* recalled several Parties of Indians from the Main, and kept them in the Woods near the Town. We cut down the small Wood to the Eastward, which hindered the Town from seeing the *Savannah*, having before show'd the Inconveniency of it, for the People being tired of Guards, to make them alert, he one Day, in his return from viewing the Sea Coast, discovered a Branch of the River that ended in the *Savannah*, and rowing up it landed with the Men, and under the shelter of that Wood came to the farther end of the Town without being discovered, having surpris'd the Centry that was without the Wood, and sent him into the Town crying the Enemy was upon them. The Men who were with Mr. *Oglethorpe* fired a Volley, falling in with a Spanish Cry, the People ran to the Fort, the very Women took Arms to help the Defence of the Fort, and the whole Colony was thoroughly alarm'd.

One *Walker*, then sick of a Fever, in his Bower, which was nearest the Wood, took up his Musquet, (which the People here were order'd to keep loaded by them) and being scarce able to stand, kneeling at his Door upon one Knee, he presented his Piece at the first Man he saw; at which Mr. *Oglethorpe* calling to him, he in the surprise scarcely knew his Voice, but hearing his own Name called he recover'd his Arms, and was glad to find they were Friends; being asked what he intended to have done, he said, that thinking the Town lost, he was resolved to die like a Man with his Arms in his hand, and to kill a *Spaniard* before he died.

A Magazine for the Powder was begun under one of the Bastions, made of solid thick Timber, with several feet of Earth over it; a Smith's Forge also was getting up in the Fort; the Storehouse being rais'd and cover'd we began to bring in Provisions, *&c.*

This House was flat roofed and covered with Boards, to be laid over with Turpentine, and above that a Composition of Tar and Sand, the Boards were already laid, but the Tar and other things were not come from *Carolina*; notwithstanding that we thought it best to get every thing into the Fort, particularly Provisions, for fear of Accidents.

I lay in the Storehouse, but the Rain came in between the Boards, so that a good many of the Stores were damaged, tho' we took all possible Care to prevent it.

The 17th we landed some Sheep, which arrived the Night before in a Sloop from *Carolina*, they were about forty, bought for the use of the Colony. Mr. *Oglethorpe* had ordered a Penn to be made for them, to keep them in till they were acquainted with the Place, the People appointed to do it and take care of them, thought they might spare the trouble of making a Penn, and govern them as they do English Sheep without it, but as soon as they were landed, they came with terrible Complaints to Mr. *Oglethorpe*, that they were not Sheep but Devils, that they had run directly into the Woods, and were as wild as Bucks. Mr. *Oglethorpe* taking some of the Indians and others, went himself, and with much difficulty brought up most of them, but some were lost. And this Experience made them mind Mr. *Oglethorpe*'s Advice, who knew the nature of the Country and the Cattle. About this time the Acre-Lots were run out, and each Freeholder that desired to have them near the Town had one, but those who were desirous of having more than one Acre for their Gardens were oblig'd to have it farther off the Town, where they had five Acres, which was part of the fifty Acres promised to them, the remainder was to be in Farm at something farther distance.

On the 18th the Flies began to plague the Horses, so as to make them almost unserviceable, Mr. *Oglethorpe* had a Stable made at the end of the Town for them. There was a Fence sometime ago begun, design'd to be carried all round the Town by joint Labour, but the Alarms making it necessary to finish the Fortifications, and put the Place into a posture of Defence (and for which there were scarce Hands sufficient) the Enclosure was obliged to be left unfinished, by which means most of the Corn, and other Things that had been planted, were destroy'd by the Cattle. The Magazine for Powder being finish'd, as also a Lodgment Bomb-proof in the hollow of another of the Bastions, the Smith's Forge in a working Order, the Fort in a posture of Defence, and Provisions sufficient for the whole Colony.

On the 25th Mr. *Oglethorpe* went down to *Saint Andrews* in a Scout-Boat, with some other Boats, to see what farther Works were necessary for that Place, and also to have the Entrance from the Sea into *Jekyl-Sound*, better view'd and sounded.

On the 26th Advice came from Ensign *Delegal*, at the Sea-Point, that he had discovered a Ship at Sea; Mr. *Tanner* went down in a Scout-Boat to see what she was, but she was stood out to Sea, upon which he returned to the Town.

The 29th Mr. *Oglethorpe* returned from *Saint Andrews*, in going down he had very bad Weather, great Storms of Thunder, Lightnings, Wind and Rain. The Scout-Boat was forced to take shelter amongst Oyster-Banks over against *Jekyl* Island, where they rode out the Night. They saw a Fire upon that Island, on which, notwithstanding the roughness of the Weather, they row'd a-cross the Sound (which is three Miles wide) with much difficulty, and could not gain the Island till Nine in the Morning; they found a Creek which carried them up to the very heart of it, and there landing found a large Field of rich Ground, formerly cleared by the Indians: They saw the footsteps of a Man where the Fire had been; Mr. *Oglethorpe* walked thro' the Island but could not make out the Track: He went on to *Saint Andrews*, and sent *Ferguson*'s Scout-Boat to Captain *Hermsdorf*; he sent off another Boat to Sound; he ordered a Ravelin to be added to the Fort at *Saint Andrews*, and also a Palisade round the bottom of the Hill. They saw some Sails from *Saint Andrews*, on which Mr. *Oglethorpe* immediately returned for *Frederica*, but by stress of Weather was forced into *Jekyl* Island, blowing and raining very hard; however at last they row'd thro' it and got up to the Town.

Mr. *Tanner* was sent down with Captain *Dymond*'s long Boat to go out at *Jekyl* Entry, to see what the Sails were. At the same time another Boat was sent down to go out at *Cumberland* Entry, and see if any Ships attempted to come in there, and to give notice thereof. Also Mr. *Delegal* was ordered to send over a Party to view *Jekyl* Island. Mr. *Oglethorpe* himself staid at *Frederica*, to take such Measures as should be necessary for the Defence of the whole, if these Ships shou'd not be Friends and Land.

On the 30th Mr. *Tanner* returned with an account that he reached *Jekyl* Island in the Evening, and saw a two Mast Vessel at an Anchor off the Bar, but being near Night could make no farther Discovery; that this Morning he went off with the Tide of Ebb being a dead Calm, so that he could get near enough to discover what she was, without any danger of being intercepted by her, he afterwards took her to be the *Hawk* Sloop, and the nearer he went to her the better satisfied he was of it; he laid two Buoys on the Breaker Heads, and then went on towards the Sloop. About Noon the Wind rising, Captain *Gascoign* in the *Hawk* weighed, came over the Bar at once, and came to an Anchor in *Jekyl* Sound.

In the middle of the Night, between the first and second of *June*, Captain *Ferguson* arrived in the Scout-Boat, with an account that Major *Richard* and Mr. *Horton*, and some others of the Men, were Prisoners at *Augustine*: That Captain *Hermsdorf* expecting every Hour to be attacked by the *Spaniards*, the Island of *St. George* not being yet in a posture of Defence, and apprehending a Mutiny amongst his Men, was come away from thence; that he had seen him safe as far as the North end of *Cumberland*, where he had left him with the *Periagua* and the *Marine* Boat; but that if he was pursued, as he believed he was, he apprehended they would easily fall into the Spaniards hands, the Men being mutinous, which was the reason he advis'd him to come up to *St. Andrews*; but the other did not think fit to conform to it. Mr. *Oglethorpe* sending for him to his Tent, enquir'd the Matter more particularly of him; after which he spent the rest of the Night in Writing, making proper Dispositions, and sending for such Assistance as he thought could be procured, resolving himself to set out in the Morning for the Southward. He spoke to the People, to take off any panick Fear that this Accident might have occasioned, tho' they were very far from being frighten'd, or even surpris'd; for they had been all along, by continual Alarms accustomed to expect that they shou'd at last be oblig'd to fight for their Lands.

Mr. *Oglethorpe* told the Particulars of the whole Story, which were, That Major *Richard*, on his arrival at *Saint George*'s, had sent over to the Spanish Side, according as he had promised to the Governour of *Augustine*, but met with no Horses or Persons at the Look-out, as was appointed: some Days passing, he being very impatient to carry his Letters, pursuant to his Promise of returning in three Weeks; and there being great danger of going in open Boats from *St. Johns* to the Bar of *Augustine*, as he had before experienc'd. Mr. *Horton* seeing it was for the Service, offered to walk to *Augustine* by Land, taking a Servant and another Man with him, to give Notice to the Governor of the Major's being arrived with the Letters. He was accordingly landed at the Spanish Look-out, from whence he was set out for *Augustine*. Some Days after two Smokes being made at the Spanish Look-out, which was the Signal agreed, Major *Richard* sent over the Marine Boat, which brought for answer, That there was a Guard and Horses ready to conduct him to *Augustine*, but that the Spaniards look'd and behav'd in such a manner as seemed to be more like Enemies than Friends. Both Men and Officers advised that Major *Richard* should not go without the Spaniards left some one as Security for his Safety, but he resolved to go.

Being landed on the other side, the Spaniards brought him a Horse, and as soon as he was mounted carried him away without taking any leave of the Boat. A few Days after this, some Smokes being made on the Spanish Side, the Boat went over to see what Message there was, and brought back a piece of dirty Paper, with something wrote in German, with a Black-lead Pencil, said by the Spaniards to be wrote to Captain *Horton* by Major *Richard*. There was nothing of consequence in those Lines, only that he was got well to the Captain of Horse's Quarters. They saw the appearance of more Spaniards than usual on the Main, and also several Fires. Mr. *Horton* not returning, the Spaniards appearing and Major *Richard* writing in so short a manner, that he was arrived at the Captain of Horse's Quarters, made Mr. *Hermsdorf* conclude that he was kept Prisoner there, and that he dared not write plainer, because the Letter passed through the Spaniards hands. Besides this, his Men being very unwilling to do their Guard exactly, or be vigilant when Centries, the Fort not being yet tenable; and being informed that there was a general Meeting designed, he thought it was best to re-embark every thing and retire to *Amelia* Sound, through which the Spaniards must pass, if they came between the Islands to attack the Colony. And if they advanced with such force as to be able to overpower him, he could perceive them soon enough to retire under the Cannon at *St. Andrews*, and there he resolv'd to stay till he had farther Orders, and sent up the Scout-Boat for them.

Mr. *Oglethorpe* having informed them of this, he farther aquainted them, that he was going down himself to set things to rights, that now the Man of War was come it would guard the entrance of *Jekyl* Sound; that the Detachment of the Independant Company would prevent landing upon the back of the Island, and that their Fort was in a good Condition to make a Defence if Men should land, and force their way through the Country; that there was sufficient Provision in the Fort of all kinds for eight Months; so they had nothing to do but to be vigilant against Surprizes. He left Orders for the Guards, and Mr. *M. Intosh*, a Scotch Gentleman who had been several Years in the King's Service, and Mr. *Auspourger* as Engineer, to instruct them in their military Duty.

The People in general answered they were under no apprehension, and were willing to die in the defence of the Place, and were only sorry that he should be exposed without them.

He set out by Eight of Clock for the Southward in Captain *Ferguson*'s Scout-Boat, and I having finished transcribing the Letters, Mr. *Tanner* in about three Hours follow'd him in the *Georgia* Scout-Boat, *John Rae* Commander.

We continued unloading the two Ships, and bringing every thing into the Storehouse, which was now finished on the outside, but the covering was not yet quite Water-proof.

The People were employ'd in building a Wheel-Wrights Shop, and a Cornhouse, being apprehensive that the Indian Corn (which is very bulky) and the Geer, would suffer by being expos'd to the wet. Several Periagua's and Boats arriv'd from *Savannah* with numbers of Volunteers on Board, they having heard many Reports by way of *Charles-Town*, and by the Indians that the Spaniards intended to attack us. And it was confidently reported there, that the Town was taken and Mr. *Oglethorpe* kill'd.

On the 8th there was a large Boat with four Pieces of Cannon, and full of Men, attempted to come in at *Jekyl-Sound*, without Colours; Ensign *Delegal* fired to make her bring too (and give an account of herself, and to know whether she was a Pirate, or what she should be) which she did not do, but row'd on; at the same time she discover'd the *Hawk-Sloop* in the Harbour, and she, instead of coming in, or showing Colours, ran out to Sea, round *Jekyl-Sound*, and into *Cumberland-Sound*, it being then Night, she came pretty near *St. Andrews* before she was discovered; but being challeng'd by them, a Man answered in English, and they row'd away with the utmost Precipitation. On board this Boat, as we heard afterwards, was *Don Ignatio*, with a Detachment of the *Spanish* Garison, and as many *Indians* and Boat-men as the Launch could hold.

The same Afternoon arriv'd the King of the *Uchee Indians*, in a large *Periagua*, with a great many of his Men, and one *Chevers* a white Man who traded amongst them. Arriv'd also Lieutenant *Delegal*, with the remainder of the Independant Company, with 13 Pieces of Cannon belonging to them, he passed on to the Sea-Point. The *Indians* and the Volunteers staid for Mr. *Oglethorpe*'s return; so that we were increased in strength.

On the 9th Mr. *Oglethorpe* return'd. I procured an account of his Journey from those that went with him, as follows,

When he set out he went first on board Captain *Gascoign*; he left *Ferguson*'s Scout-Boat, taking with him *Rae*'s Scout-Boat, and Captain *Gascoign*'s six Oar'd Yawl, on board the which was Mr. *Moore* Lieutenant of the Man of War, and a Crew of very good Men. They came to *St. Andrews* in the Night, and hastning forward, the next Day about Noon having reached the South-end of *Cumberland*, they met the *Periagua* and *Marine* Boat at Anchor, there Mr. *Oglethorpe* asking how all went on board, Mr. *Hermsdorf* answering, Well, not to lose Time, he ordered them to weigh Anchor and follow him out to Sea, the Wind being then fair. They stood out accordingly, after they were out at Sea the Wind changing, the *Periagua* was not able to reach the South-end of *Amelia*, but the Scout-Boat and Yawl got into the Inlet, and waited the next Day for the *Periagua*. In the mean time stopping a little Creek that fell into the Sea, upon the ebbing of the Water, the Men caught more Fish with their Hands, their Oars, and a Sail, for they had no Net, than all the Men on Board, the three Boats and the *Periagua* could eat. When the *Periagua* came up, and the Men were come on Shore, Mr. *Oglethorpe* inquired into the past Transactions, and having quieted the mutinous Humour among the Men, occasion'd by a Misunderstanding, fomented only by one of them who was punish'd, they resolv'd all to do their utmost; and on the fifth, at Noon, arriv'd at *St. George*'s.

He immediately landed, and viewing the Ground, found but very little cleared, but there was a Mount just upon the edge of the River, which was Salt-water, and the Ruins of a Rampart and Ditch about 25 or 30 Foot from the bottom of the Ditch to the top of the ruin'd Rampart. There was upon the top of the Hill another Mount cast up by Hands, like the Bulwarks with which they fortify'd in Queen *Elizabeth*'s Time, from whence the Hill descended on one side to the Water; from thence, if the Woods were cleared, one could overlook the Inside of the Island; and from this Bulwark you could also see the *Spanish* Look-out, and discover far into the Ocean, for it over-looks *Talbot* Island, which is narrow in that Place, and lies between that and the Sea. They immediately mounted one Piece of Cannon, on the lower Mount Bulwark, which commanded the River, and a couple of Swivel-Guns on the upper Mount, several of the Men were set to clearing, in order to judge better of the Ground.

Leaving Mr. *Hermsdorf* with the *Periagua* and *Marine* Boat, Mr. *Oglethorpe* set out with the *Scout* Boat and *Yawl* for the *Spanish* Side, carrying a Flag of Truce, in order to inquire what was become of Major *Richard* and Mr. *Horton* and his Men. There was no Body at the *Spanish* Look-out; they row'd up to a Pallmetto Hut. Mr. *Oglethorpe* went ashore about a Musket-Shot from it, and climbing one of the Sand-Hills, to see if there were any People, He ordered Mr. *Tanner* and four Youths that belong'd to him to come on Shore, making the Boats to keep at a Grapling, to prevent being surpris'd, in case of Accidents. He sent forward the White-Flag, and having examined well the Country, he pass'd thro' a little Wood into an open *Savannah*. There was no Body in the *Palmetto* Hut, nor could they discover any Men, finding only two Horses tied with

Hobbles amongst the Sand-Hills. He staid upon a rising Ground, from whence he could see both the Boats and the *Savannah*, and sent one of his Lads with a White Flag, as far down the *Savannah* as he could keep him in sight, to see if he could draw any People to a Conference, but no Body appearing, he called in his Servants in order to return. A Boy named *Frazier* was not yet come back, for whom he staid, and in a little time saw him returning through the Wood, driving before him a tall Man with a Musket upon his Shoulder, two Pistols stuck in his Girdle and a long Sword, and a short Sword. *Frazier* coming up to Mr. *Oglethorpe* said, *Here, Sir, I have caught a Spaniard for you.* Mr. *Oglethorpe* treated this Man very civilly, gave him Wine and Victuals, and asked concerning Major *Richard* and Mr. *Horton*; on which the Fellow pulled out a Letter, which he said was from Mr. *Horton, whom the Governor of* St. Augustine *had put under Arrest, as also Major* Richard. *The Man said he had watched some Days for an opportunity to deliver the Letter.* Mr. *Oglethorpe* rewarded him well, and appointed to send him an Answer by the next Day at Noon to the same place, which he agreed to come to receive. He would have given him a Letter to the Governor of *Augustine*, but the Man said, that none could be carried, for that a Troop of Horse under the Command of *Don Pedro* kept all the Passages, so that all Letters must go to him. They returned to *St. George*'s. Mr. *Oglethorpe* had great Fires made on *Talbot* Island, another on *St. George*'s, each a Mile below the Fort, and another a Mile and half in the Woods; so that any Boat coming up the River, between them and the Fort would be discovered by the Light of them. That Night the Men lay upon their Arms, strict Centries were kept; the Seamen having the Charge of the lower Mount, and Mr. *Hermsdorf*'s Men of the upper. There were Centries placed 200 Yards into the Woods every way; and either Mr. *Hermsdorf* or Mr. *Oglethorpe* kept going the Rounds all Night. One Scout-Boat was anchored near half a Mile below them, and the *Marine* Boat about half a Mile above, to watch the River.

On the 6th before Day-break, all Hands set to cut down the Wood, and with it they rais'd Barricades from the upper Mount to the lower; and all Trees that were fit for it they cut into Palisades by eight of the Clock. Mr. *Oglethorpe* ordered seven Shots to be fired out of the two Swivel Guns, which for that purpose were ordered to be carried farther into the Woods; and then at a moderate distance of time five Shots to be fired out of the four Pounder, which also was hauled into the Wood, and the Muzzle turned another way, that the Flash might not be discovered from the *Spanish* Look-out. This seemed to be Guns from different Distances;

for the small Report of the Swivel Guns made them appear farther off, and the four Pounders to be nearer; so that it appeared to be a Ship saluting at some distance behind the Island, and that returned by a Fort. At ten of the Clock Mr. *Oglethorpe* stood down with the Scout-Boat, and Lieutenant *Moore* in the Yawl, with the *Marine* Boat in Company; they went to the *Spanish* Main, but did not see the *Spaniard* at the Place appointed, but discovered some Horsemen that were conceal'd behind the Sand Hills. Mr. *Oglethorpe* would not suffer the Boats to go near where there was any Shelter, but to go to the landing Place, where there was a plain Sand for a Musket-shot round. There we made Signals carrying a Flag of Truce, but no Body would appear. After that, some Horsemen made Signals about two Miles below, but there was a close brushy Wood just behind them, made it not proper to trust the Boats there. Whilst they were looking at these Horsemen, Mr. *Oglethorpe* discover'd something which looked like a Bank with Pelicans upon it; but looking more attentively he saw it was a Launch full of Men, lying under the shelter of a Sand-Bank, near the mouth of the River *St. Johns*, within Shot of which Bank he must have passed to come to the Place where the Horsemen had made the Signals. There was a strong Tide of Ebb, and if the Boat had stood down to the Horsemen, the *Spaniards* might have cut them off from returning, since they must have row'd up against Tide, and she would have been above them. Mr. *Oglethorpe*, upon this, asked Mr. *Moore* if he was for examining the Launch first, which Mr. *Moore* readily agreed to, and Mr. *Oglethorpe* sent off the *Marine* Boat, to order the *Periagua* to weigh Anchor and come down directly. As soon as the *Marine* Boat was gone off from them, they row'd toward the Launch: As they came nearer the Men who before had kept themselves so low that they could only see their Heads, started up at once and row'd out to Sea. Upon this the two Boats stop'd, that they might not be carried too far down with the Ebb, and put in where the Horsemen were, but would not go within danger of an Ambuscade from the Bushes, or Sand Hills. Upon which two Horsemen came up to the open Point of a level Sand, where Mr. *Oglethorpe* had before made the Signals. The Boat rowing up to them, Mr. *Oglethorpe* had a Conference with one of them, a Gentleman dress'd in Blue, and very well mounted: He sent Letters on Shore to him, which he promis'd to deliver, and that he should have an Answer in a Day's time. The Boats returned to *St. George's*, and meeting the *Periagua* which was come half way towards them, as soon as they landed they fell all to work, Mr. *Oglethorpe* as well as the rest: He marked out the Ground for the Fort, enclosing the lower Mount, and joining it to the upper Mount by a Line of Palisadoes, marking it out, as also where the Breast-works should be; and clearing the old Ditches, palisading the Breaches and the Rampart; having begun by palisading the side towards the Water.

Having staid for the *Spaniard*'s Answer till the 8th in the Evening, and it not arriving, Mr. *Oglethorpe* and Mr. *Moore* set out in Captain *Gascoign*'s Yawl, leaving all the other Boats and Men at *St. George's*, under the Command of Mr. *Hermsdorf*. He landed on the Main, and there made great Fires in different Places, which could be seen as far as the *Spanish* Look-out; Mr. *Hermsdorf* having been ordered to do the same at several Places on *St. George's* Island. After which they went down to the North-end of *Talbot* Island, and there set all the Wood on fire, which also could be seen from the *Spanish* Look-out: They slept some Hours upon the Sea-Sand, and about an Hour before Day-break, the Weather being boisterous, and the Boat rather overloaded, they set several of the Men on Shore upon the South-end of *Amelia*, ordering them to march along the Sand-Beach, to the North-end. Mr. *Oglethorpe* then went out to Sea with the Yawl, and got into the opening between *Cumberland* and *Amelia*, where they took in the Men; and, rowing all Day, passed *St. Andrews*, and a violent Storm of Thunder, Lightning and Rain overtook them in *Cumberland* Sound, the Weather growing so dark that they could not see any Land; notwithstanding which they still row'd on, and got that Night on Board the *Hawk*. Mr. *Oglethorpe* having first spoke to Captain *Gascoign* went forward to *Frederica*, where he arriv'd three Hours after midnight.

On the 10th he found here the *Uchee Mico*, with his Men, and the others which waited his Arrival. He wrote a great number of Letters upon this new situation of Affairs, which confirmed all the Reports of the *Spaniards* beginning to commit Hostilities against us. It was necessary therefore to stop them nearer Home; and for that purpose to make the great Push at *St. George's*; since whilst we held that Passage from the River *St. John's*, it was difficult for them to come in open Boats to us, there being forty Miles from *St. Augustine* to *St. John's*, where they can have no Port, but must keep out at Sea, where every Squall is dangerous; but from *St. John's* there is a Passage through Channels, within the Islands as far as *Charles-Town*. If open Boats could not come up, Ships would be very cautious of venturing in upon an unknown Coast.

Mr. *Oglethorpe* therefore prepar'd for the supporting of *St. George's*, being resolv'd to have those of his Men who were Prisoners at *Augustine* brought back to him.

If the *Spaniards* could Arm the *Florida Indians*, or have gain'd the upper Creeks, it would have been of great Danger to the Colony; for the *Florida's* amount to several Thousand Men; but they have few or no Fire-Arms. The next Danger was from the Troops which would have come from *Havannah*. As there was no more Provisions at *Augustine* than what was necessary for the People already there, therefore if they could be prevented from receiving such Supplies, a large number of Men from *Havannah* would be of no service to them, if we could spin out a Defence till their Provision were wasted. To obtain these two Purposes Mr. *Oglethorpe* first wrote to the Lieutenant Governor of *Carolina*, advice of the *Spaniard*'s Intention to provide themselves with Arms and Ammunition, and *Indian* Presents, at *Charles Town*; which was the only Place they could have them from, time enough to do us any mischief; and therefore desired him to hinder the Exportation of them.

At the same time he wrote to Mr. *Eveleigh*, a publick-spirited man and a Merchant in *Charles Town*, that if the Governor and Council of *Carolina* could not prevent the sending out Arms, Ammunition, *&c.* that he should buy up what was in Town, and thereby prevent the *Spaniards* from being at present supplied with them.

He also wrote to the Governor at *New-York* on account of this matter, that he might take such measures for his Majesty's Service as his Prudence should direct; the *Spaniards* expecting to be supplied with Flower and other Provisions from their Correspondents at that Place.

On the 11th *Toma Chi Chi Mico*, with *Hyllispilli* his chief War Captain, newly come from the *Indian* Nation, and who had been with him in *England*, and a great many other Warriors arrived here; as also Mrs. *Musgrove* and her Brother, an half *Indian*, called *Griffin*, and several other *Indians*.

The *Uchee Indian* King and his People had a Conference with Mr. *Oglethorpe*; they had taken some Disgust at this Colony, by reason of an indiscreet Action of one of the *Saltzburghers*, who had cleared and planted four Acres of Land beyond the *Ebenezer* River, contrary to Mr. *Oglethorpe*'s Order, and without his knowledge; they had also turn'd their Cattle over the River, some of which had stray'd away and eat the *Uchee*'s Corn twenty Miles above *Ebenezer*. But what vex'd the *Uchees* most was, that some of the *Carolina* People swam a great Herd of Cattle over *Savannah* River, sent up Negroes and began a Plantation on the *Georgia*-side, not far from the *Uchees* Town. Mr. *Oglethorpe* had heard these matters from *Toma Chi Chi*, and had given Orders for the remedy of them, as I mentioned before.

The *Uchee* King in the Conference said, that he came to give him Thanks, for having ordered back the Cattle and sent away the Negroes, which he did on his first arrival; and then told him, that he having done them Justice before they ask'd it, made them love him, and not believe the Stories that were told them against him; and that instead of beginning a War with the *English*, they were come down to help him against the *Spaniards*; and if they wanted them they would bring fourscore more of their Warriors, and stay with him a whole Year.

All hands were employ'd in putting on Board Arms, Ammunition, Tools, *&c.* for *St. George's*: and on the 12th Mr. *Oglethorpe* set out, accompanied by *Toma Chi Chi Mico* and his *Indians*, by the *Uchees*, and a Body of White-men, with Stores of all kinds. *Toma Chi Chi* and his Men went in their Boats.

Nothing material happen'd whilst Mr. *Oglethorpe* was absent, only that I made an end of unloading the two Ships, *James*, Captain *Yoakley*, and the *Peter and James*, Captain *Dymond*, settled their Accounts and discharg'd them. Lieutenant *Delegal* was now with the whole Independant Company at the Sea-point, and the Man of War Sloop so anchored as to secure the Entry from *Jekyl-Sound*, and the Storehouse being then finished, we therefore could discharge the Ships which hitherto had serv'd both for Storehouses and Guard-Ships. The Colony was chiefly taken up with preparing for their Defence, Mr. *M. Intosh* exercising the Men daily.

On the 14th at Night, to our great Joy, Mr. *Horton* arriv'd at

Frederica, from among the *Spaniards*, and gave us an account, that he had met Mr. *Oglethorpe* at Sea, and that he would be very soon back. He told me,

That at his arrival at *St. George*'s Point, in *April* last, he sent over to the *Spaniards* Look-out, expecting to find Horses there, according to the Governor's appointment, but there being none, nor no Guard, nor Persons to be seen, after having expected them four Days in vain, and Major *Richard* having no means of sending Advice to the Governor of *Augustine* of his arrival, Mr. *Horton* offer'd to go, and set out on foot with two Servants. The *Sunday* he left the *Spanish* Look-out, he arriv'd at *Augustine*, being upwards of forty Miles; the Way he walked lay all along the Seashore, one Servant kept up with him, the other not being able to hold out. There is a River runs near the Castle of *Augustine*, which must be passed by those who go from the *Spanish* Look-out: He arriv'd at the River within sight of the Castle about four in the Evening, and fired his Gun several times as a Signal for a Boat to come and carry him over; at last one came, and carrying him over, he was conducted to the Governor, who receiv'd him very civilly. From whence he went to *Don Carlos Dempsey*'s House, who went immediately to the Governor's House, to desire a Party might be sent out to fetch in the Man who was left behind; for at that time the *Spaniards* were so apprehensive of the Indians, that they did not venture to go over the River but in Bodies. The Governor granted his Request, and the next Day ordered a Detachment for him, who found and carried him to *Don Carlos*'s House, who applied also for Horses to fetch up Major *Richard* from the Look-out; which were accordingly sent.

They were received very Civilly by the Governor, and with the greatest Joy by the People, who looked upon them as the Messengers of their Deliverance, for bringing them the news that the *English* Boats patrole upon the River, to hinder the barbarous *Indians* from passing and molesting them. Major *Richard* and Mr. *Horton* waited for the Governor's Answer to Mr. *Oglethorpe*'s Letter, which was daily promis'd them. One Night, being invited, they went to a general Dancing, at the House of the Governor's Interpreter, where they staid till three o'Clock in the Morning; when they return'd they went to Bed, and before they awaked, about eight o'Clock the same Morning, *Diego Paulo*, Town Major, came from the Governor to *Don Carlos Dempsey* with a File of Musketeers, and acquainted him with the *Spaniard*'s false Pretence, which was, that Major *Richard*, Mr. *Horton* and their Servants, had that very Morning been taking a Plan of their Town and Castle, (tho' they having sate up late and were then a-Bed) the Governor had sent a Serjeant and twelve Men to make them Prisoners, one Centry being set at the foot, and another at the head of the Stairs. The Town Major then told *Don Carlos* that he needed to fear nothing, but was at liberty to come and go as he always had done since his arrival there.

The same Morning, about Ten, the Governor came to *Don Carlos*'s Lodging, accompany'd by some Officers and the publick Scrivener of the Garison, and having sat down, began a formal Information and Examination of Major *Richard*. The Governor ask'd him, what brought him there, he answer'd, that he was come pursuant to his Promise to his Excellency of returning to him with Letters from Mr. *Oglethorpe*. He then asked where Mr. *Oglethorpe* was? He answered, he could not tell where he then was, but he had left him at *Frederica*. Upon which he asked, what Fortifications and number of Men were at *Frederica*? To which the Major answered, he did not know. He then asked, what Fortifications and number of Men were at *Jekyl-Sound*, *Cumberland Island*, *Amelia Island* and *St. John's*? To which the Major answered the same as before. Whereupon the Governor retired; and some time after sent for the Major to his House. He then examined Mr. *Horton* to the Strength of *Georgia*; but he refus'd to give them any answer: Upon which they threaten'd to send him to the Mines. To which he answer'd, that he was a Subject of *Great Britain*, and his Sovereign was powerful enough to do him Justice.

The next Day, upon *Don Carlos*'s application, the Guards were taken off, he undertaking for them, and promising, upon Honour, that they should not walk about the Town, nor leave it without his Excellency's Permission. Some Days after they sent out *Don Ignatio Rosso*, Lieutenant Colonel of the Garison, with a Detachment of it, in a large Boat called a Launch; he staid out about five Days, and returned extreamly fatigu'd, the Men having row'd the Skin off their Hands; and reported, that the Islands were all fortified and full of Men and arm'd Boats. After this, *Don Carlos* spoke to the Governor, Bishop and the rest of the Officers, a Council of War was call'd, and it was resolv'd to send back Major *Richard*, Mr. *Horton*, and the other Men; and also Letters of Civility to Mr. *Oglethorpe*, with *Don Carlos Dempsey*, *Don Pedro Lamberto*, Captain of Horse, and *Don Manuel d'Arcy* Adjutant of the Garison, and to desire Friendship. Mr. *Horton* was accordingly releas'd, arriv'd at *St. George's*, from whence he came in a Boat mann'd with his own Servants, and meeting Mr. *Oglethorpe* at Sea, as above mentioned, he had sent him forwards to have the

Spaniards receiv'd on Board Captain *Gascoign* (they being on the way in a Launch) that they might not get any Information either of our Strength or Situation.

Mr. *Oglethorpe* return'd on the 17th. On leaving this Place he went first on Board Captain *Gascoign*'s Ship, and from thence proceeded to *Cumberland*, where landing at *St. Andrews*, he took on Board Captain *Hugh Mackay*. The 13th in the Evening the *Periagua* in which Mr. *Mackay* was on Board grounded near the South of *Cumberland*; and getting her off on the 14th they stood to Sea on the outside of *Amelia*: The Weather being rough, the *Indian* Canoos landed several Men, that they might be the better able to bear the Weather, for they were too much throng'd to bear the Sea. They saw a Boat, and making up to it found it to be Mr. *Horton* return'd from the *Spaniards*. At the South-end of *Amelia* Mr. *Oglethorpe* (the Scout-Boat being foremost) saw a Launch coming down from *Saint George's*, bearing up to her; she hoisted *Spanish* Colours, and challenging her they found she had *Don Carlos Dempsey* and *Spanish* Commissaries a-board her, Mr. *Oglethorpe*, to avoid the Ceremony which must have passed on his owning himself there, and which would have prevented his going to *Saint George's*, caused Mr. *Mackay* to speak to them without going on Board: He advis'd them to come to an Anchor, till a Safe-guard should be sent to them, for that the Country was full of *Indians*. They accordingly did so; in a very short time after Mr. *Oglethorpe* met with *Rae*'s Scout-Boat, and putting Mr. *Tanner* on Board her, together with a Jar of Wine, and other Refreshments, bade them go on Board the *Spaniards*; and ordered Mr. *Tanner* to take Care and acquaint the *Indians* not to molest them, and to desire Captain *Gascoign* to entertain them till his Return. Mr. *Oglethorpe* lay at a grapling till he should see the Boat join her. The *Indians*, who were by this time come up, some by Land and some by Water, seeing a *Spanish* Launch, some of the Boats went to Shore to take in those who came by Land, but *Toma Chi Chi* with the great Boat in which he was, came up towards her; the other *Indian* Canoos, as fast as they could get their Men on Shore, row'd after him; but Mr. *Tanner* being on Board letting him know that they were Friends, he follow'd Mr. *Oglethorpe*, who soon after arriv'd at *Saint George's*, where he met Major *Richard*, who had staid there. All the Men and Stores being arriv'd, he gave the best Directions that short time would permit, and using the utmost Diligence, return'd to *Frederica* in order to receive the *Spaniards*; but being oblig'd to pass by the Man of War, on board of which the *Spaniards* already were, by making certain Signals their Boat came off to him, and he went by without being remark'd by the *Spaniards,* who were receiv'd in a very handsome manner by Captain *Gascoign.*

As soon as he came back he sent Ensign *Mackay* up to *Darien,* that he might return with some of the genteelest Highlanders and be present at the Conference. Then he ordered two handsome Tents lined with *Chinese,* with Marquises and Walls of Canvas, to be sent down and pitched upon *Jekyl* Island, and also a Present of Refreshments, and two Gentlemen to acquaint them, that he would wait upon them the next Day.

The 18th Mr. *Oglethorpe,* with seven Horses and Men upon them (which were all we had) went down to the Sea-Point, that the *Spaniards* might see that there were Men and Horses there. At his setting out a number of Cannons were fired, which they also could hear at *Jekyl* Island. When he arriv'd at the Point the Independant Company was under Arms, being drawn up in one Line at double Distances, to make them appear a larger Number to the *Spaniards,* who lay upon *Jekyl* Island. The Independant Company saluting him with their Cannon, managing them so as to seem to have many more Guns by reloading. Captain *Gascoign* came with his Boat and two Scout-Boats, and he going with Captain *Gascoign* on Board his Boat, the other attending, landed on *Jekyl* Island. He welcomed the *Spanish* Officers and made a Complement to them, making them Presents of some Refreshments; and Captain *Gascoign* invited them to Dinner on Board the *Hawk* Sloop the next Day, where Mr. *Oglethorpe* told them he would receive their Message.

The 19th Ensign *Mackay* arriv'd on Board the Man of War with the Highlanders, and a Detachment of the Independant Company in their Regimentals lined the one side of the Ship, as the Highlanders with their broad Swords, Targets, Plads, *&c.* did the other. The sailors manned all the Shrowds and the rest of the Ship, and kept Centries at the Cabin Door with drawn Cutlasses. The *Spanish* Commissaries were very handsomly entertained; and after Dinner deliver'd their Messages in Writing.

They drank the Healths of the King of *Great Britain* and the Royal Family, as Mr. *Oglethorpe* did those of the King and Queen of *Spain*. The Cannons of the Ship fired, which were answered (as before agreed upon) by such Cannon as were within hearing. Next Day they were entertained in like manner, and had long Conferences with Mr. *Oglethorpe*.

On the 21st he gave them their Answer. They made him some Presents of Snuff, Chocolate, *&c.* and he returned them very handsome ones. All the time they were there we sent down Sheep, Hogs and Poultry, with Garden-stuff in plenty for all their Men; as also Butter, Cheese, Wine, Beer, and all other Refreshments.

Toma Chi Chi, *Hyllispilli* and near thirty of the chiefest *Indians*, being returned from the Southward, came on Board, painted and dress'd as they are for War; *Hyllispilli* demanded Justice for killing the *Indians*, and other Outrages. The *Spanish* Commissary, *Don Pedro*, knowing some of the Facts, but seeming to doubt the rest, he having his Interpreter, who spoke *Indian*, *Spanish* and *English*; and the *English* having theirs, who spoke *Indian* and good *English*. The *Indians* proved, *That a Party of forty* Spaniards *and* Indians *had fallen upon some of their Nation, who then lay depending upon the general Peace between the* Spaniards, *the* Indians *and the* English, *without Suspicion, and consequently without Guard: That thus surprised several were killed and several were taken: That they murdered the Boys who were taken, by dashing out their Brains, as also the wounded Men: That they satisfied their Lusts with the Women; and that one of them being so abused as not any longer to be capable of it, they ript her up with a Knife, and not long after finished her Murder.* Don Pedro *struck with Horror at the Cruelty, asking how they could know this, they produced a young* Indian *who was wounded upon that occasion, the Scar of which he showed:* He said, *That he escaped in the Confusion by lying close amongst some Bushes; that he followed them for two Days hiding himself in the Thickets and seeing all that had passed, intending if any had straggled to revenge himself upon them.* They farther said, *That an* Indian *who had been on that Party, bragged of it at* Saint Marks *to one of the Upper Creeks, who went down to Trade there with the* Spaniards: *at the same time saying, that they were sent out from* Augustine, *which the* Indians *said was so known a thing that it could not be denied.* Upon this Mr. *Oglethorpe* desired *Don*

Pedro to represent this to the Governor of *Augustine*, for that he should expect Satisfaction to be given to them for this Insult, they being Subjects to the King of *Great Britain.* — What Mr. *Oglethorpe* said was interpreted to the *Indians.* On which *Hyllyspilli* said, *He hoped Mr.* Oglethorpe *would go with them, and then he should see what they could do to the* Spaniards; *but if he would not go with them, they would go by themselves and take Revenge.*

When this happened (said he) *I was gone with you to* England, *had I not been with you this would not have happened; for had I been there my Men should not have been so surpriz'd. You will go with me and you shall see how I will punish them; but if you will not help me, I have Friends enough that will go with me to revenge the Murder. At which all the young* Indians *gave a Shout.*

Don Pedro *said that there was a Party of* Indians *which he knew went from the Neighbourhood of* Augustine, *but that they were not* Spaniards*: That he himself at that time was at* Mexico, *on a Message from the Governor: That such Cruelty must be abhorred by every Christian; and that he would take it upon him that the People who had committed it should be punished: That the* Pohoia *King of the* Florida's *was the Man who Commanded that Party; and that if he ever came into* Augustine, *so as the* Spaniards *could secure him, the Governor and Council of War should punish him as his Cruelty deserved; and if he came not within their Power they would Banish him.*

To this *Hyllyspilli* said, *We hear what you say, when we see it done we will believe you.* Toma Chi Chi *perswaded them to be Contented.* Umpeachy *added, That he suppos'd there would be notice given to the* Pohoia *King not to come into* Augustine; *but if he does not, there is no other Place in* Florida *where he shall be safe from our Revenge.*

This Night a Party of *Indians* coming up from the Southward, landed on *Jekyl* Island, and were going to attack the *Spaniards*, with whom they began to quarrel, by taking their Victuals from them; but the *Spaniards* quietly retired from it: Notwithstanding which the *Indians* were going to fall upon them, and were with great difficulty prevented from it.

The *Spaniards* set out on the 22nd very well satisfy'd with their Reception. *Don Pedro Lamberto* is a little Man, of very good Sense, and well bred; he never was in *Europe*: He was born in *Florida*, his Father being Captain General of it: He has great Herds of Cattle in *Florida*, and a House not far distant from *Augustine*, which is fortify'd: He hath an Estate in *Mexico*, and is Captain of a Troop of Horse which belongs to the Garison, the Appointments of which amount to about two thousand Pieces of Eight *per Annum*.

FINIS.

Mr. Ingham's Journal of His Voyage to Georgia.

1 May 1736
Mr. Inghams
journal of his
voyage to
Georgea

To my much hon^rd Mother, my dearly beloved Brethren and Sisters, and all my Christian Friends, Grace, Mercy, and Peace be multiplied from Almighty God the Father, and from our Lord Jesus Christ with the Holy Ghost, to whom be Glory, Honour, and Praise for ever & ever. Amen.

Blessed, for ever blessed be the God and Father of our Lord Jesus Christ, the Father of mercy and the God of all Consolation, who of his great goodnesse has been graciously pleas'd to conduct us safe thro' the terrors of the great Deep. "They that go down to the "Sea in Ships, and occupy their busi: "ness in great waters; these men see "the works of the Lord, and his won: "ders in the deep. For at his word "the Stormy wind ariseth, which lif: "teth up the waves thereof, they are "carried up to the Heavens & down "again to ye deep, their Soul melteth "away because of the trouble. They "reel to & fro, and are tost up & "down, so that they are at their "wit's end. Then they cry unto y^e "Lord in their trouble, and he deli: "vereth them out of their distresse. "For he maketh the storm to cease "so that the waves thereof are "still: Then they are glad, becau:

Mr. Ingham's Journal of His Voyage to Georgia.

MAY 1, 1796: To my much honoured Mother, my dearly beloved Brethren and Sisters, and all my Christian Friends, Grace, Mercy, and Peace be multiplied from Almighty God the Father, and from our Lord Jesus Christ with the Holy Ghost, to whom be Glory, Honour, and Praise for ever & ever. Amen.

Blessed, for ever blessed be the God and Father of our Lord Jesus Christ, the Father of Mercy and the God of all Consolation, who of his great goodnesse has been graciously pleas'd to conduct us safe thro' the terrors of the great deep. "They that go down to the Sea in Ships, and occupy their business in great waters; these men see the works of the Lord, and his wonders in the deep. For at his word the stormy wind ariseth, which lifteth up the waves thereof, they are carried up to the Heavens & down again to the deep, their Soul melteth away because of the trouble. They reel to & fro, and are tost up & down, so that they are at their wits end. Then they cry unto the Lord in their trouble, and he delivereth them out of their distresse. For he maketh the Storm to cease so that the waves thereof are still: Then they are glad, because they are at rest, and so he bringeth them unto the Haven where they would be. O that Men would therefore praise the Lord for his Goodness, and declare the wonders that he doth for the Children of Men."

I can now inform You that we are all arriv'd in safety & in good Health in Georgea. But because I believe that a Relation of our Voyage will not be unacceptable to You, I shall with God's assistance, set down both the Chief Occurrences thereof, and also the Reasons which mov'd me undertake it. But least you should think of me or my designs, more highly than you ought to think, I do assure You that I am a very grievous & abominable Sinner, proud, sensual, self-will'd: And O! that I was truly sensible and heartily sorry of being so: O that it please Almighty God of his great grace to make me throughly humble & contrite. O that my Sins were done away, that my nature was changed, that I was a new Creature, in Christ Jesus, then perhaps God would make me an Instrument to his Glory. O my dear Friends, I beg of You, I intreat You, I beseech You, pray mightily to God in my Behalf that I be not a Castaway.

About 6 weeks before we took Shipping for Georgea, I receiv'd a letter from the Revd. Mr. John Wesley Fellow of Lincoln College, Oxon; the Substance whereof was as follows — "Fast & pray, and then send me Word whether You dare go with me to the Indians." Having observ'd his directions, about 3 days after the receipt of his, I answer'd him to this effect. "I am satisfied that God's providence has placed me in my present Station; whether he would have me go to the Indians, or not, I am not yet inform'd; I dare not go without being call'd." I kept his letter secret for some days, I was utterly averse from going; I did not in the least intend it; I thought we had Health enough at home: However I continued to pray that God would be pleas'd to direct me, whether he would have me go or not.

About a Fortnight after this, Mr. John Wesley came to London, as also his Brother Charles, and Mr. Salmon, a Gentleman of Brazen-nose College, Oxo. The first time I was with them, I desired to know the reasons which mov'd them to leave England; they answer'd they thought they could be better Christians, alledging several particular advantages which they might reasonably expect would farther their spiritual progress by going among the Indians. Some of their Reasons I approv'd of, to others I objected alleging, that a man may be a Christian in any place, but chiefly insisting upon this, That no one ought to go without being call'd of God. They told me if I required a Voice or a Sign from Heaven, That was not now to be expected; and that a man had no other way of knowing God's will, but by consulting his own reason, his Friends, and observing the order of God's Providence. They therefore thought it a sufficient call to choose that way of life, which they had reason to beleive would most promote their Christian welfare. Our Conversation being ended, they lent me several letters written by Mr. Oglethorpe relating to the Indians, their manner of living, their Customs and their great Expectations of having a white man come amongst them to teach them wisdom. All this mov'd me little, I had no mind to leave England: However I now began to pray more frequently and fervently that God would be pleas'd to direct me to do his will.

Besides the 3 Gentlemen aforesaid, there was also one Mr. Hall, Brother in Law to Mr. Wesley's resolutely determined to go. When they had been in London about 10 days, in which time I frequently conversed with them, I found my Heart so mov'd one night by being with Mr. John Wesley, that almost without thinking it, I said to him, "If neither Mr. Hall nor Mr. Salmon go along with you, I will go." At that time there seem'd no probability that either of them would draw back. They were both of them ordained by the Bishop of London in order to go; Mr. Salmon deacon, Mr. Hall, both deacon and Priest; But lo! Mr. Salmon was immediately seiz'd upon by his Relations in Town, and sent down Poste Haste to his Parents in Cheshire. Upon his arrival his Father left the House furious and distracted, protesting he would not return unless his Son would Stay; his Mother was labouring under a fever. In this distresse he knew not what to do; he promis'd his Parents to Stay, writing Mr. Wesley word he hop'd to follow him next Spring. Tho' since then he was writ to him, telling him, he doth not think himself as yet at liberty to leave Father and Mother. However Mr. Hall still continued Steady. Neither his wife nor mother, nor Brother, nor Uncle, nor all his Friends, either by Prayers, Tears, Threats, or Entreaties, could in the least turn him aside from his purpose.

A few days after this Mr. Wesley began to be more importunate with me, urging me with my Promise, telling me he had now little hope of Mr. Salmon, and as for Mr. Hall, he could not properly be said to go with him; for his design was to go amongst the Indians, whereas Mr. Hall was only to go to Savannah and be Minister there; and as for his Brother Charles he went over only as Secretary to the Trustees for the Colony of Georgea. I still refusing, telling him, "If Mr. Hall went I would not go." Nevertheless I pray'd very earnestly, almost night and day resolving upon it: My Head began now to be more and more affected; it pleas'd God to let me see I might be a better Christian by going with Mr. Wesley. I thought by living with him, and having his Example always before mine Eyes I should be enabled to rise regularly and early, and spend all my time carefully, which are great and necessary points in Christianity, and wherein I grew very deficiant by living in London. Besides these there were three other Reasons which mov'd me; I thought I should not meet with so many temptations to Sensuality and Indulgence among the Indians, as in England. Hereby likewise I see I should be freed from the Slavery of worldly Interest, and the danger and drudgery of hunting for preferment, which hinders so many from being Christians, making them to betray the Church to serve the State, and deny Jesus Christ to please worldly-minded men. The last and chief reason was the Goodness of the work and the great and Glorious promises that are made to those who forsake all for the Sake of the Gospel. Notwithstanding all these reasons I was not yet fully determin'd to go. But what is very remarkable, the Psalms, the Lessons, and all that I read then suggested to me that I should go: So that being at morning Prayers in Westminster Abbey Tuesday Oct. 7, 1735, the 10 Chapter of St. Mark, which was then read, made so strong and vigorous an impression upon me, that at the hearing of these words ("And Jesus answer'd and Said, verily, I say unto You, there is no man that hath left house, or Brethren, or Sisters, or Father, or Mother, or Wife or Children, or Lands for my Sake and the Gospels, but he shall receive an hundred-Fold Now in this time, Houses & Brethren and Sisters, and Mothers and Children, and Lands with Persecutions;

and in the world to come Eternal life.") I determin'd in my Heart that I would go. I may likewise observe here that without any intention or design, I read the same Chapter next day at St. Sepulchre's Church, which did not a little strengthen my resolution.

Tho I was thus determined in my own mind, yet I did not immediately make known my purpose to Mr. Wesley; but told him there were 3 Objections against my going with him at present. The School at Osset was not yet finish'd; my Mother and Mr. Nicolson knew nothing of the matter, whereas I ought to have acquainted them both, & obtained their Consent. To these Mr. Wesley answer'd, he did not doubt but God would provide better for the School in my Absence than if I Stay'd, especially if I recommended it to His Care in my Prayers, which I have constantly done. Mr. Morgan, likewise (a gentleman of Lincoln College, Oxford, who came up to London to take leave of Mr. Wesley's) A Zealous and Sincere Christian, being very earnest with me to go, promis'd himself to make a journey into Yorkshire to see my Mother, and to do what he could towards settling the School. As to having my Mother's Consent, he said, if I thought it was God's will, I must obey my Master, & go wherever I could do him most service, whether my Relations were willing or not. But however I could not go without Mr. Nicolson's knowledge & Consent, because that would be leaving the Parish unprovided, which would be unlawfull: We therefore put the matter upon this Issue, If Mr. Nicolson consented, I might go; if not, then there was a reasonable hindrance against my going at this time.

Mr. Nicolson had been some weeks at his Parish of Matching in Essex, whereof I was curate, he usually came to town on Saturdays; but by a wonderfull providence he was now brought to town on Monday night; his Intent was to have return'd the next day; but he was strangely detain'd by one thing or another till Wednesday. I would gladly have met with him on Tuesday, but could not find him at home; however I writ a letter and order'd it to be given him as soon as he came; next morning he came to my Lodgings at Mr. Sissons, he told me he had receiv'd my letter; which had acquainted him with my designs, he was Sorry to part with me, my warning was Short, my departure Suddain, yet as I was going about a good work, he would not oppose me, provided I could preach the Sunday following, he wou'd give me his Consent. I went to Mr. Oglethorpe to know if I could stay so long, he said I might. I return'd, acquainted Mr. Nicolson, and so parted with him very friendly, he going directly into the Country. After this I made known my designs, and got things in readinesse as fast as I could. My Friends in town endeavour'd to dissuade me, but I did not consult them but God.

On Friday Oct. 10 1735 I made my will, which I sent enclosed in a letter to you at Osset.

SUNDAY OCT. 12: I preach'd at St. Mary Somerset's in the morning, & at St. Sepulchres in the afternoon. Service being ended I took leave of my good old Friend Mrs. Sissons and her Family, who wept much, my cousin Robt. Harrap and some other Friends. Thence I went to Sr. John Philips a very worthy Gentleman & devout Christian, who shew'd me a great deal of Respect, and did me many Favours when I was in London, where having exhorted one another we kneeled down to prayer & so parted. Thence I went with Mr. Morgan to Mr. Hutton's, a good Family in Westminster, where we spent the next day with Mr. Wesley's chiefly in private; but there happen'd such a remarkable Circumstance on it as I can not pass over in Silence. Mr. Hall who had made great preparations for the Voyage, and had now got all things ready for his departure, having this very morning hired a Coach to carry himself & wife down to Gravesend, where the Ship lay, in the very hour, wherein they should have gone, drew back. He came unexpectedly and told Mr. Oglethorpe his Uncle and Mother would get him a living, & therefore he would not go. So he, whom all his Friends could not dissuade before, lost himself, & dropt all his resolutions in the very last moment.

This Strange occurrence which was so much beyond all expectations, was a Strong & fresh demonstration to me, that it was God's will that I should go; Because as I observed, I had said to Mr. Wesley some time ago: "If neither Mr. Hall nor Mr. Salmon go along with you, I will go." And again, "If Mr. Hall goes, I will not go."

TUESDAY OCT. 14: Having now no further doubt but that I was intended by Providence to accompany Mr. John Wesley; on Tuesday, Oct. 14, We, his Brother Mr. Charles, my self and Mr. Delamotte, Son of a Merchant in London, who had a mind to leave the world, & give himself up entirely to God; being accompanied by Mr. Morgan, Mr. Burton one of the Trustees, & Mr. James Hutton, took boat at Westminster for Gravesend. We arrived there about 4 in the afternoon, & immediately went on board the Ship call'd the Simonds. We had two Cabins allotted us in the Fore-Castle, I & Mr. Delamotte having the first, and Mr. Wesley's the other. Theirs was made pretty large, so that we could all meet together to read or pray in it. This part of the Ship was assign'd to us by Mr. Oglethorpe, as being most Convenient for privacy.

Wednesday & Thursday we spent chiefly with Mr. Morgan & Mr. Hutton, exhorting & encouraging one another; we also receiv'd the Lord's Supper with them each day, thereby to encrease our Spiritual Strength and resolution. They were both Sorry to part with us & I believe Mr. Morgan would have been very glad to have gone with us.

FRIDAY OCT. 17: Mr. John Wesley began to learn the German tongue, in order to converse with the Moravians, a good, devout, peaceably & heavenly minded people, who were persecuted by the Papists, and driven from their Native Country upon the account of their Religion; they were graciously receiv'd and protected by Count Zinzendorff of Hernhouth, a very holy man, who sent them over into Georgia, where lands will be given them. There were 26 of them in our Ship, and almost the only time you could know they were in the Ship, was when they were harmoniously singing the praises of their great creatour, which they constantly do in publick twice a day, wherever they are: Their example was very edifying. They are more like the primitive Christians than any other Church now in the world: for they retain both the Faith, practice & Discipline deliver'd by the Apostles. They have regularly ordain'd Bishops, Priests & deacons; Baptism, Confirmation, & the Eucharist are duly administred; discipline is strictly exercised without respect of person, they all submit themselves to their Pastors, being guided by them in every thing. They live together in perfect love and peace, having for the present all things in common: they are more ready to serve their neighbour than themselves; In their businesse they are diligent and industrious in all their dealings strictly just and conscientious; in every thing they behave themselves with great meekness, Sweetness and Humility.

SATURDAY OCT. 18: This morning Mr. John Westley and I began to read the Old Testament, which we finish'd during our Voyage; Mr. Wesley likewise baptized a Man of 30, who before had only receiv'd Lay Baptism; I was witness.

SUNDAY OCT. 19: Mr. John Wesley began to preach without Notes, expounding a Portion of Scripture extempore, according to the Antient Usage. During our Passage, he went over our Saviour's Sermon on the Mount: he also constantly explain'd the second Lesson, except when he Catechiz'd the Children; whereby all that heard with sincere hearts were much edified. To day being the first time we celebrated the Lord's Supper publickly (which we did constantly every Lord's day afterwards) we had but 3 Communicants besides our selves; a small number; yet God has been graciously pleas'd to add unto them. All Love, all Glory be to thee O Lord.

MONDAY OCT. 20: I began to teach & Catechize the Children on Board our Ship, being in number about 12. I likewise help'd two or three of the Moravians to learn English. This I continued to do several weeks, till we came out to Sea, and then I could do it but seldome by reason of the Rolling of the Ship. O that we were all like little Children, willing to be instructed & guided by our Heavenly Father. O that we were truly Sensible of our own Ignorance and how very little the wisest of us knows that is worth knowing. "It is God that teacheth man knowledge."

TUESDAY OCT. 21: We left Gravesend & went down the River tho' very slowly, the wind not being favourable to us. We now began to be more in earnest: we resolv'd to rise early & spend our time regularly and carefully. The first hour we allotted to prayer for ourselves & absent friends; the next we read the Scriptures; and from 6 to Breakfast we generally read some thing relating to the primitive Church. At 8 we had publick prayers; the Forenoon I spent either in teaching or instructing the Children, or reading antiquity. Mr. John Wesley in learning German; Mr. Charles Westley in writing; Mr. Delamotte in learning Greek or Navigation. At 12 we all met together to joyn in prayer, & to exhort one another, consulting both how to profit our Neighbours & our Selves. After dinner I taught the Children, or conversed religiously with some of the Passengers as also Mr. Wesley constantly did. At 4 we had publick prayer; from 5 to 6 we spent in private, then we supped. At 7 I read to as many of the Passengers as were willing to hear, and instructed them in Christianity. Mr. John Wesley joyn'd with the Moravians in their publick devotion. At 8 we all met together again to give an Account of what we had done, whom we had conversed with, deliberating upon the best method of proceeding with such and such persons; what advice, direction, Exhortation, or Reproof was necessary for them; & some times we read a little, concluding with prayer, and so went to Bed about 9, sleeping soundly upon Matts, and Blankets, regarding neither the noise of the Sea, nor the Sailors. "The Angels of the Lord are round about them that fear him."

MONDAY OCT. 27: We Sail'd from Margaret Road to the downs. A Gentleman Passenger strongly opposed our having prayers in the great Cabin; and indeed he half carried his point, so that we were forced to submit to the Inconvenience of having them between decks in the afternoons, till it pleas'd God to remove him out of the Ship.

SUNDAY, NOV. 2: We past the Fleet at Spithead, and came into Cows-Road off the Isle of Wight, where we lay till the 10 of December. During our Stay here, we had an excellent opportunity of promoting the work of God among our fellow Passengers. We met with both opposition and success, passing thro' evil report and good report. May it please the Almighty to give us all an abundant measure of his grace, zealously to preserve in his Service to the end of our days. Every Christian must be perfected thro' Sufferings either inward or outward, for even the Captain of our Salvation was made perfect thro' sufferings, and we are to be like him.

Mr. Charles Wesley being known to the Minister of Cows, preached several times in the Island, and also read at a poor woman's house to a good number of the people there assembled. Before he came away, he left a few Books among them; The poor people were very glad, express'd much thankfulnesse, & I believe were not a little edified by his admonition and Exhortation.

MONDAY NOV. 3: We took a walk into the Isle, where we agreed upon the following resolutions.

In the name of God, Amen. We whose names are underwritten being fully convinced that it is impossible either to promote the work of God among the Heathen without an entire union amongst our Selves, or that such an Union should subsist, unlesse each one will give up his single Judgement to that of the Majority, do agree by the help of God—

1. That none of us will undertake any thing of Importance, without first proposing it to the other three.

2. That wherever our Judgements or inclinations differ, any one shall give up his Single judgement or Inclination to the others.

3. That in case of an equality after begging God's direction, the matter shall be decided by Lot.

J.W. C.W. B.I. C.D.

The wind was now fair, but the Man of War which was to convoy us over was not yet ready. The Passengers grew impatient of delay; but our Heavenly Father intended it for our Good. "Known unto God are all his works from everlasting: Unsearchable are thy ways, O Lord, God of Hosts: Blessed art thou for ever."

SATURDAY, NOV. 8: I went upon quarter deck after dinner to teach the Children; but because some gentlemen were there who laugh'd at me for it, I was asham'd to proceed. O! what a dreadful Thing is the fear of Men! how doth it stagger our Stoutest Courage! O how deceitfull is my Heart! If thou, O lord, shouldst withdraw thy grace from me but one day I should utterly renounce thee, and commit the most enormous Crimes.

SUNDAY NOV. 16: Mr. John Wesley baptized Thomas Hird and Grace his wife, Mark his Son, & Phebe his daughter, both adults, having prepared them for it, by private instruction. To this I was a Witness; they were brought up Quakers, but are now Serious people and constant Communicants. Prais'd be the Lord who hath turned their hearts from Error, and put them in the right way.

THURSDAY NOV. 20: The Man of War being come we left Cows End got down to Yarmouth, where they cast anchor: but next morning the wind being contrary, we were forced back again into Cow's Road. During this our latter stay here, there were several Storms, in one of which two Ships that ventured out, were stranded upon the Island; notwithstanding this several of my people murmered at our delay. If God would deal with us according to our deservings, we should be consumed in a moment.

SUNDAY NOV. 23: We had besides our selves 8 Communicants; The Tuesday following I got a Boy well whip't, by Mr. Oglethorpe's orders, for Swearing & Blasphemy. Private admonition had no effect upon him, so that I was forced to have recource to publick Correction.

SUNDAY NOV. 30: I preach'd on board the other Ship, and read prayers, which I did several times while we lay at Cows. We now again had prayers in the great Cabin, the gentleman aforemention'd having yesterday left the Ship. Blessed be God who delivered us from him, for he very much oppos'd us. I did think, and I told it my friends, that we could not Sail while he was in the Ship. This perhaps might be one reason why we were kept from Sailing so long.

MONDAY DEC. 1, 1735: We agreed on the following resolution: "If any one upon being reproved, or upon any other Occasion Shall feel any Sort or degree of Anger or Resentment, he Shall immediately, or at the next meeting, frankly and fully confesse it."

The second Mate a very insolent and ill natur'd fellow, who had abus'd many of the Passengers, and also Mr. Wesley, at last affronted even Mr. Oglethorpe to his face. The next day he was Sent aboard the Man of War; The people rejoyced at this, and praised be God who delivered them from his power. "The fierceness of man Shall turn to thy Praise, & the fierceness of them shallt thou restrain." This I think was another reason why we were kept still at Cows.

SUNDAY DEC. 7: We were 15 Communicants; This Evening we resolved to leave off eating suppers, till we found some inconvenience from it, which none of us did to the end of the Voyage. Since our Settling in America Mr. Wesley and Mr. Delamotte have resum'd them. As yet it agrees perfectly well with my health, and I still continue it.

MONDAY DEC. 8: A Young Man very providentially was taken into our Ship; I perceiving that he was a Stranger, began to converse with him; He gave me an Account of himself, and the reason of his Coming. He had left his Parents he said, who were rich (tho he was their only Son) because they would not let him Serve God as he had a mind. He us'd to spend good part of the Night in prayer, not having opportunity to do it by day. When he left home he did not know where he should go, having no Cloaths with him; but he did not seek for money or worldly enjoyments, he desired only to save his Soul. When he was travelling he pray'd that he might go to some place where he could have the advantage of publick prayers, and the holy Sacrament. Several times he had had thoughts of turning Hermit, but Providence had brought him to us, and he was glad to meet with Ministers with whom he could freely converse about spiritual things: And indeed I was glad to meet with him: this I think was another reason of our delay: all Love, all Glory be to thee, O Lord.

WEDNESDAY DEC. 10, 1735: Now at length it pleas'd our Heavenly Father to Send us a fair wind; we left Cows about 9 in the Morning. Two Gentlemen, Passengers of the other Ship, were left behind, having the night before gone to Portsmouth; we waited for them near two hours, but they not coming, we made the best of our way, running between 7 & 8 miles an hour.

Friday in the afternoon we left the Man of War, he not being able to sail as fast as our Ships. Most of the Passengers were now Sick; I was so for about half an hour, Mr. John Wesley scarce at all.

FRIDAY DEC. 19: Mr. Wesley & I, with Mr. Oglethorpe's approbation, undertook to visit each of us a part of the Ship, and daily to provide the Sick people with Water, Grace and such other things as were necessary for them. At first we met with some difficulties, but God enabled us to persevere in the constant performance the rest to the end of our Voyage. Mr. Oglethorpe likewise himself went several times about the Ship, to comfort and encourage the people, and indeed he has never been wanting in this respect: He is a pattern of fatherly Care and tender compassion, being always ready night or day to give up his own ease or Conveniencys to serve the poorest Body among the people. He seldom eat above once a day, and then he usually chose Salt provisions, tho' not so agreeable to his health, that he might give the fresh to the sick; But more will appear from the following instance.

One Mrs. Welsh, who was believed to be at the point of death, being big with Child, in a high fever, attended with a violent Cough, was by Mr. Oglethorpe's Order, remov'd into his own Cabin, which was the best in the Ship, he himself lying several nights in a Hammock, till another Cabin was got ready for him; He also constantly supplied her with all the best things in the Ship. Some of the Gentlemen seem'd disgusted at this; but that only made him the more resolute. Yet notwithstanding all possible Care was taken of her, human means failed. The doctor gave her up, every Body thought she would die. Mr. Oglethorpe only continued in hope; nay he said he was sure God would raise her up to manifest his power in her. She had a desire to receive the Lord's supper before she died; and lo! from the moment she receiv'd, she began to recover, & is now safely deliver'd of a daughter, and in perfect Health. "Gracious is the Lord, and merciful, Long suffering and of great goodness; the Lord is loving unto every man, and his Mercy is over all his works."

SUNDAY DEC. 21: We were 21 Communicants: This, as well as yesterday, was an exceeding calm & pleasant day. The Sky appear'd to me mor beautiful than ever I had observ'd it in England. We were likewise got to far to the Southward, that the weather was as warm now as it is there in the Spring. This being Mr. Oglethorpe's Birthday, he gave a Sheep and wine to the people, which with the smoothness of the Sea, and the Serenity of the Skie, so enliven'd them, that they perfectly recover'd from their Sea Sickness. On Christmas day also Mr. Oglethorpe gave a Hog and wine to the people.

MONDAY DEC. 29: We are now past the Latitude of 25 degrees and are got into what they call the Trade winds, which blow much the same way all the Year round. The Air is balmy, soft and sweet. The Ship glides smoothly & quickly along; the Clouds are finely variegated with numbers of pretty colours. The nights are mild and pleasant, being beautifully adorned with the shining Host of Stars. "The Heavens declare the Glory of God, and the firmament sheweth his handy work. One day telleth another, & one Night certifieth another."

SUNDAY JAN: 4, 1735/6: A Gentleman was very angry with me for accusing his Servant of swearing before Mr. Oglethorpe. The next day Mr. John Wesley began to Catechise the Children publickly after the second Lesson, Evening Service, which he continued to do every day for about 3 weeks.

MONDAY JAN. 12: I began to write out the English dictionary, in order to learn the Indian tongue. O! Who is sufficient for these things! When the Ship roll'd so that we could not well go about to visit the people, we generally spent the evenings in Conversation with Mr. Oglethorpe from whom we learn't many particulars concerning the Indians.

SATURDAY JAN. 17: The wind was very Strong; about half an hour after 10 at night, we encountered such a wave, as we did not meet with in all our passage besides: it shook the whole frame of the Ship from Stem to Stern; The water sprung thro' the Sides of the Ship which before were tight, and was also toss'd above the main Yard; falling down it cover'd the decks, broke into the great Cabin, fill'd Mrs. Welshe's Bed; Mr. Oglethorpe was gone to Bed, but he got up and resign'd his own dry Cabin to the Sick, betaking himself once more to his Hammock. Hitherto we had had a very fine passage, but now approaching near Land, we met with contrary winds, which kept us above a Fortnight longer at Sea than otherwise we should have been.

TUESDAY JAN. 20: I baptized a Child which was thought to be at the point of death, nay some thought it was dead; but from the moment it was baptized it began to recover.

WEDNESDAY JAN. 21: This Evening Mr. Oglethorpe call'd together the Heads of families, as he did also at some other times, and gave them several excellent and usefull instructions relating to their living in Georgea, exhorting them likewise to love God, and one another.

SUNDAY JAN. 25: We were 20 Communicants. Towards Evening we had a terrible Storm, which lasted several hours. I observ'd it well, and truly I never Saw any thing hitherto so solemn and majestick. The Sea Sparkled and Smoak'd as if it had been on fire; the Air darted forth Lightening, and the wind blew so fierce that You could scarce look it in the face and draw your Breath. The waves did not swell so high as at some other times being press'd on by the impetuosity of the Blast; neither did the Ship roll much, but it quiver'd, jarr'd & Shak'd. About half an hour after 7, a great Sea broke in upon us, which split the main Sail, carried away the Companion, fill'd between decks, and rush'd into the great Cabin. This made most of the people tremble, and I believe they would have been then glad to have been Christians, how light soever they made of Religion before. I myself was made Sensible that nothing will enable us to smile in the face of death, but a life of extraordinary holiness. I was under some fear for a little while, but I recollected my self again by reflecting that every thing came by the will of God, and that whatever he willed was the best for me. If therefore he was pleas'd to take me off at this very time, so much the better, I should be deliver'd from many Evils, & prevented from committing many Sins to come. Betwixt 4 & 12 I recommended my self to God and went to bed, resting satisfied with whatever should befall me. Towards 3 the wind abated; In the morning we returned publick thanks for our deliverance, and before night most of the people had forgot they were ever in a Storm. "If they hear not Moses and the Prophets, neither will they be persuaded tho' one rose from the dead."

WEDNESDAY JAN. 28: Being a calm day I went on board the other Ship, read prayers and visited the People. At my return I acquainted Mr. Oglethorpe with their State, and he sent them such things as they wanted.

SUNDAY FEB. 1, 1735/6: Three Sail appearing we made up toward them, and got what letters we could write, in hopes some of them might be bound for England. I writ a short one to You at Osset. One of them that was bound for London made towards us, & we put our Letters on Board her. On Tuesday we found Ground; on Wednesday we Saw Land, & on Thursday afternoon Feb. 5, we got safe into the Tybe Road in the mouth of the River Savannah in the Province of Georgea in America. Mr. Wesley, Mr. Delamotte and I, had some discourse about our manner of going in this new Country. I was strick with a deep religious awe, considering the greatness and Importance of the work I came upon; but was comforted with these words in the Psalms. "O Tarry thou the Lord's leisure, be strong and he shall comfort thy heart, and put thou thy trust in the Lord." From the whole Service I was mov'd to think that the Gospel would be propagated over the whole world: May God of his great Mercy be pleas'd to grant it.

FRIDAY FEB. 6: We went on Shore and had prayers, where we were comforted by the second lesson. Next day I receiv'd a letter from my Brother William, one from my Sister Hannah, & another from Mr. H. Washington, whereby I was very much affected. I call'd to mind several things past, reflected upon the sweet happinesse of true friendship, and pray'd earnestly for my dear Friends in England with tears.

SATURDAY FEB. 14: This Morning as well as yesterday we met with several remarkable passages in our Course of reading in the Prophets relating to the propagation of the Gospel, which not a little comforted & encouraged us; I was also Strongly affected by the second lesson, Mark 13.

A little in the afternoon, some Indians came to make us a Visit, we put on our gowns and Cassocks, spent some time in prayer, and then went into the great Cabin to receive them. At our Entrance they all rose up, & both Men and Women shak'd hands with us. When we were all seated, Tomo Chachee their king, spoke to us to this effect, (his Interpreter was one Mrs. Musgrove who lives about 5 Miles above Savannah, she is descended of a white man by an Indian woman. She understands both languages, being educated amongst the English, she can read and write, and is a Sensible well civiliz'd woman. She is likewise to teach us the Indian tongue.)

Ye are welcome. I am glad to see you here. I have a desire to hear the *great word*: for I am ignorant. When I was in England I desired that some might speek the *Great Word* to me, our nation was then Willing to hear: Since that time we have been in trouble, the French on one Hand, and the Spaniards on the other, and the Traders that are amongst us have caus'd great Confusion, and have set our people against hearing the great word, their tongues are useless; Some say one thing and some another. But I am glad Ye are come; I will assemble the great men of our Nation, and I hope by degrees to compose our differences, for without their Consent I can not hear the *great word*. However in the mean time, I shall be glad to see You at my town, and I would have You teach our Children, but we would not have them made Christians as the Spaniards make Christians, for they baptize without Instruction; but we would hear & be well instructed first; and then be Baptized when we understand.

All this he Spake with great earnestness and with much action both of his head and hands.

Mr. John Wesley made a Short answer, "God only can teach You Wisdom, & if You be sincere, perhaps he will do it by us." We then shak'd Hands with them, and so withdrew.

The Queen made us a present of a Jar of Milk, and another of Honey: "that we might feed them," she said, "with Milk, for they were but Children, and that we might be sweet to them."

About 3 next day in the afternoon, just before they went away, we put on our Surplices, at Mr. Oglethorpe's desire, and went to take leave of them.

MONDAY FEB. 16: About 7 this Evening, I set forward with Mr. Oglethorpe, and some others in a ten oar'd Boat for the Alatamaha, the Southermost part of Georgea. At 11 we arriv'd at a place call'd Skiddowa, where we went ashore into the woods, and kindled a Fire under a lofty Pine tree. Having writ some Letters and eaten something, we laid down to sleep upon the cold Ground, without either Bed or board, having no other Covering besides our Cloths, but a Single Blanket each and the Canopy of Heaven. About 8 next day we set forward again, passing several marshes beset on both sides with Trees of various Sorts, whose leaves being guilded with the glorious Rays of the Sun, yielded a beautiful prospect. About 12 the wind blew so high that we were driven upon an Oyster Bank, where we could not get a stick to make a Fire; here we dined very Comfortably. Near 2 we set forward again and with great difficulty cross'd over the Mouth of the River Ogeechee. The wind was exceeding high & the water very rough; almost every wave drove over the Side of the Boat, so that every moment we were in Jeopardy of our lives: And truly if Mr. Oglethorpe had not rouz'd up himself and struck life into the Rowers, I do not know but most of us might have here made our Exit. Towards 6 we got to a little place call'd Bear's Island, where we encamp'd all night round a roaring fire in a Bed of Canes where the wind could not reach us. Here also we came up with a large Boat, call'd a Pettiaugur, loaded with people for the Alatamaha, who had set out before us.

Next morning after prayers, Mr. Oglethorpe considering that our own Boat was overloaded, and also that I might probably be of some Service to the People, ask'd me if I was willing to go on Board the Pettiaugur, whereto I readily consented. Here during the remainder of our Passage I read to the people and instructed them as I had opportunity. This Evening we lay upon St. Catherines, a very pleasant Island where we met with 2 Indians a hunting. I took one of them on Board the Pettiaugur and gave him some Bisket & wine, and he in return sent us the greatest part of a deer.

SUNDAY MORNING FEB. 22: We arriv'd at the Island of St. Simons upon the River Alatamaha, a pleasant & fertile place, which Mr. Oglethorpe had reach'd the Thursday night before. Several of the people were firing Guns, but upon my Landing, I ask'd Mr. Oglethorpe if Sunday was a proper day for Shooting. We immediately put a Stop to it. Having breakfasted, we joyn'd in the Litany, and then he return'd to Savannah, having already put the people into a method of proceeding.

Next day in the Forenoon we were alarm'd by a Sail appearing in the River. We call'd all the people together, and after consultation, we threw up a Trench strengthening it with Barrels of Beef and Pork, which we had here in abundance, we also sent a Canoo down the River, and several men into the woods for Scouts, to bring us Intelligence: in the mean time we got all our Arms in readinesse providing for the worst. About half an hour past 12 the Canoo return'd, and brought us word, that it was the Sloop which brought the Provisions, that had turn'd back to take in Ballast.

Two or three of the first days the People spent in building Palmetto Bowers; we enclosed a little round place with Myrtle Bags, and Laurel, in the midst whereof we nightly kept a great fire, round which I lay several weeks in the open air, my whole Bed consisting of two Blankets, and never had I health better in my life. Now we had short prayer early in the morning before they began, & at night after they had done working. My chief Businesse was daily to visit the People, to take care of those that were sick and to Supply them with the best things we had: for a few days at the first I had every

Body's good word; but when they found that I watch'd narrowly over them and reprov'd them sharply for their faults, immediately the Scene changed; instead of blessing came cussing, and my Love and Kindnesse was repay'd with Hatred and ill will.

SUNDAY FEB. 29: After morning Prayers which we had pretty early, I told the people that it was the Lord's day, and therefore ought to be Spent in his Service, that they ought not to go ashouting or walking up & down the woods and that I would take notice of all those that did. One man answer'd that these were new laws in America; this man, as well as Several others went out, but he, I think, was two days before he could find his way back again. I reprov'd most of them afterwards privately in a friendly manner, laying before them the Heinousness of the Sin, and the dreadfull consequences that would necessarily follow. One or two took my advice well, but the rest were harden'd, & instead of reforming, rais'd heavy complaints and accusations against me to the Gentleman that was left chief in Commission, that I had made a black List, and that I intended to ruin them. This caus'd a very sharp contest between that Gentleman & me, wherein God enabled me boldly & couragiously to vindicate the Honour of his day and worship, without regarding the favour or displeasure of any man. So soon as I was retired, I pray'd earnestly from my heart, that God would forgive him, and also give him a new mind; which prayer God heard, (Blessed be his Goodnesse,) for since I came away, he frankly confess'd that he was in the wrong, that his Passions carried him to too great a height, that I was certainly in the right, & had only done what was my duty.

I mentioned this to show the great use of praying for our Enemies. Who knows how much such prayers will avail before God? Certainly it purifies our own heart, and is the only sure remedy to keep out hatred, malice and Revenge.

TUESDAY MARCH 2d: This morning I pray'd that God would be pleas'd to send home the lost man, and also make him sensible of his Sin. About breakfast time he came, looking very ghastly, sadly affrighted, telling me he was resolved never more to prophane the

Sabbaoth. God grant he may keep his word: This Example would not make others take Warning: next Sunday 3 more went a Shooting, who were all lost till next day. Nothing but the Almighty grace of God is sufficient to turn one Sinner from the Error of his ways.

MONDAY MARCH 8: Mr. Oglethorpe arrived with 4 Pettiaugurs, and next day my dear friend Mr. Charles Wesley with another, wherein were all the married men, women and Children, that came over in our two Ships. Mr. Oglethorpe immediately lay'd out the new town Frederica in a neat and regular method, and kept the people to strict work in building themselves Palmetto Houses; during the 3 weeks longer which I spent here, there happen'd such variety of Incidents that it would be too tedious to relate them. Only I will add that Mr. Charles Wesley and I had the happiness of undergoing for the Truth's Sake the most glorious trial of our whole lives, wherein God enabled us exceedingly to rejoyce, and also to behave ourselves throughout with undaunted Courage and Constancy, for which may we ever love and adore him. NB. The Book of God was our Support, wherein as our necessities required, we always met with direction, Exhortation, and Comfort. "Thy Word is a Lanthorn to my feet, and a light unto my Paths." "In God's Word Will I comfort me."

SUNDAY MARCH 28, 1736: About 7 in the Evening, I left Frederica, and took Boat for Savannah; we had a fair wind, & if we had not run twice a ground, I believe we should have got thither in 24 hours. Towards 4 on Tuesday morning it began to Thunder and Lighten, and rain in the most dreadfull manner I ever beheld since I was born; Ours was a little open Boat without any Cover: The rest of the people wrapt themselves up head and ears in Blankets and Sails, whatever they could get, and laid down in the bottom of it: I pluck'd up a good heart, threw my Cloak over me, and stood up as Still as I could in the midst of it, that I might behold the Majesty of God in Thunder. And duely so glorious a Scene I never saw. I dare not attempt to describe. However I pass'd the time very comfortably in praising God, and whereas the rest were all well wet, I was pure and dry all over, except my Cloak & Shoes.

Betwixt 7 & 8 we arriv'd at Savannah, where I was kindly receiv'd by Mr. John Wesley & Mr. Delamotte; the latter had begun to teach a few little orphans and the Former had brought the people to short prayer morning and night. I now again entred upon a manner of life more acceptable to me than what I had spent at Frederica, having both time & convenience for regular retirement.

SUNDAY APRIL 4: This afternoon Mr. Wesley and Mr. Delamotte took Boat for Frederica: in their absence I took care both of the Church and School.

MONDAY APRIL 5: After Evening Prayers I began to catechise at our own House all Young persons that were willing to come as well Children, as Servants, and Apprentices, who could not come in the day time. I have continued to do this every night since. On Sundays I do it after dinner & also publickly in the Church after second lesson.

SUNDAY APRIL 11: After Evening Service I made a visit to a few people who had formed themselves into a sort of a Society meeting together Wednesday, Friday and Sunday nights. I found their design was good; they read, prayed, & sung Psalms together: accordingly I exhorted them to go on, promising myself to meet with them sometimes, and to give them such helps and directions as I could. I have joyn'd them every Sunday since, and I hope it will be a means of some good. God grant it.

WEDNESDAY APRIL 14: I baptiz'd a Child by wine Immersion, being the first I ever did that good old way.

SUNDAY APRIL 18: This afternoon there was an allarm made in time of divine Service, whereupon several people went out of Church. The Cause of it was a Young lad that had run away from his Master. He had broken into our House, under which he said he had lain a Fortnight, and Stole provisions when I was at prayers. He had taken down a Pistol, and loaded it with a design I suppose to shoot in the Woods, for he had got the powder flask; and as he was getting out of the window, somehow he Slipt and fired off the Pistoll, which broke his arm to Shivers. He then call'd out aloud for help; whereupon some people that heard, went to see what was the matter. He begg'd of them to drag him out of the window, which they did, and found him in a bad Condition; they carried him to a Surgeon who cut off his Arm. In the night not having due attendance, he loosed it, whereby he lost so much blood that he died the next morning. I was very sorry for the unfortunate wretch, for he came to be catechiz'd the night before he ran away, and I being inform'd that he had done so several times before, talk'd to him a good while to behave himself well, and to obey his Master. But not having Grace, he did the very reverse to what I exhorted him. A sad Example, whereby others ought to take warning.

This being the great and Holy week, I dedicated to devotion, observing the discipline of the primitive Church. On Tuesday Evening Mr. John Wesley & Mr. Delamotte arrived from Frederica. Next day Mr. Wesley gave me an account of what had pass'd there since my departure. O what Secrets will come to light in the last day!

EASTER SUNDAY APRIL 25, 1736: We were 34 Communicants. Our Constant number is about a dozen. Next day Mr. Wesley and I went up to Cowpen in a Boat, bought for our Use, to converse with Mrs. Musgrove about learning the Indian Language. I agreed to teach her Children to read, and to make her whatever recompence she designed more for her trouble. I am to spend three or four days a week with her, and the rest at Savannah in communicating what I learn to Mr. Wesley; because he intends as Yet wholly to reside there. The Moravians being inform'd of our design, desired me to teach one of the Brethren along with Mr. Wesley; to this I consented at once with my whole heart; And who think Ye is the Person intended to learn? Their lawfull Bishop. O! how am I surprized! How do I rejoyce at this! The right hand of the Lord hath the Preeminence, the right hand of the Lord bringeth mighty things to pass.

FRIDAY APRIL 30: Mr. Wesley and I went up again to Cowpen: taking along with us Tomo Chachee and his Queen. Their town is about 4 miles above Savannah in the way to Mrs. Musgrove's. We told them we were about to learn their language. I ask'd them if they were willing that I should teach the Young Prince: they consented, desiring me to check & keep him in, but not to Strike him. The Indians never Strike their Children, neither will they suffer any one to do it. I told them I would do my best as far as gentleness and good advice would go. How I shall manage God alone can direct me. The Youth is sadly corrupted, and excessively addicted to drunkennesse, which he has learn't of our Christian Heathen. Nay the whole Creek Nation is now generally given to this Brutal sin, whereto they were utter Strangers before Christians came among them. O! what a work have we before us! Who is sufficient for these things? I am nothing. I have nothing. I can do nothing. O my dearest Friends pray for us, pray earnestly for us, and more especially for me Your very weak, tho

Most dutiful Son &
affectionate Brother
Benjamin Ingham

Savannah
May 1, 1736.

An Extract of the
Rev. Mr. John Wesley's Journal

AN

EXTRACT

OF THE

Rev. Mr. JOHN WESLEY'S

JOURNAL

From his Embarking for GEORGIA

To his Return to LONDON.

What ſhall we ſay then?——That Iſrael *which follow'd after the Law of Righteouſneſs, hath not attained to the Law of Righteouſneſs.—— Wherefore? Becauſe they ſought it not by Faith, but as it were by the Works of the Law.* Rom. ix. 30, 31.

BRISTOL:

Printed by S. and F. FARLEY.

And ſold at their Printing-Office in *Caſtle-Green*; at the New School-Houſe in the Horſe-Fair; and by the Bookſellers in Town and Country.

JOURNAL

From *Oct.* 14. 1735, to *Feb.* 1. 1738.

UESDAY, *Oct.* 14. 1735. Mr. *Benjamin Ingham*, of Queen's College, *Oxford*, Mr. *Charles Delamotte*, Son of a Merchant in *London*, who had offered himself some Days before, my Brother *Charles Wesley*, and myself, took Boat for *Gravesend*, in order to imbark for *Georgia*. Our End in leaving our Native Country, was not to avoid Want (God having given us Plenty of Temporal Blessings) nor to gain the Dung or Dross of Riches or Honour: But singly this, To save our Souls, To live wholly to the Glory of God. In the Afternoon we found the *Simmonds* off *Gravesend*, and immediately went on board.

Wednesday and *Thursday* we spent with one or two of our Friends; partly on board and partly on Shore, in exhorting one another, to *shake off every Weight, and to run with Patience the Race set before us.*

Friday 17. I began to learn *German*, in order to converse with the *Moravians*, Six and Twenty of whom we had on board. On *Sunday*, the Weather being fair and calm, we had the Morning Service on Quarter Deck. I now first preach'd *ex tempore*, and then administer'd the Lord's Supper to six or seven Communicants. A little Flock. May God increase it!

Monday 20. Believing the denying our selves even in the smallest Instances, might, by the Blessing of God, be helpful to us, we wholly left off the Use of Flesh and Wine, and confined our selves to Vegetable Food, chiefly Rice and Bisket. In the Afternoon *David Nitchman*, Bishop of the *Moravians*, and two others began to learn *English*. O may we be, not only of one Tongue, but of one Mind and of one Heart!

Tuesday 21. We sail'd from *Gravesend*. When we were past about half the *Goodwin Sands*, the Wind suddenly fail'd. Had the Calm continued till Ebb, the Ship had probably been lost. But the Gale sprung up again in an Hour, and carried us into the *Downs*.

We now began to be a little Regular. Our Common Way of living was this. From Four in the Morning till Five, each of us used Private Prayer. From Five to Seven we read the Bible together, carefully comparing it (that we might not lean to our own Understandings) with the Writings of the Earliest Ages. At Seven we breakfasted. At Eight were the Publick Prayers. From Nine to Twelve I usually learn'd *German*, and Mr. *Delamotte*, *Greek*. My Brother writ Sermons, and Mr. *Ingham* instructed the Children. At Twelve we met, to give an Account to one another, what we had done since our last Meeting, and what we designed to do before our next. About One we dined. The Time from Dinner to Four, we spent in reading to those of whom each of us had taken Charge, or in speaking to them severally, as Need required. At four were the Evening Prayers; when either the Second Lesson was explained, (as it always was in the Morning) or the Children were catechised, and instructed before the Congregation. From Five to Six we again used Private Prayer. From Six to Seven I read in our Cabin to two or three of the Passengers (of whom there were about Eighty *English* on board), and each of my Brethren to a few more in theirs. At Seven I joined with the *Germans* in their Publick Service; while Mr. *Ingham* was reading between the Decks, to as many as desir'd to hear. At eight we met again, to exhort and instruct one another. Between Nine and Ten we went to Bed, where neither the roaring of the Sea, nor the Motion of the Ship, could take away the refreshing Sleep which God gave us.

Friday 24. Having a rolling Sea, most of the Passengers found the Effects of it. Mr. *Delamotte* was exceeding sick, for several Days: Mr. *Ingham* for about half an Hour. My Brother's Head ached much. Hitherto it has pleased God, the Sea has not disorder'd me at all; nor have I been hinder'd one Quarter of an Hour from reading, writing, composing, or doing any Business I cou'd have done on Shore.

During our Stay in the *Downs*, some or other of us went, as often as we had Opportunity, on board the Ship that sail'd in Company with us, where also many were glad to join in Prayer and hearing the Word.

Friday Oct. 31. We sailed out of the *Downs*. At Eleven at Night I was waked by a great Noise. I soon found, there was no Danger. But the bare Apprehension of it, gave me a lively Conviction, what manner of Men those ought to be, who are every Moment on the Brink of Eternity.

Sat. Nov. 1. We came to St. *Helen*'s Harbour, and the next Day into *Cow*'s Road. The Wind was fair, but we waited for the Man of War, which was to sail with us. This was a happy Opportunity of instructing our Fellow-Travellers. May he whose Seed we sow, give it the Increase!

Sund. 16. *Thomas Hird*, and *Grace* his Wife, with their Children, *Mark*, aged 21, and *Phebe*, about 17, late Quakers, were, at their often-repeated Desire, and after careful Instruction, admitted to Baptism.

Thu. 20. We fell down into *Yarmouth* Road; but the next Day were forced back to *Cows*. During our Stay here, there were several Storms: In one of which two Ships in *Yarmouth* Road were lost.

The Continuance of the contrary Winds gave my Brother an Opportunity, of complying with the Desire of the Minister of *Cows*, and preaching there three or four Times. The poor People flock'd together in great Numbers. We distributed a few little Books among the more serious of them, which they receiv'd with all possible Expressions of Thankfulness.

Fr. 21. One recovering from a dangerous Illness, desired to be instructed in the Nature of the Lord's Supper. I thought it concern'd her to be first instructed, in the Nature of Christianity: And accordingly fixt an Hour a Day to read with her in Mr. *Law*'s Treatise on Christian Perfection.

Sun. 23. At Night I was waked by the tossing of the Ship and roaring of the Wind, and plainly shew'd I was unfit, for I was unwilling to die.

Tu. Dec. 2. I had much Satisfaction in conversing with one that was very ill and very serious. But in a few Days she recovered from her Sickness and from her Seriousness together.

Sund. 7. Finding Nature did not require so frequent Supplies as we had been accustom'd to, we agreed to leave off Suppers; from doing which we have hitherto found no Inconvenience.

Wed. Dec. 10. We sail'd from *Cows*, and in the Afternoon past the *Needles*. Here the ragged Rocks, with the Waves dashing and foaming at the Foot of them, and the white Side of the Island rising to such a Height, perpendicular from the Beach, gave a strong Idea of *Him that spanneth the Heavens, and holdeth the Waters in the Hollow of his Hand!*

To Day I spoke closely on the Head of Religion, to one I had talked with once or twice before. Afterwards she said, with many Tears, "My Mother died when I was but Ten Years old. Some of her last Words, were, 'Child, fear GOD; and though you lose me, you shall never want a Friend.' I have now found a Friend, when I most wanted, and least expected one."

From this Day to the 14th, being in the Bay of *Biscay*, the Sea was very rough. Mr. *Delamotte* and many others were more sick than ever: Mr. *Ingham* a little; I not at all. But the 14th being a calm Day, most of the Sick were cured at once.

Th. 18. One who was big with Child, in a high Fever, and almost wasted away with a violent Cough, desired to receive the Holy Communion before she died. At the Hour of her receiving, she began to recover, and in a few Days was entirely out of Danger.

Sund. 21. We had Fifteen Communicants, which was our usual Number on *Sundays*: On *Christmas Day* we had Nineteen; but on *Newyear's Day*, Fifteen only.

Th. Jan. 15. 1736. Complaint being made to Mr. *Oglethorpe*, of the unequal Distribution of the Water among the Passengers, he appointed new Officers to take Charge of it. At this the old ones and their Friends were highly exasperated against us, to whom they imputed the Change. But *the Fierceness of Man shall turn to thy Praise.*

Sat. Jan. 17. Many People were very impatient at the contrary Wind. At Seven in the Evening they were quieted by a Storm. It rose higher and higher till 9. About 9, the Sea broke over us from Stem to Stern: burst through the Windows of the State Cabin, where three or four of us were, and cover'd us all over, tho' a Bureau shelter'd me from the main Shock. About 11, I lay down in the great Cabin, and in a short time fell asleep, tho' very uncertain whether I should wake alive, and much ashamed of my Unwillingness to die. O how pure in Heart must he be, who wou'd rejoice to appear before God at a Moment's Warning! Toward Morning, *He rebuked the Winds and the Sea, and there was a great Calm.*

Sund. 18. We returned God Thanks for our Deliverance, of which a few appear'd duly sensible. But the rest (among whom were most of the Sailors) denied we had been in any Danger. I could not have believed that so little Good would have been done by the Terror they were in before. But it cannot be that they should obey God from Fear, who are deaf to the Motives of Love.

Frid. 23. In the Evening, another Storm began. In the Morning it increased, so that they were forced to let the Ship drive. I could not but say to myself, *How is it that Thou hast no Faith?* being still unwilling to die. About One in the Afternoon, almost as soon as I had stept out of the Great Cabin Door, the Sea did not break as usual, but came with a full, smooth Tide over the Side of the Ship. I was vaulted over with Water in a Moment, and so stunn'd, that I scarce expected to lift up my Head again, till the Sea should give up her Dead. But, Thanks be to God, I receiv'd no Hurt at all. About Midnight the Storm ceased.

Sund. 25. At Noon, our 3d Storm began. At Four it was more violent than any before. Now indeed we cou'd say, *The Waves* of the Sea were *mighty and raged horribly*. They *rose up to the Heavens above, and* clave *down to Hell beneath.* The Winds roar'd round about us, and (what I never heard before) whistled as distinctly as if it had been a human Voice. The Ship not only rocked to and fro with the utmost Violence, but shook and jarr'd with so unequal, grating a Motion, that one cou'd not but with great Difficulty keep one's Hold of any thing, nor stand a Moment without it. Every ten Minutes came a Shock against the Stern or Side of the Ship, which one wou'd think shou'd dash the Planks in Pieces. At This Time, a Child, privately baptized before, was brought, to be receiv'd into the Church. It put me in mind of *Jeremiah*'s buying the Field, when the *Chaldeans* were on the Point of destroying *Jerusalem*, and seem'd a Pledge of the Mercy GOD design'd to show us, even in the Land of the Living.

We spent two or three Hours after Prayers, in conversing suitably to the Occasion, confirming one another in a calm Submission, to the wise, holy, gracious Will of GOD. And now a Storm did not appear so terrible as before. Blessed be the GOD of all Consolation!

At Seven I went to the *Germans*. I had long before observed, The great Seriousness of their Behaviour. Of their Humility they had given a continual Proof, by performing those servile Offices for the other Passengers, which none of the *English* wou'd undertake; for which they desir'd, and would receive no Pay, saying, "It was good for their proud Hearts," and "Their loving Saviour had done more for them." And every Day had given them Occasion of shewing a Meekness, which no Injury cou'd move. If they were pushed, struck, or thrown down, they rose again and went away; but no Complaint was found in their Mouth. There was now an Opportunity of trying, Whether they were deliver'd from the Spirit of Fear, as well as from that of Pride, Anger and Revenge. In the Midst of the Psalm wherewith their Service began, the Sea broke over, split the Main Sail in Pieces, cover'd the Ship, and poured in between the Decks, as if the great Deep had already swallow'd us up. A terrible Screaming began among the *English*. The *Germans* calmly sung on. I asked one of them afterwards, "Was you not afraid?" He answer'd "I thank GOD, No." I asked, "But were not your Women and Children afraid?" He replied mildly, "No; our Women and Children are not afraid to die."

From them I went to their crying, trembling Neighbours, and

pointed out to them the Difference, in the Hour of Trial, between him that feareth God, and him that feareth him not. At Twelve the Wind fell. This was the most glorious Day which I have ever hitherto seen.

Mond. 26. We enjoy'd the Calm. I can conceive no Difference, comparable to that between a smooth and a rough Sea, except that which is between a Mind calmed by the Love of God, and one torn up by the Storms of Earthly Passions.

Thurs. Jan. 29. About Seven in the Evening, we fell in with the Skirts of a Hurrican. The Rain as well as the Wind, was extremely violent. The Sky was so dark in a Moment, that the Sailors could not so much as see the Ropes, or set about furling the Sails. The Ship must in all Probability have overset, had not the Wind fell as suddenly as it rose. Toward the End of it, we had that Appearance on each of the Masts, which (it is thought) the Antients call'd *Castor* and *Pollux*. It was a small Ball of White Fire, like a Star. The Mariners say, it appears either in a Storm (and then commonly upon the Deck) or just at the End of it: And then 'tis usually on the Masts or Sails.

Fr. 30. We had another Storm, which did us no other Harm, than splitting the Fore Sail. Our Bed being wet, I laid me down on the Floor, and slept sound till Morning. And I believe, I shall not find it needful to go to Bed (as it is call'd) any more.

Sund. Feb. 1. We spoke with a Ship of *Carolina*; and *Wed.* 4. came within Soundings. About Noon the Trees were visible from the Mast, and in the Afternoon from the Main Deck. In the Evening Lesson were these Words, *A great Door and Effectual is opened.* O let no one shut it!

Thurs. Feb. 5. Between Two and Three in the Afternoon, God brought us all safe into the *Savannah* River. We cast Anchor near *Tybee*-Island, where the Groves of Pines, running along the Shore, made an agreeable Prospect, shewing, as it were, the Bloom of Spring, in the Depth of Winter.

Fr. 6. About Eight in the Morning, we first set Foot on *American* Ground. It was a small, uninhabited Island, over-against *Tybee*. Mr. *Oglethorpe* led us to a rising Ground, where we all kneel'd down to give Thanks. He then took Boat for *Savannah.* When the rest of the People were come on Shore, we called our little Flock together to Prayers. Several Parts of the Second Lesson, *Mark* vi. were wonderfully suited to the Occasion; in particular, the Account of the Courage and Sufferings of *John* the Baptist, our Lord's Directions to the first Preachers of his Gospel; and their toiling at Sea, and Deliverance with those comfortable Words, *It is I, be not afraid.*

Sat. Feb. 7. Mr. *Oglethorpe* return'd from *Savannah*, with Mr. *Spangenberg*, one of the Pastors of the *Moravians.* I soon found what Spirit he was of; and asked his Advice with regard to my own Conduct. He said, "My Brother, I must first ask you one or two Questions. Have you the Witness within your self? Does the Spirit of God bear Witness with your Spirit that you are a Child of God?" I was surprised, and knew not what to answer. He observed it, and asked, "Do you know Jesus Christ?" I paused and said, "I know he is the Saviour of the World." "True"; reply'd he; "but do you know He has saved You?" I answer'd, "I hope, he has died to save me." He only added, "Do you know Your self?" I said, "I do." But I fear, they were vain Words.

Mond. 9. I asked him many Questions, both concerning Himself, and the small Remains of the *Moravian* Church. The Substance of his Answers was this.

At Eighteen Years old I was sent to the University of *Jena*, where I spent some Years in learning Languages, and the vain Philosophy, which I have now long been labouring to forget. Here it pleased God by some that preached his Word with Power, to overturn my Heart. I immediately threw aside all my Learning, but what tended to save my Soul. I shunn'd all Company, and retired into a solitary Place, resolving to spend my Life there. For three Days I had much Comfort here; but on the fourth it was all gone. I was amazed, and went for Advice to an experienced Christian. When I came to him, I could not speak. But he saw my Heart, and advised me to go back to my House, and follow the Business Providence called me to. I went back, but was fit for nothing. I could neither do Business, nor join in any Conversation. All I could say to any one, was Yes, or No. Many times I could not say That, nor understand the plainest Thing that was said to me. My Friends and Acquaintance looked upon me as dead, came no more to me, nor spoke about me.

When I grew better, I began teaching some poor Children. Others joining with me, we taught more and more, till there were above Thirty Teachers and above Two Hundred Scholars. I had now Invitations to other Universities. But I could not accept of any; Desiring only, if it were the Will of God, to be little and unknown. I had spent some Years thus, when Professor *Breithaupt* of *Halle* died: Being then prest to remove thither, I believed it was the Call of God, and went. I had not been long there, before many Faults were found, both with my Behaviour and Preaching: And Offences increased more and more, till after half a Year, a Petition against me was sent to the King of *Prussia*, who sent an Order to the Commander at *Halle*, in Pursuance whereof, I was warn'd to leave the City in forty-eight Hours. I did so, and retired to *Hernhuth*, to Count *Zinzendorf*.

The Village of *Hernhuth* contains about a Thousand Souls, gather'd out of many Nations. They hold fast the Discipline, as well as the Faith and Practice of the Apostolical Church. I was desir'd by the Brethren there last Year, to conduct Sixteen of them to *Georgia*, where two Lots of Ground are assign'd us, and with them I have stay'd ever since.

I asked, "Whither he was to go next?" He said, "I have Thoughts of going to *Pennsylvania*. But what God will do with me, I know not. I am blind. I am a Child. My Father knows, and I am ready to go, where ever he calls."

Frid. 13. Some of the *Indians* sent us Word of their Intention to come down to us. In our Course of Reading to Day, were these Words: *Thus saith the Lord of Hosts, it shall yet come to pass that there shall come People, and the Inhabitants of many Cities. And the Inhabitants of one City shall go to another, saying, Let us go speedily to pray before the Lord, and to seek the Lord of Hosts: I will go also. Yea many People and strong Nations, shall come to seek the Lord of Hosts and to pray before him.* Zech. viii. 20. *&c.*

Sat. Feb. 14. About One, *Thomo-Chachi*, *Thleeanouhee*, *Sinauky*, with two more Women and two or three *Indian* Children, came on board. As soon as we came in, they all rose, and shook us by the Hand, and *Tomo Chachi* (one Mrs. *Musgrove* interpreted) spoke as follows.

I am glad you are come. When I was in *England* I desir'd that some would speak *the Great Word* to me. And my Nation then desir'd to hear it. But now we are all in Confusion. Yet I am glad you are come. I will go up and speak to the Wise Men of our Nation. And I hope they will hear. But we would not be made *Christians*, as the *Spaniards* make *Christians*. We would be taught, before we are baptized.

I answered, "There is but One, He that sitteth in Heaven, who is able to teach Man Wisdom. Tho' we are come so far, we know not whether he will please to teach you by us or no. If He teaches you, you will learn Wisdom; but we can do nothing." We then withdrew.

Sund. 15. Another Party of *Indians* came. They were all tall, well-proportion'd Men, and had a remarkable Softness in their Speech, and Gentleness in their whole Behaviour. In the Afternoon they all return'd home, but Three, who stay'd to go with Mr. *Oglethorpe*.

Mond. Feb. 16. Mr. *Oglethorpe* set out for the New Settlement on the *Alatamahaw* River. He took with him 50 Men; besides Mr. *Ingham*, Mr. *Hermsdorf* and the Three *Indians*.

Thursd. 19. My Brother and I took Boat, and passing by *Savannah*, went up to pay our first Visit in *America*, to the poor *Heathens*. But neither *Tomo-Chachi* nor *Sinauky* were at home. Coming back, we waited upon Mr. *Causton*, the Chief Magistrate of *Savannah*. From him we went with Mr. *Spangenberg* to the *Moravian* Brethren. About Eleven we returned to the Boat, and came to our Ship about Four in the Morning.

Sat. 21. *Mary Welch*, aged Eleven Days, was baptized according to the Custom of the First Church, and the Rule of the Church of *England*, by Immersion. The Child was ill then, but recover'd from that Hour.

Tu. 24. Mr. *Oglethorpe* return'd. The Day following I took my Leave of most of the Passengers of the Ship; who all appear'd serious. It may be, all the Seed is not fallen upon stony Ground.

In the Evening I went to *Savannah* again, whence Mr. *Spangenberg*, Bishop *Nitschman* and *Andrew Dober*, went up with us to Mrs. *Musgrove*'s, to chuse a Spot for the little House, which Mr. *Ogle-*

thorpe had promis'd to build us. Being afterward disappointed of our Boat, we were obliged to pass the Night there. But wherever we are, it is the same thing, if it be the Will of our Father which is in Heaven.

At our Return the next Day, (Mr. *Quincy* being then in the House wherein we afterwards were) Mr. *Delamotte* and I took up our Lodging with the *Germans*. We had now an Opportunity Day by Day, of observing their whole Behaviour: For we were in one Room with them from Morning to Night, unless for the little Time I spent in walking. They were always employ'd, always cheerful themselves, and in good Humour with one another. They had put away all Anger and Strife and Wrath and Bitterness and Clamour and Evilspeaking. They walk'd worthy of the Vocation wherewith they were call'd, and adorn'd the Gospel of our Lord in all Things.

Sat. Feb. 28. They met to consult concerning the Affairs of their Church: Mr. *Spangenberg* being shortly to go to *Pensylvania*, and Bishop *Nitschman* to return to *Germany*. After several Hours spent in Conference and Prayer, they proceeded to the Election and Ordination of a Bishop. The great Simplicity as well as Solemnity of the whole, almost made me forget the Seventeen Hundred Years between, and imagine myself in one of those Assemblies, where Form and State were not; but *Paul* the Tent-Maker or *Peter* the Fisherman presided; yet with the Demonstration of the Spirit and of Power.

Sund. 29. Hearing Mr. *Oglethorpe* did not come any more to *Savannah*, before he went to *Frederica*, I was obliged to go down to the Ship again, (Mr. *Spangenberg* following me thither) and receive his Orders and Instructions on several Heads. From him we went to Publick Prayers; after which we were refreshed by several Letters from *England*. Upon which I could not but observe, How careful our Lord is, to repay whatever we give up on his Account. When I left *England*, I was chiefly afraid of Two Things; One, That I should never again have so many faithful Friends as I left there: The other, That the Spark of Love which began to kindle in their Hearts, would cool and die away. But who knoweth the Mercy and Power of God? From Ten Friends I am a while secluded; and he hath opened me a Door into the whole *Moravian* Church. And as to the very Persons I left behind, his Spirit is gone forth so much the more, teaching them not to trust in Man, but *in him that raiseth the Dead, and calleth the Things that are not, as tho' they were.*

About Four, having taken Leave of Mr. *Spangenberg*, who was the next Morning to set out for *Pensylvania*, I return'd to *Savannah. Satur. March* 6. I had a long Conversation with *John Reinier*, the Son of a Gentleman, who being driven out of *France*, on Account of his Religion, settled at *Vivay* in *Swisserland*, and practised Physick there. His father died while he was a Child. Some Years after he told his Mother, he was desirous to leave *Swisserland*, and to retire into some other Country, where he might be free from the Temptations which he could not avoid there. When her Consent was at length obtain'd, he agreed with a Master of a Vessel, with whom he went to *Holland* by Land; thence to *England*, and from *England* to *Pensylvania*. He was provided with Money, Books and Drugs, intending to follow his Father's Profession. But no sooner was he come to *Philadelphia*, than the Captain who had borrow'd his Money before, instead of repaying it, demanded the full Pay for his Passage, and under that Pretence seized on all his Effects. He then left him in a strange Country, where he could not speak to be understood, without Necessaries, Money or Friends. In this Condition he thought it best to sell himself for a Servant, which he accordingly did, for seven Years. When about five were expired, he fell sick of a lingring Illness, which made him useless to his Master; who after it had continu'd Half a Year, wou'd not keep him any longer, but turn'd him out to shift for Himself. He first tried to mend Shoes, but soon after joined himself to some *French* Protestants, and learned to make Buttons. He then went and lived with an Anabaptist; but soon after hearing an Account of the *Moravians* in *Georgia*, walk'd from *Pensylvania* thither, where he found the Rest, which he had so long sought in vain.

Sund. March 7. I entered upon my Ministry at *Savannah*, by preaching on the Epistle for the Day, being the 13th of the First of *Corinthians*. In the Second Lesson, *Luke* xviii. was our Lord's Prediction of the Treatment which He Himself (and consequently his

Followers) was to meet with from the World; and his gracious Promise to those who are content *Nudi Nudum Christum sequi: Verily I say unto You, There is no Man that hath left House or Friends or Brethren or Wife or Children for the Kingdom of* GOD'*s Sake, which shall not receive manifold more in this present Time, and in the World to come Everlasting Life.*

Yet notwithstanding these plain Declarations of our Lord, notwithstanding my own repeated Experience, notwithstanding the Experience of All the sincere Followers of Christ, whom I have ever talk'd with, read or heard of; nay, and the Reason of the Thing, evincing to a Demonstration, That all who love not the Light must hate him, who is continually labouring, to pour it in upon them: I do here bear Witness against Myself, That when I saw the Number of People crowding into the Church, the deep Attention with which they receiv'd the Word, and the Seriousness that afterwards sat on all their Faces; I could scarce refrain from giving the Lie, to Experience and Reason, and Scripture all together. I could hardly believe that the Greater, the far Greater Part of this Attentive, Serious People, would hereafter trample under Foot that Word, and say all manner of Evil falsly of him that spake it. O who can believe, what their Heart abhors? Jesus, Master, have Mercy on us! Let us love thy Cross! Then shall we believe, *If we suffer with Thee, we shall also reign with Thee!*

This Evening one of the *Moravians*, who had been long ill of a Consumption, found himself much worse. On my mentioning it to Bp. *Nitschman*, he smiled and said, "He will soon be well; he is ready for the Bridegroom."

Sund. Mar. 14. (Having before given Notice of my Design to do so, every *Sunday* and Holiday, according to the Rules of our Church) I administer'd the Holy Communion to eighteen Persons. Which of these will endure to the End!

Mond. Mar. 15. Mr. *Quincy* going for *Carolina*, I remov'd into the Minister's House. It is large enough for a larger Family than ours, and has many Conveniences, besides a good Garden. I could not but reflect on the well-known Epigram,

'Αγρὸς 'Αχαιμενιδου γενομην, ποτε νυν δὲ Μενιππου.

How short a Time will it be, before its present Possessor is removed! Perhaps, to be no more seen!

Sund. 28. A Servant of Mr. *Bradley*'s sent to desire to speak with me. Going to him, I found a young Man, ill, but perfectly sensible. He desired the rest to go out, and then said, "On *Thursday* Night, about Eleven, being in Bed, but broad awake, I heard one calling aloud, '*Peter! Peter Wright!*' And looking up, the Room was as light as Day, and I saw a Man in very bright Cloaths stand by the Bed, who said, '*Prepare yourself; for your End is nigh;*' and then immediately all was dark as before." I told him, "The Advice was good, whence-soever it came." In a few Days he recover'd from his Illness: His whole Temper was changed as well as his Life; and so continued to be, till after three or four Weeks, he relapsed and died in Peace.

Tuesd. Mar. 30. Mr. *Ingham* coming from *Frederica*, brought me Letters, pressing me to go thither. The next Day Mr. *Delamotte* and I began to try, Whether Life might not be as well sustained, by one Sort as by Variety of Food. We chose to make the Experiment with Bread; and were never more vigorous and healthy, than while we tasted nothing else. *Blessed are the Pure in Heart!* who whether they eat or drink, or whatever they do, have no End therein but to please God! To them all Things are pure. Every Creature is good to Them, and nothing to be rejected. But let them who know and feel, that they are not thus pure, use every Help and remove every Hindrance: Always remembring, *He that despiseth little Things, shall fall by little and little.*

Sund. Apr. 4. About Four in the Afternoon, I set out for *Frederica*, in a Pettiawga (a sort of flat-bottom'd Barge). The next Evening we anchor'd near *Skidoway* Island, where the Water at Flood was twelve or fourteen Foot deep. I wrapt myself up from Head to Foot, in a large Cloak, to keep off the Sand-Flies, and lay down on the Quarter Deck. Between One and Two I waked under Water, being so fast asleep that I did not find where I was till my Mouth was full of it. Having left my Cloak, I know not how, upon Deck, I swam round to the other Side of the Pettiawga, where a Boat was ty'd, and climb'd up by the Rope, without any Hurt, more than wetting my Cloaths. Thou art the God of whom cometh Salvation: Thou art the Lord by whom we escape Death.

The Winds were so contrary, that on *Sat.* 10 we could but just get over-against *Doboy* Island, twenty Miles from Frederica, but could not possibly make the Creek, having a strong Tide also against us. Here we lay beating off till past One; when the Lightning and Rain which we had long seen at a Distance, drove down full upon us; till after a Quarter of an Hour, the Clouds parted, some passing on the Right, and some on the Left, leaving us a clear Sky, and so strong a Wind right after us, as in two Hours brought us to *Frederica.*

A little before we landed, I open'd my Testament on these Words, *If* God *be for us, who can be against us?* Coming on Shore, I found my Brother exceeding weak, having been for some Time ill of a Flux. But he mended from the Hour he saw me. *This* also *hath* God wrought!

Sund. April 11. I preached at the New Storehouse, on the first Verse of the Gospel for the Day, *Which of you convinceth me of Sin? And if I say the Truth, why do you not believe me?* There was a large Congregation, whom I endeavoured to convince of Unbelief, by simply proposing the Conditions of Salvation, as they are laid down in Scripture, and appealing to their own Hearts, whether they believed they could be saved on no other Terms.

In every one of the six following Days, I had some fresh Proofs of the absolute Necessity of following that wise Advice of the Apostle, *Judge nothing before the Time; until the Lord come, who both will bring to Light the hidden Things of Darkness, and will make manifest the Counsels of the Hearts.*

Sat. April 17. We set out for *Savannah*, and reach'd it on *Tuesday* Evening. O blessed Place, where having but one End in View, Dissembling and Fraud are not; but each of us can pour out his Heart without Fear into his Brother's Bosom!

Not finding as yet any Door open, for the pursuing our main Design, we considered, In what Manner we might be most useful to the little Flock at *Savannah.* And we agreed, 1st. To advise the more serious among them, to form themselves into a Sort of little

Society, and to meet once or twice a Week, in order to reprove, instruct and exhort one another. 2. To select out of these a smaller Number for a more intimate Union with each other, which might be forwarded, partly by our conversing singly with each, and partly by inviting them all together to our House; and this accordingly we determined to do every *Sunday* in the Afternoon.

Wed. May 5. I was ask'd to baptize a Child of Mr. *Parker*'s Second Bailiff of *Savannah.* But Mrs. *Parker* told me, "Neither Mr. *P.* nor I will consent to its being dipp'd." I answer'd. "If you *certify that your Child is weak, it will suffice* (the Rubrick says) *to pour Water upon it.*" She reply'd, "Nay, the Child is not weak; but I am resolv'd it shall not be dipp'd." This Argument I could not confute. So I went home; and the Child was baptized by another Person.

Sund. 9. I began dividing the Publick Prayers, according to the Original Appointment of the Church (still observ'd in a few Places in *England*). The Morning Service began at Five. The Communion Office (with the Sermon) at Eleven. The Evening Service, about Three. And this Day I began reading Prayers in the Courthouse; a large and convenient Place.

Mond. 10. I began visiting my Parishioners in order, from House to House; for which I set apart the Time (when they can't work, *viz.*) from Twelve, till Three in the Afternoon.

Sund. May 16. We were surpriz'd in the Evening by my Brother just come from *Frederica.* After some Conversation, we consulted how the poor People there might be taken Care of, during his Absence. And it was at last agreed, that Mr. *Ingham* and I should take our Turns in assisting them; and the First was allotted me. Accordingly on *Tuesd.* 18. I walk'd to *Thunderbolt*; whence the next Afternoon we set out in a small Boat: In the Evening we touched at *Skidoway*, and had a small, but attentive Congregation, to join with us in Evening-Prayer.

Sat. May 22. About Four in the Afternoon we enter'd upon *Doboy* Sound. The Wind, which was right a Head, was so high, *when we* were in the Middle of it, and the Sea so rough, being driven in at the Inlet, that the Boat was on the Point of sinking every

Moment. But it pleased God to bring us safe to the other Side in half an Hour, and to *Frederica* the next Morning. We had Publick Prayers at Nine, at which nineteen Persons were present; and (I think) nine Communicants.

Frid. 28. I read the Commendatory Prayer by Mr. *Germain*, who lay at the Point of Death. He had lost his Speech and his Senses. His Eyes were set, neither had he any discernible Motion, but the heaving of his Breast. While we stood round him, he stretched out his Arms, rubb'd his Head, recovered his Sight, Speech and Understanding; and immediately sending for the Bailiffs, settled the Affairs of his Family; and then lay down and died.

At the first Service on *Sund. May* 30. were only Five, at the Second twenty-five. The next Day, I made Mr. *Lassel*'s Will; who notwithstanding his great Weakness, was quite revived, when any Mention was made of Death, or of Eternity.

Tuesd. June 1. After praying with him, I was surprized, to find one of the most controverted Questions in Divinity, disinterested Love, decided at once by a poor, old Man, without Education or Learning or any Instructor, but the Spirit of God. I asked him, What he thought of Paradise (to which he had said he was going)? He said, "To be sure, it is a fine Place. But I don't mind that. I don't care what Place I am in. Let God put me where he will, or do with me what he will, so I may but set forth his Honour and Glory."

Th. June 3. Being Ascension Day, we had the Holy Communion; but only Mr. *Hird*'s Family joined with us in it. One Reason why there were no more, was because a few Words which a Woman had inadvertently spoken, had set almost all the Town in a Flame. Alas! How shall a City stand that is thus divided against itself! Where there is no brotherly Love, no Meekness, no forbearing or forgiving one another: But Envy, Malice, Revenge, Suspicion, Anger, Clamour, Bitterness, Evilspeaking, without End! Abundant Proof, that there can be no true Love of Man, unless it be built on the Love of God.

Sund. 6. Calling on Mr. *Lassels*, and asking how he did, "My Departure (said he) I hope is at Hand." I asked, "Are you troubled at that?" He reply'd, "O no; to depart and to be with Christ, is far better. I desire no more of this bad World. My Hope and my Joy and my Love is there." The next time I saw him he said, "I desire nothing more, than for God to forgive my many and great Sins. I would be humble. I would be the humblest Creature living. My Heart is humble and broken for my Sins. Tell me, teach me, what shall I do to please God. I would fain do whatever is his Will." I said, "It is his Will, you should suffer." He answer'd, "Then I *will* suffer. I will gladly suffer whatever pleases him."

Mond. 7. Finding him weaker, I asked, "Do you still desire to die?" He said, "Yes; but I dare not pray for it, for fear I should displease my heavenly Father. His Will be done. Let him work his Will, in my Life, or in my Death."

Th. 10. We began to execute at *Frederica*, what we had before agreed to do at *Savannah*. Our Design was on *Sundays* in the Afternoon, and every Evening after Publick Service, to spend some time with the most Serious of the Communicants, in singing, reading and Conversation. This Evening we had only *Mark Hird*. But on *Sunday* Mr. *Hird*, and two more desired to be admitted. After a Psalm and a little Conversation, we read the *Christian Perfection*, and concluded with another Psalm.

Sat. June 12. Being with one who was very desirous to converse with me, "but not upon Religion," I spoke to this Effect:

Suppose you was going to a Country, where every one spake *Latin* and understood no other Language, neither would converse with any that did not understand it: Suppose one was sent to stay here a short time, on purpose to teach it you: Suppose that Person, pleased with your Company, should spend his time in trifling with you, and teach you nothing of what he came for: Would that be well done? Yet this is our Case. You are going to a Country, where every one speaks the Love of God. The Citizens of Heaven understand no other Language. They converse with none who do not understand it. Indeed none such are admitted there. I am sent from God to teach you this. A few Days are allotted us for that Purpose. Would it then be well done in me, because I was pleased with your Company, to spend this short time in trifling, and teach you nothing of what I came for? God forbid! I will rather, not converse with you at all. Of the two Extremes, This is the best.

Wed. June 16. Another little Company of us met, Mr. *Reed*, *Davison*, *Walker*, *Delamotte*, and myself. We sung, read a little of Mr. *Law*, and then convers'd. *Wednesdays* and *Fridays* were the Days we fixt for constant Meeting.

Th. 17. An Officer of the Man of War, walking just behind me with two or three of his Acquaintance, curs'd and swore exceedingly; but upon my reproving him, seemed much moved, and gave me many Thanks.

Sat. 19. Mr. *Oglethorpe* returned from the South, and gave Orders, on *Sunday* the 20th, That none should profane the Day (as was usual before) by fishing or fowling upon it. In the Afternoon-Sermon I sum'd up, what I had seen or heard at *Frederica*, inconsistent with Christianity, and consequently with the Prosperity of the Place. The Event was as it ought: Some of the Hearers were profited, and the rest deeply offended.

This Day, at half an Hour past Ten, God heard the Prayer of his Servant, and Mr. *Lassels*, according to his Desire, was *dissolved that he might be with Christ.*

Tu. 22. Observing much Coldness in Mr. ——'s Behaviour, I asked him the Reason of it. He answer'd,

I like nothing you do; all your Sermons are Satires on particular Persons. Therefore I will never hear you more. And all the People are of my Mind. For we won't hear ourselves abused.

Beside, they say, They are Protestants. But as for You, they can't tell what Religion you are of. They never heard of such a Religion before. They don't know what to make of it. And then, your Private Behaviour — All the Quarrels that have been here since you came, have been long of You. Indeed there is neither Man nor Woman in the Town, who minds, a Word you say. And so you may preach long enough; but no body will come to hear you.

He was too warm for hearing an Answer. So I had nothing to do, but to thank him for his Openness, and walk away.

Wed. 23. I had a long Conversation with Mr. ——, upon the Nature of True Religion. I then asked him, "Why he did not endeavour to recommend it, to all with whom he convers'd." He said,

I did so once; and for some time I thought, I had done much Good by it. But I afterwards found, They were never the better, and I myself was the worse. Therefore now, tho' I always strive to be inoffensive in my Conversation, I don't strive to make People Religious, unless those that have a Desire to be so, and are consequently, Willing to hear me. But I have not yet (I speak not of You or your Brother) found One such Person in *America*.

He that hath Ears to hear, let him hear! Mark the Tendency of this accursed Principle! If you will speak only to those who are *Willing to hear*, see how Many you will turn from the Error of their Ways! If therefore, striving to do Good, you have done Hurt, what then? So did St. *Paul*. So did the Lord of Life. Even HIS Word was *the Savour of Death, as well as the Savour of Life*. But shall you therefore strive no more? GOD forbid! Strive more humbly, more calmly, more cautiously. Do not strive, *as you did before*,——but strive, while the Breath of GOD is in your Nostrils!

Being to leave *Frederica* in the Evening, I took the more Notice of these Words in the Lesson for the Day. *Whereunto shall I liken the Men of this Generation? They are like unto Children sitting in the Market-Place, and saying, We have piped unto you, and ye have not danced; we have mourned to you, and ye have not wept. For John the Baptist came neither eating Bread, nor drinking Wine, and ye say, He hath a Devil. The Son of Man is come eating and drinking; and ye say, Behold a gluttonous Man and a Wine-Bibber, a Friend of Publicans and Sinners.* Luke vii.

About Eleven at Night we took Boat. And on *Sat.* 26, about One in the Afternoon, came to *Savannah*. O what do we want here, either for Life or Godliness! If Suffering, GOD will send it in *His* time.

Sun. June 27. About Twenty join'd with us in Morning Prayer. An Hour or two after, a large Party of *Creek Indians* came, the Expectation of whom depriv'd us of our Place of Publick Worship, in which they were to have their Audience.

Wed. 30. I hoped a Door was opened, for going up immediately to the *Choctaws*, the least polish'd, *i. e.* the least corrupted of all the *Indian* Nations. But upon my informing Mr. *Oglethorpe* of our Design, he objected, not only the Danger, of being intercepted, or killed by the *French* there; but much more, the Inexpediency of leaving *Savannah*, destitute of a Minister. These Objections I related to our Brethren in the Evening, who were all of Opinion, "We ought not to go yet."

Th. July 1. The *Indians* had an Audience, and another on *Saturday*, when *Chicali*, their head Man, dined with Mr. *Oglethorpe*. After Dinner, I asked the Greyheaded Old Man, "What he thought he was made for?" He said, "He that is above, knows what he made us for. We know nothing. We are in the Dark. But White Men know much. And yet White Men build great Houses, as if they were to live for ever. But White Men can't live for ever. In a little time White Men will be Dust as well as I." I told him, "If Red Men will learn the Good Book, they may know as much as White Men. But neither We nor You can understand that Book, unless we are taught by him that is above: And he will not teach, unless you avoid, what you already know is not Good." He answer'd, "I believe that; He will not teach us, while our Hearts are not white. And our Men do, what they know is not Good. They kill their own Children. And our Women do what they know is not good. They kill the Child before it is born. Therefore, He that is above, does not send us the Good Book."

Hearing the Younger of the Miss *Boveys* was not well, I called upon them this Evening. I found, she had only The Prickly Heat, a sort of Rash very common here in Summer. We soon fell into serious Conversation, after I had asked, "If they did not think they were too young, to trouble themselves with Religion yet? And, whether they might not defer it, Ten or a Dozen Years?" To which one of them reply'd, "If it will be reasonable Ten Years hence, to be Religious, it is so now: I am not for deferring one Moment."

Wed. July 7. I called there again, being determin'd now, to speak more closely. But meeting Company there, *Prudence* induced me to put it off, till another Opportunity.

Thur. 8. Mr. *O.* being there, and casually speaking of sudden Death, Miss *Becky* said, "If it was the Will of God, I should chuse to die without a lingring Illness." Her Sister said, "Are you then always prepared to die?" She replied, "Jesus Christ is always prepared to help me. And little Stress is to be laid on such a Preparation for Death, as is made in a Fit of Sickness."

Saturd. July 10. Just as they had done drinking Tea, Mrs. *Margaret* seeing her Colour change, asked, If she was well? She did not return any Answer; and Dr. *Tailfer* soon after going by, she desir'd him to step in, and said, "Sir, My Sister, I fear is not well." He looked earnestly at her, felt her Pulse, and replied, "Well, Madam! Your Sister is dying." However he thought it not impossible, Bleeding might help. She bled about an Ounce, lean'd back and died.

As soon as I heard of it, I went to the House, and begg'd they would not lay her out immediately, there being a Possiblility, at least, she might only be in a Swoon: Of which indeed there was some slight Hope, she not only being as warm as ever, but having a fresh Colour in her Cheeks, and a few Drops of Blood starting out, upon bending her Arm: But there was no Pulse and no Breath; so that having waited some Hours, we found her *Spirit was indeed return'd to* GOD *that gave it.*

I never saw so beautiful a Corpse in my Life. Poor Comfort to its late Inhabitant! I was greatly surpriz'd at her Sister. There was in all her Behaviour, such an inexpressible Mixture of Tenderness and Resignation. The first Time I spoke to her, she said, "All my Afflictions are nothing to this. I have lost not only a Sister, but a Friend. But 'tis the Will of GOD. I rely on Him; and doubt not but he will support me under it."

This Evening we had such a Storm of Thunder and Lightning, as I never saw before even in *Georgia*. This Voice of GOD too, told me I was not fit to die; since I was afraid, rather than desirous of it! O when shall I wish to be dissolved and to be with Christ! When I love him with all my Heart.

Almost the whole Town was the next Evening at the Funeral: Where many doubtless made a World of Good Resolutions. O how little Trace of most of these will be left in the Morning! 'Tis a true Saying, "Hell is paved with good Intentions."

Tuesd. July 20. Five of the *Chicasaw Indians* (twenty of whom had been in *Savannah* several Days) came to see us, with Mr. *Andrews*, their Interpreter. They were all Warriors; Four of them, Head Men. The two chief were *Paustoobee* and *Mingo Mattaw*. Our Conference was as follows.

Q. Do you believe, There is One Above, who is over all Things?

Paustoobee answer'd, We believe, there are Four Beloved Things above; The Clouds, the Sun, the Clear Sky, and He that lives in the Clear Sky.

Q. Do you believe, there is but One that lives in the Clear Sky?

A. We believe, there are Two with him, Three in all.

Q. Do you think, He made the Sun, and the other Beloved Things?

A. We cannot tell. Who hath seen?

Q. Do you think, He made You?

A. We think, He made all Men at first.

Q. How did he make them at first?

A. Out of the Ground.

Q. Do you believe, He loves You?

A. I don't know. I cannot see him.

Q. But has He not often saved Your Life?

A. He has. Many Bullets have gone on this Side, and many on that Side, but he would not let them hurt me. And many Bullets have gone into these young Men; and yet they are alive.

Q. Then, can't he save You from your Enemies now?

A. Yes, but we know not, if he will. We have now so many Enemies round about us, that I think of nothing but Death, And if I am to die, I shall die, and I will die like a Man. But if He will have me to live, I shall live. Tho' I had ever so many Enemies, He can destroy them All.

Q. How do you know that?

A. From what I have seen. When our enemies came against us before, then the Beloved Clouds came for us. And often much Rain, and sometimes Hail has come upon them, and that in a very hot Day. And I saw, when many *French* and *Choctaws* and other Nations, came against one of our Towns. And the Ground made a Noise under them, and the Beloved Ones in the Air behind them. And they were afraid, and went away, and left their Meat and Drink and their Guns. I tell no Lie. All these saw it too.

Q. Have you heard such Noises at other Times?

A. Yes, Often: Before and after almost every Battle.

Q. What Sort of Noises were they?

A. Like the Noise of Drums and Guns and Shouting.

Q. Have you heard any such lately?

A. Yes; four Days after our last Battle with the *French.*

Q. Then you heard nothing before it?

A. The Night before I dream'd I heard many Drums up there, and many Trumpets there, and much stamping of Feet and shouting. Till then I thought we should all die. But then I thought the Beloved Ones were come to help us. And the next Day I heard above a hundred Guns go off, before the Fight begun. And I said, "When the Sun is there, the Beloved Ones will help us; and we shall conquer our Enemies." And we did so.

Q. Do you often think and talk of the Beloved Ones?

A. We think of them always, wherever we are. We talk of them and to them, at home and abroad; in Peace, in War, before and after we fight; and indeed whenever and wherever we meet together.

Q. Where do you think your Souls go after Death?

A. We believe the Souls of Red Men walk up and down near the Place where they died, or where their Bodies lie. For we have often heard Cries and Noises near the Place where any Prisoners had been burnt.

Q. Where do the Souls of White Men go after Death?

A. We can't tell. We have not seen.

Q. Our Belief is, That the Souls of Bad Men only walk up and down; but the Souls of Good Men go up.

A. I believe so too. But I told you the Talk of the Nation.

(Mr. *Andrews.* They said at the Burying, "They knew what you was doing. You was speaking to the Beloved Ones above to take up the Soul of the young Woman.")

Q. We have a Book that tells us many Things of the Beloved One above. Wou'd you be glad to know them?

A. We have no Time now, but to fight. If we should ever be at Peace, we should be glad to know.

Q. Do you expect ever to know what the White Men know?

(Mr. *Andrews.* They told Mr. *O.* They believe the Time will come, when the Red and the White Men will be One.)

Q. What do the *French* teach you?

A. The *French Black* * *Kings* never go out. We see you go about. We like that. That is good.

* *So they call the Priests.*

Q. How came your Nation by the Knowledge they have?

A. As soon as ever the Ground was found, and fit to stand upon, it came to us, and has been with us ever since. But we are Young Men. Our Old Men know more. But all of them do not know. There are but a Few; whom the Beloved One chuses from a Child, and is in them, and takes care of them and teaches them. They know these Things: And our Old Men practise; therefore they know: But I don't practise. Therefore I know little.

Mond. July 26. My Brother and I set out for *Charles-Town*, in order to [begin] his embarking for *England*. But the Wind being contrary, we did not reach *Port-Royal*, 40 Miles from *Savannah*, till *Wedn.* Evening. The next Morning we left it. But the Wind was so high in the Afternoon, as we were crossing the Neck of St. *Helena*'s Sound, that our oldest Sailor cry'd out, "Now every one must take Care for himself." I told him, "GOD would take Care for us all." Almost as soon as the Words were spoken, the Mast fell. I kept on the Edge of the Boat, to be clear of her her when she sunk, (which we expected every Moment) tho' with little Prospect of swimming to Shore, against such a Wind and Sea. But *How is it that thou hadst no Faith?* The Moment the Mast fell, two Men caught it and pull'd it into the Boat; the other three rowed with all their Might, and GOD *gave Command to the Winds and Seas*, so that in an Hour we were safe on Land.

Sat. July 31. We came to *Charles-Town*. The Church is of Brick, but plaister'd over like Stone. I believe it would contain three or four Thousand Persons. About three Hundred were present at the Morning Service the next Day, (when Mr. *Garden* desired me to preach) about fifty at the Holy Communion. I was glad to see several Negroes at Church; one of whom told me, "She was there constantly; and that her old Mistress (now dead) had many Times instructed her in the Christian Religion." I ask'd her, what Religion was? She said, "She could not tell." I ask'd, if she knew what a Soul was? She answered, "No." I said, "Don't you know there is something in you, different from your Body? Something you can't see or feel?" She reply'd, "I never heard so much before." I added,

"Do you think then, a Man dies all together as a Horse dies?" She said, "Yes, to be sure." O God, where are thy tender Mercies? Are they not over all thy Works? When shall the Sun of Righteousness arise on these Outcasts of Men, with Healing in his Wings!

Mond. August 2. I set out for the Lieutenant Governor's Seat, about thirty Miles from *Charles-Town*, to deliver Mr. *Oglethorpe*'s Letters. It stands very pleasantly, on a little Hill, with a Vale on either Side, in one of which is a thick Wood; the other is planted with Rice and Indian Corn. I design'd to have gone back by Mr. *Skeene*'s, who has about fifty Christian Negroes. But my Horse tiring, I was obliged to return the streight Way to *Charles-Town*.

I had sent the Boat we came in, back to *Savannah*, expecting a Passage thither myself in Col. *Bull*'s. His not going so soon, I went to *Ashley-Ferry* on *Thursday*, intending to walk to *Port-Royal*. But Mr. *Belinger* not only provided me a Horse, but rode with me himself ten Miles, and sent his Son with me to *Cumbee-Ferry*, twenty Miles farther; whence having hired Horses and a Guide, I came to *Beaufort* (on *Port-Royal*) the next Evening. We took Boat in the Morning; but the Wind being contrary, and very high, did not reach *Savannah* till *Sunday* in the Afternoon.

Finding Mr. *Oglethorpe* was gone, I stay'd only a Day at *Savannah:* And leaving Mr. *Ingham* and *Delamotte* there, set out on *Tuesday* Morning for *Frederica*. In walking to *Thunderbolt*, I was in so heavy a Shower, that all my Cloaths were as wet as if I had gone thro' the River. On which Occasion I can't but observe that vulgar Error, concerning the Hurtfulness of the Rains and Dews of *America*. I have been thro'ly wet with these Rains more than once; yet without any Harm at all. And I have lain many Nights in the open Air, and received all the Dews that fell. And so I believe might any one, if his Constitution was not impaired by the Softness of a genteel Education.

At *Thunderbolt* we took Boat, and on *Frid. Aug.* 13, came to *Frederica*, where I delivered to Mr. *O.* the Letters, I had brought from *Carolina*. The next Day he set out for *Fort St. George*. From that Time I had less and less Prospect of doing good at *Frederica*; many there being extremely zealous, and indefatigably diligent to prevent it: And few of the rest daring to shew themselves of another Mind, for Fear of their Displeasure.

Saturday. 28. I set apart, (out of the few we had) a few Books towards a Library at *Frederica.* In the Afternoon I walked to the Fort on the other Side of the Island. About Five we set out homeward. But my Guide not being perfect in the Way, we were soon lost in the Woods. We walked on however as well as we could, till between Nine and Ten; when being heartily tired, and thro'ly wet with Dew, we lay down and slept till Morning.

About Day-break, on *Sunday* the 29th, we set out again, endeavouring to walk streight forward, and soon after Sun-Rise found ourselves in the *Great Savannah* near *Frederica.* By this good Providence I was deliver'd from another Fear, That of lying in the Woods, which Experience shew'd was to one in tolerable Health, a meer *Lion in the Way.*

Thurs. Sept. 2. I set out in a Sloop, and about Ten on *Sunday* Morning, came to *Skidoway*; which (after reading Prayers and preaching to a small Congregation) I left and came to *Savannah* in the Evening.

Mond. 13. I began reading with Mr. *Delamotte*, Bp. *Beveridge*'s *Pandectæ' Canonum Conciliorum.* Nothing could so effectually have convinced us, That both Particular and *General Councils may err, and have erred: And that Things ordained by them as necessary to Salvation, have neither Strength nor Authority, unless they be taken out of Holy Scripture.*

Mond. 20. We ended (of which also I must confess, I once thought more highly than I ought to think) the Apostolical Canons; so call'd, as Bp. *Beveridge* observes, *because partly grounded upon, partly agreeing with, the Traditions delivered down from the Apostles.* But he observes farther, (in the 159th Page of his *Codex Canonum Ecclesiæ Primitivæ*: And why did he not observe it in the first Page of the Book?) *They contain the Discipline used in the Church at the Time when they were collected; not when the Council of* Nice *met; for then many Parts of it were useless and obsolete.*

Tuesd. October 12. We considered if any Thing could yet be done, for the poor People of *Frederica.* And I submitted to the

Judgment of my Friends, which was, That I should take another Journey thither: Mr. *Ingham* undertaking to supply my Place at *Savannah*, for the Time I should stay there. I came thither on *Sat.* the 16th and found few Things better than I expected. The Morning and Evening Prayers, which were read for a while after my leaving the Place, had been long discontinued, and from that Time, every Thing grew worse and worse: Not many retaining any more of the Form than of the Power of Godliness.

I was at first a little discouraged, but soon remember'd the Word which cannot fail, *Greater is he that is in you than he that is in the World*. I cried to God to *Arise and maintain his own Cause*: And after the Evening Prayers were ended, invited a few to my House (as I did every Night while I stay'd in *Frederica*). I read to them one of the Exhortations of *Ephrem Syrus*, the most awakening Writer (I think) of all the Antients. We concluded our reading and Conversation with a Psalm, and I trust, our God gave us his Blessing.

Mond. 18. Finding there were several *Germans* at *Frederica*, who not understanding the English Tongue, could not join in our Publick Service, I desired them to meet at Noon, in my House; which they did every Day at Noon from thence forward. We first sung a *German* Hymn, then I read a Chapter in the New Testament, then explain'd it to them as well as I cou'd. After another Hymn we concluded with Prayer.

Mond. 25. I took Boat, and after a slow and dangerous Passage, came to *Savannah* on *Sunday* the 31st.

Tuesd. November 23. Mr. *Oglethorpe* sail'd for *England*, leaving Mr. *Ingham*, Mr. *Delamotte* and me at *Savannah*, but with less Prospect of preaching to the *Indians*, than we had the first Day we set Foot in *America*. Whenever I mentioned it, it was immediately replied, "You can't leave *Savannah* without a Minister." To this indeed my plain Answer was, "I know not that I am under any Obligation to the contrary. I never promised to stay here one Month. I openly declared both *before*, *at*, *and ever since* my coming hither, That I neither would nor could take Charge of the *English* any longer than 'till I could go among the *Indians*." If it was said

"But did not the Trustees of *Georgia* appoint you to be Minister of *Savannah*?" I replied "They did; but it was not done by my Sollicitation: It was done without either my Desire or Knowledge. Therefore I cannot conceive that Appointment to lay me under any Obligation of continuing there, any longer than 'till a Door is opened to the Heathens: And this I expressly declared, at the Time I consented to accept of that Appointment." But tho' I had no other Obligation not to leave *Savannah* now, yet that of Love I could not break thro': I could not resist the importunate Request of the more serious Parishioners, "To watch over their Souls yet a little longer, 'till some one came who might supply my Place." And this I the more willingly did, because the Time was not come to preach the Gospel of Peace to the Heathens; all their Nations being in a Ferment; and *Paustoobee* and *Mingo Mattaw*, having told me, in Terms, in my own House, "Now our Enemies are all about us, and we can do nothing but fight: But if the Beloved Ones should ever give us to be at Peace, then we would hear *the Great Word*."

Thursday, *December* 9. Hearing of one dangerously ill, I went to her immediately: She told me, "That she had many Things to say:" But her Weakness prevented her saying them then; and the next Day God required her Soul of her.

Wednesday 23. Mr. *Delamotte* and I, with a Guide, set out to walk to the *Cowpen*; when we had walk'd two or three Hours, our Guide told us plainly, "He did not know where we were." However, believing it could not be far off, we thought it best to go on. In an Hour or two we came to *Cypress-Swamp*, which lay directly across our way: There was not Time to walk back to *Savannah* before Night; so we walk'd thro' it, the Water being about Breast-high. By that Time we had gone a Mile beyond it, we were out of all Path; and it being now past Sun-set, we sat down, intending to make a Fire, and to stay there 'till Morning; but finding our Tinder wet, we were at a Stand; I advis'd to walk on still; but my Companions being faint and weary, were for lying down, which we accordingly did about Six o'Clock: The Ground was as wet as our Cloaths, which (it being a sharp Frost) were soon froze together; however, I slept 'till Six in the Morning. There fell a heavy Dew in the Night, which cover'd us over as white as Snow. Within an Hour after Sun-rise, we came to a Plantation, and in the Evening, without any Hurt, to *Savannah*.

Tuesday 28. We set out by Land with a better Guide for *Frederica*. On *Wednesday* Evening we came to *Fort-Argyle*, on the Back of the River *Ogeechy*. The next Afternoon we crost *Cooanoochy River* in a small Canoo, our Horses swimming by the Side of it. We made a Fire on the Bank, and notwithstanding the Rain, slept quietly 'till the Morning.

Saturday, *January* 1. 1737. Our Provisions fell short, our Journey being longer than we expected: But having a little barbecued Bears-flesh (i. e. dried in the Sun) we boil'd it and found it wholsome Food. The next Day we reached *Darien*, the Settlement of the *Scotch Highlanders*, a sober, industrious, friendly, hospitable People; whose Minister, Mr. *Mac-leod*, is a serious, resolute, and (I hope) a pious Man.

On *Monday* Evening we left *Darien*, and on *Wednesday* 5, came to *Frederica*. Most here were as we expected, cold and heartless: We found not one who retained his first Love. O send forth thy Light and thy Truth, that they may guide them! Let them not yet follow their own Imaginations!

After having *beaten the Air* in this unhappy Place for twenty Days, on *January* 26, I took my final Leave of *Frederica*. It was not any Apprehension of my own Danger (tho' my Life had been threatned many Times) but an utter Despair of doing Good there; which made me content with the Thought of seeing it no more.

In my Passage home, having procured a celebrated Book, the Works of *Nicolas Machiavel*, I set myself carefully to read and consider it. I began with a Prejudice in his Favour; having been inform'd, he had often been misunderstood, and greatly misrepresented. I weigh'd the Sentiments that were less common; transcribed the Passages wherein they were contained; compared one Passage with another, and endeavour'd to form a cool, impartial Judgment: And my cool Judgment is, That if all the other Doctrines of Devils which have been committed to Writing, since Letters were in the World, were collected together in one Volume, it would fall short of this: And, That should a Prince form himself by this Book, so calmly recommending Hypocrisy, Treachery, Lying, Robbery, Oppression, Adultery, Whoredom and Murder of all Kinds; *Domitian* or *Nero* would be an Angel of Light, compared to that Man.

Mond. Jan. 31. We came to *Savannah. Tues. Feb.* 1. being the Anniversary Feast, on Account of the first Convoy's Landing in *Georgia*, we had a Sermon and the Holy Communion. *Thur.* 24. It was agreed, Mr. *Ingham* should go for *England*, and endeavour to bring over (if it should please God) some of our Friends to strengthen our Hands in his Work. *Sat.* 26. he left *Savannah*.

By Mr. *Ingham* I writ to Dr. *Bray*'s Associates, who had sent a Parochial Library to *Savannah*. It is expected of the Ministers who receive these, to send an Account to their Benefactors of the Method they use in catechizing the Children, and instructing the Youth of their respective Parishes. That Part of the Letter was as follows:

Our General Method is this: A young Gentleman who came with me, teaches between Thirty and Forty Children, to read, write and cast Accounts. Before School in the Morning, and after School in the Afternoon, he catechises the Lowest Class, and endeavours to fix something of what was said, in their Understandings as well as their Memories. In the Evening he instructs the Larger Children. On *Saturday* in the Afternoon I catechise them all. The same I do on *Sunday* before the Evening Service. And in the Church, immediately after the Second Lesson, a select Number of them having repeated the Catechism and been examin'd in some Part of it, I endeavour to explain at large, and to inforce that Part, both on them and the Congregation.

Some time after the Evening Service, as many of my Parishioners as desire it, meet at my House (as they do also on *Wednesday* Evening) and spend about an Hour in Prayer, Singing and mutual Exhortation. A smaller Number (mostly those who design to communicate the next Day) meet here on *Saturd.* Evening: And a few of these come to me on the other Evenings, and pass half an Hour in the same Employment.

Frid. Mar. 4. I writ the Trustees for *Georgia* an Account of our Year's Expence from *March* 1. 1736, to *March* 1. 1737. Which, deducting Extraordinary Expences (such as, Repairing the Parsonage House, and Journeys to *Frederica*) amounted for Mr. *Delamotte* and me to 44*l*. 4*s*. 4*d*.

From the Directions I receiv'd from God this Day, touching an Affair of the greatest Importance, I could not but observe (as I had done many Times before) the entire Mistake of those, who assert, "God will not answer your Prayer, unless your Heart be wholly resign'd to his Will." My Heart was not entirely resign'd to his Will. Therefore, not daring to depend on my own Judgment, I cried the more earnestly to him, To supply what was wanting in me. And I know and am assured, He heard my Voice, and did send forth his Light and his Truth.

Thurs. 24. A Fire broke out in the House of *Robert Hows*, and in an Hour burnt it to the Ground. A Collection was made for him the next Day; and the Generality of the People shew'd a surprizing Willingness, to give a Little out of their Little for the Relief of a Necessity greater than their own.

About this Time Mr. *Lacy* of *Thunderbolt* call'd upon me; when observing him to be in a deep Sadness, I asked, What was the Reason of it? And a terrible one indeed he gave in the Relation following.

In 1733 *David Jones*, a Sadler, a middle-aged Man, who had for some Time before lived at *Nottingham*, being at *Bristol*, met a Person there; who after giving him some Account of *Georgia*, asked, Whether he would go thither? Adding, His Trade (that of a Sadler) was an exceeding Good Trade there, upon which he might live, creditably and comfortably. He objected his Want of Money to pay his Passage, and buy some Tools which he should have need of. The Gentleman told him, He would supply him with That, and hire him a Shop when he came to *Georgia*, wherein he might follow his Business, and so repay him, as it suited his Convenience. Accordingly to *Georgia* they went; where soon after his Arrival, his Master (as he now stiled him) sold him to Mr. *Lacy*, who set him to work with the rest of his Servants in clearing Land. He commonly appear'd much more thoughtful than the rest, often stealing into the Woods alone. He was now sent to do some Work on an Island, three or four Miles from Mr. *Lacy*'s Great Plantation. Thence he desir'd the other Servants to return without him, saying, *He would stay and kill a Deer.* This was on *Saturday*. On *Monday* they found him on the Shore, with his Gun by him, and the Forepart of his Head shot to Pieces. In his Pocket was a Paper-Book, all the Leaves whereof were fair, except one, on which ten or twelve Verses were written; two of which were these, (which I transcribed thence, from his own Hand Writing)

Death could not a more sad Retinue find;
Sickness and Pain before, and Darkness all behind!

Sund. April 3. And every Day in this Great and Holy Week, we had a Sermon and the Holy Communion. *Mond.* 4. I began learning *Spanish*, in order to converse with my *Jewish* Parishioners: Some of whom seem nearer the Mind that was in Christ, than many of those who call him Lord.

Tues. 12. Being determin'd, if possible, to put a Stop to the Proceedings of one in *Carolina*, who had married several of my Parishioners without either Banns or Licence, and declared, "He would do so still:" I set out in a Sloop for *Charles-Town*. I landed there on *Thursday*, and related the Case to Mr. *Garden*, the Bp. of *London*'s Commissary, who assur'd me, "He would take Care no such Irregularity should be committed for the future."

Sund. 17. Mr. *Garden* (to whom I must ever acknowledge myself indebted for many kind and generous Offices) desiring me to preach, I did so, on those Words of the Epistle for the Day, *Whatsoever is born of* God, *overcometh the World.* To that plain Account of the Christian State which these Words naturally led me to give, a Man of Education and Character seriously objected (what is indeed a great Truth) '*Why if this be Christanity, a Christian must have more Courage than* Alexander the Great.'

Tu. 19. We left *Charles-Town*; but meeting with stormy and contrary Winds, after losing our Anchor, and beating out at Sea all Night, on *Thursd*, 21. we with some Difficulty got back into *Charles-Town* Harbour.

Frid. 22. It being the Time of their Annual Visitation, I had the Pleasure of meeting with the Clergy of *South-Carolina*: Among whom in the Afternoon there was such a Conversation for several Hours, on "Christ, Our Righteousness," as I had not heard at any Visitation in *England*, or hardly on any other Occasion.

Sat. 23. Mentioning to Mr. *Thompson*, Minister of St. *Bartholomew*'s, near *Ponpon*, my being disappointed of a Passage Home by Water, he offer'd me one of his Horses, if I would go by Land, which I gladly accepted of. He went with me twenty Miles, and sent his Servant to guide me the other twenty to his House. Finding a young Negroe there, who seem'd more sensible than the rest, I ask'd her how long she had been in *Carolina*? She said, Two or three Years; but that she was born in *Barbados*, and had lived there in a Minister's Family from a Child. I ask'd, Whether she went to Church there? She said, Yes, every *Sunday*,—to carry my Mistress's Children. I asked what she had learn'd at Church? She said, *Nothing: I heard a deal; but did not understand it.* But what did your Master teach you at Home? *Nothing.* Nor your Mistress? *No.*

I ask'd, "But don't you know, that your Hands and Feet and this you call your Body, will turn to Dust in a little Time? She answered, *Yes.* But there is something in you that will not turn to Dust, and this is what they call your Soul. Indeed, you can't see your Soul, tho' it is within you, as you can't see the Wind, tho' it is all about you. But if you had not a Soul in you, you could no more see, or hear, or feel, than this Table can. What do you think will become of your Soul, when your Body turns to Dust? *I don't know.* Why, it will go out of your Body, and go up there, above the Sky, and live always. God lives there. Do you know who God is? *No.* You can't see him, any more than you can see your own Soul. It is He that made you and me, and all Men and Women, and all Beasts and Birds, and all the World. It is He that makes the Sun shine, and Rain fall, and Corn and Fruits to grow out of the Ground. He makes all these for us. But what do you think he made us, what did He make you and me for? *I can't tell.* He made you to live with himself, above the Sky. And so you will, in a little Time,—if you are good. If you are good, when your Body dies, your Soul will go up, and want nothing, and have whatever you can desire. No one will beat or hurt you there. You will never be sick. You will never be sorry any more, nor afraid of any Thing. I can't tell you, I don't know, how happy you will be: For you will be with God."

The Attention with which this poor Creature listen'd to Instruction is inexpressible. The next Day she remembered all, readily answered every Question; and said, *She would ask Him that made her, to shew her how to be good.*

Sund. 24. I preached twice at *Ponpon* Chappel, on the 13th Chapter of the 1st Epistle to the *Corinthians.* O how will even these Men of *Carolina*, who come eight, ten, or twelve Miles to hear the Gospel, rise in Judgment against those who hear it not, when it is preach'd at their own Doors!

Wedn. 27. I came to Mr. *Belinger*'s Plantation at *Chulifinny*, where the Rain kept me till *Friday*. Here I met with an half-*Indian*, (one that had an *Indian* Mother, and a *Spanish* Father) and several Negroes, who were very desirous of Instruction. One of them said, "When I was at *Ashley-Ferry*, I went to Church every *Sunday*. But here we are buried in the Woods. Tho', if there was any Church within five or six Miles, I am so lame, I can't walk, but I would crawl thither."

Mr. *Belinger* sent a Negro-Lad with me to *Purrysburg*, or rather to the poor Remains of it. O how hath God stretched over this Place *the Lines of Confusion and the Stones of Emptiness!* Alas for those whose Lives were here vilely cast away, thro' Oppression, thro' divers Plagues and Troubles! O Earth! How long wilt Thou hide their Blood! How long wilt Thou cover thy Slain?

This Lad too I found both very desirous and very capable of Instruction. And perhaps one of the easiest and shortest Ways, to instruct the *American* Negroes in Christianity, would be first to enquire after and find out, some of the most serious of the Planters. Then having inquired of them, which of their Slaves *were best inclined* and understood *English*, to go to them from Plantation to Plantation, staying as long as appear'd necessary at each. Three or four Gentlemen in *Carolina* I have been with, that would be sincerely glad of such an Assistant; who might pursue his Work with no more Hindrances than must every where attend the Preaching of the Gospel.

Satur. 30. I came to *Savannah*, and found my little Flock in a better State than I could have expected: God having been pleased greatly to bless the Endeavours of my Fellow-Labourer, while I was absent from them.

Wed. May 18. I discovered the first Convert to Deism that (I believe) has been made here. He was one that for some time had been zealously and exemplarily religious. But indulging himself in harmless Company, he first made shipwreck of his Zeal, and then of his Faith. I have since found several others that have been attack'd. They have as yet maintain'd their Ground. But I doubt the Devil's Apostles are too Industrious to let them long halt between two Opinions.

Wed. 25. I was sent for by one who had been several Years of the Church of *Rome*: But was now deeply convinced (as were several others) by what I had occasionally preach'd, of the grievous Errors that Church was in, and the great Danger of continuing a Member of it. Upon this Occasion I could not but reflect on the many Advices I had receiv'd, To beware of the Increase of Popery: But not One (that I remember) to beware of the Increase of Infidelity. This was quite surprizing, when I consider'd, 1. That in every Place where I have yet been, the Number of the Converts to Popery bore no Proportion to the Number of the Converts to Infidelity. 2. That as bad a Religion as Popery is, no Religion is still worse; a baptized Infidel being always found upon the Trial, twofold worse than even a bigotted Papist. 3. That as dangerous a State as a Papist is in, with Regard to Eternity, a Deist is in a yet more dangerous State, if he be not (without Repentance) an assured Heir of Damnation. And lastly, That as hard as it is to recover a Papist, it is still harder to recover an Infidel: I myself having known many Papists, but never one Deist, re-converted.

May 29. Being *Whitsunday*, four of our Scholars, after having been instructed daily for several Weeks, were at their earnest and repeated Desire, admitted to the Lord's Table. I trust their Zeal hath stirr'd up many, to remember their Creator in the Days of their Youth, and to redeem the Time, even in the Midst of an evil and adulterous Generation.

Indeed about this Time, we observ'd the Spirit of God, to move upon the Minds of many of the Children. They began more carefully to attend to the Things that were spoken both at Home and at Church; and a remarkable Seriousness appear'd in their whole Behaviour and Conversation. Who knows but some of them may *grow up, to the Measure of the Stature of the Fulness of Christ!*

June 25. Mr. *Causton* (the Store-keeper and Chief Magistrate of *Savannah*) was seized with a slow Fever. I attended him every Day (as I did any of my Parishioners, who were in any painful or dangerous Illness) and had a good Hope from the Thankfulness he shew'd, that my Labour was not in vain.

Sunday, July 3. Immediately after the Holy Communion, I mention'd to Mrs. *Williamson* (Mr. *Causton*'s Niece) some Things which I thought reproveable in her Behaviour. At this she appear'd extremely angry, said, *She did not expect such Usage from me*; and at the Turn of the Street (thro' which we were walking Home) went abruptly away. The next Day Mrs. *Causton* endeavour'd to excuse her, told me, She was exceedingly grieved for what had past the Day before, and desired me to tell her in writing what I disliked; which I accordingly did the Day following.

But first, I sent Mr. *Causton* the following Note:

Sir,

To this Hour, you have shewn yourself my Friend: I ever have and ever shall acknowledge it. And it is my earnest Desire, that he who hath hitherto given me this Blessing would continue it still.

But this cannot be, unless you will allow me one Request, which is not so easy an one as it appears, *Don't condemn me for doing in the Execution of my Office, what I think it my Duty to do.*

If you can prevail upon yourself to allow me this, even when I act without Respect of Persons, I am persuaded there will never be, at least not long, any Misunderstanding between us. For even those who seek it, shall I trust, find no Occasion against me, *except it be concerning the Law of my* God.

July 5, 1737. I am, *&c.*

Wedn. 6. Mr. *Causton* came to my House, with Mr. Bailiff *Parker*, and Mr. Recorder; and warmly ask'd, "How could you possibly think I should condemn you, for executing any Part of your Office?" I said short, "Sir, what if I should think it the Duty of my Office, to repell one of your Family from the Holy Communion?" He replied, "If you repell me or my Wife, I shall require a legal Reason. But I shall trouble myself about none else. Let them look to themselves."

Sat. 9. Meeting with a *Frenchman* of *New Orleans* on the *Missisippi*, who had lived several Months among the *Chicasaws*, he gave us a full and particular Account of many Things which had been variously related. And hence we could not but remark, What is the Religion of Nature, properly so called; or, That Religion which flows from Natural Reason, unassisted by Revelation. And that, even in those who have the Knowledge of many Truths; and who converse with their Beloved Ones Day and Night. But too plainly does it appear by the Fruits, That *the* Gods *of these Heathens too are but Devils*.

The Substance of his Account was this:

Some Years past the *Chicasaws* and *French* were Friends. The *French* were then mingled with the *Nautchee Indians*, whom they used as Slaves; till the *Nautchees* made a general Rising, and took many of the *French*, Prisoners. But soon after, a *French* Army set upon them, killed many, and carry'd away the rest. Among those that were kill'd were some *Chicasaws*, whose Death the *Chicasaw* Nation resented: And soon after as a *French* Boat was going thro' their Country, they fired into it, and kill'd all the Men but two. The *French* resolved on Revenge, and Orders were given for many *Indians* and several Parties of White Men, to rendezvous on the 26th of *March*, 1736, near one of the *Chicasaw* Towns. The first Party, consisting of fifty Men, came thither some Days before the Time. They staid there till the 24th, but none came to join them. On the 25th, they were attack'd by two hundred *Chicasaws*. The *French* attempted to force their Way thro' them. Five or six and twenty did so; the rest were taken Prisoners. The Prisoners were sent two or three to a Town to be burnt. Only the Commanding Officer, and one or two more were put to the Death on the Place of the Engagement.

I (said he) and one more, were saved by the Warrior who took us. The Manner of burning the rest was, Holding lighted Canes to their Arms and Legs and several Parts of their Bodies for some Time, and then for a while taking them away. They likewise stuck burning Pieces of Wood into their Flesh all round, in which Condition they kept them from Morning till Evening. But they commonly beat them before they burn them. I saw the Priest that was with us carried to be burnt; and from Head to Foot, he was as black as your Coat with the Blows which they had given him.

I asked him, "What was their Manner of Life?" He said, "They do nothing but eat and drink and smoak from Morning till Night, and in a Manner from Night till Morning. For they rise at any Hour of the Night when they wake; and after eating and drinking as much as they can, go to sleep again." See *The Religion of Nature* truly *Delineated!*

Saturday 23. Reflecting on the State I was now in, I could not but observe in a Letter to a Friend, "How to attain to the being crucified with Christ, I find not, being in a Condition I neither desired, nor expected in *America*, in Ease and Honour and Abundance. A strange School for him who has but One Business, Γυμναζειν ἑαυτὸν πρὸς ἐυσέβειαν.*

Wednesd. 27. I rejoiced to meet once more with that Good Soldier of Jesus Christ, *August Spangenberg:* With whom on *Monday August* 1. I began my long-intended Journey to *Ebenezer.* In the way I told him, "The Calm we had so long enjoyed, was now drawing to an End: That I hoped he would shortly see I was not (as some had told him) a Respecter of Persons; but was determin'd (GOD being my Helper) to behave Indifferently to all, Rich or Poor, Friends or Enemies." I then asked his Advice as to the Difficulty I foresaw, and resolved, by GOD's Grace to follow it.

In the Evening we came to *New Ebenezer*, where the poor *Saltzburghers* are settled. The Industry of this People is quite surprizing. Their Sixty Huts are neatly and regularly built; and all the little Spots of Ground between them, improv'd to the best Advantage. One Side of the Town, is a Field of *Indian* Corn; on the other are the Plantations of several Private Persons: All which together one would scarce think it possible for a Handful of People to have done in one Year.

Wed. 3. We return'd to *Savannah. Sund.* 7. I repelled Mrs. *Wil-*

* *To exercise himself unto Godliness.*

liamson from the Holy Communion. And *Mond.* 8. Mr. Recorder of *Savannah*, issued out the Warrant following:

Georgia, Savannah ss.

To all Constables; Tythingmen and others whom These may concern:

You and each of you are hereby required, to take the Body of *John Westley*, Clerk:

And bring him before one of the Bailiffs of the said Town, to answer the Complaint of *William Williamson* and *Sophia* his Wife, for defaming the said *Sophia*, and refusing to administer to her the Sacrement of the Lord's Supper, in a Publick Congregation, without Cause; by which the said *William Williamson* is damag'd One Thousand Pounds Sterling. And for so doing, this is your Warrant, certifying what you are to do in the Premises. Given under my Hand and Seal the 8th Day of *Aug. Anno Dom.* 1737.

Tho. Christie.

Tues. 9. Mr. *Jones* the Constable served the Warrant, and carried me before Mr. Bailiff *Parker* and Mr. Recorder. My Answer to them was, That "The giving or refusing the Lord's Supper, being a Matter purely Ecclesiastical, I could not acknowledge their Power, to interrogate me upon it." Mr. *Parker* told me, "However, you must appear at the next Court holden for *Savannah*." Mr. *Williamson* (who stood by) said, "Gentlemen, I desire Mr. *Wesley* may give Bail for his Appearance." But Mr. *Parker* immediately reply'd, *Sir, Mr.* Wesley'*s Word is sufficient.*

Wednes. 10. Mr. *Causton* (*from a just Regard*, as his Letter express'd it, *to the Friendship which had subsisted between us, till this Affair*) required me, To give the Reasons in the Court-House, why I repell'd Mrs. *Williamson* from the Holy Communion? I answer'd, "I apprehend many ill Consequences may arise from so doing. Let the Case be laid before the Trustees."

Thursd. 11. Mr. *Causton* came to my House, and among many other sharp Words said, "Make an End of this Matter, Thou hadst best. My Niece to be used thus! I have drawn the Sword, and I will never sheath it, till I have Satisfaction."

Soon after he added, "Give the Reasons of your repelling her, before the whole Congregation." I answer'd, "Sir, If you insist upon it, I will; and so you may be pleased to tell her." He said, "Write to her, and tell her so yourself." I said, *I will*; and after he went, I wrote as follows.

To Mrs. Sophia Williamson.

At Mr. *Causton*'s Request, I write once more. The Rules whereby I proceed are these:

So many as intend to be Partakers of the Holy Communion, shall signify their Names to the Curate, at least some Time the Day before. This you did not do.

And if any of these——have done any Wrong to his Neighbours by Word or Deed, so that the Congregation be thereby offended, the Curate——shall advertise him, that in any wise he presume not to come to the Lord's Table, until he hath openly declared himself to have truly repented.

If you offer yourself at the Lord's Table on *Sunday*, I will advertise you (as I have done more than once) wherein you *have done Wrong*. And when you have *openly declared yourself to have truly repented*, I will administer to you the Mysteries of God.

Aug. 11. 1737. *John Wesley.*

Mr. *Delamotte* carrying this, Mr. *Causton* said, among many other warm Sayings, "I am the Person that am injured. The Affront is offered to me; and I will espouse the Cause of my Niece. I am ill used; and I will have Satisfaction, if it be to be had in the World."

Which way this Satisfaction was to be had, I did not yet conceive. But on *Friday* and *Saturday* it began to appear; Mr. *Causton* declaring to many Persons, That *Mr.* Wesley *had repelled* Sophy *from the Holy Communion, purely out of Revenge; because he had made Proposals of Marriage to her, which she rejected, and married Mr.* Williamson.

I could not but observe the gracious Providence of God, in the Course of Lessons all this Week. On *Mond.* Evening God spake to us in these Words, *Call to Remembrance the former Days, in which you endured a great Fight of Afflictions: Partly whilst ye were made a Gazing-flock, both by Reproaches and Afflictions, and partly whilst ye became Companions of them that were so used.——Cast not away therefore your Confidence, which hath great Recompence of Reward.*

For ye have Need of Patience, that after ye have done the Will of God, *ye might receive the Promise.*

The Evening Lesson on *Tuesday*, was the 11th of the *Hebrews*; in reading which I was more particularly encouraged by His Example, who *chose rather to suffer Affliction with the People of* God, *than to enjoy the Pleasures of Sin for a Season: Esteeming the Reproach of Christ greater Riches than the Treasures of* Egypt.

The Lesson on *Wednesday* began with these Words, *Wherefore seeing we are compast about with so great a Cloud of Witnesses, let us lay aside every Weight—and run with Patience the Race that is set before us: Looking unto Jesus the Author and Finisher of our Faith, who for the Joy that was set before him, endured the Cross, despising the Shame, and is set down at the Right Hand of the Throne of* God.

In the *Thursday*-Lesson were these comfortable Words, *I will never leave Thee nor forsake Thee. So that we may boldly say, the Lord is my Helper, and I will not fear what Man shall do unto me.*

The Words of St. *James*, read on *Friday* were, *Blessed is the Man that endureth Temptation:* And those on *Saturday*, *My Brethren, Have not the Faith of our Lord Jesus Christ—with Respect of Persons.*

I was only afraid, lest those who were weak, should *be turned out of the Way*; at least, so far as to forsake the Publick *assembling of themselves together*. But I feared where no Fear was. God took Care of this also. So that on *Sunday* 14. more were present at the Morning Prayers, than had been for some Months before. Many of them observed those Words in the First Lesson, *Set Naboth on high among the People; and set Two Men, Sons of Belial, before him, to bear Witness against him.*

Tuesd. 16. Mrs. *Williamson* swore to and sign'd an Affidavit, insinuating much more than it asserted: But asserting, "That Mr. *Wesley* had many Times propos'd Marriage to her, all which Proposals she had rejected." Of this I desired a Copy: Mr. *Causton* reply'd, "Sir, You may have one from any of the News-Papers in *America*."

On *Thursday* or *Friday* was deliver'd out a List of Twenty-Six Men, who were to meet as a Grand Jury, on *Monday* the 22d. But this List was called in the next Day, and Twenty-Four Names added to it. Of this Grand Jury (Forty-Four of whom only met) One was a *Frenchman*, who did not understand *English*, One a *Papist*, One a *profest Infidel*, Three *Baptists*, Sixteen or Seventeen others, *Dissenters*, and several others who had Personal Quarrels against me, and had openly vow'd Revenge.

To *this* Grand Jury, on *Monday* the 22d, Mr. *Causton* gave a long and earnest Charge, *To beware of Spiritual Tyranny, and to oppose the New, Illegal Authority, which was usurped over their Consciences.* Then Mrs. *Williamson*'s Affidavit was read: After which Mr. *Causton deliver'd to the Grand Jury*, a Paper intitled "A List of Grievances, *presented by* the Grand Jury for *Savannah*, this Day of *Aug.* 1737."

This the Majority of the Grand Jury alter'd in some Particulars, and on *Thu. Sept.* 1. deliver'd it again to the Court, under the Form of Two Presentments, containing Ten Bills, which were then read to the People.

Herein they asserted, upon Oath,

That *John Wesley*, Clerk, had *broken the Laws of the Realm, contrary to the Peace of our Sovereign Lord the King, his Crown and Dignity,*

1. By speaking and writing to Mrs. *Williamson*, against her Husband's Consent:
2. By repelling her from the Holy Communion:
3. By not declaring his Adherence to the Church of *England*:
4. By dividing the Morning Service on *Sundays*:
5. By refusing to baptize Mr. *Parker*'s Child otherwise than by Dipping, except the Parents would certify it was Weak, and not able to bear it.
6. By repelling *Wm. Gough* from the Holy Communion:
7. By refusing to read the Burial-Service over the Body of *Nathaniel Polhill*:
8. By calling himself *Ordinary* of *Savannah*:
9. By refusing to receive *Wm. Aglionby* as a Godfather, only because he was not a Communicant:
10. By refusing *Jacob Matthews* for the same Reason; and baptizing an *Indian* Trader's Child with only Two Sponsors.

(This, I own, was wrong; for I ought, at all Hazards, to have refused baptizing it, till he had procured a Third.)

Frid. 2. Was the Third Court, at which I appear'd, since my being carried before Mr. *P.* and the Recorder.

I now moved for an immediate Hearing on the First Bill, being the only one of a Civil Nature: But it was refused. I made the same Motion in the Afternoon; but was put off till the Next Court Day.

On the next Court Day I appear'd again; as also at the Two Courts following: But could not be heard, *because* (the Judge said) *Mr.* Williamson *was gone out of Town.*

The Sense of the Minority of the Grand Jurors themselves (for they were by no Means unanimous) concerning these Presentments, may appear from the following Paper, which they transmitted to the Trustees.

To the Honourable the Trustees for Georgia.

Whereas Two Presentments have been made, the one of *August* 23, the other of *August* 31, by the Grand Jury for the Town and County of *Savannah* in *Georgia*, against *John Wesley*, Clerk.

We whose Names are underwritten, being Members of the said Grand Jury, do humbly beg Leave to signify our Dislike of the said Presentments; being by many and divers Circumstances thro'ly persuaded in ourselves, That the whole Charge against Mr. *Wesley*, is an Artifice of Mr. *Causton*'s, design'd rather to blacken the Character of Mr. *Wesley*, than to free the Colony from Religious Tyranny, as he was pleas'd in his Charge to us to term it. But as these Circumstances will be too tedious to trouble your Honours with, we shall only beg Leave to give the Reasons of our Dissent from the Particular Bills.

With regard to the First Bill, we do not apprehend, That Mr. *Wesley* acted against any Law, by Writing or Speaking to Mrs. *Williamson*, since *it does not appear* to us, *That* the said *Mr. Wesley has either spoke in private, or wrote to*, the said *Mrs. Williamson, since March* 12, (the Day of her Marriage,) *except one Letter of July the 5th, which he wrote at the Request of her Aunt, as a Pastor to exhort and reprove her.*

The Second we do not apprehend to be a true Bill, because we humbly conceive Mr. *Wesley* did not assume to himself any Authority contrary to Law: For we understand, *Every Person intending to communicate, should "signify his Name to the Curate, at least some time the Day before,"* which Mrs. *Williamson* did not do; altho' Mr. *Wesley* had often in full Congregation declared, He did insist on a Compliance with that Rubrick, and *had before repell'd divers Persons, for Noncompliance therewith.*

The Third we do not think a true Bill, because several of Us, have been his Hearers, when he has declared his Adherence to the *Church of England.* in a stronger Manner than by a formal Declaration; by explaining and defending the *Apostles, the Nicene* and the *Athanasian Creeds,* the *Thirty-nine Articles,* the *whole Book of Common-Prayer,* and the *Homilies* of the said Church: And because we think a formal Declaration is not required, but from those who have receiv'd Institution and Induction.

The Fact alledged in the Fourth Bill we cannot apprehend to be contrary to any Law in being.

The Fifth we do not think a true Bill, because we conceive Mr. *Wesley* is justified by the Rubrick, viz. "*If they* (the Parents) *certify that the Child is weak, it shall suffice to pour Water upon it.*" Intimating (as we humbly suppose) it shall not suffice, if they do not certify.

The Sixth cannot be a true Bill, because the said *William Gough,* being one of our Members, was surprised to hear himself named, without his Knowledge or Privity; and did publickly declare, *It was no Grievance to him, because the said* John Wesley *had given him Reasons with which he was satisfied.*

The Seventh we do not apprehend to be a true Bill, for *Nathaniel Polhill* was an *Anabaptist,* and desir'd in his Life-time, That he might not be interr'd with the Office of the *Church of England.* And farther, we have good Reason to believe, That Mr. *Wesley was at* Frederica, or on his Return thence, *when* Polhill *was buried.*

As to the Eighth Bill we are in doubt, as not well knowing the Meaning of the Word Ordinary. But for the Ninth and Tenth, we think Mr. *Wesley* is sufficiently justified by the Canons of the Church; which forbid *any Person to be admitted Godfather or Godmother to any Child, before the said Person has received the Holy Communion*; whereas *William Aglionby* and *Jacob Matthews,* had never certified Mr. *Wesley,* That they had receiv'd it.

This was sign'd by twelve of the Grand Jurors, of whom three were Constables, and six more, Tythingmen: Who consequently would have made a Majority, had the Jury consisted, as it regularly should have done, of only fifteen Members, viz. the four Constables and eleven Tythingmen.

Friday, Sept. 30. Having ended the Homilies, I began reading

Dr. *Rogers*'s eight Sermons to the Congregation: Hoping they might be a timely Antidote against the Poison of Infidelity, which was now with great Industry propagated among us.

October the 7th I consulted my Friends, whether GOD did not call me, to return to *England*? The Reason for which I left it had now no Force; there being no Possibility as yet of instructing the *Indians*: Neither had I as yet found or heard of any *Indians* on the Continent of *America*, who had the least Desire of being instructed. And as to *Savannah*, having never engaged myself, either by Word or Letter, to stay there a Day longer than I should judge convenient, nor ever taken Charge of the People any otherwise, than as in my Passage to the Heathens, I looked upon myself to be fully discharged therefrom, by the vacating of that Design. Besides, there was a Probability of doing more Service to that unhappy People, in *England* than I could do in *Georgia*, by representing without Fear or Favour to the Trustees, the real State the Colony was in. After deeply considering these Things; they were unanimous, *That I ought to go. But not yet.* So I laid the Thoughts of it aside for the present: Being persuaded, that when the Time was come, GOD would *make the Way plain before my Face.*

Sat. Oct. 15. Being at *Highgate*, a Village five Miles from *Savannah*, consisting of (all but one) *French* Families, who, I found, knew but little of the *English* Tongue, I offer'd to read Prayers there in *French*, every *Saturday* in the Afternoon. They embrac'd the Offer gladly. On *Saturday* the 22d I read Prayers in *German* likewise, to the *German* Villagers of *Hampstead*: And so continued to do, once a Week. We began the Service (both at *Highgate* and *Hampstead*) with singing a Psalm. Then I read and explain'd a Chapter in the *French* or *German* Testament, and concluded with Prayers and another Psalm.

Sat. Oct. 9. Some of the *French* of *Savannah* were present at the Prayers at *Highgate*. The next Day I receiv'd a Message from them all, That as I read Prayers to the *French* of *Highgate*, who were but few, they hop'd I would do the same to those of *Savannah*, where there was a large Number who did not understand *English*. *Sunday*, 30, I began so to do: And now I had full Employment for that Holy Day. The first *English* Prayers lasted from Five 'till Half an Hour past Six. The *Italian* (which I read to a few *Vaudois*) began at Nine. The second Service for the *English* (including the Sermon and the Holy Communion) continu'd from Half an Hour past Ten, till about Half an Hour past Twelve. The *French* Service began at One. At Two I catechised the Children. About Three began the *English* Service. After this was ended, I had the Happiness of joining with as many as my largest Room would hold, in Reading, Prayer, and singing Praise. And about Six the Service of the *Moravians* began: At which I was glad to be present, not as a Teacher, but a Learner.

Thursd. Nov. 3. I appear'd again, at the Court holden on that Day: And again, at the Court held, *Tuesday, Nov.* 22. On which Day Mr. *Causton* desired to speak with me. He then read me some Affidavits which had been made, *Sept.* 15. last past: In one of which it was affirm'd, "That I then abused Mr. *Causton* in his own House, calling him Liar, Villain, and so on." It was now likewise repeated before several Persons, (which indeed I had forgot) That I had been reprimanded at the last Court, for an Enemy to, and Hinderer of, the Publick Peace."

I again consulted my Friends, who agreed with me, That the Time we look'd for was now come. And the next Morning calling on Mr. *Causton*, I told him, "I design'd to set out for *England* immediately." I set up an Advertisement in the Great Square to the same Effect, and quietly prepared for my Journey.

Friday, Dec. 2. I propos'd to set out for *Carolina* about Noon, the Tide then serving. But about Ten the Magistrates sent for me, and told me, I must not go out of the Province; for I had not answer'd the Allegations laid against me I replied, *I have appeared at six or seven Courts successively, in order to answer them. But I was not suffer'd so to do, when I desired it Time after Time.* They then said, However, I must not go, unless I would give Security to answer those Allegations at their Court. I asked, "What Security?" After consulting together about two Hours, the Recorder shew'd me a kind of Bond, engaging me, under a Penalty of fifty Pounds, to appear at their Court when I should be required. He added, *But*

Mr. Williamson *too has desired of us, that you should give Bail to answer his Action.* I then told him plainly, *Sir, You use me very ill, and so you do the Trustees. I will give neither any Bond, nor any Bail at all. You know your Business, and I know mine.*

In the Afternoon the Magistrates publish'd an Order, requiring all the Officers and Centinels, to prevent my going out of the Province; and forbidding any Person to assist me so to do. Being now only a Prisoner at large, in a Place where I knew by Experience, every Day would give fresh Opportunity, to procure Evidence of Words I never said, and Actions I never did; I saw clearly the Hour was come for leaving this Place: And as soon as Evening Prayers were over, about Eight o'Clock, the Tide then serving, I shook off the Dust of my Feet, and left *Georgia*, after having preach'd the Gospel there (not as I ought, but as I was able) one Year, and nearly nine Months.

During this Time I had frequent Opportunities of making many Observations and Enquiries, concerning the Real State of this Province, (which has been so variously represented) the *English* Settlements therein, and the *Indians* that have Intercourse with them. These I minuted down from Time to Time; a small Extract of which I have subjoined.

1. *Georgia* lies in the 30 and 31st Degree of North Latitude. The Air is generally clear, the Rains being much shorter, as well as heavier, than in *England*. The Dews are very great. Thunder and Lightning are expected almost every Day, in *May*, *June*, *July*, and *August*. They are very terrible, especially to a Stranger. During those Months, from Ten in the Morning to Four in the Afternoon, the Sun is extremely scorching. But the Sea-Breeze generally blows, from Ten till Three or Four. The Winter is nearly of the same Length as in *England*. But the Mid-day Sun is always warm, even when the Mornings and Evenings are very sharp, and the Nights piercing cold.

2. The Land is of four Sorts, Pine-barren, Oakland, Swamp and Marsh. The Pine-Land is of far the greatest Extent, especially near the Sea-Coasts. The Soil of this, is a dry, whitish Sand, producing Shrubs of several Sorts, and between them a spiry, coarse Grass, which Cattle do not love to feed on. But here and there is a little of a better Kind, especially in the Savannahs (so they call the low, watry Meadows, which are usual-

ly intermixt with Pine-Lands). It bears naturally two Sorts of Fruit, Hurtle-Berries (much like those in *England*) and Chincopin-Nuts; a dry, harsh Nut, about the Size of a small Acorn. A laborious Man may in one Year clear and plant four or five Acres of this Land: It will produce the first Year, from two to four Bushels of *Indian* Corn, and from four to eight of *Indian* Pease *per* Acre. The second Year it usually bears half as much; the Third, less; the Fourth nothing.

3. Vines, Mulberries and Peach-Trees it bears well. The White Mulberry is not good to eat. The Black is about the Size of a Blackberry, and has much the same Flavour. In fresh Pine-Land, *Indian* Potatos grow well (which are more luscious and larger than the *Irish*). And so do Water-melons and Sewee Beans, about the Size of our Scarlet, but to be shell'd and eaten like *Windsor* Beans.

4. Oak-Land commonly lies in narrow streaks between Pine-Land and some Swamp, Creek or River. The Soil is a blackish Sand, producing several Kinds of Oak (tho' none exactly like the *English*) Bay, Lawrel, Ash, Walnut, Sumac-Trees, Gum-Trees (a fort of Sycamore) Dog-Trees (cover'd in Spring with large white Flowers) and many Hickary-Trees, which bear a bad Kind of Walnut. In the moistest Part of this Land, some Porsimmon-Trees grow, (which bear a sort of yellow, clear, luscious Plum) and a few Mulberry and Cherry-Trees. The common Wild-Grapes are of Two Sorts, both Red: The Fox-Grape grows two or three only on a Stalk, is thick-skin'd, large-ston'd, of a harsh Taste, and of the Size of a small *Kentish* Cherry. The Cluster-Grape is of a harsh Taste too, and about the Size of a White Currant.

5. This Land requires much Labour to clear; but when it is clear'd, it will bear any Grain, for three, four, or sometimes five Years, without laying any Manure upon it. An Acre of it generally bears ten Bushels of *Indian* Corn, beside five of Pease, in a Year. So that this at present is justly esteemed the most valuable Land in the Province.

6. A Swamp is, any low, watry Place, which is cover'd with Trees or Canes. They are here of three Sorts, Cypress, River and Cane-Swamps. Cypress-Swamps are, mostly, large Ponds, in and round which Cypresses grow. Most River-Swamps are over-flown every Tide, by the River which runs thro' or near them. If they were drain'd, they would produce Good Rice; as would the Cane-Swamps also; which in the mean time are the best Feeding for all Sorts of Cattle.

7. The Marshes are of Two Sorts: Soft Marsh, which is all a Quagmire, and absolutely good for nothing: And Hard Marsh, which is a firm, but

barren Sand, bearing only sower Rushes. Marshes of both Sorts abound on the Sea-Islands, which are very numerous, and contain all Sorts of Land. And upon these chiefly, near Creeks and Runs of Water, Juniper-Trees and Cedars grow.

8. *Savannah* stands on a flat *Bluff* (so they term any high-Land hanging over a Creek or River) which rises 45 Feet perpendicular from the River, and commands it several Miles both upward and downward. The Soil is a white Sand for above a Mile in Breadth, South-East, and North-Westward. Beyond this, Eastward, is a River-swamp; Westward a small Wood, in which was the old *Indian* Town. On the other Side of the River is a Marshy Island, cover'd with large Trees. South-West of the Town is a large Pine-barren, which extends backward to a Branch of the *Alatamahaw* River.

9. St. *Simon*'s Island, having on the South-East the Gulph of *Florida*; on the other Sides, Branches of the *Alatamahaw*, is about 100 Miles South of *Savannah*, and extends in Length about 20, in Breadth from two to five Miles. On the West-side of it, on a low Bluff, stands *Frederica*, having Woods to the North and South; to the East, partly Woods, partly Savannahs, and partly Marshes. The Soil is mostly a blackish Sand. There is not much Pine-Land on the Island; the greatest Part being Oak-Land, intermixt with many Savannahs, and old *Spanish* or *Indian* Fields.

10. On the Sea-Point, about five Miles South-East of the Town, is the Fort where the Soldiers are station'd. The But-Storehouse in *Frederica* better deserves that Name; being incompast with regular Ramparts of Earth, and a Palisaded Ditch, and mounted with Cannon, which intirely commands the River.

11. About twenty Miles North-West from St. *Simon*'s is *Darien*, the Settlement of the *Scotch Highlanders*, a Mile from *Fort King George*, which was built about seventeen, and abandoned about eleven Years since. The Town lies on the Main-Land, close to a Branch of the *Alatamahaw*, on a Bluff thirty Feet above the River, having Woods on all Sides. The Soil is a blackish Sand. They built at first many scatter'd Huts; but last Spring, (1736) expecting the *Spaniards*, they built themselves a large Fort, and all retired within the Walls of it.

12. *Augusta*, distant from *Savannah* one hundred and fifty Miles, and five from old *Savana* Town, is designed to stand in an old *Indian* Field, on a Bluff, about thirty Feet high. A small Fort of Wooden Piles was built there in 1737; but no House was then built, nor any more Ground clear'd, than Mr. *Lacy* and his Men found so.

13. *Old Ebenezer*, where the *Saltzburghers* settled at first, lies twenty-five Miles West of *Savannah*. A small Creek runs by the Town, down to the River, and many Brooks run between the little Hills: But the Soil is a hungry, barren Sand; and upon any sudden Shower, the Brooks rise several Feet perpendicular, and overflow whatever is near them. Since the *Saltzburghers* remov'd, two *English* Families have been placed there: But these too say, *That the Land is good for nothing; and that the Creek is of little Use; it being by Water twenty Miles to the River; and the Water generally so low in Summer-time, that a Boat cannot come within six or seven Miles of the Town.*

14. *New Ebenezer*, to which the *Saltzburghers* removed, in *March* 1736, lies six Miles Eastward from the *Old*, on a high Bluff, near the *Savannah* River. Here are some Tracts of fruitful Land, tho' the greatest Part of that adjoining to the Town, is Pine-barren. The Huts, 60 in Number, are neatly and regularly built; the little Piece of Ground allotted to each for a Garden, is every where put to the best Use, no Spot being left unplanted. Nay, even one of the main Streets, being one more than was as yet wanted, bore them this Year a Crop of *Indian Corn*.

15. About ten Miles East of this, on a Creek, three Miles from the River, was the Village of *Abercorn*. Ten Families settled here in 1733; but it is now without Inhabitant. Four Miles below the Mouth of *Abercorn*-Creek is *Joseph's-Town*, the Settlement of two *Scotch* Gentlemen. A Mile below was Sir *Francis Bathurst*'s Plantation. And a Quarter of a Mile from this, *Walter Augustin*'s Settlement. But both these are left without Inhabitant.

16. A Mile below this is Capt. *Williams*'s Plantation: A Mile from thence, Mrs. *Matthew*'s (late *Musgrove*) commonly known by the Name of the *Cowpen*: Adjoining to which is the Land belonging to Capt. *Watson*; on which is an unfinish'd House, swiftly running to Ruin. A Mile from this is *Irene*, a House built for an *Indian* School, in the Year 1736. It stands on a small, round Hill, in a little Piece of fruitful Ground, given by the *Indians* to Mr. *Ingham*. The *Indian* Town is within a Furlong of it.

17. Five Miles South-West of *Savannah*, on a small Rise, stands the Village of *Highgate*. It has Pine-Land on three Sides, and a Swamp on the fourth. Twelve Families were placed here in 1733; nine whereof remain there. A Mile Eastward of this is *Hampstead*, settled with twelve Families also, a little before Highgate; five of which are still remaining.

18. Six Miles South-East of *Savannah* is *Thunderbolt*. Three Families are settled here, near a small, ruinous, Fort: Four Miles South of this, is

the Island of *Skidoway*: On the North-East Point whereof Ten Families were placed in 1733-4; (a small Fort was built here likewise) but nine of them are either dead, or removed to other Places. A small Creek divides *Skidoway* from *Tybee* Island, on the South-East Part of which, fronting the Inlet, the Light-House is built. Ten Families were settled here in 1734; but they are Part dead, and Part removed, so that the Island is now again without any fixt Inhabitant.

19. Twelve Miles Southward from *Savannah* (by Land) is Mr. *Houstoun*'s Plantation: And forty or fifty Miles from him, up Ogeechy River, that where Mr. *Sterling* for some time lived. Fort *Argyle* stands twenty Miles from this, on a high Bluff, by the River *Ogeechy*. 'Tis a small, square, Wooden Fort, Musket-Proof. Ten Freeholders were settled near it; but eight of them are gone, and the Land they had cleared lying waste, will in a few Years be as it was before.

20. The Southermost Settlement in *Georgia*, is *Fort St. Andrews*. It stands fifty Miles South of *Frederica*, on the South-West Side of *Cumberland* Island, upon a high Neck of Land, which commands the River both Ways. The Walls are of Wood, fill'd up with Earth, round which are a Ditch and Palisade.

21. 'Tis hard to pick out any consistent Account of the *Georgian Indians*, from the contradictory Relations of their Traders. The following is extracted, partly from those wherein all, or the Generality of them agree; partly from the Relations of such as have been occasionally amongst them, and have no Interest in making them better or worse than they are.

22. Of the *Georgian Indians* in general it may be observed, That they are not so properly Nations, as Tribes or Clans, who have wandered thither at different Times; perhaps expell'd their Native Countries by stronger Tribes; but how or when they cannot tell, being none of them able to give any rational Account of themselves. They are inured to Hardship of all Kinds, and surprisingly patient of Pain. But as they have no Letters, so they have no Religion, no Laws, no civil Government. Nor have they any Kings or Princes, properly speaking; their Meeko's or Head-men, having no Power either to command or punish, no Man obeying them any farther than he pleases. So that every one doth what is right in his own Eyes; and if it appears wrong to his Neighbour, the Person aggrieved usually steals on the other unawares, and shoots him, scalps him, or cuts off his Ears: Having only two short Rules of Proceeding, To do what he will, and what he can.

23. They are likewise all, except (perhaps) the *Choctaws*, Gluttons,

Drunkards, Thieves, Dissemblers, Liars. They are Implacable, Unmerciful; Murderers of Fathers, Murderers of Mothers, Murderers of their own Children: It being a common Thing for a Son to shoot his Father or Mother, because they are old and past Labour; and for a Woman either to procure Abortion, or to throw her Child into the next River, because she will go with her Husband to the War. Indeed Husbands, strictly speaking, they have none; for any Man leaves his Wife (so call'd) at Pleasure; who frequently, in Return, cuts the Throats of all the Children she has had by him. Whoredom they account no Crime, and few Instances appear of a young *Indian* Woman's refusing any one. Nor have they any fixt Punishment for Adultery; only if the Husband take his Wife with another Man, he will do what he can to both, unless speedily pacified by the Present of a Gun or a Blanket.

24. The *Choctaws* only have some Appearance of an intire Nation, possessing a large Extent of Land, eight or nine hundred Miles West of *Savannah*, and many well inhabited Towns. They are said to have six thousand fighting Men, united under one Head. At present they are in League with the *French*, who have sent some Priests among them; by whom (if one may credit the *Choctaw* Traders) ten or twelve have been baptized.

25. Next to these, to the North-East, are the *Chicasaws*. Their Country is flat, full of Meadows, Springs and Rivers. In their Fields, tho' six or seven hundred Miles from the Sea, are found Sea-Shells in great Numbers. They have about nine hundred fighting Men, ten Towns, and one *Meeko* (at least) in every one. They are eminently Gluttons, eating, drinking, and smoaking all Day, and almost all Night. They are extreme indolent and lazy, except in War; then they are the most indefatigable, and the most valiant of all the *Indians*: But they are equally cruel with the rest, torturing and burning all their Prisoners, whether *Indian* or *European*.

26. East of them, in the Latitude of 35 and 36, about three or four hundred Miles from *Savannah*, lie the *Cherikees*. Their Country is very mountainous, fruitful, and pleasant. They have fifty-two Towns, and above three thousand fighting Men. In each Town are three or more Head-men, who keep up a sort of Shadow of Government, having Power to set the rest to work, and to punish such as will not join in the common Labour. They are civil to Strangers, and will do any thing for them, *for Pay*; being always willing, for a small Piece of Money, to carry a Message for 50 or 60 Miles, and, if required, a heavy Burthen too: But they are equally cruel to Prisoners with the *Chicasaws*, tho' not equally valiant. They are

seldom intemperate in Drinking, but when they can be so on Free-Cost. Otherwise, Love of Drink yields to Covetousness; a Vice scarce to be found in any *Indian* but a *Cherikee.*

27. The *Uchees* have only one small Town left (near 200 Miles from *Savannah*) and about forty fighting Men. The *Creeks* have been many Times on the Point of cutting them off. They are indeed hated by most, and despis'd by all the other Nations, as well for their Cowardice, as their Superlative Diligence in Thieving, and for Out-lying all the *Indians* upon the Continent.

28. The *Creek-Indians* are about 400 Miles from *Savannah.* They are said to be bounded to the West by the *Choctaws,* to the North by the *Chicasaws,* to the East by the *Cherikees,* and to the South by the *Alatamahaw* River. They have many Towns, a plain, well-water'd Country, and fifteen hundred fighting Men. They have often three or four Meeko's in a Town; but without so much as the Shadow of Authority, only to give Advice, which every one is at Liberty to take or leave. But Age and Reputation for Valour and Wisdom, have given *Chicali,* a Meeko of the *Coweta*-Town, a more than ordinary Influence over the Nation; tho' not even the Show of Regal Power. Yet neither Age, Wisdom nor Reputation can restrain him from Drunkenness. Indeed All the *Creeks,* having been most conversant with White Men, are most infected with Insatiate Love of Drunkenness, as well as other *European* Vices. They are more exquisite Dissemblers than the rest of their Countrymen. They know not what Friendship or Gratitude means. They shew no Inclination to learn any thing; but least of all, Christianity; Being full as opinionated of their own Parts and Wisdom, as either Modern *Chinese,* or Antient *Roman.*

Saturd. Dec. 3. We came to *Purrysburg* early in the Morning, and endeavour'd to procure a Guide for *Port-Royal.* But none being to be had, we set out without one, an Hour before Sunrise. After walking two or three Hours, we met with an old Man, who led us into a small Path, near which was a Line of *blazed* Trees, (i. e. mark'd by cutting off Part of the Bark) by following which, he said, we might easily come to *Port-Royal* in five or six Hours.

We were four in all; one of whom intended to go for *England* with me; the other two to settle in *Carolina.* About eleven, we came into a large Swamp, where we wander'd about 'till near Two. We then found another *Blaze,* and pursued it, 'till it divided into two; one of these we followed thro' an almost impassable Thicket, a Mile beyond which it ended. We made thro' the Thicket again, and traced the other *Blaze*, 'till that ended too. It now grew toward Sun-set, so we sat down, faint and weary, having had no Food all Day, except a Gingerbread Cake, which I had taken in my Pocket. A third of this we had divided among us at Noon; another third we took now; the rest we reserved for the Morning; but we had met with no Water all the Day. Thrusting a Stick into the Ground, and finding the End of it moist, two of our Company fell a digging with their Hands, and at about three Feet depth, found Water. We thank'd GOD, drank, and were refreshed. The Night was sharp; however, there was no complaining among us; but after having commended ourselves to GOD, we lay down close together, and (I at least) slept 'till near Six in the Morning.

Sunday, Dec. 4. GOD renewing our Strength, we arose neither faint nor weary, and resolved to make one Tryal more, to find a Path to *Port-Royal*. We steer'd due East; but finding neither Path nor Blaze, and the Woods growing thicker and thicker, we judg'd it would be our best Course to return, if we could, by the Way we came. The Day before, in the thickest Part of the Woods, I had broke many young Trees, I knew not why, as we walk'd along: These we found a great Help in several Places, where no Path was to be seen; and between One and Two GOD brought us safe to *Benjamin Arieu*'s House, the old Man we left the Day before.

In the Evening I read *French* Prayers to a numerous Family, a Mile from *Arieu*'s; one of whom undertook to guide us to *Port-Royal*. In the Morning we set out. About Sun-set, we ask'd our Guide, If he knew where he was? Who frankly answer'd, No. However, we push'd on 'till about Seven we came to a Plantation, and the next Evening (after many Difficulties and Delays) we landed on *Port-Royal* Island.

Wednesd. 7. We walk'd to *Beaufort*; where Mr. *Jones* (the Minister of *Beaufort*) with whom I lodg'd during my short Stay here, gave me a lively Idea of the old *English* Hospitality. On *Thursday* Mr. *Delamotte* came; with whom, on *Friday*, 9th, I took Boat for *Charles-Town*. After a slow Passage by Reason of contrary Winds, and some Conflict (our Provisions falling short) with Hunger as well as Cold, we came thither early in the Morning, on *Tuesday* the 13th. Here I expected Tryals of a different kind, and far more dangerous. For Contempt and Want are easy to be borne: But who can bear Respect and Abundance?

Wednes. 14. Being desir'd to read Publick Prayers, I was much refreshed with those glorious Promises, contained both in the 72d *Psalm*, and in the first Lesson, the 40th Chapter of *Isaiah.* Yea, *they that wait upon the Lord shall renew their Strength, and mount up with Wings as Eagles; they shall run and not be weary; they shall walk and not faint!*

In the Afternoon visiting a dying Man, we found him still full of the Freshest Advices (and busy in settling the Affairs of the *Czarina*, Prince *Thamas*, and the *Ottoman Port*). How natural then is the Thought

———————*Quæ cura nitentes*
Pascere equos, eadem sequitur tellure repostos?

For if a Soul quivering on the Verge of Life, has still Leisure for these Impertinencies, one might almost believe the same Dreams would continue, even in the Sleep of Death!

Frid. 16. I parted from the last of those Friends, who came with me into *America*, Mr. *Ch. Delamotte*, from whom I had been but a few Days separate, since *Oct.* 14. 1735.

Sund. 18. I was seiz'd with a violent Flux, which I felt came not before I wanted it. Yet I had Strength enough given to preach once more to this careless People: And a few *believed our Report.*

Thurs. 22. I took my Leave of *America*, (tho', if it pleased God, not for ever) going on board the *Samuel*, Capt. *Percy*, with a young Gentleman who had been a few Months in *Carolina*, One of my Parishioners of *Savannah*, and a *Frenchman*, late of *Purrysburg*, who was escaped thence with the Skin of his Teeth. *Sat.* 24. we sail'd over *Charles-Town* Bar, and about Noon, lost Sight of Land.

Journal of Thomas Causton Esq.
1st Bailif of Savannah

urnal of Thomas
ston Esq 1st Bailif
Savannah
1737

Journal

from 25 May 1737 to 24 July following

Wednesday

25 May

John Sindall Officer of ye Guard.
Began to unload ye Sloop from N. York — Monday in ye evening, as ye Saltzburgers were rolling a hhd. of Molasses to ye water side, one of ye Staves press'd in, by wch near half of it was entirely lost.
Sundry Stores issued & receiv'd as ℘ day book;

a Mr. Wesley having ask'd Mr. Jones to set out ye Glebe Land, wch being done, he desired ye some part of it might be fenced in — Cha. Britton being in debt to ye Trustees, has undertook to split Rails for ye same, on Condition yt. I support him wth provisions — Mr. Wesley having also desired a School room for ye Children, to be built by his house; John Desborough has undertook it for 14 £ St. he being likewise in Debt to ye Trustees; I am to allow him provisions only.

26. James Campbell (for Austin Widdal) Officer of ye Guard.

b Wm. Sterling complaind to me yt. Mr. Bradley had taken possession of some lands on Vernon River, by wch he apprehended he sh'd be defeated of his right of being first seated, his grant being prior to that of Bradley's — I ask'd him, if he was sure of it — he said he was so sure yt. he had laid aside all thoughts of

Journal of Thomas Causton Esq. 1st Bailif of Savannah

from 25 May 1737 to 24 July following

MAY 25: John Lindall officer of Guard. Began to unload the Sloop from New York. Monday in the evening, as the Saltzburghers were rolling a hogshead of Molasses to the water Side, one of the Staves pressed in by which near half of it was entirely lost. Sundry Stores issued & received as per day book.

Mr. Wesley having asked Mr. Jones to Set out the Glebe Land, which being done, he desired that some part of it might be fenced in. Charles Briton being in debt to the Trustees, has undertook to split Rails for the same, on Condition that I support him 10 pound provisions. Mr. Wesley having also desired a Schoolroom for the Children, to be built by his house, John Desborough has undertook it for 14 £ Sterling he being likewise in Debt to the Trustees, I am to allow him provisions only.

26 MAY: James Campbell (for Austin Weddal) officer of the Guard. William Sterling complained to me that Mr. Bradley had taken possession of some lands on Vernon River, by which he apprehended he should be defeated of his right of being first Seated, his Grant being prior to that of Bradleys. I asked him, if he was sure of it— he said he was so sure that he had laid aside all thoughts of Settling there, & that he had pitch'd on another place, which was part of

Wilmington Island, & was a large Tract of Land, sufficient for himself & brother, & some other friends, who would come here immediately if they were sure they could have Lands to joyn theirs. He said he desired nothing more of me yet, that it might be mentioned to the Trustees, & that I would take notice of the time of this application, that no other person might take possession of, or claim the Same land on pretence of any request prior to his. He told me, the reason for leaving their Settlement on the Argyle River, was, that they suffered very much by being So far distant from any market. I told him I would acquaint the Trustees of the matter, & that it would be proper to acquaint them himself, as well as of the reasons why he had left his former Settlement: as of this request.

A periaguer arrived with Sawed Timber for Mr. Robert Williams from Carolina. Sundry Stores issued & received as per Day book.

27 MAY: James Carwell Officer of the Guard.

Colonel Beamor arrived with Butter & Fowls: as he is a planter who has always Seemed willing to Serve the Colony, I bought them; he offered me a Draft which I have made in his favour on Mr. Jennys on account of the Rumm Duty being value for Sundry provisions bought of him for the Store telling me Mr. Jennys refused payment because I had drawn for more money than the Government of Carolina had granted to the Colony; I thereupon wrote out the Rum Duty Account and Sent it him by the Colonel with an Explanatory Letter, to which I referr.

Sundry Stores issued & received as per day book.

28 MAY: Walter Fox Officer of the Guard.

Thomas Ware, Master of the Sloop from New York, having delivered his Cargo, I certified his Account for which I received in the Store.

I received a letter from Captain Ferguson desiring Latter's Muster Roll, & that he would go down to Charles Town with him to be Sworn to it; for now he had an opportunity of getting the money.

John Rea being here with Mr. Horton brought me his Establishment & Accounts.

Sundry Stores issued & received as per Day book.

SUNDAY 29TH MAY 1737: John Vanderplank Officer of the Guard.
Nothing material.

30 MAY: William Cooksey officer of the Guard.

William Bollinger Junr. arrived from Purrysburgh with 2 Steers killed last night which I received in the Store, at 12 Shillings Currency per lb. He told me he had 11 more at Purrisburgh which he kept on purpose for me, if I wanted them. I agreed to take 'em on Condition he would kill once a week, at which time I ordered him to deliver to the Millwrights & Cowkeeper at Old Ebenezer, & to the Saltzburghers at St. Ebenezer Such proportions as they should Severally have occasion to take, which they should fetch; I pressed very much that he would drive 'em over the River; he Said it was almost impossible at present, & that it was too Small a number to Answer so much trouble.

Sundry Stores, &c.

31 MAY: Noble Jones, officer of the Guard.

The mill wrights who are building the Sawmill at Ebenezer River, acquainted me that the waters there had overflown the Lands very much, & rose 4 foot higher, than (as they were informed) was ever known. They Said they had brought all their Clay to the Mill which they fetched 6 Miles below it: that as soon as the waters were down again, they would lay the Foundation, having every thing ready to raise; There having been opinions spread in town that it was an improper place, I was the more particular in asking Richard Cooper his opinion, who gave it me for certain that the place would do very well, & that any Timber might be easily rafted from it into the main River, that being the chief objection I had heard of; He further Said, he had often been up the whole River, that the obstructions were only Brushwood, & might be easily removed, that the Mill was too far from the main River for any rise of water there ever to choak it, & that he did not perceive there would be any want of water to drive it.

James Smithe, one of the above mentioned mill wrights complained that William Sterling had assaulted & abused him with a great Stick without any provocation. I sent for Stirling by the officer of the Guard to answer the Complaint, & it appeared that Sterling with others of his Country men were walking up & down Bull street, while Smithe & others with him were Sitting on a piece of Timber by the water side: that Smith held a Stick, which he pointed towards Sterling, who came to him directly, asked him what he meant, held up his stick & threatned him. That Smith said he did not fear him for all he was a Scotch man: upon which Sterling beat him, & bruised his Shoulder. Smith said the pointing his Stick was occasioned by his Company then being in discourse about Gunning, & that he said (when he pointed the stick) if that was a Gun, he could shoot them two men. Sterling said that the night before, Smith & others were together, while he and Some of the Scotch Gentlemen were walking in the Street; that Smith, (as he believed by his voice) said, if the Devil was to cast his net, what a parcell of Scotchmen he would catch. That he apprehended the pointing the Stick was another instance of Reproach which he & his Countrymen had frequently met with & that it was very hard that they could not walk up & down the Streets without being reproached for their Country. Both partys were very warm; the complainant as he was a young Lad well behaved, & very Industrious, gave me reason to believe what he Said was true; I therefore ordered Sterling to appear at the next Court, having first tryd all means of reconciliation in Vain.

In half an hour after this, one of the millwrights labourers being drunk at the water Side, & Seeing Mr. Cuthbert & Andrew Grant coming down Bull Street, he shook a hammer which he had in his hand, & swore if he could have his will, he would knock them Scotch Sons of Bitches brains out. Edward Jenkins overhearing these words, brought him before me, & he appearing to be very Drunk, I Sent him to the Stocks, which made all easy: a Great many of the Scotch Gentlemen being at my house on this occasion, & appearing very warm, I therefore took this opportunity, as I had on other occasions frequently done, to represent to them the imprudence of thinking any trifling Reproach given to any one of them an injury done to the whole body of Scotchmen.

N.B. Their Daily spending their time in walking the Streets, Drinking at publick houses, ingrossing the Conversation of all Strangers, and an imperious manner of Behaviour, I fear has rendred them odious to too many. The wives of Joseph Simmonds, Joseph Pavay, & Thomas Reale came before me on a warrant for an assault & scandalous words committed & spoken by Simons on Pavay; they were too warm to give any intelligible account of the matter; I therefore told 'em (after much noise) that as to the assault, they must call their witnesses to prove it, & as to the Scandal, they must make it appear there was a probability of Damages, otherwise I would discharge the warrant. That in England there was an Ecclesiastical Court, where Such Sort of things were prosecuted, that there was none Such here; but that one Court was to preserve the properties, & to repair them in Damages (when committed) that common Disturbers indeed might be indicted, men might be fined & women might be ducked. I recommended an agreement, but in vain, Mr. Vanderplank at last offered to prove that Simmonds did assault Pavay; I therefore ordered her to appear at next Court.

Sunday Stores &c.

I continued the License of Robert Perryman, a Trader at the Euchee Town.

1 JUNE 1737: Edward Jenkins, officer of the Guard.

Thirteen Jews, men & women, arrived here from Charles Town. They came from England by Captain Caruthers, & reported that Captain Diamond Set out a fortnight before 'em.

Donald Stewart returned from Charles Town, with Sundrys from Mr. Eveleigh for the Store.

Daniel Demetrie being come from Port Royal, advised me that Mr. Woodward could get no kind of Provisions & that Corn was Sold for 30 shillings Currency per Bushel.

Sundry Stores &c.

2 JUNE: William Gough officer of the Guard.

Mr. Bradley came to ask for Corn, Pease, & Rice, complaining that this was the 7th day that his Horses, Hogs, poultry, & Dogs had no victuals; I told him I had none in the Stores, & I perceived there would be great Difficulties in getting any; after a good deal of discontented talk; he Said, he would e'en go & kill a Sow to feed his Dogs.

Sundry Stores &c.

3 JUNE: Elisha Foster officer of the Guard.

In Conversation with Mr. Horton, Mr. Robert Williams, & Mr. Christie, a discourse began concerning the Tenure of lands, particularly by Mr. Horton, that the people were not legally put in possession, therefore their titles are all liable to be defeated. Mr. Horton asserted he did not know any one person in the whole Colony, who was legally put in possession: the Reason he gave was, that the true way of giving possession, was, by a Twigg & a Tuef, & that no other way was legall. As this Seemed to Stick with the other two, I Said that we had all the Right in Effect, & I did not know who could dispute it. The discourse ceased. *Opinions* of this kind are continually flying about in ill shapes past my Representation.

I received a letter from Mr. Woodward that he could not get any Corn, Pease, Rice, or other Provisions.

Sundry Stores &c.

4 JUNE: Robert Potter, officer of the Guard.

Mr. Tolson came up from Tybee & advised me of the arrival of Captain Diamond there this morning at 9 o'Clock, & delivered his letters relating to himself & Recruits; on which I immediately ordered boats & a Guard to be ready to attend 'em to the Company, as Soon as they came up.

Several people Demanding Extravagant pay to guard these Recruits, I was obliged to order the Constable to press men for that purpose.

Sundry Stores &c.

SUNDAY 5 JUNE: John Fallowfield officer of the Guard.

I spent this morning in writing letters to the Southward, that they might go with the boats that were to convey the Recruits.

About Noon, the *Poker* & *James* Anchored before the Town, & Captain Diamond dyn'd with me, & delivered me all his Letters, with the Box of Accounts & Sola bills.

In the Evening the boats fell down the River, with Mr. Tolson & his Recruits.

The passengers as per list arrived all in good health. Some of the Sailors being on Shore, got drunk; & making a noise in the Streets about Midnight, were confined in the Guard House till morning.

6 JUNE: William Parker, officer of the Guard.

Last night having been very Stormy, the periaguer with her Recruits were drove from her grapling, & obliged to return back under the town: They proceeded again in the afternoon. Mr. Venables, one of Captain Diamond's passengers complained, that having been ashore yesterday, & returning on board at night, the Mate used him very ill, & beat him, & added that he had done the same all the passage. I referred this complaint 'till I spoke with Captain Diamond.

Last night 2 Servants of Mr. Robert Lacy, one of Robert Williams, & one of George Smith, ran away from their respective Services. It appeared that they had met at the house of George Roane, & had been there drinking till 3 o'Clock in the morning. I acquainted the Masters present that they might raise Hue & Cry and publish that I would pay £ 50 Currency reward for each of them taken out of the province.

Sundry Stores &c.

7 JUNE: Patrick Grant, officer of the Guard.

Mr. Kent who went in the Boat to guard the Recruits, returned & acquainted me the periaguer had lost her grapling, & that she must return back, unless one could be got. As the boat belonged to the Trustees, I bought one.

I dispatched a boat with the 2 Servants for the mill-wrights at Ebenezer, & Letters for Mr. Boltzius.

I paid off the Georgia Scout Boat.

Sundry Stores &c.

8 JUNE: William Woodroofe officer of the Guard.

Mr. Horton went from hence to Frederica in the Georgia Scout boat. Yesterday the Ranger Sailed for Frederica, having taken on board on the Stores, which the officer of ordnance had shipped on board Captain Dymond for the *Hawk*, & also Provisions for Frederica Store.

I sent Searles Boat to the Settlement to endeavour to get provisions, & gave him £ 20 Sterling towards paying for what he Should buy.

Adjusted all accounts with Robert Williams, & Company and gave him a Certified Copy of his Leidgar Accounts.

I Continued the Licence for Jacob Morris.

Barker James Beamore, Thomas Holmes, Cornelius Decharty, Gregory Hains, Locklaw, Mr. Bean, Traders in the Cherokee Nation: Docharty requested that a Small town which had about 6 houses in it, might be added to his License. I told him he must apply to Mr. Oglethorpe when he came. Mr. Lacey made Several Drafts on me in favour of these Traders for necessaries at Augusta, which I paid.

Sundry Stores &c.

9 JUNE: John Coates, officer of the Guard.

Mr. Wesley intimated to me that I Stood accused among the people of Several Acts of injustice, and intending Revenge to Several people, which by his discourse he Seemed to believe; upon my promise of not mentioning it again to the partys, he told me that he had it from Mr. Bradley, who he said had given him instances of short measure & short weights, & that because Said Bradley had made a Complaint of me to Mr. Oglethorpe when here, I had hindered the building of his house. I told him that he knew very well Mr. Oglethorpe had entered into Bradley's complaints & that his Determination was, that whatever Mr. Bradley met with amiss, he should first make his complaint to me, & if I did not redress him, then he might make his complaint to the Trustees; if therefore there was any thing now that regarded the Store, Bradley Should complain to me himself; I added that Mr. Bradley's large Demands on the Store without any evident Cause, had given me Sufficient uneasiness; but I defied him to mention anything wherein I had not kept within yet bounds of Civility. Mr. Wesley then urged the house, saying, that in his hearing Mr. Oglethorpe ordered it to be finished with all speed. I told him, I was a stranger to it; that Mr. Oglethorpe's orders to me, were, that whatever Mr. Bradley had to offer to me, my best way was to referr him to the Trustees. I asked Mr. Wesley, if he found me charged with so many crimes of injustice & Revenge; and whether he had heard no Accusations of me in regard to the Magistracy; his answer was, *An artfull man could avoid that.* I did not think it worth my while to shew any uneasiness to him, because he had now fully discovered himself; but I let him know, if I was charged at any time with behaviour in a Sour manner it might be a just charge, because I had had so many unreasonable demands that it was very difficult to distinguish whether I could be justified by the people's necessitys, or whether I should not stand charged by the Trustees for doing things without their orders; & particularly in Bradley's affair, I now found I had far exceeded the Trustees' agreement with him, likewise Brown of Highgate, & several others who are daily making demands on the Store, & I think I might be allowed, when I know things were without order, to act cautiously, & shew an unwillingness in the Execution; I added that I perceived by this, that there were Some people endeavouring to raise an ill opinion in him of me, which hitherto I had endeavoured to prevent, and I thought it was as much his business as mine to do the same; that for my part I had ever espoused his Character, & always discouraged those who lessened it.

Mr. Boltzius arrived, having received my letters, & took with him several parcells which came in Captain Dymond from England, & promised to come down next week to Settle the General accounts. He acquainted me that he had received a letter from Captain Coram, which he had orders to deliver with his own hands to Captain Watson; I told him where to find him, & that he was a prisoner by the Trustees' orders; but that he might deliver the letter if he pleased.

Sundry Stores &c.

10 JUNE: Samuel Mercer officer of the Guard.

Mr. Boltzius told me he had been with Captain Watson, & that he very much abused the Trustees, Mr. Oglethorpe, & me; & added that he believed he was a very artful man; & said that if he talked to other people in the manner he had done to him, he must necessarily do a great deal of mischief, & that it was a misfortune he was confined here.

I received a letter from Colonel Barnwell, that he had 400 Bushels of Corn to dispose of, which I might have at 17. 6 Currency per Bushell present money. I immediately answered him & sent a periaguer for it.

Having paid Mr. Bellinger for Some fresh meat delivered here, I agreed with him for 30 Steers to be delivered alive at Savannah at £3 Sterling per head each Steer to weigh 500 w. or upwards; I also agreed with him for 20 other Steers to be delivered at Mr. Bryan's landing, & put on board periaguers for the Southward at £ 2. 8. Sterling a head of the Same weight, on Account of which I advanced him £ 50 Sterling.

Mr. Horton not being gone to the Southward he again came to take his leave of me. Mr. Venables a passenger by Captain Dymond came to inform me that he did not understand labour, that he was an upholsterer by trade, & could get his bread better elsewhere. I told him I thought it would be better to take his friend's advice, & tarry here till he had acquainted them of it; & that if he appeared industrious I would do what I could to serve him. He said he would go to Charles Town, & from thence intends to return to England, & accordingly he went in Lacey's periaguer.

Joseph West, a Child of 3 years old was accidentally drowned in a well in his father's farm Lott.

11 JUNE: Robert How, officer of the Guard.

John White, a Labourer with the mill-wrights at Ebenezer, who was apprehended last Monday on a violent Suspicion of Felony (Goods being found on him), could not be examined till this day, the owner of the Goods being absent, being brought before me, It appeared that he got in at the window of the Hutt of William

Aglionby, & intended to Steal Several things which he had bundled up in the absence of Said Aglionby. He had confessed that he had broke open a Chest in Said Hutt, which belonged to James Corneck, & took the things which he had bundled up; that he had a shirt on his back when he was taken which belonged also to Said Corneck; he was therefore committed, & the Evidences bound over to prosecute him at next Court.

The Said White is the Mill-wrights labourer mentioned the 31 last month. It being the king's accession to the Throne, the officer applyed to Mr. Vanderplank for leave to hoist the Colours, but he ordered him to deferr it to the 15th being the day the king was proclaim'd, & to avoid Strife, I did not interpose.

Sundry Stores &c.

12 JUNE: John Lyndall officer of the Guard.

Captain McIntosh Sent his Brother & 2 Men from Fort prince George, with 2 Runaway Servants, who belonged to Mr. Robert Williams & George Smith. They were carried before Mr. Parker, and their Masters not appearing, he committed them to the workhouse for further Examination.

Sundry Stores &c.

13 JUNE: Austin Waddell, officer of the Guard.

Mr. Gronau came from Ebenezer & reported all there were in good health; he took with him the money & Several things which came per Captain Dymond. Mr. Bradley's wife having some time Since miscarried, & since that fell into the Jaundice, dyed this Evening. Her latter complaints were violent pains in her Stomach, attended with an intermitting fever; her pains Seemed to be eased by vomiting, & she was judged by the Doctor to be out of Danger 2 hours before She dyed.

I paid Captain McIntosh's brother £ 100 Currency reward for taking the 2 runaway men Servants mentioned yesterday.

Sundry Stores &c.

14 JUNE: James Carwells officer of the Guard.

Thomas Ellis, Mr. Jones the Surveyor's Servant acquainted me he had been Setting out Mr. Houstoun's land, & running Some other Lines on Vernon River, & had his Master's orders to run out the land for the lower new ward, which he was now going about; that Mr. Christie had desired him to Shew him his land, & that he intended to go that way & shew it him: Mr. Christie accordingly went with him, & in about 3 hours time, returned, & complained that he had been waiting in the woods but could not proceed, because Ellis's people were got drunk & did not come. Mrs. Bradley was buried.

Mr. Mathews & his Wife, & Thomas Jones & his Wife dined with me; they were very glad to hear the news from England, & I acquainted them with Mr. Watson's petition, & agreed to assist in answering Several parts of it.

Sundry Stores &c.

15 JUNE: Walter Fox officer of the Guard.

This day was observed as the king's accession to the Throne; on which occasion the Guns were fired, & Mr. Vanderplank asking for something for the Guard to Drink, I ordered a Barrell of Beer at the Disposal of himself and all the officers.

Mr. Parker & Mr. Christie being with me, we examined the Runaway Servants: It appeared that 2 of Mr. Lacey's Servants (not taken) and these, had consulted about Running away at the house of George Roan on Sunday the 5 inst; that Lacey's 2 Servants had been most of the day drinking there, that Roan & his Wife were privy to their Designs; that Williams' Servant was unacquainted with the Consultation till 10 at night, when being in pursuit of John White, who was committed the 11 Inst. he came by the Door of Said Roan, & hearing folks up, went in to get further assistance; that he there Saw Lacey's Servants & Smiths's Servant; that Said Smith's Servant went with him, & told him that he was just then going off with Lacey's Servants, & asked him if he would go with them; to which he agreed. There was found on Smith's Servant, a Gun belonging to Mr. Lacey, he was therefore committed to Goal by the name of Benjamin Groom for Felony, and William's Servant having given an ingenuous account of all their proceedings, & promising amendment, he was at his Master's request, discharged.

The magistrates on this occasion were of opinion that the Trustees have paid £ 50 Currency for the taking Smith's Servant, & Smith being no proper habitant of this Province, & the Servant being a Dangerous fellow, & having committed the like offences before, it was ordered that Said Servant Should be committed to hard labour for 6 months, & unless Mr. Smith would repay the £ 50 the Said Labour Should be performed in publick Service at St. Andrews or elsewhere; & if Said Smith Should pay £ 50, then Said Labour to be for his Benefit, he was therefore ordered to consider of the matter.

Mr. Vanderplank complained that he met George Roan Drunk in the Streets who had assaulted him, & torn his Cloaths, that with much difficulty he had brought him with him that he had charged John Thomson to assist him, who had neglected it, & by his behaviour encouraged Roan, by Saying, Are you a Freeholder, meaning (as Vanderplank Supposed) that Freeholders were to do as they pleased, & were not to be apprehended. As an Insult on a Constable whose ward was then upon Duty, required further notice that the punishment due to Drunkenness, & Roan not being in a Condition to be examined, I committed him to Goal. John Thomson appearing to be one of the Guard on Duty, I examined him as to Mr. Vanderplank's complaint, & it appearing that he saw the assault & did not assist, I bound him over to answer the Complaint at next Court.

A Child of a Woman Servant of Mr. Houston dyed aged about 2 years.

Mr. Patrick Grant complained that he had no 5 Acre lot, or other land yet Set him out: he owned he had formerly refused any, not then intending to cultivate it, thinking he could Spend his time better, but that now he had altered his mind, & desired he might have it Set out; I told him I would take care about it.

Sundry Stores &c.

16 JUNE: Juhn Vanderplank officer of the Guard.

James Carwells, keeper of the workhouse complained that he

had been obliged to hire assistants to dress the Victuals, & carry necessarys to Several prisoners, for which he demanded £25 for 5 Months being £5 Sterling per month. I told him if he would bring a particular account of it I believed the magistrates would consider of it, but in the light he put it in it looked like a raising his Salary which I had no power to do; whereupon he shewed himself very angry & delivered me up his Keys.

In the afternoon Mr. Parker & Mr. Christie being with me, we sent for him: & convinced him of his mistake; the magistrates ordered that the £25 might be paid for the present for the assistance he mentioned; but that for the future, if there was any extraordinary trouble with any particular prisoner, he should acquaint the magistrates of it before the Discharge that they might better judge by whom such Charges Should be born, & the keys were again delivered him.

George Roane was brought to be examined, and was bound over to answer the assault; he having a house built, his own Bond was taken for his appearance at next Court; and in regard to his Drunkeness, not being able to pay 2 Shillings according to the statute, he was Set in the Stocks.

Sundry Stores &c.

17 JUNE: William Cooksey officer of the Guard.

John Desborough's wife complained that in a Reckoning with Henry Lloyd, one of the Victuallers, for Carpenter's work done by her husband & Sons, Said Lloyd had charged 'em 6/9 for 9½ pounds meat; as I believed it to be extortion, I issued a Warrant against Said Lloyd, & he being brought before me, it appeared that Desborough had importuned Said Lloyd Several times to let him have Some Bacon & some Smoked Beef which he had bought for his own use, & was unwilling to sell; that he had let him have 3½ pounds of beef, for which he charged 6 p, & 6 pounds of Bacon, for which he had charged 10 per pound. As it did not appear that Lloyd made any Common practice of Selling provisions, & that this was at the importunity of the Complainant, & that the provisions Sold was an extravagant kind of food, & not necessary, I discharged the warrant, recomending it to the Plaintiffs to be more frugal of their money, and at the same time cautioned Lloyd not to encourage the people to spend their time in his house in an idle manner, agreeable to the Trustees Orders of the 15 May 1735.

William Cooksey complained that he did not know where his 45 Acre Lot was; that as his 5 Acre Lot was very wet, & he unable at present to do any thing with it, he wanted to be Shearing of the other; I promised to give orders in the matter, & that it should be Shewn him.

Mr. Wesley lately acquainted me that there were Several Deists in the place, & now gave me a long account of a discourse between him & Dr. Garratt: I told him I did not doubt but he would be able to Set people right in these matters, & that I should be always ready to give the assistance of a Civil magistrate in discountenancing & punishing bad morals whenever any particular Fact should make it necessary. Donald Stewart complained that he had not received his Cow & Calf according to a written order I had Sent to Mercer as Pindar; that he carried Said order to Mercer, who went with him to Mr. Bradley, who upon reading Said he would not deliver one without seeing Mr. Oglethorpe's Order: but told Joseph Stewart that he would let him have a Cow & Calf on his own Account if he would give him his note or Bond that Mr. Oglethorpe should agree to it when he came.

Thomas Devall, John Lacy, & William Kellihorn, Traders in the Creek Nation, arrived & delivered me their Licences to be continued.

Sundry Stores &c.

18 JUNE: Thomas Ellis officer of the Guard for Noble Jones now at Augusta.

I continued the Licences of Thomas Deval, & William Kellihorn, & delivered them, & told 'em to tell Lacy his was also ready. Lacy was in liquor when he came yesterday, & behaved in a ludicrous manner, at first pretending he had lost his Licence, then that he had left it behind him, & after some Reprimands for his Behaviour he confess'd he had it in his pocket, & then left it.

Thomas Ellis Shewed me his work concerning the lower new

ward. I ordered him to Shew Mr. Christie & Mr. Cooksey their Lotts, & to call upon Mr. Grant, & set him out a five Acre Lott, & when that was done, he said he would proceed in Setting out the 500 Acre Tracts on Vernon River according to his Master's orders.

Mr. Purry proposed to send the *Peter & James*, Captain Dymond, to New York, or Philadelphia for Provisions for the Colony on his own Risque & Freight, I only agreeing to receive the Provisions on account of the Trustees at a Stated price, viz. Beef at 30 Sterling per pound; Pork at 35 Sterling per pound; Butter at 6 Sterling per pound; Chese at 4 Sterling per pound; Flour at 10/6 per pound; Midling Biscuit at 13 Sterling, & Brown Biscuit at 10/6 per pound all 10 ch. being agreeable to the market price. I agreed to take them, but insisted on the Delivery at Frederica, because whatever might be wanted here might come in the Bark Carriage of Perriaguas that were continually going thither, which would be much cheaper than sending them from home; to which he agreed, but insisted that in case he could not get loaded at New York, but should be obliged to proceed to Philadelphia, I should allow 5 per cent on the price of the Goods. This last is not yet agreed to.

I examined with Mr. Purry some Gun powder which he brought from Charles Town during the late Alarms; I totally rejected some blds, & he took Several others, viz: FF & EEE to dry & desired I would then see if they might not be taken for Cannon powder.

A Child of William Frigden about 5 months old dyed & was buryed.

Sundry Stores &c.

SUNDAY 19 JUNE: Edward Jenkins officer of the Guard.

Alexander Wood & Patrick Graham, Traders from the Creek Nation, & Thomas Andrews, a Trader from the Chickasaw Nation, & George Cozens from New Windsor arrived here. Cozens brought a Draft on me for £   sterling from Mr. Lacey which I paid.

Mr. Andrews brought him 4 Chickasaw Indians, who, he said, were come to be paid for French prisoners they had taken, which he also brought with him.

Mr. Weddall arrived with the Garrison boat from Augusta. He

reports every body in health; that they could get meat kind enough, but that Bread kind was very scarce; he therefore brought down the great Boat to carry some up. Mr. Lacey advises me that they had cleared the Ground for the Fort, and had begun to Set up the Puncheons, & that they were 5 more hands wanting to assist the Surveyor. That their neighbouring Indians, who are a branch of the Chickasaw Nation (& are the same who lately came down with Captain Grey) received them very kindly, & promised them their assistance.

Sundry Stores &c.

20 JUNE: William Gough officer of the Guard.

Alexander Wood & Patrick Brown brought me their Licences which I continued. Wood brought a Draft on me from Anthony Willey with Certificates of his men's Service & a Bill of Expences of Mr. Tanner, all which amounted to £ Sterling which I paid.

Sundry Stores &c.

21 JUNE: Elisha Forster officer of the Guard.

Mr. Robert Williams in his passage to Carolina met with the 2 runaway Servants that belonged to Mr. Lacey, & Sent 'em hither. On their Arrival I committed them to the work house; Mr. Williams drew a Bill on me for £ 50 Currency to defray the Charges of bringing them, which I paid. Mr. Lacey coming to town in the Evening, the Servants were examined, they each of them discovered the whole Transaction, & upon their promise of good Behaviour for the future, which Seemed to be Sincere, they were discharged.

Sundry Stores &c.

22 JUNE: Robert Potter officer of the Guard.

James Searles arrived with 350 Bushels of Corn from Colonel Barnwell; he acquainted me there were Pease enough to be got at Port Royal, but people had not time enough to thrash them, but that they had promised to get some ready against his return. I ordered him to Cask up 200 Bushels of the Corn, & to proceed with it immediately to Frederica; I also ordered 50 Bushels to be Casked up for Augusta, & 50 for Ebenezer, & the Remainder to be delivered at the Store.

A Periagua arrived from Charles Town on board of 13 Arrived Mr. Hugh Anderson & his family, with several other passengers as per list, all in good health. Mr. Anderson produced the Trustees' appointment under Seal to him as Inspector of the publick Gardens, and of the Mulberry Planters in Georgia. They left Scotland the latter end of March, & after 9 weeks passage arrived at Charles Town, where he & his Company received the usual Discouragements as to their settling in Georgia. Mr. Anderson delivered me the Letter from Mr. Verelst to him, dated 8 March 1736, of which I have not as yet received any advice.

Sundry Stores &c.

23 JUNE: John Fallowfield officer of the Guard.

Mrs. Lacey having complained that she suspected her 2 Servants, who had lately run away, were contriving to do the same again: at her request I ordered Mr. Woddall to take them to Augusta & deliver them to their Master, & to secure them in the work house till he went.

A complaint was made by Thomas Atwell's wife in his Absence, against William Bradley, that he refused to deliver a Calf which her Husband had bought of Joseph Pavay for 2 Steers delivered to him. Bradley asserted that Pavay had some long time since (before Atwell's claim) made a present of it to his Daughter Jannet, & therefore had no right to Sell it afterwards to Atwell; Pavay allowed the Bargain made with Atwell but denyed the gift to Bradley's Daughter. Bradley insinuated that he was not at all obliged to Pavay for the Gift, for that he had made him an sole Amends, & there Seemed to be accounts between 'em unadjusted. Upon the whole, Pavay agreed to pay Atwell the value of the Calf, & to let Mr. Bradley keep it as his own, which Atwell chose to accept, rather than have any difference, tho' thereby she was deprived of last of her Stock.

This was not her original Stock, but arose from Increase. Mr. Wesley having lately intimated that Mr. Brown of Highgate had complained to Bradley that he had lately received short weight, & short measure at the Store, I therefore wrote to Mr. Brown, requiring him to give me an account that I might rectifie it. I referr to his Letter as to the Answer he gave me, dated 20 June 1737, upon the Receipt of which I examined into the particular Charges therein: As to the Soap, my Servant at the Store proved that he saw Mr. Brown's Servant put some in his pocket, which he then told him was for his own use. My Servant also insisted that he gave him full weight, & that it was impossible he could mistake 2 pounds in 6. As to the Vinegar it appeared that the Cask brought was filled, supposing it held 4 Gallons, but in reality it held 4 7½ wine measure, which is the measure that Comodity is now bought & issued by. I could See no reason to think these Complaints just, the Entries of both being fair & the Delivery 2 months past; but I acquainted Mr. Brown that I was always ready to hear any Complaints of that kind, & that I would certainly do every one justice, that applyed to me: But on the Contrary as I could not deliver the Stores my Self, I ought not to be charged from 2. & 3. hands as I had been now, viz., from him to Bradley, & from Bradley to Mr. Wesley, & perhaps to others, therefore I insisted that if he had any complaints of that kind to make, they ought to be made first to me.

John Desborough complained that he received Molasses at the Store, & there being some spilt by my Servants out of his Bag into a puddle of water, he saw them take up water and dirt to fill it again. I examined into the matter, and found that some of the Molasses had been spilt, but in a clean place, & they did take up what they could of it, & put it in the bag again, but when Desborough found fault with it, they emptyed the whole bag again, & filled it with fresh Molasses.

My Servants on this occasion complained that notwithstanding they had behaved in this manner to please him: both he & his wife had grossly abused them, called them Thieves, Cheats, & Rogues, & included me with them. I repremanded the Servants for taking Molasses from the Ground, which must unavoidably have dirt in it, & mixing it with the pure; because tho' it might be fit for Brewing, it could not be fit for those who eat it; and I ordered that in such Cases for the future they should put such damaged Molasses into a Cask by it self, and when my own people wanted any to brew to deliver it them, & charge it to my account. I acquainted Desborough that he might see I was ready to do him justice if he had been injured; but told him if he expected to have any goods from the Store, he must come for 'em in a quiet manner; as I would not encourage any one in the Store in any Crime whatsoever, I would never Suffer them to be insulted in their Duty.

Sundry Stores &c.

24 JUNE: William Parker officer of the Guard.

The Society of Free Masons held their Annual Feast after had been at Church & heard a Sermon, & broke up about 3 o'Clock. Mr. Wesley dined with us, & received the Thanks of the Society for his Suitable Sermon. A Periagua arrived from Charles Town with Sundry European Goods for Mr. Brownfield.

Sundry Stores issued & received as per day Book.

25 JUNE 1737: Patrick Grant officer of the Guard.

Thomas Andrews, the Chickasaw Trader, the 4 Indians, the 2 French Captives, Tomochachi, & Thomas Wiggan a Creek Trader dined with me.

Tomochachi requested a Goose & Gander for one of the Chickasaw Indians, who he Said was an old friend, which I gave him.

Thomas Wiggan delivered me the written account of the danger he had been in because his horse had accidentally killed an Indian Child.

Thomas Andrews gave me an account of Sundry presents the Indians expected for the Ransom of the 2 Frenchmen and that they insisted on coming down with him; and as to the Goods, he Said, he would let them have them out of his Store in the Nation, & would Submit his account to Mr. Oglethorpe. I agreed to this, Supposing he might expect thereby Some Benefit to himself for his trouble.

Sundry Stores issued & received as per day Book.

SUNDAY 26 JUNE: William Woodroofe officer of the Guard.

Mr. Mathews & his wife, & Thomas Jones & his wife dined with me. I gave each of them a Dozen bottles of English beer which I lately bought of Mr. Brownfield.

I had some appearance of a Fever on Friday last, & was this day Seized with a violent Fitt, which continued 'till next morning.

One of my women Servants who lately arrived per Captain Dymond, dyed this day of a fever, which had some appearances of a Malignancy.

Ambrose Morrison's wife dyed this day; her Illness was chiefly the Flux, which probably proceeded from a disorderly course of life, being much addicted to Drinking.

Sundry Stores issued as per day Book.

27 JUNE: John Coates, officer of the Guard.

Daniel Demetree's periager arrived with 9 fat Steers from Mr. Belinger; the weather being very bad I was obliged to impress 4 hands in towing him to Frederica, least the Steers Should Suffer by delay.

I also dispatched James Sarle's Boat with 200 Bushell of Corn for the Southward, being part of the Cargo lately bought of Mr. Barnwell, & sundry other provisions & ammunition.

Sundry Stores &c.

28 JUNE: Samuel Mercer officer of the Guard.

The wife of George Symmes dyed of a violent Flux, which she had laboured under above a month.

A Stranger from Purrisburgh coming here for his health, dyed in his passage.

Sundry Stores &c.

29 JUNE: Robert Howes, officer of the Guard.

I continued the Licenses of August McPherson & William Williams, 2 Creek Traders, & delivered them.

Sundry Stores &c.

30 JUNE: John Lindall, officer of the Guard.

Colonel Beamore arrived & acquainted me that Mr. Jennys, notwithstanding the account delivered, had again refused payment of my Draft on account of Rum Duty; I therefore gave him Cash for the same.

The wife of Thomas Antrobus dyed of a Fever.

Sundry Stores &c.

1 JULY: Austin Weddal officer of the Guard.

Mr. John Darne, the 3d Bailiff, dyed; & in regard that he had born a military Commission, the Great Guns were fired at his Funeral. His illness was a flux, attended with several Gripings, which he had been frequently Subject to.

I certified Mr. Purry's accounts to the 25th of March & desired he would make out his Account to the 24th of June, the Trustees having ordered all their accounts to that time, to be remitted with what speed they could.

Sundry Stores &c.

2 JULY: James Carwell, officer of the Guard.

The *Ranger* Sloop brought me Captain Gascoigns Lee advising me he had furnished provisions of Frederica to the value of £ 11/2/0. about which he supposing I was not able to repay in the same species, said he was willing to take the value in money, which I accordingly paid.

I certified Mr. Brownfield's Account to the 24 June.

Sundry Stores &c.

3 JULY: Walter Fox officer of the Guard.

Mr. Vanderplank having acquainted me that the people were desirous to cutt a way for their Cattle to be brought home that lay on the Lands by Thunderbolt, he now told me they were going out, & desired I would issue them Some Provisions & Strong Beer for Refreshment, which I accordingly did.

Austin Weddal returned last night with the Garrison boat to

Augusta, having on board Such provisions & other necessarys as were wanting.

Sundry Stores &c.

4 JULY: John Vanderplank officer of the Guard.

I renewed the Licences of Archibald McGilbury, a Trader in the Creek Nation.

Mr. Jones, the Surveyor desired me to advance him some money, which I told him I could not comply with, unless he would give me some particular reasons for it. He insisted that Mr. Oglethorpe had ordered that I should pay for all the people's Lands he had run out. I told him, if he would let me know who the people were, whose Lands were Set out, & had not paid him, I would give him Credit for it in the Store & he might at any time see his account but that he must bring a Certificate from every such person, because Mr. Oglethorpe's intention was, that they should be charged therewith. He insisted I had Mr. Oglethorpe's orders to pay him, & therefore complained that he was ill used. I told him I always had been & should be ready to do him any Service in my power, but the General Expences were so great, that I was necessitated to be cautious of Disposing of the Trustees' money, & besides he knew very well, that the hands which he hired had been duly paid & Victualled, & his family Supported; by which there was little prospect of any thing being due to him, unless he could make his Demands appear to the Trustees & obtain their orders. He urged Sundry difficulties in the business of Surveying, wherein he had received no recompense. I told him I could not judge for the Trustees, but advised him to think of returning his plans, & endeavour to remove the people's complaints, which for the Generality I believed were just.

The Relict of Nathaniel Polhill who is now married to Robert Redford, having applyed for relief in behalf of Polhill's Children, I ordered the usual allowance till Mr. Oglethorpe's Arrival.

Sundry Stores &c.

5 JULY: William Cooksey, officer of the Guard.

Mr. Wesley having sent a letter to Mrs. Williamson, containing several Charges, & Demands of a Confession, the particulars of which I believe her husband will take notice of. In about 2 hours after I received the letter from him of this date, at which I was much surprized.

Sundry Stores &c.

6 JULY: Noble Jones, officer of the Guard.

I waited on Mr. Wesley with the Magistrates to acquaint him that tomorrow was the Anniversary on which the Court of Record was first opened here, and the first people put in possession of their Lands, & the power given for the administration of Justice. That the people thought it incumbent on them to continue their Religious observation of the Day, & therefore desired that Divine Service might for that purpose be performed in the morning before the Court Satt. To which he readily agreed. As I would industriously remove all misunderstandings between Mr. Wesley & myself, I took this opportunity to ask him the meaning of his letter to me yesterday, particularly that part of it wherein he seemed to place his future friendship with me upon my Compliance with something which he called *Doing his Duty*. I farther told him, I had neither done or Said any thing from whence he could think I would oppose any thing that he Should do in the Execution of his office. He was silent for some time. Upon which I again told him, that to prevent any misunderstandings & ill Conjectures concerning his letter, & to vindicate my own Actions, I had acquainted the Magistrates, then present, with the Contents of his Letter; & that I must insist upon an Explanation before them that they might witness for me in time to come. After some further pause, he said: *Suppose I should refuse to administer the Sacrament to Some body in your Family*. I answered, if it was my Self or my wife, or my Child, that was to undergo any Censures of that kind, I expected to be acquainted with the Reasons. I believed it would be advisable in him to do the Same to every one in the Town before he refused either of the Sacraments, or used any Church Discipline, because I apprehended that by the Cannon Law itself he was enjoyned thereto. He replyed that he hoped I should have no Occasion to give my self any uneasiness about the matter.

Sundry Stores &c.

7 JULY: Edward Jenkins, officer of the Guard.

Divine Service was performed early in the morning, & Mr. Wesley preached a Sermon Suitable to the occasion, after which the Court Sate.

Sundry Stores &c.

8 JULY: William Gough officer of the Guard.

Nothing material.

9 JULY: Elisha Forster officer of the Guard.

The Court Sate according to adjournment. Vide proceedings annexed. Daniel Demetree's periaguer arrived from Frederica; Mr. Horton by a letter dated 29 June, relates the Distresses of the people for want of provisions. By another dated 4 inst. he complains that the men pressed into Demetrees Periaguer (the better to Expedite his passage with the Live Steers) was an injury to the publick service, asserting that they belonged to one of the Scout Boats, & were thereby taken from that Service. In this he was mistaken for tho' they had belonged to one of the Scout boats, they had received their pay, & had quitted the Service, & it was with much difficulty the officer found 'em out, & when they were pressed, they Seemed unwilling to Serve in that part of the province, & had they been in the publick service, as Mr. Horton reports, then they were the more proper to be employed on this occasion. In this last he relates the Satisfaction of the people on the Receipt of Some provisions I lately Sent.

The Wife of John Wright complained that having heard her Husband was dangerously ill at Augusta: she had asked for a passage in a Carolina Trading Boat that was going to N. Windsor, & that the Patroon had demanded £ 20 Currency for her passage, & even when she had complyed with the Extravagant Demand, he refused to Land her at Augusta, and at last would not carry her thither at any Rate.

As this Seemed to be an ill natured action, I persuaded her not to trouble herself about it, for that she might soon meet with another passage.

Sundry Stores &c.

10 JULY: Robert Potter officer of the Guard.

Serles periaguer arrived from Frederica having delivered the Corn & other provisions there.

A young Child of The Antrobus, & a young Girl of Robert Howe, dyed.

Joseph Barker keeper of the Cowpen at Ebenezer reported that the Cattle under his Care were all in good health, but that there were some Steers that were unruly, which perhaps might be a means of making the rest go astray. He therefore advised some of them to be killed. He also reported that Captain McPherson had crossed the River with his Cattle, & was gone forward with them to the Darien.

Sundry Stores &c.

11 JULY: John Fallowfield, officer of the Guard.

John Hughes complained that William Bradley had Seized his Goods on pretence of some Demands he had on him for his Board and passage, & that he kept from him the Utensils in his Business as a Tallow Chandler which he had from the Store. As the Young man Seemed very much grieved, I sent for Bradley, hoping to accomodate the matter. Upon Examination I found that Bradley demanded the Charges of Hughes's passage & Board Since their Setting out from England, Saying that he stood Chargeable with it in his Account to the Trustees. I endeavoured to reconcile them, but to no purpose. Hughes insisted that he had Expectation that he Should receive his passage & provisions of the Trustees as their bounty, being one of Bradley's family. As to this Demand, I could form no judgement, having never received a perfect List of Bradley's family. This difference seemed to arise from other Causes: Hughes intimating that he had refused to testifie according to Bradley's desire in a dispute between him & Mr. Woodroffe's wife. Bradley insisting on his Demand, I ordered the Goods to be bailed, & the Cause to be tryed at next Court. Mr. West being Bail for the Goods, who without Doubt is as Sufficient a man as any in the place for Such a Sum, yet Bradley not contented, Demanded that West Should justifie, which he accordingly did.

N.B. This point of the Law was never practiced here before; Neither can there be the same Reasons for the Demand as there is in England, because every one here is Sufficiently known without it.

This Evening Bradley killed one of the Trustees' Steers, which he had delivered him for Labour. One Side thereof he Sold, one Quarter he gave away, & kept the other Quarter for the use of his family.

Donald Stewart arrived from Charles Town with Bushels of Rice. I ordered him to compleat his Loading, & to proceed to Frederica.

Sundry Stores &c.

12 JULY: William Parker, officer of the Guard.

A Sloop arrived from New England with provisions &c. but last from St. Augustine, of which one Francis Johannott was Supercargo, who delivered me a letter from Caleb Davis, & another from Mr. William Kelliway, both at St. Augustine: In which they give an Account that the pay ships lately arrived, brought 35,000 pieces of Eight, which was not half enough to pay their Debts due to the English. Davis reports every thing to be at peace, & that the new Governor is a man of a great Deal of Honour, & Justice, & punctual to his word. Mr. Kelliway says, all is Said to be at peace. But that Since Sunday last, all the English were confined to their Lodgings (Except the New York Factor). The Reasons unknown. They both recommended Johannet for the Sale of his Cargo, & say the Governor would not permit him to trade there.

In Discourse with Johannet, I find the Spaniards are in continual apprehensions of mischief from the Creek Indians, and their Behaviour Shews them very jealous of the English, & that notwithstanding the Confinement mentioned by Kelliway the English were free to pass any where about the Backside of the town.

Davis in his Letter desires me to buy Some Cables for him of Johannet, and to Send 'em to him to St. Augustine. As they were naval Stores, I excused my Self from Acting therein.

Lopes D'Castro delivered the letter enclosed as his answer, concerning the Sale of his wive's Lott.

I renewed the Licences of Alexander McQueen, & William Allen, two Traders in the Creek Nation.

Sundry Stores &c.

13 JULY: Patrick Grant, officer of the Guard.

I renewed the Lycence of Theophilus Perryman, Trader at the Euchee town. I dispatched Donald Stewart to Frederica with provisions out of Johannet's Sloop, having agreed with him for such part of his Cargo, as was proper for the magazine, & I ordered Daniel Demetree, to take out another Loading for the same place.

John Latter, Master of the Carolina Scout Boat Shewed me a note, whereby Michael Martin had entered himself in his Service on the 6th of June last, and complained that he heard that Mr. Horton had obliged him to Serve with John Ray, Master of the Georgia Scout Boat. This appearing to be one of the men who had been obliged to go with Demetree to the Southward; I told him that when he came to the Southward, Mr. Horton would Set that matter right.

Talking with Several Inhabitants concerning the improvement of Lands, I proposed that A Society might frequently meet on that Subject, & assist each other, which might in time prove of general Service.

Sundry Stores &c.

14 JULY: William Woodroffe officer of the Guard.

Mr. Boltzius came from Ebenezer & I went thro' the private Accounts of him, Mr. Gronau, & the School master.

A woman belonging to the Savannah Indians, complained that She being at Skidoway Island, some of Mrs. Mouse's Daughters had beat her. Mrs. Mouse being in town, I Sent for her (Mrs. Mathews being present to interpret, as also the Indian woman's husband). Upon examining into the matter I found that they had frequently bartered with Mouse for trifling things, and had received Strong liquors at that time, & were drunk. I gave Mrs. Mouse a Severe reprimand for giving Strong liquors to Indians, & for dealing with them in any Sort, assuring her that if any Such practices were carried on for the future, they must expect not only to lose their License, but to be prosecuted.

The Indians Seemed very well Satisfied, & Mrs. Mouse promised to take more care for the future.

Sundry Stores &c.

15 JULY: John Coates officer of the Guard.

Mr. Robert Williams arrived from Charles Town & acquainted me that 15 of the Creek Indians were then at Charles Town, under the Conduct of Alexander Wood, who is a Trader Lycensed from this Province. That he perceived Several Differences were Subsisting & likely to increase between the assembly & the Lieutenant Governor & that he believed the Assembly would be dissolved.

One of Robert Parker's Servants informed me that he had been with his Master at Bistow in Carolina, & that he had given him up his Indenture, as also those of his Fellow Servants. He asked me what should be done with his Master's Corn on the Ground, which I was informed would come to little. I referred him to those of his Master's Creditors who had power to Act in the matter. He informed that his Master was hired to teach School at Bistow at £ 150 Currency per Annum.

Sundry Stores &c.

16 JULY: Samuel Mercer, officer of the Guard.

I received a letter from Mr. David Provost, desiring that his account might be certified. I accordingly answered his request, & advised the Trustees of it.

Captain Parminter, who was Master of a Sloop, & had some time Since brought Several European Goods to Mr. Brownfield which had been consigned to Mr. Savage of Charles Town, delivered me a Letter from Mr. Jennys, wherein Said Jennys Set forth that the freight of Said Goods from Charles Town hither was not paid, & desired me to procure the payment. Upon Examining into the matter, I found that Parminter had Signed the Bill of Lading for the Goods in good order, & that on opening them they appeared to be damaged; the Reason Parminter insisted on the freight, was, that according to the Judgement of Several Merchants who had viewed the Goods & Package, Said Goods were damaged in the voyage from London to Charles Town & in no wise while under his Care: to which Brownfield answered, that either Savage, Parminter, or Somebody had discharged the Bill of Lading from England, and therefore it was of the power of the Shippers to receive any Recompence. He also produced Letters from his Correspondents in England, explaining what he said, to be the Case, & approving of his not paying the Freight from Charles Town. I told Captain Parminter that the Case was So plain that I could Say nothing to it; but my opinion was that as Savage had employed him he ought to be his Paymaster, & if he was a Sufferer, he might thank himself for Discharging the Bill of Lading.

Sundry Stores &c.

17 JULY: Robert Howes, officer of the Guard.

I received the letter from Mr. Jacob Mathews of this Date, on which I immediately went up to Tomochachi's & took him with me to Mr. Mathews to examine into the matter. Upon my Arrival at Tomochachi's, I saw the man who had been shot; the Bullet went in under his Jaw, near the Ear, & out at his mouth; upon the Enquiry I found that Tomochachi's Indians had frequently got liquor at Mr. Mackay's plantation, which lies on Carolina Side of the River, & that one Daniel Mackay who was lately a Servant to Mr. Patrick McKay, & is Still supposed to Act by his Countenance & direction, Supplys them with liquor, & frequently Trades with them, & particularly had invited Tomochachi & the Queen to trade, & bring their people with them. The present case was a Savannah & a Nauchee Indian had been at Mackay's, & being in liquor, were wrestling together at Tomochachi's; The Nauchee threw the Savannah down; a Brother to the Savannah Seeing him fall, took a Bottle of Rum out of the Nauchee's hand, & throwed it into the River. The Nauchee went away in a Sullen humour, Seeming to mutter; packed up what he had, and carried his pack out, Returned again, took his Gun, & went out again into a peice of Corn, & under Cover of the Corn, came near a Hutt, open on all

Sides, in which was a woman & a man, & shot the man, who was one of the Creeks with whom I can not find he had any difference. Two other Nauchee Indians, as soon as the Gun went off, took their Guns, & went away, and the other is Supposed to be gone with them. Tomochachi first intended to have taken Satisfaction of the Rest of the Nauchees that were Settled by him, but finding the wounded man in a way to recover, he had Shook hands, & smoked with them. I apprehended the Sole meaning of the Letter was to find out how it would be taken, if they should pursue their Revenge, & do mischief any where among the English Settlements. I shewed Mr. Patrick McKay Mathews's letter, & desired he would not Suffer such practices. He said, it was without his knowledge, but that he would enquire into it.

Sundry Stores &c.

18 JULY: John Lindall, officer of the Guard.

Peter Mailliet from Purrysburgh informed me that Weddall with the Augusta Boat was prevented from proceeding for want of hands, one of them having been bit by an allegator, & another left sick. He therefore had procured him other hands before he could proceed.

Theophiles Hetherington Sent me a Letter to the Trustees, as his answer to that part of the Trustees' Letter to me relating to his affair.

John Latter with the Carolina Scout Boat having been fully paid, returned to his Station at the Southward.

John Latter during his stay here went to Mr. Ferguson at Port Royal who was the late Commander of the Boat, to return the Muster Roll for that part of his Service, whilst under the pay of the Government of Carolina; This being the Desire of Said Ferguson whereby he might be enabled to repay the Trustees the money advanced.

Sundry Stores &c.

19 JULY: James Campbell, for Austin Weddal, officer of the Guard.

Benjamin Appleby with a small Sloop of about 110 tun, arrived with provisions from New York which I bought.

I had now been long in Expectation of Provisions, either from Philadelphia or New York, & had received Advice that one Vessel from Philadelphia which Mr. Ellis had ordered to be freighted for this place, having touched at Charles Town, was obliged by the Government there to dispose of her Cargo, they being in great want of Provisions (as they pretended). This we thought very unfair, being Sensible that Several Merchants in Charles Town had great Stores of Rice which they kept for Shipping, & thereby kept up the provision market.

Sundry Stores &c.

20 JULY: James Carwells, officer of the Guard.

Robert Williams informed me that whilst he was at Charles Town, a vessel having come in there with Corn, it was Sold at 30 Shillings Currency per Bushel. That he had been in Company with some people there who gave out that they understood Mr. Ellis had another Sloop designed for this place, & that the Government would likewise make her come in there & dispose of her Cargo. He said further that such a Vessel had been 6 weeks on her Voyage for this place, & they now believed she was lost. Mr. McKay Sent me the letter of this Date, which I could not comply with not having the quantity of Corn desired in the Store, having distributed the Corn bought of Johannet, 300 Bushels of which went to Frederica. Notwithstanding this answer given in a Civil manner, in the presence of Mr. Hugh Anderson, I in half an hour received the other Letter, to which I added the Date. As this is a Specimen of many things of the like nature from others as well as him, I think it plainly shews upon what little reasons the people are apt to take umbrage, & how difficult it is for any one that Executes a publick office to gain the good will of those who take the priviledge of judging every thing for their own private advantage, without having any regard to that of the publick.

Mr. Bradley having Sent his Servant to me to desire to know if I had any meat for his family, I returned my Service; & desired to speak with him. Accordingly he came. I acquainted him that at present there was little or no Salt meat to be got, the Sloops that had lately been here having brought no more than what I was obliged to send to the Southward: But that I had bought some good dried fish, of which he might have any quantity. He answered, that he, nor any of his family never was used to any such food. I told him I had likewise bought Some Sweet Oyl, because I found it cheaper than butter, and I believed would make the Fish very good food. He said it might be very good, but answered as above; & then added that he must kill a Cow or Calf to feed his family. I told him, I desired whenever he killed any Cattle he would let me know what it was he did kill, and the weight, because it was necessary there should be an Account made of it. To this he answered, that he did not think there was any Occasion for it, for if he killed what had been delivered to him by order of Mr. Oglethorpe, he supposed himself to be answerable for it, & there was no occasion for any further account. I found he intended to dispute a matter which was part of the Trustees' orders, & Mr. Jones only being present at the beginning, I sent for Mr. Christie, Mr. Vanderplank, & Mr. Wesley, resolving (if possible) either to convince him of the Error he seemed likely to fall in, or to take necessary precautions for my own Vindication.

Mr. Vanderplank & Mr. Wesley Soon came, & it was then with much importunity I persuaded Bradley to tarry any longer; but after laying open the matter in dispute & urging the Trustees' late orders relating to his family, which I found then necessary to acquaint him of, he Sate down; and I further acquainted him, that having received the Trustees' Directions, it was necessary that we Should come to account, & desired that he would appoint a time. He at first told me, he would not account with me, for that he had settled that matter with the Trustees before he left England, & that Lord Percival had told him he had nobody to apply to but Mr. Oglethorpe. I told him, I asked him nothing but what was in pursuance of the Trustees' Orders & read him their Letter. He said that was only Mr. Verelst's letter, of which he had a Copy; but that he had the Trustees' broad Seal for what he did. I told him, I had often heard him talk of a broad Seal, but if he would Shew me any such thing, that contradicted either what I did, or endeavoured to do, I should be very glad to be set right. He answered, he had a broad Seal, but was particularly ordered by the Trustees, & by Mr. Oglethorpe not to shew it to me. I told him, I did not doubt but that the Trustees had very good Reasons for every thing they said or did: But he must excuse me if I thought that any of his Concerns were of equal Consequence with those they had already thought fit to entrust me with; as I best knew my own Integrity, I must be so plain to tell him I did not believe him. I also told him, I understood by the Trustees' Directions that in the first place there was an agreement subsisting between him & them for the Cultivation of Land, that they had also limited the Provisions for himself & family, That his pay for the Cultivation of the Land was to come out of the produce, according to the Rate there set down; That I was to deliver to him all things that should be necessary for such Cultivation which they particularly say shall be charged to him for the use of the Trustees, & not as his own Property; Therefore as there was a long account Subsisting, it was necessary he should let me know what part of his account should be carried over to the Cultivation of Land, whereby I might be enabled to make out his private account. I again urged, that whenever he killed any Cattle, which was put in his Care for the Trustees' use, as it was not his own property, he ought to let me know, because by killing, selling, or Eating thereof, he made it his own property, & it therefore ought to be placed to his separate Account. He answered to this as he had done before, & neither I, or the Company could convince him of his Error, or rather remove his obstinacy. At length he agreed to Examine what he had received of me, & acknowledge the Receipt: but said he would never Submit his accounts to me. I told him that when they were put into Such form as the Trustees had ordered, I should return 'em to them, & he might then say or do as he pleased; & that I should always think the less I had to do with him, the better. I again urged that he would appoint a time to settle the Account for that I should not be easy 'till it was transmitted, & desired that it might be done within a fortnight, & that he would give me two

days' notice. He objected against two days' notice, & I then desired only 6 hours. At length after a good deal of Contradiction, he agreed to appoint a time within a Fortnight.
Sundry Stores &c.

21 JULY: Walter Fox, officer of the Guard.
I examined the Accounts of Samuel Montaigut & Company to the 24th of June last & certified the same.
I also certified to the board of Ordinance that I received their Stores, which they sent per Captain Dymond, for the use of the *Hawk* Sloop, pursuant to their request.
Sundry Stores &c.

22 JULY: John Vanderplank officer of the Guard.
I dispatched Mr. Aglionby (who is owner of a large Boat) to Frederica with Provisions.
Colonel Beamore arrived with some Fowls and about 5 Bushels of pease which I bought of him. He reports the Rains had been so heavy in the Spring that their Rice had suffered very much, & that now they were like to suffer in their Corn, thro' the great Drowth. It is much the same with our Corn, & those who expected 100 Bushels will Scarce have above 10.
Sundry Stores &c.

23 JULY: William Cooksey officer of the Guard.
I received advice of Mr. Jenny's Death, & that Mr. Eveleigh was dangerously ill.
Sundry Stores &c.

24 JULY: Noble Jones, officer of the Guard.
I certified the account of Trander Johannet & advised the Trustees thereof, & in the afternoon his Sloop Sailed for New England.
Sundry Stores Issued as per Day book.

A Journal of a Voyage from *London* to *Savannah* in Georgia.

A

JOURNAL

OF A

VOYAGE

FROM

LONDON

TO

Savannah in GEORGIA.

In two PARTS.

PART I. From *London* to *Gibraltar.*
PART II. From *Gibraltar* to *Savannah.*

By GEORGE WHITEFIELD, *A. B.*
of *Pembroke-College, Oxford.*

With a short Preface, shewing the Reason of its Publication.

The FOURTH EDITION.

LONDON,
Printed for JAMES HUTTON at the *Bible* and *Sun* next the *Rose Tavern* without *Temple-Bar.* MDCCXXXIX.
(Price Six-Pence.)

A Journal of a Voyage from *London* to *Savannah* in Georgia.

S*ATURDAY*, *Jan.* 14. Hasted on board about Eleven, (the Wind promising fair) to take us out of the Channel, and was affectionately received by the People. I was greatly delighted to see all the Ships sail together from the *Downs*.

Sunday, *January* 15. All the Day the Sea was entirely becalm'd; every Thing about us seem hush'd and quiet, as though it would remind us of that sacred Rest the Day was set apart to commemorate. In the Evening the Wind blew very fresh, but being full against us, we were obliged to sail back to the *Downs* (though we had got near fifty Miles) where we arrived about Twelve a-Clock.

Monday, *January* 16. Was a little affected by seeing a poor Soldier tied Neck and Heels, for several mutinous Words he had spoken. The Captain related the Case to me, and said, if I could make him sensible of his Crime, I might beg him off. I endeavoured to do it, but, alas, in vain; he continued obstinate, and thereby hindered my Design taking Effect. After this, the Captain ordered him to be tied down between Decks; from whence I took Occasion, in my Morning Sermon, to exhort the Soldiers to obey them that *had the Rule over them* and to avoid those Sins, that would provoke

GOD to command them to be *tied Hand and Foot, and to be cast into outer Darkness, where would be weeping and gnashing of Teeth.*

Wednesday, January 18. About Eleven at Night went and sat down among the Sailors in the Steerage, and reasoned with them *about Righteousness, Temperance, and a Judgment to come*; at which some of them almost *trembled.*

Monday, Jan. 23. Was much comforted by receiving five more Letters; answered some of them; and about Eleven in the Morning went on board the *Amy*, to pay my Respects to Colonel *C.* and to visit the Soldiers, whom I looked upon as Part of my Charge. I was received very civilly by the Officers; went among the Soldiers, enquired into the State of their Souls, gave them a Word or two of Exhortation; promised to bring them some Books (I saw their Wants,) and (at the Officer's Request) to come and preach to them, if Opportunity should offer, before we left the *Downs.*

After this, I visited the *Lightfoot*, our other Transport Ship, in which were about twelve Soldiers and a Serjeant: they received me kindly. I sat down and conversed with them; promised to send them some Books, and to come and preach to them also, if Providence should permit. The *Downs* being exceeding calm, and the Weather clear, going from Ship to Ship was very pleasant.

Tuesday, Jan. 31. The Weather being fair, we went on board with Pleasure: The Ship was under Sail, but we met with it, and were received affectionately.

Our Ship sailed briskly for a few Hours; but the Wind shifting again, was obliged to return back once more, and we cast Anchor in the *Downs* about Nine at Night.

Thursday, Feb. 2. About Ten o'Clock there sprung up a pleasant fair Gale, which carried us from the *Downs* near forty Miles that Day.

Friday, Feb. 3. Let this Day be noted in my Book; for GOD wrought for us a wonder Deliverance! About Seven in the Morning, the Men upon Deck not keeping a good lookout, one of the *East-India* Ships in shifting to the Wind ran near us so very briskly, that had not Captain *W.* providentially been on Deck, and beseeched them for GOD's sake to tack about, both the Ships must inevitably have split one against another. They were within four Yards of each other. The Captain said he never was in so great Danger in his Life. God so ordered it, that Mr. *H.* and I knew nothing of it 'till it was over: But when I was apprised of it, I endeavoured to excite all to Thankfulness, and returned publick Thanks at Prayers.

Tuesday, *Feb.* 14. May I never forget this Day's Mercies, since the Lord was pleased to deal so lovingly with me! About Twelve at Night a fresh Gale arose, which increased so very much by Four in the Morning, that the Waves raged horribly indeed, and broke in like a River on many of the poor Soldiers, who lay near the Main Hatch Way. Friend *H.* and I knew nothing of it, but perceived ourselves restless, and could not sleep at all; he complained of a grievous Headach. I arose and called upon God for myself and those that sailed with me, absent Friends, and all Mankind. After this I went on Deck; but surely a more noble awful Sight my Eyes never yet beheld! for the Waves rose more than Mountain high, and sometimes came on the Quarter-Deck. I endeavoured all the while to magnify God, for thus making his Power to be known: And then creeping on my Knees (for I knew not how to go otherwise) I followed my Friend *H.* between Decks, and sung Psalms and comforted the poor wet People. After this, I read Prayers in the great Cabbin; but we were obliged to sit all the while. Then thinking I should be capable of doing nothing, I laid myself across the Chair reading; but God was so good, so to assist me by his Spirit, that tho' Things were tumbling, the Ship rocking, and Persons falling down unable to stand, and sick about me; yet I never was more chearful in my Life, and was enabled, though in the midst of Company, to finish a Sermon before I went to Bed, which I had begun a few Days before: So greatly was God's Strength magnified in my Weakness! *Praise the LORD, O my Soul, and all that is within me praise his holy Name!*

Thursday, *Mar.* 9. Married a Couple on Deck. I endeavoured to give them a suitable Exhortation after the Solemnity was over, and hope this Couple will call Christ to their Marriage.

The contrary Winds still continuing, my Sea-sickness encreased;

so that I was obliged to omit reading Prayers to the Soldiers, and go to Bed sooner than usual. I find this Sickness will purge my Body, and hope, through Grace, it will purify my Soul.

Saturday, Mar. 18. The Weather being exceeding fair, and the Sea calm, I went with Capt. *W.* on board the *Lightfoot*, dined with the Gentlemen belonging to the Ship and Colonel *C.* who came on board to pay them a Visit: Married a Couple; dispersed *Bibles, Testaments, Soldiers Monitors* amongst the Men; exchanged some Books for some Cards, which I threw over board; preached a Sermon against Drunkenness, which God enabled me to finish yesterday; and returned in the Evening, highly delighted with seeing the Porpoises roll about the great Deep.

Sunday, Mar. 19. Went with Captain *W.* on board the *Amy*; read Prayers and preached to above two hundred and twenty Hearers; and married a Couple, who did not behave so well as I could wish: The Bridegroom laughed several Times in the midst of the Solemnity, upon which I shut up my Prayer-book: But he shewing his Concern by weeping, I then proceeded, gave him and the Bride a Bible, as the best Present I could make them; and exhorted all to Holiness of Life.

Monday, Mar. 20. To-day Colonel *C.* came to dine with us, and in the midst of our Meal we were entertained with a most agreeable Sight; it was a Shark about the Length of a Man, which followed our Ship, attended with five little Fishes called the Pilot Fish, much like a Mackarel, but larger. These I am told always keep the Shark company; and what is most surprising, though the Shark is so ravenous a Creature, yet let it be ever so hungry, it never touches one of them. Nor are they less faithful to him: For if at any Time the Shark is hooked, these little Creatures will not forsake him, but cleave close to his Fins, and are often taken up with him. *Go to the Pilot Fish, thou that forsakest a Friend in Adversity, consider his Ways and be abashed.* This simple Sight one would think sufficient to confute any Atheist (if there be such a Fool as a speculative Atheist) in the World.

Friday, March 24. To-day the Sick still increased, and Friend *H.* was very ready to assist and carry Things to them. We begin now to live so happy on Shipboard, that I believe we shall part with each other with Regret. Sailed an hundred and fifty four Miles the last twenty four Hours: And was much delighted in seeing many Porpoises playing about the Ship, one of which Captain *W.* catched, and Part of its Liver we had dressed for Dinner: It had a Head much like a Pig, and was about six Foot long.

Sunday, March 26. This Day GOD I trust magnified his Power in the Conversion of a young Gentleman on board, whom he has been pleased to visit with a Fever. His Convictions were strong, and as far as I could find, a thorough Renovation begun in his Heart.

Exchanged some bad Books that were on board (which I threw immediately into the Sea) for some good ones, blessed be GOD; all that I have found them with, as yet, have been ready to surrender them up. And I find it by daily Experience more and more that People who are truly awakened to a Sense of the Divine Life, cannot bear to read any thing trifling; but throw away their useless Books, as those did the Books of Divination and curious Arts, whose Conversion we read in the *Acts*, Chap. v.

Monday, March 27. Last Night GOD was pleased to take away a black Boy of Capt. *W*'s after he had been ill of a violent Fever for some Days— He was never baptised, but I had a Commission from his Master, who seemed much affected at his Death, to instruct, and baptise him, if it had pleased the Most High that he should recover; but GOD saw fit to order it otherwise. About Ten in the Morning he was wrapt up in a Hammock and thrown into the Sea. I could not read the Office over him being unbaptised, but Capt. *M.* ordered the Drum to beat, and I exhorted all the Soldiers, Sailors, *&c.* as GOD gave me Utterance, to *Remember their Creator in the Days of their Youth*, and to prepare for that Time, *when the Sea should give up its Dead, and all Nations be called together to appear before the Son of God.*

Wednesday, March 29. Sailed near an hundred and sixty Miles every twenty-four Hours, for several Days, most delightful pleasant Weather; and had much of GOD's Presence amongst us.

Friday, March 31. Had a good Instance of the Benefit of breaking Children's Wills betimes. Last Night going between Decks (as I do every Night) to visit the Sick and to examine my People, I asked one of the Women to bid her little Boy that stood by her, say his Prayers, she answered, his elder Sister would, but she could not make him. Upon this, I bid the Child kneel down before me, but he would not till I took hold of its two Feet and forced it down. I then bid it say the *Lord's Prayer*, (being informed by his Mother he could say it if he would) but he obstinately refused, till at last after I had given it several Blows, it said its Prayers as well as could be expected, and I gave it some Figs for a Reward. And this same Child, tho' not above four Years of Age, came to Night on Deck, when the other Children came to say their Prayers to my Friend *H.* and burst out into a Flood of Tears, and would not go away till he had said his too. I mention this as a Proof of the Necessity of early Correction: Children are sensible of it sooner than Parents imagine. And if they would but have Resolution to break their Wills thoroughly when young, the Work of Conversion would be much easier, and they would not be so troubled with perverse Children when they are old.

April 14. To-day, I could have wished for some young Prodigals on board the *Whitaker*, to see one of our Soldiers dying. Alas, how did his Breast heave, his Heart pant, and great Drops of Sweat trickle down his Face! his Eyes looked ghastly, and the whole Man was in a bitter Agony. Captain *W.* went down between Decks once or twice to see him: And I used the last Prayer several Times. About Nine at Night he expired, I fear without Hope; for he killed himself by Drinking. *Oh that all Drunkards would learn from him to be wise in time, and practically consider their latter End.*

April 15. This Morning I buried the dead Soldier in time of publick Prayers, chose proper Lessons, and gave the Soldiers a suitable Exhortation; but I was so affected with a Sense of the Misery of fallen Man, that I could not speak with my usual Vigour.

Exercised a little Discipline this Evening on a Boy, whom Captain *M.* took notice of above a Week ago for behaving ill at Church, and said he would deliver him up to me: I therefore, by the Advice of his Master, ordered him to be tied, till he could say the 51*st*

Psalm, which he repeated to Night very solemnly in the midst of the Congregation. May it be a Warning to him for the future!

Saturday, *April* 22. Fled as it were on the Wings of the Wind for three Days past, sailing sometimes an hundred and seventy, sometimes an hundred and eighty Miles in twenty-four Hours. I find that God generally sends us strongest Winds, when nearest our Port.

Monday, *May* 1. This Morning went out upon Deck, after being confined to my Bed a Week by a violent Fever, with which all except three or four in the Ship have been visited. I was blooded thrice, and blistered and vomited once, and, blessed be God, I can say, *It is good for me that I have been afflicted*: For as Afflictions abounded, Consolations much more abounded; and God enabled me to rejoice with Joy unspeakable and full of Glory.

Friday, *May* 5. About Ten o'Clock this Morning buried the Cook of the Ship, who expired last Night. I could have wished for a hundred Tongues to have sounded a loud Alarm to the People; but the Sight of the Corpse, and the Weakness of my Body, would but just permit me to read out the Office.

In the Afternoon I privately baptized a new-born Infant. Thus it is, some coming into the World, others going out of it continually.

This Afternoon, after having lain about a Week on this Coast, we saw *Savannah* River, and sent off for a Pilot. Oh what Joy appeared in every one's Countenance! How infinitely more joyful will the Children of God be, when having passed through the Waves of this troublesome World, they arrive at the Haven of everlasting Rest?

Sunday, *May* 7. Last Night, by the Blessing of God, we cast Anchor near *Tyby* Island, about fourteen Miles off *Savannah*; and to-day God gave me Strength to preach my Farewel Sermon, (which I have sent you,) at which many wept.

Arrived at *Savannah* Town about seven this Evening, and joined in Prayer, and a Psalm of Thanksgiving with Mr. *Delamotte*, and some pious Souls that were rejoiced at my Arrival.

Spent the remainder of the Evening in taking sweet Counsel with Mr. *Delamotte*, who seems providentially left behind at *Sa-*

vannah against my coming. How sweetly does Providence order Things for us!

Monday, May 8. Begun to read publick Prayers and expound the second Lesson at Five in the Morning to seventeen Adults and twenty five Children.

In the Afternoon Mr. *Causton* sent Word that he and the Magistrates would wait upon me, but I chose rather to wait upon them. I was received with great Civility, and our chief Conversation ran upon the Place of my Settlement; at last it was resolved that I should have a House and Tabernacle built at *Frederica*, and serve at *Savannah*, when, and as long as I pleased. I find there are many Divisions amongst the Inhabitants, but God, I hope, will make me an Instrument of composing them.

Sunday, May 14. After another Weeks Confinement, by the Return of my Fever, under which God shewed me great Mercies, and which went off with a Fit of the Ague, I attempted to read Prayers, but was so exceeding faint and weak, that I was obliged to leave off before I begun the second Service.

Tuesday, May 16. Having by the Blessing of God gotten a little Strength, I went to see *Tomo Chachi*, who, I heard, was near expiring at a Neighbour's House. He lay on a Blanket thin and meagre, and little else but Skin and Bones. *Senauki* sat by fanning him with some *Indian* Feathers. There was no Body that could talk *English*, so I could only shake Hands and leave him.

Friday, May 19. God still strengthening me more and more, I went this Morning to two little Villages, *Hampstead* and *Highgate*, about Five Miles off *Savannah*: The former consists of three Families, making in all eleven Souls, one Man a *Jew*; two Men, one Woman and seven Children *Swissers*. I was much delighted with seeing the improvements a few pair of Hands had made in their respective Plantations, and was surprized to see what Industry will do. Surely they speak not Truth, who say that the *Georgia* People have been idle; for I never saw more laborious People than are in these Villages. They live exceeding hard, but with a little Assistance may do very well. I was at a Loss, because I could not talk *French*; but however I resolved, under God, to follow my worthy

Predecessor's Example, and to visit them once a Week, and read Prayers to as many as could understand me. I also enquired into the State of their Children, and found there were many who might prove useful Members of the Colony, if there was a proper Place provided for their Maintenance and Education. Nothing can effect this but an Orphan-House, which might easily be erected at *Savannah*, would some of those that are rich in this World's Good, contribute towards it.

Saturday, *May* 20. Went once more to see *Tomo Chachi*, hearing his Nephew *Tooanoowee* was there, who could talk *English*. I desired of him to enquire of his Uncle, Whether he thought he should die; who answer'd, He could not tell: I then asked where he thought he should go after Death? He replied, to Heaven. *But alas, how can a Drunkard enter there!* I then exhorted *Tooanoowee* (who is a tall proper Youth) not to get drunk, telling him, he understood *English*, and therefore would be punished the more if he did not live better. I then asked him, Whether he believed a Heaven? He answer'd, Yes. I then asked, Whether he believed a Hell? and described it by pointing to the Fire, he replied, No. From whence we may easily gather how natural it is to all Mankind to believe there is a Place of Happiness, because they wish it may be so, and on the contrary, how averse they are to believe a Place of Torment, because they wish it may not be so. But God is true and just, and as surely as the Good shall go into everlasting Happiness, so the Wicked shall go into everlasting Punishment.

Wednesday, *May* 24. Went to Day to *Thunderbolt*, a Village about six Miles off *Savannah*, situated very pleasantly near the River, and consisting of three Families, four Men and two Women, and ten Servants; I was kindly received, expounded a Chapter, used a few Collects, called on a Family or two that lay near our Way, and returned home to *Savannah* very comfortably, with my Friend *Delamotte*, about six o'Clock in the Evening.

Friday, *June* 2. This Evening parted with kind Captain *Whiting* and my dear Friend *Delamotte*, who embarked for *England* about seven at Night. The poor People lamented the Loss of him, and went to the Water-side to take a last Farwel. And good Reason had they to do so: For he has been indefatigable in feeding CHRIST's Lambs with the sincere Milk of the Word, and many of them (*Blessed be GOD*) have grown thereby. Surely I must labour most heartily, since I come after such worthy Predesessors. The Good Mr. *John Wesly* has done in *America*, under GOD, is inexpressible. His Name is very precious among the People; and he has laid such a Foundation, that I hope neither Men nor Devils will ever be able to shake.

Monday, *June* 5. Had a Conference with a certain Person of the Parish, who, I heard last Night, had been broaching many heretical Doctrines to one of my Friends, particularly in denying the Eternity of Hell Torments. I therefore invited him this Morning to Breakfast; and after imploring GOD's Assistance, in the Spirit of Meekness, I asked him, Whether he believed the Eternity of Hell Torments? He answer'd frankly, No. I replied, What do you mean, Sir, when you repeat the 12th Article of our Creed? He said, he believed wicked Men were to be annihilated. I then read *Pearson*'s Exposition of the last Article, but he denied it all, said he thought himself in the right, and believed it his Duty to inform Mankind, that they were to be annihilated. Upon which I repeated to him that Passage out of the *Revelations*. "If any Man shall take away from or add unto the Words that are written in this Book, GOD shall take away his Name out of the Book of Life, and add unto him all the Plagues that are written in this Book." This he said he believed. Afterwards we discoursed afresh, but finding him resolute to propagate his Principles, I then told him with the utmost Calmness, that I was sorry that I gave him the Cup yesterday at the Sacrament; but for the future, he must pardon me if I refused ever to give it him again. This stagger'd him a little, but he bore it pretty patiently, yet thought me uncharitable. But I told him I should meet him at the Judgment-Seat of CHRIST, and then he would see upon what Principles I acted.

Saturday, *June* 10. Placed one that came with me, at *Highgate*, to teach the Children *English*, that belong to that Village and *Hampstead*. They are about twenty in all, of *French* Extraction, but some few of them are able to speak a little in our vulgar Tongue.

I thought placing a Master there, would be of great Consequence. *First*, Because I cannot think Children will ever be naturaliz'd to the Colony, till they can talk our Language. *Secondly*, Because the present Generation will soon wear off, and these Children being well instructed in ours, will make them forget their own Tongue, and should they marry and have Children, they would naturally teach their Children the same; so that at length we shall all be of one Speech. *Thirdly*, As they are but few in Number, and no likelihood of any *French* Minister to come amongst them; I or my Successors shall be unable to Catechise or bring them to hear the Word of God at our Church, unless they are acquainted with the *English* Tongue.

Monday, *June* 11. Opened a School to Day for the Girls of *Savannah*, a Friend, whose Heart God was pleased to touch on Board the Ship, having at my Request undertaken to teach them. The Work is for my Master, and therefore I doubt not of being supplied some Way or another with a sufficient Fund for the Support of it.

Thursday, *June* 22. Was taken (as all about me thought for Death) with a violent Purging and Vomiting, which in the Space of five Hours quite exhausted my Spirits, and brought me in appearance almost to the Point of Death. But God supported me by his inward Comforts, caused me to rejoice in it; and cast me into a deep Sleep, out of which I awoke perfectly well, to the Surprize of all about me. My Parishioners in general shewed they loved me; for they seem'd most sollicitous for my Welfare. For their Sake, as well as for my own, I hope God has so suddenly restored me.

Friday, *June* 24. To the great Surprise of myself and People, was enabled to read Prayers and preach with Power before the Free-Masons, with whom I afterwards dined, and was used with the utmost Civility.

Friday, *July* 7. Being the Anniversary for opening the Court, I preached in the Morning at the Magistrate's Request, and endeavoured with all Plainness and Humility to shew both them and the People what they ought to do to promote their Temporal and Eternal Welfare.

Tuesday, *July* 11. Returned this Evening from *Ebenezer* (whither I went Yesterday) the Place where the *Saltzburghers* are settled; and was wonderfully pleased with their Order and Industry. Their Lands are improved surprisingly for the Time they have been there, and I believe they have far the best Crop of any in the Colony—They are bless'd with two such pious Ministers, as I have not often seen: They have no Courts of Judicature, but all little Differences are immediately and implicitly decided by their Ministers, whom they look upon and love as their Fathers. They have likewise an Orphan-House, in which are seventeen Children, and one Widow, and I was much delighted to see the Regularity wherewith it is managed,—*Oh that GOD may stir up the Hearts of his Servants to contribute towards that and another which we hope to have erected at* Savannah.—Mr. *Boltzius*, one of their Ministers, being with me on *Saturday*, I gave him some of my Poor's Store for his Orphans, and when I came to *Ebenezer*, he call'd them all before him, catechised and exhorted them to give God Thanks for his good Providence towards them; then prayed with them, and made them pray after him; then sung a Psalm, and afterwards the little Lambs came and shook me by the Hand one by one, and so we parted, and I scarce was ever better pleased in my Life—Surely whoever contributes to the Relief of the *Saltzburghers* will perform an acceptable Sacrifice to our Blessed Master. They are very poor; but with a little Assistance might live comfortably and well. They want a Place for Publick Worship, and Money to buy Cattle and other Necessaries for the Orphan-House and People.

Tuesday, *July* 18. About ten o'Clock this Evening returned to *Savannah*, having set out from thence Yesterday to visit four or five Families that live at some of the outward Settlements about twelve Miles off.—Their Beginnings as yet are but small, but I cannot help thinking there are Foundations laying for great temporal and spiritual Blessings in *Georgia*, when the Inhabitants are found worthy.—Blessed be God, in *Savannah* they will hear the Word gladly, and People every where receive me with the utmost Civility and are not angry when I reprove them.

Tuesday, *July* 25. I am now waiting for the Scout-Boat which Mr. *Horton* has sent to take me to *Frederica*, to preach the Gospel there also. For therefore am I sent.—I should part with regret from the People of *Savannah*, did I not know God call'd me from them. For they seem to have a sincere Affection for me, and flock (especially every Evening) to hear the Word of God.— I have endeavoured to let my Gentleness be known amongst them, because they consist of different Nations and Opinions.—And I have strove to draw them by the Cords of Love, because the Obedience resulting from that Principle I take to be most genuine and lasting. My ordinary way of dividing my ministerial Labours has been as follows,—

On *Sunday* Morning at five o'Clock, I publickly expound the second Lesson for the Morning or Evening Service as I see most suited to the Peoples Edification; at Ten I preach and read Prayers, at Three in the Afternoon I do the same, and at Seven expound Part of the Church Catechism, at which great Numbers are usually present. I visit from House to House, read publick Prayers and expound twice and catechise (unless something extraordinary happens,) visit the Sick every Day, and read to as many of my Parishioners as will come thrice a Week,—and blessed be God my Labours have not been altogether vain in the Lord. For he has been pleased to set his Seal to my Ministry in a Manner, I could not, I dared not in *America* expect.

Tuesday, *August* 8. After a pleasant Passage of five or six Days arrived at *Frederica*, a Town situated southwardly above an hundred Miles from *Savannah*, and consisting of about an hundred and twenty Inhabitants. The People received me most gladly, having had a Famine of the Word for a long Season.

In the Evening we had publick Prayers, and expounding of the second Lesson under a large Tree, and many more present than could be expected.

Wednesday, *August* 9. Began to Day visiting from House to House, and found the People in Appearance desirous of being fed with the sincere Milk of the Word, and sollicitous for my Continuance amongst them. Poor Creatures! my Heart ached for them, because I saw them and their Children scatter'd abroad as Sheep having no Shepherd.

This Evening had Prayers in a House which Mr. *Horton* hired for us during my Stay, and most of the Inhabitants, I believe, were present. Blessed be God, Timber is sawing for the erecting a more commodious Place for publick Worship, 'till a Church can be built.

Friday, *August* 11. Went in the Morning to, and returned in the Evening from the *Darien*, a Settlement about twenty Miles off from *Frederica*, whither I went to see Mr. *Macloud* a worthy Minister of the *Scotch* Church, and God gave me a most pleasant Passage.

Saturday, *August* 12. This Afternoon was alarmed with the News of a Family Disaster. My dear Friend *H*'s Brother going to find a Horse that was lost in the Woods, was lost himself, and many Guns shot after him for several Days, but in vain. I endeavoured to give Thanks to God for this and every Thing that befals me, because it is his Will, and resolved to set out for *Savannah* immediately, knowing what Concern my dear Friend *H*. must be in at so sudden a Loss.

In the Evening, because I was to go about Midnight, I gave Notice I would preach as well as expound, at which almost all the Inhabitants were present; for many were obliged to stand without the Door. The Lesson was very applicable to my Circumstances. It was the first of St. *James* wherein the Apostle bids us *rejoice when we fall into divers Temptations*. God enabled me to enlarge on it pretty much. I told the People that God called me and I must away, at which some wept.

Sunday, *Aug*. 13. Being disappointed of going by the Boat last Night, I read Prayers and preached to my dear little Flock twice, which caused great Joy among them. Mr. *Horton* was extreamly civil and did every Thing he could to oblige me. This Afternoon after Sermon intended to go with him to preach to the Soldiers at the Fort of St. *Simon*'s, and then the next Day to go to St. *Andrew*'s, *but Lord thou callest me elsewhere*. Had an Alarm brought to *Frederica* that the *Spaniards* had taken Possession of *Fort St. George*, and fired at one of our Boats: But this was quickly found to be entirely groundless.

About Two in the Afternoon having first read Prayers, and preached, most of the Inhabitants accompanied me to the *Bluff* and took their Leaves of me in an affectionate Manner, and laded me with Things convenient for my Journey.

Wednesday, *August* 16. Arrived this Day at *Savannah*, and had the Pleasure of meeting my Friend who had been lost, he was from *Tuesday* 'till *Friday* roving about the Woods, during which Time the great Guns were fired according to Custom, and the People shewed what a great Respect they had for me and my Friends. Many of them going out all Day and Night after him.—As soon as I had refreshed myself I went and visited my Parishioners from House to House to return them Thanks for their Kindness to my Friends. An unusual Joy appear'd in their Faces at my unexpected Return, and they were ready to say, *How beautiful are the Feet of him that bringeth the glad Tidings of Salvation!* At Evening Prayers (and a very large Congregation was present) I returned my dear Hearers hearty Thanks for the late Instance of their sincere Affection, I publickly exhorted my Friend that was lost to shew forth his Thankfulness not only with his Lips but with his Life, and desired their Prayers to GOD for me that I might now more and more devote myself to my Blessed Master's Service, and study daily to purify my corrupt Nature, that I might be made an Instrument under him of winning their Souls to GOD.

Wednesday, *August* 23. A Necessity was laid on me to Day to express my Resentment against Infidelity by refusing to read the Burial Office over the most professed Unbeliever I ever yet met with.—GOD was pleased to visit him with a lingring Illness, in which Time I went to see him frequently.—Particularly about five Weeks agone, I asked him what Religion he was of, he answered, "Religion was divided into so many Sects he knew not which to chuse."—Another Time, I offer'd to pray with him, but he would not accept it, upon which I resolv'd to go see him no more;—But being told two Days before he dyed, that had an Inclination to see me, I went to him again, and after a little Conversation, I put to him the following Questions, "Do you believe JESUS CHRIST to be GOD, the one Mediator between GOD and Man?" He said, "I believe CHRIST was a good Man."—"Do you believe the Holy Scriptures"? "I believe," replied he, "something of the Old Testament, the New I do not believe at all."—"Do you believe, Sir, a Judgment to come?" he turn'd himself about and replied, "I know not what to say to that."—Alass said I, Sir, "if all these Things should be true—" which Words I believe gave him Concern, for he seemed after to be very uneasy, grew delirious, and departed in a Day or two.—Unhappy Man, how quickly was he convinced that all I said was true. Now he and I are of one Mind: The Day after his Decease he was carried to the Ground, and I refused to read the Office over him, but went to the Grave and told the People what had passed between him and me, warned them against Infidelity, and asked them whether I could safely say, "as our Hope is this our Brother doth," upon which I believe they were thoroughly satisfied that I had done right.—*GOD grant this may be a Warning to surviving Unbelievers.*

Thursday, *Aug.* 24. This Day went to *Highgate* with a Friend or two more, and read Prayers, preach'd and baptized a Child, and catechised in a House lately erected by the Inhabitants. For upon my sending a Master to teach their Children, one offer'd to give me a part of his Lot, and the rest to give their Labour. Accordingly I accepted of it, found Materials, and to Day it was fit to preach in, and be made a School-House of. The Children tho' Foreigners answer'd admirably well, which gave me great Hopes that the other foreign Children of the Colony may also learn our *English* Tongue when a proper Master is provided.—After Service we refreshed ourselves together, thanked our good God, and eat our Bread with Gladness of Heart.

Sunday, *August* 27. God having now shewn both me and my Friends that it was his Will I should return for a while to *England*: This Afternoon I preached my Farewel Sermon, to the great Grief of my dear Parishioners, for their Hearts I found were very full as well as mine, which they expressed by shedding many Tears. But a sensible Alteration appear'd in their Countenances, when I promised them solemnly before God to return as soon as possible.

The Weather was exceeding hot, and the Greatness of the Congregation made it still hotter, but God enabled me to preach with Power.

Monday, *August* 28. This being the Day of my Departure, it was mostly spent in taking Leave of my Flock, who expressed their Affection now more than ever. For they came to me from the Morning to the Time I left them with Tears in their Eyes, wishing me a prosperous Voyage and safe Return, and gave me other Tokens of their Love. For they brought me Wine, Ale, Cake, Coffee, Tea, and other Things proper for my Passage, and their Love seem'd without Dissimulation.

About Four in the Afternoon I went into the Boat provided for me by Mr. *Causton*, who with the Recorder came to my House and took their Leave. A great Number of People came to the *Bluff* and wish'd me a good Voyage with all their Souls, and a speedy Return; I thanked them, and having desired their Prayers, blessed them in the Name of God and took my Leave.

My Heart was full and I took the first Opportunity of venting it by Prayers and Tears. I think I never parted from a Place with more Regret; for *America* in my Opinion is an excellent School to learn Christ in; and I have great Hopes some good will come out of *Savannah*, because the longer I continued there, the larger the Congregations grew. And I scarce know a Night, though we had Divine Service twice a Day, when the Church-House has not been near full—A Proof, this, I hope, that God has yet Spiritual and Temporal Blessings in store for them. *Hasten*, *O LORD that blessed Time!*

FRIDAY, *January* 11. 1739-40. Went this Morning with some Friends to view a Tract of Land, consisting of 500 Acres, which Mr. *H*— whom I left School-Master of *Savannah*, was directed, I hope by Providence, to make Choice of for the *Orphan-House*. It is situated on the Northern Part of the Colony, about 10 Miles off *Savannah*, and has various Kinds of Soil in it; a Part of it very good. —Some Acres, through the Diligence of my Friend, are cleared. He has also stock'd it with Cattle and Poultry. He has begun the Fence, and built a Hut; all which will greatly forward the Work. I choose to have it so far off the Town, because the Children will then be more free from bad Examples, and can more conveniently go upon their Lands to work. For it is my Design to have each of the Children taught to labour, so as to be qualified to get their own Living.

Thursday, *January* 24. Went this Morning and took Possession of my Lot. I called it *Bethesda*, that is, *the House of Mercy*. For I hope many Acts of Mercy will be shewn there, and that many will thereby be stirred up *to praise the LORD, as a GOD whose Mercy endureth for ever*.

Tuesday, *January* 29. Took in three *German* Orphans, the most pitiful Objects, I think, that I ever yet saw.—No new Negroes could possibly look more despicable, or require more Pains to instruct them.—They have been used to exceeding hard Labour, and tho' supplied with Provisions from the Trustees, yet treated in a Manner unbecoming even Heathens.—Was all the Money I have collected, to be spent in freeing these three Children from Slavery, it would be well laid out.—I have also in my House near twenty more, who, in all Probability, if not taken in, would be as ignorant of God and Christ, comparatively speaking, as the *Indians*. Blessed be God, they begin to live in order.

Tuesday, *January* 29. This Day I began the Cotton Manufacture, and agreed with a Woman to teach the little ones to spin and card.—I find annual Cotton grows indifferently well in *Georgia*: And to encourage the People, I this Day bought three hundred Pounds Weight, and have agreed to take all the Cotton, Hemp, and Flax that shall be produced the following Year through the whole Province.—I see more and more the Excellency of the Charity in which I am engaged. I trust it will make *Savannah* lift up her drooping Head. Tho' there are fewer Inhabitants, yet I think they are in a better Situation than when I was here last.—They now live independent on a Public Store. Provisions, (Flour especially) are much cheaper, Cattle more plentiful; and by the Divine Blessing, if any Manufacture can be raised amongst themselves, to prevent their exporting so much Money, they may yet do well.—I bless GOD my Congregations are as large as usual.—The Court-House is generally full, and I keep as near as may be, to my old Way of Proceeding.—We have the Sacrament every *Sunday*, and the public Prayer and Exposition twice every Day in the Week.

Wednesday, *January* 30. Went this Day with the Carpenter and Surveyor, and laid out the Ground whereon the Orphan-House is to be built. It is to be sixty Feet long, and forty wide. A Yard and Garden before and behind. The Foundation is to be Brick, and is to be sunk four Feet within, and raised three Feet above the Ground. —The House is to be two Story high, with an Hip-Roof: The first ten, the second nine Foot high.—In all, there will be near twenty commodious Rooms.—Behind are to be two small Houses, the one for an Infirmary, the other for a Work-house. There is also to be a Still-House for the Apothecary; and I trust ere my Return to *England*, I shall see my Children and Family quite settled in it.—I find it will be an expensive Work: But it is for the LORD CHRIST. He will take Care to defray all Charges. The Money that will be spent on this Occasion, will keep many Families from leaving the Colony, and in all Probability bring many others over. There are near thirty working at the Plantation already, and I would employ as many more, if they were to be had.—Whatsoever is done for GOD, ought to be done speedily, as well as with all our Might.

Monday, *February* 4. Met, according to Appointment, with all the Magistrates, and the former Trustee of the Orphans, who heard the Recorder read over the Grant given me by the Trustees, and took a Minute of their Approbation of the same.

Monday, *February* 11. Had much of the Divine Presence Yesterday, both at Morning and Evening Service. Took in four fresh Orphans, and set out with two Friends to *Frederica*, in order to pay my Respects to General *Oglethorpe*, and to fetch the Orphans that were in the Southern Parts of the Colony.

Tuesday, *February* 12. Lay here last Night at a Planter's House, expecting to meet the Scout Boat this Morning, but finding it did not come at the Time appointed, I and my Friends went to *Bethesda*, and I hope spent the Day to GOD's Glory and our own Good.

At Night we returned to *Providence*.—About eight o'Clock the Scout Boat came; but it being late, we chose to defer going till next Morning.—In the mean while, God was pleased to give us refreshing Sleep, and to fill my Soul, after it had been much cast down, with unspeakable Peace and Joy in the Holy Ghost.

Friday, *February* 15. Lay on the Water two Nights, and reached the *Scots* Settlement To-day at Noon.—Was kindly received by Mr. *Macleod* the Minister, and those of his House.—Engaged to take four Orphans which were in his Flock; and about seven in the Evening, after some edifying Conversation and friendly Offices of Love, I took Boat for *Frederica*, where we arrived about two in the Morning; and having warmed and refreshed ourselves, retired to Bed, blessing God for the bodily and spiritual Comforts which he from time to time imparted to us.

Saturday, *February* 16. Waited upon and was courteously received by the General, with whom I and my Friends breakfasted and dined, and spent most Part of the Day. At Night God was pleased to visit me with a Fever, which obliged me to go to Bed sooner than usual. My Mind was also exercised with inward Trials: But in a few Hours my Pain both of Body and Mind, were somewhat abated, and the Remainder of the Night I was blessed with sweet Repose.

Sunday, *February* 17. Found myself better in Body, tho' somewhat weak.—Preach'd in the Morning in a Room belonging to the Store-House.—God was pleased to give me much Freedom, and the People seemed very attentive.—The General, Soldiers and People attended very orderly.—After Sermon I married a Couple, baptized a Child, and spent the Remainder of the Evening with my two Friends.

Monday, *February* 18. Rose this Morning by one o'Clock.—Took Boat in order to go to *St. Andrew's*; but the Rudder breaking, we were obliged to return back and desist from our intended Voyage.—Went to Bed and slept for a few Hours. Spent a good Part of the Day with the General. Received from him a Bill of Exchange for £ 150 which he advanced me in order to begin a Church at *Savannah*. About seven o'Clock set off for the *Darien*, whither I promised to return, to take Mr. *Macleod* and the Orphans with me to *Savannah*.—The Passage to that Place is generally about four Hours: But the Wind being high and contrary, we were obliged to come to a Grapling, near an open Reach, and did not get to *Darien* till the next Day at Noon.—Mr. *Macleod* and his Friends received us with Joy, and finding me ill, advised me to lie down; by which I was much refreshed, and was thereby enabled at Night to give God Thanks in Family Prayer.

Wednesday, *February* 20. Preached about ten in the Morning to Mr. *Macleod*'s Congregation, who seemed rejoiced at what God enabled me to deliver.—About two o'Clock took Boat for *Savannah*.—But after we had rowed about twelve Miles, the Wind grew rough, and the Water beat so fast into our Boat, which was but small, and very heavy laden, that we were obliged to put in at a Place called *Doboy Island*; where we sat very comfortably round a large Fire, and praised the Lord with joyful Lips, for providing such a Place for our Safety.

Friday, *February* 21. Continued all Day Yesterday, to my abundant Satisfaction, and Spiritual Advantage on *Doboy Island*, and finding the Wind still continue high and contrary, we thought it best to return back to *Darien*, where we arrived this Day about Noon.—The People were much pleased at our Return; and tho' I wanted to see my dear Family at *Savannah*, yet I felt such a peculiar Satisfaction within myself, as gave me Hopes God intended some Good for the *Scots* People at *Darien*.

Sunday, *February* 24. Preached once Yesterday and twice To-day. Prayed with a sick Person. Spent some Hours in discoursing with a well-disposed Family.— Was enabled to see more of the Vileness of my Heart and Nature.—Felt God's Spirit striving with my Spirit; and upon many Accounts, both bodily and spiritual, had Reason to bless God for bringing me to, and detaining me at *Darien*.—I have Reason to say, *It is good for me that I have been here*.—Retirement is a sweet Means to keep up and quicken the Divine Life.

Thursday, *February* 28. Preached on *Monday*, and on *Tuesday* settled a School both for grown Persons and Children at the *Dari-*

en, to the great Satisfaction of the Inhabitants—Set out with my Friends and four Orphans on *Tuesday* Evening.—Had pleasant Weather.—Lay two Nights in the Woods.—Reached *Bethesda* about Noon; was pleased with the Improvements that had been made in my Absence.—Was refreshed with some comfortable Christian Letters that I received from *New-York*.—Took Horse and came home to my dear Family at *Savannah*; who received me with abundance of Love and Joy.—The People also of the Parish I found were rejoiced at my Coming.—They flocked to and seemed very attentive at Public Worship.—God also was pleased to grant me some peculiar Vouchsafements of his Blessed Presence in my Soul, and I was comforted on every Side.

Tuesday, *March* 11. Buried this Evening one of the Women that came over with me, who I trust died in the Lord.—The Orphans sung before the Corpse from our House to the Court-House, where I preached, and after that gave another Word of Exhortation at the Grave.—My Soul was much affected with the Awfulness of the Solemnity.—The Word came with Power.

Tuesday, *March* 25. Went this Day to *Bethesda*, and with full Assurance of Faith laid the first Brick of the great House. The Workmen attended, and with me kneeled down and prayed. After we had sung a Hymn suitable to the Occasion, I gave a Word of Exhortation to the Labourers, and bid them remember to work heartily, knowing that they worked for God and not for Man. Much Satisfaction seemed to be amongst them, and blessed be God's holy Name, his Work prospers much in our Hands! Near twenty Acres of Land are cleared, and almost ready for Planting. Two Houses are already raised, and one near upon being finished. All the Timber for the Frame of the great House is sawn, and most of it brought to the Place where it is to be built. A good Part of the Foundation is dug, and many Thousands of Brick ready for Use. Near forty Children are now under my Care. I have many Pounds of Cotton spun ready for the Loom; and near a hundred Mouths are daily supplied with Food from our Store.—The Expence is great; but our Great and Good God, I am persuaded, will enable me to defray it. As yet I am kept from the least doubting. The more my Family encreases, the more Enlargement and Comfort I feel. And tho' what has been hitherto done, comparatively speaking, may be only like a Grain of Mustard Seed, yet I believe it will, in GOD's due Time, take Root and fill the Land, and many poor distressed Souls will come and lodge under the Branches of it.

Sunday, *March* 30. Found my self very sick and weak in Body; but was strengthened notwithstanding, to go through most of the Duties of the Day, and to take an affectionate Leave of my dear Parishioners, because it appeared that Providence called me at this Time towards the Northward. An unspeakable Trouble and Agony of Soul did I feel most Part of the Day, and was enabled to wrestle with my LORD in behalf of the People in general, and those belonging to the *Orphan-House* in particular. Blessed be GOD he has already, and I trust in a great Measure, heard my Prayer. All Things belonging to the *Orphan-House* succeed beyond Expectation, and some of my little Flock have lately (as far as I can judge) been effectually called of GOD. One Woman, that had been a constant Attender on the Means of Grace, and thought herself a Christian for many Years, came to me acknowledging, that she had been a Self-Deceiver, and knew nothing of the Righteousness or true living Faith in JESUS CHRIST. A Tradesman of the same Stamp, having felt the Power of the Doctrines of Grace, sent me seventeen Volumes of Archbishop *Tillotson*'s Sermons, of which he had been a great Admirer, to do what I would with them. A Captain of a Ship, who had been a strong Opposer of the Truth, wrote and came to me under great Convictions, confessing his Sin, and desirous to be a Christian indeed. Some others also there are who have received the Love of GOD in the Truth of it. So that I hope, if ten Saints could preserve *Sodom*, the few righteous Souls left behind, will prevent the utter Desolation of declining *Savannah*.

Wednesday, *April* 3. Read Prayers, as usual, as soon as it was light, expounded the Lesson, and then went on board with several of my Family and my Parishioners, whose Hearts GOD has touched by his Grace. The Weather was very pleasant, and we spent the Day to our mutual Edification and Comfort.—In the Evening we wept over and took Leave of each other; and the Searcher of

Hearts only knows what yearnings I felt in my own Soul. I have always observed, that I am under a greater Concern, when leaving *Savannah*, than any other Place in the World: For it has proved a blessed Place for my Soul; and leaving my Companions, and more particularly familiar Friends, gives Nature a deeper Wound than any other outward Trial.

Wednesday, *June* 4. Cast Anchor about Midnight, at *Tybee Island*, fifteen Miles from *Savannah*, after a short Passage of nine Days, a Thing very extraordinary at this Time of the Year. But our God is a God hearing Prayer.

Thursday, *June* 5. Took Boat at *Tybee*, about one in the Morning, and arrived at *Savannah* about eight. But oh what a sweet Meeting had I with my dear Friends. What God has prepared for me I know not; but surely I cannot well expect a greater Happiness till I embrace the Saints in Glory. When I parted, my Heart was ready to break with Sorrow, but now it almost burst with Joy. All Things concurred to render our Meeting exceeding happy.—None of my Letters had come to Hand, so that my Family did not expect me for a long Season. They had also been informed that I was cast away; so that they received me as one rising from the dead. Oh how did each in Turn, hang upon my Neck, kiss and weep over me with Tears of Joy. And my own Soul was so full of a Sense of God's Love, when I embraced one Friend in particular, that I thought I should even have expired in the Place. All that *Joseph* felt, when he wept over his Brother *Benjamin*, or *David*, when making a Covenant with *Jonathan*, did I feel, and I could almost say, far more. In short, my Soul was quite full with Peace, with Love and Joy; and I took the first Opportunity of kneeling down with my dear Family, and venting my Heart before them. Several of my Parishioners came with great Joy to see me, and after we had wept and prayed and gave Thanks for a considerable Time, I took a little Refreshment for my Body; but felt my Soul so full of a Sense of the Divine Love, that I wanted Words to express myself!

Friday, June 6. Blessed be the GOD of all Grace, who continues to do for me marvellous Things! This Day I hope Salvation is come to many in my House.—Long have I interceded for poor *Savannah.* Strong Wrestlings have I had with GOD Time after Time, both in public and private, on the Inhabitants Behalf; and this Night GOD has most remarkably answered my Requests.—Ever since my Arrival, my Soul has been quite carried out with a Sense of GOD's Love, in bringing me back so opportunely. And all this Day, one or two of my Friends perceived a Divine Power coming gradually amongst us.—In the Afternoon, one of the Men that I brought over, was enabled to wrestle with GOD exceedingly, both for himself and others.—About four, GOD gave me to pray earnestly, and particularly with strong Cryings and Tears for my Friends, who were in the Room with me.—Many came into the Passage near us, and wept much before the LORD, deeply labouring in their Souls.—After this I went up and pray'd for near half an Hour with some of the Women of the House, and three Girls, who seemed to be weary with the Weight of their Sins. But when we came to public Prayer, the HOLY GHOST seemed to come into the Congregation like a mighty rushing Wind, carrying all before it.—I was so carried out in Exposition, that the Sweat poured most plentifully from my Face, till my animal Spirits were almost exhausted.—I had not begun long before several fell a crying sorely; and the Number still increased, till young Men and Maidens, old Men and Children, were all dissolved in Tears and Mourning after JESUS. I believe there were scarce half a Dozen in the whole Congregation, but what were deeply affected. I think I never saw the like before. It amazed me, and must have affected the Heart of any one not quite dead to GOD, to behold the little Lambs crying most bitterly. And what was more extraordinary, after Church, several of my Parishioners, all my Family, and the little Children, came crying along the Street, and many could not avoid praying very loud.—Being come home, I laid myself upon the Bed, weak in Body, and astonished at the Power of GOD. But finding so many come up in such a Condition, I rose from Bed, and betook myself to Prayer again. But had I not lifted up my Voice like a Trumpet, the Groans and Cries of the Children would have prevented my being heard. This continued for near an Hour, till at last, finding their Concern rather increase than abate, I desired all to retire. But oh how was I delighted afterwards, to hear some or other praying most earnestly to GOD in every Corner of the House; And it surprized me to hear what a Spirit of Supplication was put into the Hearts of some of the Boys and Girls. It happened also to thunder and lighten, which added much to the Solemnity of the Night, and reminded us more of the Coming of the Son of Man. After my Parishioners had been gone, and the Family retired for about an Hour, when I thought their Spirits were composed, I called all together, and sung an Hymn to our dear LORD JESUS, whose Hand alone had brought such mighty Things to pass. My exerting myself so much, threw my Body into a Fever; and GOD's Comforts so refreshed my Soul, that I slept but little the whole Night. The next Day the Concern still continued, especially amongst the Girls, four of whom I have great Reason to believe are coming home truly to JESUS CHRIST, with as many Boys. Their Convictions increase. They are even now in frequent Agonies, when lying and groaning under the Sense of their original and actual Sins. The next Day after this Awakening, for near two Hours, they cried out as violently as they did the Night before. One has been so filled with Love, Peace and Joy, that she has continued almost whole Nights in Prayer. Her Heart burns with longing Desire for the Salvation of her dear Relations and Fellow-Creatures; she is surprisingly enabled to pray to GOD for them, and has wrote such Truths, as I am persuaded none could write without an inward Feeling of the Spirit of GOD in the Heart. The Boys also go on well. I walk out with them or the Girls under Conviction once every Day, and am delighted to find what a rational Account they give me of the Work of GOD, and how they are let to see the Corruption of their Nature. They are observed frequently to retire, and some of them have prayed sweetly before me, and at other Times they have been overhead wrestling with GOD in the strongest Manner, and praying to JESUS CHRIST to deliver them from the bottomless Pit.— Several also of my Parishioners are under great Concern: But I mention my Orphans in particular, that their Benefactors may rejoice in hearing what God is doing for their Souls. Blessed be his holy Name! our Affairs are now carried on with Decency and Order, and I really believe *Savannah* will yet become the Joy of the Earth. Ere long, I trust, the Lord will take it into his own Hands, and then the Curse which I believe has hitherto been lying on it, will be taken off. I am now beginning to build a Church, and when Matters are brought to a sufficient Extremity, then I believe will be the Lord's Opportunity to save and deliver us. He seems to be purging the Province apace. The Sword will sweep away the Refuse of Lies, and I trust a Rest will yet be prepared in this despised Place, for our dear Lord's own People.— Blessed be God, the Children are industrious. We have now in the House near 100 Yards of Cloth spun and weaved. We have also several Tradesmen belonging to the House, much Cattle on our Plantation, and I hope ere long we shall live amongst ourselves. There are several Masters set over the Children, who watch over them both in and after School Hours. Generally once a Day, if I do not, they walk with their respective Charges, tell them of the Glory of God in the Creation, and praise him by singing a Hymn. But I shall give a more particular Account when I send my next Journal.—As it is uncertain when I shall return to my native Country, I thought it my Duty to send this in the mean while, that my dear Friends may give Thanks in my Behalf, and by their Prayers strengthen my Hands: For an effectual Door is opening in *America*; and I trust the Time is coming, when the Earth shall be filled with the Knowledge of the Lord, as the Waters cover the Sea.—We hear of Wars and Rumours of Wars, but let not the Servants of Jesus Christ be troubled; for the Lord generally ushers in his Kingdom with dreadful Pomp, and destroys those with the Sword of the Enemy, who would not be wounded with the Sword of his Spirit.—*May the LORD be glorified in all his Dispensations! and may that happy Time now hasten on, wherein the Leopard shall lie down with the Kid, and the Lion eat Straw like the Ox, and the People learn War no more!*—The Concern I have for the Church in general, and *Savannah* and the *Orphan-House* in particular, lies much upon my Heart Day and Night.

WEDNESDAY, *June* 25. Went on *Monday* to, and returned this Evening from *Ebenezer*, which I have seen with no small Satisfaction. Surely there is a Difference, even in this Life, between those that serve the Lord, and those that serve him not. All other Places of the Colony seem to be like *Egypt*, where was Darkness, but *Ebenezer* like the Land of *Goshen*, wherein was great Light. For near four Miles did I walk in almost one continued Field, with a most plentiful Crop of Corn, Pease, Potatoes, *&c.* growing upon it. All the Product of a few Months Labour. But God gives the Labourers a peculiar Blessing. They are unanimous: The Strong help the Weak: And all seem hearty for the Common-Good. In a few Years the *Saltzburghers*, I believe will be a flourishing People. Their Land is good, and lies very near the River. They already provide Food, and ere long will be capable of providing Raiment for themselves. I shall send them up Cotton, Spinning Wheels, and a Loom to begin a Manufactory for themselves; and next Year they hope their own Land will produce enough Flax, Cotton, *&c.* to carry it on. I had sweet Communication with their Ministers. Our Sister Orphan-House there is blessed by their Means. And Yesterday was set apart as a Day of Thanksgiving for some Assistances lately sent the dear Lambs from *Germany* and *Savannah*. The People seem very grateful. They willingly received me into their clean, but little Huts, and seemed proud when I would accept of any Thing from their Hands. Blessed be God, certainly some Blessings are in Reserve for *Georgia*. As I said formerly, so I say again, they who help the *Saltzburghers* will do a good Work. They want Assistance.

Friday, June 27. With great Comfort received Captain *Grant*, who has been at Cape *Fear* to fetch a Load of Boards, and returned with his Sloop in fourteen Days. He was received very courteously by the head Inhabitants; and many, he tells me, were in Expectation of seeing me at *North Carolina*.

Monday, *June* 30. For these ten Days last past, have had frequent Communications from above, both by Way of Humiliation and Exaltation. God has often been pleased, since my Return, to make himself known in our Sanctuary, and has caused a mighty Power to attend the Word preached, both in Publick and Private. I have been much refreshed with a Packet of Letters from *English* Friends. Providence seems to smile upon the Orphan-House, and to prosper every Thing I take in Hand. A wealthy, moral, civiliz'd Planter of *South Carolina* came lately to see us, and God, I believe, has been pleased to give him a true Knowledge of himself, and a true Faith in his dear Son Jesus Christ. His Wife also was much quickened, having been wrought upon by God sometime last Winter. She was a great Admirer of Archbishop *Tillotson*; but having her Eyes now opened, to discern spiritual Things, can no longer take up with such Husks, fit only for carnal, unawakened, unbelieving Reasoners to eat. With this happy Pair (hearing that *Charlestown* People were in great Expectaions of seeing me before I went to the Northward, and that God had been pleased to work by my late Ministry among them) I and a dear Friend left *Savannah* this Morning, in a large Boat, conversed with one another in the Way, and arrived at *Beaufort* in *Port-Royal* about Midnight. Our Friend and his Wife went to a Relation's House, but my Companion and I chose to continue in the Boat, where our Lord was pleased to cause us to lie down and sleep in Peace and Safety.

Friday, *July* 26. Took Boat before Day, and having fine Weather, and a favourable Gale, reached *Savannah*, and saluted my dear Family about five in the Evening. My Body being weak, it could not bear up under the Joy and Satisfaction which I felt in my

Mind. However, I kneel'd down, wept out a short Prayer and Thanksgiving, and, as well as I could, told my Assistants what God had done for my Soul. In the Evening, I expounded, and undesignedly, thinking it was the Lesson for the Night, read the last Chapter of St. *Paul*'s second Epistle to *Timothy*, in which were encouraging Words.

Thursday, *August* 1. Continued very weak, ever since my Return from *Charlestown*; but was much refreshed this Morning with the Sight of some dear Friends, (amongst whom was one Mr. *T—y*, a Baptist-Minister) who came in our Sloop to see the Orphan-House. I gave them the Meeting at early Prayers, and God enabled me to expound with Power.

Sunday, *August* 3. Felt more than common of the divine Presence in my Soul since the Arrival of *Charlestown* Friends, who brought the Orphans many Presents, and blessed God for the Footsteps of his Goodness and Providence, plainly discernible amongst us. But last Night, through Weakness of Body, and a prodigious Concern, which lay upon my Soul, just as I began Family Prayer, I was struck, as I thought, almost with Death. I put up a few broken Accents and breathed out, *Lord Jesus receive my Spirit*. This Morning my Master shewed me why I was thus humbled. Soon after I rose, I found that Mr. *J—* and his Wife of *Port-Royal*, Mr. *Jonathan B—*, Brother to Mr. *Hugh B—*, and one Mr. *B—ll*, were all come to pay us a Visit. Tho' exceeding weak, and I had almost laid aside Thoughts of officiating this Day, yet, upon Mr. *J—*'s intimating that Friends came expecting to hear me, I promised, if I could, to preach, and begg'd him to read Prayers. He did, but I found myself so ill, that I would fain have persuaded Mr. *T—y* to preach for me. He peremptorily refused, urging that God would strengthen me if I begun. Upon this I stood up, and soon found Power communicated to me from above. I felt a sweet Melting in my Soul, and ere I had prayed long, Mr. *B—ll* dropp'd down, as tho' shot with a Gun.—He soon got up, and sat attentively to hear the Sermon. The Power soon spread abroad. The greatest Part of the Congregation was under great Concern. Tears trickled down apace. God manifested himself also amongst us much during the

Time of the Sacrament, and I went home ashamed that I was so unwilling to preach. I stood justly reproved, when Mr. *T—y*, after we came home, said, "Did I not tell you, God would strengthen you?"

Monday, *August* 4. Was sent for about Noon to see Mr. *Jonathan B—n*. At my coming, I found him under great Concern, and strong Convictions of Sin. Oh! How did he reflect on his past mis-spent Life! How did he bless God for bringing him now to *Savannah*, and desire that he might be found in Christ ere he returned Home! His Wife sat weeping by, and Mr. *B—ll* lay on a Bed groaning in Bitterness of Soul, under a Sense of Guilt, and crying out for an Interest in Jesus. I asked him "what caused him to fall down Yesterday." He answered, "The Power of God's Word." After about half an Hour's Conversation on the Nature of the New-Birth, and the Necessity of a saving Closure with the Lord Christ; I kneeled down, prayed with them, and then took my Leave, well hoping, that the Lord would pluck them as Fire-brands out of the Burning.

Sunday, *August* 9th. Went on *Tuesday* with Mr. *B— J—s*, &c. to *Bethesda*, and had the Pleasure of seeing the Work of God going on in most of our Visitor's Hearts. It was but seldom I could officiate; but, when I did, the Lord generally caused the Word to come with very great Power. This Morning I expounded early as usual, and read Part of the Prayers at ten o'Clock; but got Mr. *T—y* to preach, who (tho' a Baptist Minister) joined with us in receiving the Sacrament, in the Church of *England* Way. The KING was pleased to sit at his Table: He brought us into his Banqueting House, and caused it to be a Feast of fat Things to our Souls. Many, I believe, fed on Jesus in their Hearts with Thanksgiving. After the Ordinance was over, the Lord enlarged my Heart, and I prayed as the Spirit gave me Utterance. I went Home much refreshed in my Soul, but so weak in Body that I declined going to public Worship in the Afternoon. In the mean while God gave me a fresh Supply of Strength. About the Evening, when my Friends were sitting down together, finding the Power of the Lord come upon me, I began to speak to them of the Things of God. A great

Alteration was soon discernible in most of the Company; their Concern gradually increased, till many burst into Floods of Tears, and one fell upon the Ground.—E'er I had done, some of my Parishoners came up, and the rest my Family: They also felt the divine Power. When I had done speaking to them from God, I spoke in Prayer to God for them. My Soul was carried, as it were, out of the Body, and I was enabled to wrestle mightily with our Lord in their Behalf—He did not let us go without a Blessing.—The Room was filled with the Cries of those around me, and many, I believe, at that Time sought Jesus sorrowing.—The Concern continued after the Duty was over—Several were in great Agonies of Soul, and a Cherikee *Indian* Trader, who providentially was present, desired to speak with me, saying, *he never saw or felt the like before*. Mr. *J—s* also of *Port-Royal* (who went away on *Friday*, but was forced back by contrary Winds, and officiated for me this Afternoon at *Savannah*) told a Friend that *surely God was with us of a Truth*.

Saturday, *August* 15. Parted with dear Mr. *B*— and Mr. *B—n*, on *Tuesday*, who, I hope, could say, *Lord now lettest thou thy Servants depart in Peace; for our Eyes have seen*, *our Hearts have felt thy Salvation*. Met with closer outward Tryals this Week than ever I was visited with before. Was forced several Times to come out thro' Concern of Soul, and Weakness of Body in the midst of public Worship, and, had not God uncommonly supported me, I must frequently have given up the Ghost. But, as Troubles abounded, Consolations abounded also. These Words, *But* David *strengthened himself in the Lord his God*, were pressed with a wonderful supporting Power upon my Soul. The Eleventh of *Hebrews* also was blessed to me. I found the Benefit of being afflicted. God enabled me to sanctify him in my Heart, and my greatest Grief was, that I should be so naughty as to oblige my heavenly Father to chastize and scourge me.

Monday, *August* 17. Preached Yesterday Morning, and took Leave of my Parishioners. Administer'd the blessed Sacrament, and gave a close Exhortation afterwards. Settled every Thing to the best of my Power for the Orphan-house, which succeeds beyond Expectation, and was so filled with the Love of Christ in this

Evening's Exposition, and my private Farewel-discourse, that I could almost say I was within the Veil.—My Hearers, both in public and private, were vastly affected, and a strange Woman was so touched, that she came to me confessing her Sins, and crying out *what shall I do to be saved?* When I came to converse with her, I found God had struck her the last Time I preached at *Port-Royal*, and I hope he will now effectually call her by his Grace. Pleased, and I hope, in some Measure thankful to the Lord of all Lords for setting such Seals to my Ministry just at Departure. About 10 at Night I went on Board our Sloop with my other dear Visitors, in order to go to *Charlestown*; where, by the Advice of Friends, the Captain is to take in Freight for *Boston*, for the Benefit of the Orphan-house.

Select Bibliography

Aldridge, Alfred O., "George Whitefield's Georgia Controversies," *Journal of Southern History*, 9 (Aug., 1943).

Church, Leslie F., *Oglethorpe: A Study of Philanthropy in England and Georgia* (London, 1932).

Coulter, E. Merton, ed., *The Journal of Peter Gordon 1732–1735* (Wormsloe Foundation Publications No. 6, Athens, Ga., 1963).

Ettinger, Amos A., *James Edward Oglethorpe: Imperial Idealist* (Oxford, 1936).

Fries, Adelaide L., *The Moravians in Georgia 1735–1740* (Winston-Salem, N.C., 1905).

Harrison, G. E., *Son to Susanna: The Private Life of John Wesley* (London, 1944).

Henry, Stuart C., *George Whitefield: Wayfaring Witness* (New York, 1957).

Hofer, J. M., "The Georgia Salzburgers," *Georgia Historical Quarterly*, 18 (June, 1934).

Loewald, Klaus G., Beverley Strika and Paul S. Taylor, eds., "John Martin Bolzius Answers a Questionnaire on Carolina and Georgia," *William and Mary Quarterly*, 14 (April, 1957) and 15 (April, 1958).

McCain, James R., *Georgia as a Proprietary Province: The Execution of a Trust* (Boston, 1917).

McCall, Hugh, *The History of Georgia, containing brief sketches of the most remarkable events up to the present day* (2 vols., Savannah 1811–16).

McPherson, Robert G., ed., "The Voyage of the *Anne* – A Daily Record," *Georgia Historical Quarterly*, 44 (June, 1960).

Moore, H., *Life of Rev. John Wesley, in which is included the life of his brother Charles Wesley* (2 vols., London, 1824).

Strauss, Felix P., "A Brief Survey of Protestantism in Archiepiscopal Salzburg and the Emigration of 1732," *Georgia Historical Quarterly*, 43 (March, 1959).

Strobel, P. A., *The Salzburgers and Their Descendants* (Baltimore 1855 reprint edn., Athens, Ga., 1953).

Temple, Sarah Gober, and Kenneth Coleman, *Georgia Journeys: being an account of the lives of Georgia's original settlers and many other early settlers from the founding of the colony in 1732 until the institution of royal government in 1754* (Athens, Ga., 1961).
Tyerman, Luke, *The Life of the Rev. George Whitefield* (2 vols., London, 1876–7).
Urlspurger, Samuel, ed., *Der Ausführlichen Nachrichten von der Königlich–Gross Britannischen Colonie Salzburgischer Emigranten in America* (3 vols., Halle, 1735–52).
White, George, *Historical Collections of Georgia, containing the most interesting facts, traditions, biographical sketches, anecdotes, etc., relating to its history and antiquities, from its first settlement to the present time* (3rd edn., New York, 1955).
———, *Statistics of the State of Georgia, including an account of its natural, civil and ecclesiastical history* (Savannah, 1849).
Widmann, Hans, *Geschichte Salzburgs* (3 vols., Gotha, 1907–14).

Trevor R. Reese teaches at the University of London Institute of Commonwealth Studies. He is author of *Colonial Georgia: A Study in British Imperial Policy in the Eighteenth Century* (Athens, 1963). All of the documents for this new edition of early Georgia journals have come from the collection of the University of Georgia Library, Special Collections. The text of Peter Gordon's journal follows *The Journal of Peter Gordon* (Athens, 1963) as published by the University of Georgia Press, edited by E. M. Coulter and sponsored by the Wormsloe Foundation. § This book was planned and edited at Savannah, Georgia, by The Beehive Press, which publishes sources and studies of Georgia history and literature. Its pressmark, which appears above and pictures bees busy at their hive, expresses the enthusiasm of this work; the source of the pressmark—an early Georgia colonial pamphlet entitled *An Impartial Enquiry into the State and Utility of the Province of Georgia*, London, 1741—suggests a spirit of free intellectual endeavor. § This book was printed at The Stinehour Press in Lunenburg, Vermont.

THE BEEHIVE PRESS
321 Barnard Street
Savannah, Georgia 31401